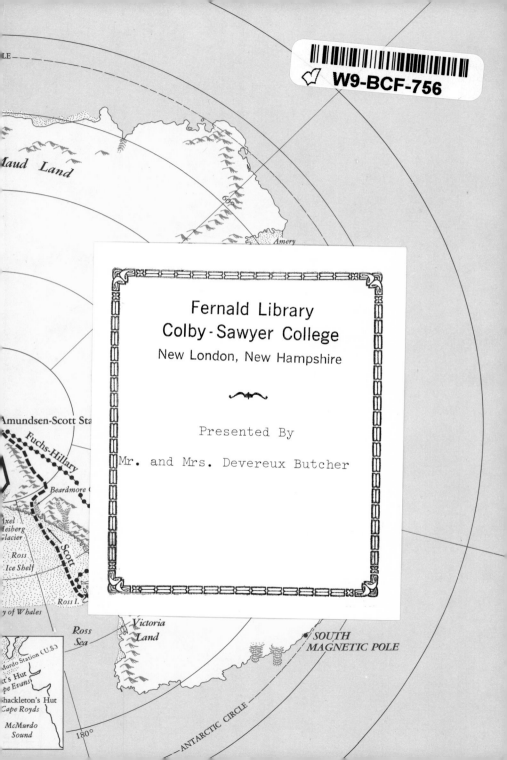

Books by CHARLES NEIDER

Fiction

Naked Eye
The Authentic Death of Hendry Jones
The White Citadel

Biography

Susy: A Childhood

Criticism

Mark Twain
The Frozen Sea: A Study of Franz Kafka

Books edited by CHARLES NEIDER

The Autobiography of Mark Twain
The Complete Short Stories of Mark Twain
Short Novels of the Masters
Man Against Nature
The Great West
Etc.

ANTARCTICA

Shackleton's hut, Cape Royds, Ross Island,
with Mount Erebus in the background.

ANTARCTICA

*Authentic Accounts of Life and
Exploration in the World's Highest,
Driest, Windiest, Coldest
and Most Remote Continent*

*Edited with an Introduction
and Notes*
by CHARLES NEIDER

RANDOM HOUSE   NEW YORK

Copyright © 1972 by Charles Neider

All rights reserved under International
and Pan-American Copyright Conventions.
Published in the United States by Random House, Inc.,
New York, and simultaneously in Canada
by Random House of Canada Limited, Toronto.

ISBN: 0-394-46831-7
Library of Congress Catalog Card Number: 73-37072

Acknowledgment is gratefully extended to the following
for permission to reprint excerpts from their works:
Cambridge University Press: From "The Voyage
of Captain Bellingshausen to the Antarctic Seas,"
by Thaddeus Bellingshausen, *The Hakluyt Society*, Volume I,
published by Cambridge University Press.
Constable Publishers: From THE WORST JOURNEY IN THE WORLD,
by Apsley Cherry-Garrard, Volume I.
Gerald Duckworth & Co Ltd.: From THE GREAT WHITE SOUTH,
by Herbert Ponting.
E.P. Dutton & Co., Inc.: and Hodder & Stoughton Ltd.:
From the book NO LATITUDE FOR ERROR, by Sir Edmund Hillary.
Copyright © 1961 by Sir Edmund Hillary.
The Macmillan Company: From SOUTH, by Ernest Shackleton.
Copyright 1920 by The Macmillan Company, renewed 1947
by Raymond S. Shackleton and Edward A.A. Shackleton.
Copyright © 1962 by The Macmillan Company.
G.P. Putnam's Sons: From ALONE, by Richard E. Byrd.
Copyright 1938 by Richard E. Byrd. Copyright renewed 1966
by Marie A. Byrd. From 90° SOUTH, by Paul Siple.
Copyright © 1959 by Paul Siple.

Manufactured in the United States of America
by the Haddon Craftsmen Inc., Scranton, Pennsylvania

Designed by Andrew Roberts
Endpaper map by Dyno Lowenstein

2   4   6   8   9   7   5   3
First Edition

ACKNOWLEDGMENTS

The United States Navy made it possible for me to visit Antarctica in November 1969. Rear Admiral David F. Welch, Commander, and Lieutenant Dan Davidson, Public Affairs Officer, United States Naval Support Force, Antarctica (Operation Deep Freeze), extended courtesies to me in the United States, in New Zealand and in the Antarctic. Jack Renirie and Kendall Moulton of the National Science Foundation were very helpful to me in connection with this visit, both in Antarctica and in the United States. Walt Seelig of the National Science Foundation was unfailingly helpful to me in Washington. E. Leitz Inc., Rockleigh, New Jersey, through Walter Heun lent me photographic equipment to supplement my own equipment. The Firestone Library of Princeton University was helpful in very important respects through Alfred Bush. Robert Axtmann of Princeton University, George Cody of RCA Laboratories, Carl Faith of Rutgers University, and Mrs. Leigh Bienen of Princeton made many useful suggestions. The MacDowell Colony, Peterborough, New Hampshire (particularly its former director, George Kendall), was of great service to me by means of three residence fellowships. Catharine Meyer of *Harper's Magazine* provided special encouragement and help. And Susan Rabiner of Random House very capably gave me the benefit of editorial aid of every sort. To these institutions and persons I wish to express my profound thanks.

CONTENTS

Contents : : x

ANTARCTICA

INTRODUCTION

White Pilgrimage

MY INTEREST IN ANTARCTICA goes back to my boyhood in Richmond, Virginia. In 1931, when I was sixteen, I heard Rear Admiral Richard E. Byrd, the Antarctic explorer and one of the Byrds of Virginia, lecture on Antarctica. He became a boyhood hero of mine. I wanted very much to go to the Antarctic, so I wrote letters to the National Geographic Society and the American Geographical Society asking to be included in an expedition. Naturally, I was turned down.

My dream of visiting the continent continued into my adult years. But I never thought it would be realized. I have long been interested in man's behavior in conditions of great stress, especially when he is pitted against nature. In 1954 I edited a book titled *Man Against Nature*, published by Harpers, which included authentic accounts of exploration. In several of these accounts Antarctica was the environment against which man struggled. It later struck me that the time had come for a literary person to go to the Antarctic.

There are tours that take you by ship from South America to the Antarctic Peninsula, but these don't go to the high latitudes. (South of the Equator, "high latitudes" describes the more southerly latitudes.) The usual way for an American to go to the high latitudes is to have the United States Navy fly him from its base in New Zealand down to Ross Island in the Ross Sea. The main United States base in the Antarctic, McMurdo Station, is on Ross Island, at a latitude of almost 78°.

In November of 1969 I went to the Antarctic as a guest of the Navy, having been invited with three newsmen to observe Operation Deep Freeze, the Navy's logistic support activity on behalf of American scientific research on the continent. The research, which is entirely basic research, is conducted by USARP, the United States Antarctic Research Program, under the supervision and with funds of the National Science Foundation. With us were four science writers who were guests of NSF.

The lure of Antarctica, that fabulous, awesome and in some ways exquisitely beautiful last frontier, is so great that the long first leg to New Zealand seems even longer despite the speed of the huge Air Force jet that takes you there. You travel with the suspense of a pilgrim eager to reach places sanctified by human and superhuman events. But the chief goal of the Antarctic pilgrim is to reach pure nature itself— from ancient, pre-human time, frozen in an incredible ice cap. Such a pilgrim goes to pay his respects to natural conditions; to take a breath of unpolluted air; and to sense how it all felt in the beginning, before the introduction of man. But he also goes to see how man survives in the world's most hostile place and does so by means of the very gadgetry which increasingly possesses and assails him. He travels, in short, from technological defilement for a glimpse of innocence, hoping to learn along the way a few things about himself.

In Christchurch, New Zealand, in the austral spring or summer you pick up a U. S. Navy plane, which in eight hours will take you the twenty-four hundred miles to "the ice," as Antarctic hands call the continent. As you board the aircraft, Christchurch is warm and it seems mildly funny to be wearing waffleweave longjohns, Seabee green shirt and trousers, pile-lined cap, cushion-sole socks and huge white rubber thermal boots called bunny boots. (You have acquired Navy-issue dunnage.) You and your fellow passengers sit in two rows on red canvas seats, facing each other across a fence of strapped-down seabags, and wonder what Antarctica will be like and what you will be like in it. The antipodean waters below are so cold that if a person is immersed he can survive only eight to ten minutes. But a plane has never gone down on this flight and everyone is cheerful even as we pass the point of safe return, beyond which the C130 Hercules, a great ski-equipped four-engine turboprop, cannot turn back. There's excitement as the first pack ice is sighted. And people nudge each other and point to and touch wall bolts that have iced up.

The plane is cool now and you put on two pairs of gloves and a parka with a fur-trimmed flying hood. In your seabag are huge gauntleted furback mittens known as bear paws and lined over-pants called many-pockets trousers or waddle pants but these are for places where it's really cold. You will not wear them on your arrival. Meanwhile one can't help but think there's a certain humor in the fact that he's approaching the world's quietest place (when the winds aren't blowing) in a craft so noisy one carries on a conversation, if at all, in shouts. The roar is varied by the sound of hissing somewhere and by the screams of wing and tail controls.

One disembarks, and there is Williams Field, afloat on the great Ross Ice Shelf, and there too is Mount Erebus, some twelve and a half thousand feet high, the largest and most active volcano on the continent. On my trip the temperature was a mild 5° F when I arrived. We boarded a bulky, fat-tired orange bus and bounced on a road carved on the annual ice of McMurdo Sound, viewing distant mountains half-veiled by luminous clouds. After six or seven miles we reached McMurdo Station, the center of American logistic and scientific activity in Antarctica, whose winter population of two hundred and summer population of almost a thousand makes it the largest station on the continent. Perched on volcanic hills on the southern tip of Ross Island, it has a severe climate, with an all-time recorded low of −59° F and with winds clocked as high as a hundred and fifty-five miles an hour. Its black hills and roads give it the look of a mining camp.

Our quarters were in the Press Hut on the station's western edge, overlooking a frozen harbor and a distant horizon of mountain ranges and glaciers. The mountains and glaciers endlessly fascinate one because, due to variations in snow fall, cloud cover, humidity and the position of the sun, they seem to change almost hourly. The hut was a Jamesway, a green, tent-like, round-topped structure of prefabricated wood and insulated canvas, almost windowless, heated by two oil-fired units and containing several tiny semi-private cubicles with two-tiered beds. After a leisurely dinner in the nearby mess hall we walked around the station. Two of us and a naval escort climbed down the snow-covered hill below the Press Hut to observe the skuas scavenging at a dump heap on the ice. They are large, dark, gull-like birds who steal Adélie penguin eggs and kill and eat Adélie chicks. A wind of some ten knots had come up and now the cold was piercing. When we turned in we were excited but slept nevertheless, despite the knowledge that the never-setting sun was circling and circling as though lost.

Early the next morning we headed for the Pole, where only the Americans have a station. To paraphrase a current politician, once you've seen one undersnow station you've seen them all, with this proviso: that you see the Pole Station first. Because of its historical significance, its remoteness, its hostility to life of every kind and degree, or if for no better reason than that, like Mount Everest, it's there, the Pole is the Mecca of all imaginative Antarctic residents and visitors, only a handful of whom get to visit it.

THE ARCTIC AND ANTARCTICA are poles apart in more ways than one readily realizes. The North Pole is a frozen, floating point on a sea some ten thousand feet deep. The South Pole is at an elevation of ninety-two hundred feet and is located on the world's windiest, driest and highest continent, whose average elevation is about seventy-five hundred feet. The Arctic is a sea surrounded by great land masses. The Antarctic is a land mass approximately as large as the United States and Mexico combined, containing great plateaus, vast mountain ranges and an ice cap that in places is almost three miles thick. Its average temperature is some 35° F lower than that of the Arctic. It is surrounded by the unbroken confluence of the Pacific, Atlantic and Indian Oceans which, with the prevailing westerlies, comprise the world's most savage sea. The lowest temperature ever recorded on earth was recorded in the Antarctic: −126.9° F. Whereas the North Pole is relatively close to places inhabited by man and is not very distant from highly developed forms of life, the South Pole is utterly remote and is roughly the center of a continent which holds life at bay, allowing survival only minimally in its interior.

It is still a difficult and hazardous traverse to the Pole from any Antarctic station. By the ski-equipped Hercules departing from McMurdo the trip takes three hours. The eight hundred miles are covered pleasantly, if noisily, but perhaps with a certain apprehension if one is making the visit for the first time. How cold will it be? Will your bronchial tubes cough up blood, as you hear can happen in very low temperatures? Was it true, as our Navy escort said, that one's lungs could freeze in certain polar conditions? How will the altitude affect you after the sudden change from sea level? Will you be blinded by the light? These and similar questions arose privately with us but were firmly dismissed in the faith that all would go well under the Navy's devoted care.

Although my flight as a flight was routine, it was unique in one respect. It was carrying the first women ever to visit the Pole: five Americans and a New Zealander. Five were scientists and one was a science writer. The Navy was nervously determined that no one of them should have the unfair if accidental distinction of being the *first* woman to step down at the Pole. After some discussion among high-ranking officers the solution to the problem was found: lower the cargo ramp in the rear of the plane, disembark all passengers with the exception of Rear Admiral David F. Welch (commander of Operation Deep Freeze) and the ladies, and have the latter descend the ramp arm in arm, the admiral in the middle. Navy photographers would record the historic moment.

As we neared the Pole we donned our waddle pants, lowered and secured our ear and neck flaps, closed the air valves in our bunny boots and checked our bear paws and fur-trimmed hoods. I glanced through one of the aft portholes and saw the vast, arid, blinding polar plateau. Warnings came over the intercom. The parka hood would eliminate our side vision, and the cap ear flaps and hood would dull our hearing, so it was best to exercise caution in one's movements. Several visitors in recent years, becoming confused, had wandered forward and had nearly been chewed up by the still-turning props. We were warned to be on guard against frostbite. The temperature at the Pole now was −49° F, the wind ten knots, making the effective temperature somewhat lower than −80° F. Unless we didn't mind losing skin we had better not touch metal with our bare hands, and if we had a rangefinder camera it was wise not to touch the finder's metal rim with our cheek. Because of the Pole's considerable altitude we were advised to move slowly and to breathe often.

But all went smoothly despite this last-minute counsel, much of which was a reiteration of earlier briefings. When we left the plane we waited for the cold to hit us but it didn't. What hit us was the light, for we had exited facing the sun.

We were on a great flat desert plain and wherever we turned, there was the same glaring white featureless northern horizon. The sun hung low in the sky like a terrible spotlight. The snow was thick and extremely dry, the sky fantastically blue. Only man lent visual interest to the barrenness: vehicle and boot tracks, communications antennas, a khaki instrument dome, black fuel drums on a huge sled, a red cleated vehicle, a khaki rubber storage bladder for fuel. Some hundred feet away was the famous "barber" pole with its red and black stripes surmounted by a gleaming chromium-plated globe. We walked toward it and felt the effects of the altitude. Our breath issued in white streamers, frosting our glasses. Diaphanous steam rose and billowed from people and machines. My companions made me think of walking tea kettles. The red beard of one of the men had turned a brilliant white.

I removed my bear paws, unzipped my parka and fumbled for the light meter and camera hanging from my neck. And now, as I shot the scenes, I at last felt the cold. My hands, even though covered by two pairs of gloves, ached and rapidly grew numb. I felt a strange satisfaction. After all, I told myself, I hadn't come more than thirteen thousand miles to experience warmth.

We were photographed individually at the barber pole by official Navy photographers. Statistics on a sign were photographed with us. The ice cap in the Pole's vicinity is over nine thousand feet thick. The average temperature is $-57°$ F. The population is twenty-one. I remembered other statistics—the highest temperature recorded at the Pole is 5.5° F, the lowest $-113.3°$ F. The annual precipitation (in terms of water equivalent) is less than 2″, as compared with Phoenix, Arizona's 7.2″. I thought of the tragic contrast between Amundsen's and Scott's arrival at the Pole and remembered Scott's words from his journal: "Great God! this is an awful place and terrible enough for us to have laboured to it without the reward of priority."

A Navy journalist, peering at my face, said the end of my

nose was very white and advised that I go inside the station temporarily. I went to a wooden door and down a precipitous flight of wooden stairs, at the foot of which stood the station's medical officer, with whom I chatted while I warmed my nose with my hand. The tunnel extending from the stairs was encrusted with ice crystals. Its temperature was thirty or forty below. Other frostbite cases descended the stairs to be advised by the officer. This same pleasant young man doubled as the station's postmaster and later cacheted the group's envelopes and led some of its members on a tour of the station, showing them the tiny infirmary (one bed, rarely occupied), the communications room, the ham radio room, the food storage area, the snow melter, and his own tight quarters, all under the ice. The station had originally been constructed on the surface of the snow (during the International Geophysical Year, 1957) but drift snow had covered it, compacted into ice and was slowly crushing it. The station would soon have to be abandoned. This was just as well in one sense, for the station had drifted with the ice cap away from the Pole. A new station, of superior design, would be built at the Pole itself in the early seventies.

We lunched in a small mess room, one wall of which was crowded with huge-breasted pinups. It was interesting to see the confrontation of these ladies of men's dreams with the real ladies casually consuming spaghetti with meat sauce, buttered bread chunks, mincemeat pie and coffee. The bread and pie were fresh out of the station's oven. We left on schedule after a visit of two hours, hearing that the ladies had been persuaded to leave souvenirs of their visit: a bobby pin, a comb, a pair of ear rings and a lipstick.

If the flight to the Pole was dull because it occurred at too high an altitude for interesting sights, the return flight to McMurdo decidedly was not. It offered those few of us lucky enough to have access to a porthole a series of spectacular views of the Beardmore Glacier, which the pilot flew over at low altitudes, descending during one sequence to three hundred feet. The Beardmore is a landmark familiar to students of Antarctic exploration because it provided first Shackleton and then Scott with access to the polar plateau through the Transantarctic Mountains. Both the Shackleton and the Scott parties were in great danger on the glacier due to exhaustion, hunger and cold as they made their way back to Ross Island. The Shackleton party survived by a hair. The Scott group was trapped and destroyed by a blizzard on the Ross Ice Shelf not long after leaving the Beardmore.

At first, after the wastes of the seemingly endless plateau, with its dead flatness except for occasional nunataks (mountain peaks visible above the ice cap), we saw delicate scenes such as the pale grays and gray-blues of a mountain range peeping out of snow. But soon we came on naked, barren, slate-gray mountains, vast, sprawled, showing the ribs of cliff edges. From a height the glacier looked like a bluish plain, behind which were serene mountains of a deeper blue, at whose foothills were the congregated gleaming points of something resembling a town. But actually these points were an array of sastrugi (wind-made waves in the snow or ice), crevasses and crumbling buttes reflecting the low-hanging sun and suggesting the vast forces involved in the ice cap's movement to the Ross Ice Shelf and eventually to the Southern Ocean. As we flew over long, parallel ice ridges the ice river's width seemed immense, the distant part looking smooth, level, fit for traverses, the foreground giving the impression of having been chewed up by a thousand half-tracks. Far away was a lesser glacier, tonguing down between mountains to add to the Beardmore's mass. A mountain range, pale slate with a hint of violet, crests capped by snow, rose out of a creamy sea. Now the plane descended rapidly and one saw pale-green, veined splotches of bare ice or splotches resembling ragged circles of boiling white metal. There were huge upward-curling ice flakes among wildly mixed-up tremendous crevasses, and gleaming wild waves, a frozen surf, great buttes, and immense sections resembling crumbling blue cheese.

ONE MORNING I received permission to walk the two miles from McMurdo to New Zealand's Scott Base alone, on the condition that I was to phone the MAC (McMurdo) duty officer when I left McMurdo, when I reached Scott Base, when I departed from Scott Base and when I returned to McMurdo. Although the walk was safe enough, the weather in Antarctica is very uncertain and I could be caught in a blizzard or a whiteout, the latter a polar phenomenon in which the sky and the snow or ice reflect each other so completely that one loses orientation and feels as if he were in a bottle of milk. If caught in a whiteout one should sit it out until it passes. It may last an hour or two or a couple of days, depending on your luck. I suspected that the real reason for the calls was that I was a member of the tenderfoot press group and therefore a prime candidate for getting into trouble through ignorance and an excited imagination. Haunted by the ghosts of Scott, Shackleton and Byrd, whose names and exploits were never distant from us on the ice, I might give way to the actor in all of us and play the role of OAE (Old Antarctic Explorer), taking a short cut across the crevassed ice or wandering off into the hills. We were told more than once that although Antarctica is infinitely safer now in the air age than it was in the heroic period of the early explorers, survival still requires constant vigilance and caution.

I left McMurdo after an early breakfast, taking outlying streets and seeing a fuel tank farm, crates stacked outside of warehouses, and fork trucks and bulldozers. As I climbed the gap between Crater Heights and Observation Hill I came upon men constructing a tank which would hold more than two million gallons of fuel. The road was dark, graded volcanic dirt and rock, with patches of snow and ice, and was persistently steep, climbing out into the countryside to a crest, where it went quickly down to the New Zealand base. I had superb views of the Western Mountains and of a seemingly interminable stretch of ice and of barren volcanic hills, sometimes snow-covered but at others naked, gaunt.

The temperature was 4° F, the wind velocity at McMurdo ten knots. But in the Gap were head winds of twenty knots and more, which brought the effective temperature down to −35° F or lower. The winds made the going slow. Also, my gear was heavy, the thermal boots caused my feet to drag and the way was still surprisingly steep. I had the neck and ear flaps of my cap down but side gusts burned my eyes, causing them to run copiously. When I put up my parka hood I discovered I couldn't secure it because one of the draw-strings was missing. The wind kept blowing it back over my shoulders. Finally I let it stay there, occasionally shielding my left eye, which felt frozen, with a hand. I had brought my bear paws along. Whenever I removed them, for example to adjust the hood, my hands in their double gloves (khaki woolen insert and black leather shell) ached, then went numb. I found myself thinking it would be nice to sit down for a bit.

On my right the island sloped away, black rock and white snow, to the bluish Ross Ice Shelf which stretched out flat and immense to the horizon. This shelf is the size of France. On my left was a mottled, flinty, dark, volcanic hill of pumice-like stuff swept clean of snow and marked by regular vertical ridges which appeared to have been made by bulldozers. A hill further along on my left was furry with snow and on my right and somewhat ahead of me, far below on the white shore, was Scott Base, looking tiny with its antennas and green huts. The pallor of the green added to the base's appearance of innocence as compared with big, bustling McMurdo. I descended the steep road, slippery with brittle shards of volcanic rock, and became aware of the pressure ice at the coast's edge, its angular, uplifted, helter-skelter and vaguely frightening forms tinted with delicate blues and greens. Skuas were wheeling above the shoreline. Far out on the ice, almost indiscernible, was a cluster of specks which was Williams Field.

On the edge of Scott Base were some young men in green parkas, repairing one of several red motor toboggans standing in a row. I was directed to the post office, where I used the dial phone. Scott Base was constructed in 1957 for the International Geophysical Year and has been occupied continuously ever since. A young man was energetically cacheting envelopes with a hammer-like instrument on a rattling wooden counter. The base is an international post office and issues the Ross Dependency stamps. There was motion picture equipment about. I spoke with a young film director, who soon afterwards was killed in a helicopter crash on the ice, together with an American geologist. The snug, simple, efficient base is a series of huts connected by a covered metal archway which affords protection against the weather.

A New Zealander showed me the adjoining communications room and, after a walk down the covered archway, a room full of scientific equipment where ionosphere research was being conducted, then led me outdoors past pressure ridges and over minor crevasses onto the ice to see some Weddell seals and their pups. The seals were massive and prone, and the ice and snow in their vicinity were stained yellow, red and brown by the afterbirth. In this world of blacks, whites, greens and blues the warm afterbirth colors are very conspicuous. A seal observed us across her wiry whiskers, bawling cries of alarm if we drew closer than some six feet. Her pup's eyes were large, dark and soulful looking. When my companion, squatting, reached out a glove the pup suddenly snapped at it, just missing it. We heard the jaws shut.

We threaded our way back among the pressure ridges with their jewel blues and cobalt shadows. I was led to a snow field north of the base to meet the huskies, who were chained at intervals to prevent them from fighting. (The American stations no longer use sled dogs.) They are large animals with coarse coats in many shades of white, tan and brown. Hearing us approach, they set up a chorus of high barks and wails. One of them bounded against me and licked my face.

I left Scott Base and reached McMurdo in time to catch a bus which took our group to Scott's hut (erected in 1902) on

Hut Point Peninsula. It is one of three such huts on Ross Island protected as historic sites under the Antarctic Treaty. The other two are Shackleton's hut on Cape Royds and Scott's 1911 hut on Cape Evans. All three were hastily abandoned and all, because of the extreme dryness of Antarctica, survived the weather well. On Cape Evans it is not uncommon to find a sock, a boot or an old bottle lying in the outdoor snow. In the austral summer there's a bustle as cargo ships unload near the 1902 hut but in November the hut sits silent and remote. It is spacious (some thirty-six feet square) and has a pyramidal roof and overhanging eaves. It was brought from Australia and was the kind of bungalow used by Australian frontier settlers of the time. Inasmuch as the ship *Discovery* was iced in and available as living quarters, the hut was not lived in during Scott's first expedition. It was used for such purposes as drying furs, skinning birds, refitting awnings and for the rehearsal and performance of various theatrical entertainments, complete with scenes and footlights. It was also utilized for gravity observations made by the swinging of pendulums.

Although Scott was based on Cape Evans in 1911, it was from the 1902 hut that he departed with his four companions on November 3, 1911 in what proved to be a death march to the Pole. Admiral Byrd, writing in 1947, reported that its timbers still looked very fresh. Mutton carcasses, cartons of biscuits, and magazines and newspapers lay strewn about. Much of it had become filled with ice and compacted snow. It was restored in 1963 and 1964 by members of the New Zealand Antarctic Society. When we entered, it was dark, gloomy, rather empty and very cold.

THE FOLLOWING MORNING we attended one of many briefings on scientific research, usually conducted in scientific stations, where the sophisticated equipment, arcane to us, was a pleasant if vague visual aid. The equipment is frostily sedate even when it contains tiny colored lights, but at the cosmic ray station in a long red hut between McMurdo Station and Scott Base it goes into an antic dance. It does this every two minutes when the digital readout (an automatic counter) whirls lighted numerals faster than the eye can catch them and punches its findings on a roll of narrow tape to be sent to the States for analysis. The new Antarctica is accustomed to complex control and instrument panels. One sees them in the cockpits of aircraft, in the small nuclear plant at McMurdo (the only one on the continent) where seawater is desalinated and electricity produced, in some of the scientific stations and at Williams Field. At this briefing we heard discussions of the next logical step: unmanned automated stations that will radio their findings to polar satellites. Meanwhile, manned American research on the continent continues in numerous fields: glaciology, oceanography, biology, cartography, meteorology, geomagnetism, seismology, aurora, upper atmosphere physics (including cosmic ray and ionosphere opacity studies), paleontology and others.

Why has Antarctica been chosen as the site upon which to conduct basic research? There are a number of reasons, among them the following: the continent comprises one-tenth of the earth's land mass; it contains significant clues to the earth's past; it greatly influences the weather patterns of the Southern Hemisphere; it is relatively free of radio static; and it is ideally suited for upper atmosphere studies. Less than three weeks after we left the ice a fossil was discovered near the Beardmore Glacier that several scientists believed established "beyond further question" proof of the theory of continental drift.

The scientists we encountered were young, eager, personable and very competent. We often saw them as a different breed from the Antarctic hands who wintered over in the old days. The tall, fit-looking young man at the cosmic ray station was about to return to the States after a stay on the ice of thirteen months, much of it in the hut. One remembered how wintering-over personnel in the past felt the prolonged absence of sunlight, some growing morose, irritable, and a few breaking down or even becoming temporarily deranged. The young man had wintered over alone, had walked now and then to McMurdo on an errand and had received supplies and an occasional visitor. Had he ever been lonely or depressed? On the contrary, he asserted, he had enjoyed the winter. There had been fewer distractions, and being without mail had its advantages: there was no mail to upset him and no cause to be disappointed because someone hadn't written. Did he smoke, drink, play cards? No. "I'm a straight arrow," he said with a candid, ironic smile. Then how had he spent his free time? Well, he had faced and stained the walls of his bedroom with veneered plywood, had kept a diary, had taken photographs. Occasionally he had spoken with his folks by ham radio. He was not only a different breed from his predecessors; he also lived under very different conditions. In the Antarctic, solitude has perhaps a less deleterious effect than the old condition of extreme crowding in tiny, primitive huts. He had electric light, a telephone and the medical facilities at McMurdo.

There were older scientists too, of course, some of whom have been going to Antarctica for years. One of them, Dr. Laurence M. Gould, who was chief scientist of the 1928 Byrd Expedition, informed the National Science Foundation from Antarctica of the recent fossil find, which he and a fellow geologist pronounced "not only the most important fossil ever found in Antarctica but one of the truly great fossil finds of all time." The find was made by an Ohio State University group under the direction of Dr. David H. Elliot.

Admiral Welch's quarters at McMurdo look modest on a little knoll. The outside of the hut is rough but the inside was graced, on the day I visited, by touches uncommon in the Antarctic: a linen table cloth, place cards with names carefully hand-printed on them, and an unobtrusive servant. On the center of the table was a vase with plastic flowers. Someone asked the admiral what problems kept him awake at night. He said there were two: the uncertain legal jurisdiction on the continent, and tourism. The admiral has complete criminal jurisdiction over the men in his command, but none over the civilians. "If you shot one of my men I doubt that you could be tried for it," he said. "The U. S. has no sovereignty here. Nor would the laws of the high seas apply. Technically we're guests of the New Zealanders, who claim the Ross Dependency, which was turned over to them by Great Britain in the twenties. But all territorial claims were frozen for thirty years by the Antarctic Treaty. Also, the U. S. has never recognized any nation's claims in the Antarctic and has never made any. Of course, I'd fly you out of here even if I had to manhandle you but that's all I'd do."

As for tourism, he had no doubt it would come to the Antarctic. The only question was how soon. "I just hope it won't happen during *my* watch. I'm responsible for the safety of all Americans in the Antarctic, yet I can't tell tourists what they can or can't do. What if they started wandering around on the ice? There's a tourist agency which wants to bring a ship down here and use it as quarters for tourists whom they'd fly down in a chartered plane. This is completely open territory—anybody can come down here if he has the means of getting here and staying here. But if they start flying a plane down I'd have to be prepared for a rescue mission in case it got into trouble. What if somebody decides to fly across the continent alone, in a private plane? I couldn't stop him, yet I'd have to be ready to help if he needed help or to find him if he went down."

There was a discussion of the Antarctic Treaty. Signed by the United States, the Soviet Union and ten other nations, it provides for the free exchange of scientific information and for international inspection, and bans military bases and maneuvers, weapons testing, nuclear explosions and the disposal of radioactive wastes. The military role is restricted to logistic support efforts.

After lunch we went to the Press Hut, gathered our survival gear (waddle pants, bear paws and scarf) and walked to the helicopter pads at the foot of McMurdo Station for a flight to Cape Evans to see Scott's hut and to Cape Royds to see an Adélie penguin rookery and Shackleton's hut. We set down first on Evans, some fifteen air miles from McMurdo. A glance around showed remarkable contrasts between the cape's blackness and its snow arms and cradles. Looking southwest, we saw a frozen white beach, a frozen gray sea and a horizon of white-capped blue mountains under a great naked sky. To the north across an inlet were the sheer seaside cliffs of the Barne Glacier, which flows from Mount Erebus. Erebus, much of it obscured by clouds, was a fat truncated hulk.

Scott's hut, constructed in January 1911, stands close to the beach. Originally it included a wardroom, a laboratory for biologists and physicists, and a darkroom. Its size is twenty-five by fifty feet. It was from this structure, on June 27, 1911, that Cherry-Garrard, Bowers and Wilson left on a winter journey to Cape Crozier to bring back Emperor penguin eggs for scientific study. (The Emperor lays and hatches a single egg each year in mid-winter while enduring the worst weather of that latitude.) They returned August 1st after experiencing temperatures as low as 77° below, having had only a tent to shelter them. Cherry-Garrard titled his account *The Worst Journey in the World.* Bowers and Wilson were to die with Scott on the South Pole traverse. On entering the hut one is reminded of familiar photographs, for example the picture of Scott, with legs crossed at a desk in his cubicle, writing in his journal. One sees mukluks, crockery, cots, cases, sleeping bags, pony traces, cans of oatmeal, socks, bottles of medicine, magazines, books, a packaged bar of Lifebuoy soap. Outside are the remains of stables; a seal head with empty eyes; a seal skeleton; an anchor and chain; the debris of crates; a sock; a boot sticking up out of the snow. Both this hut and the one on Royds were restored in 1960–61 by the New Zealand Huts Restoration Party with the aid of the United States Navy.

When we left Cape Evans and headed north toward Cape Royds some eight miles away we saw below us on our right the Barne Glacier, its cliffs cracked and flaked, its surface laced with crevasses. Beyond it was a wide plateau climbing to Erebus. In places the cliffs were shadow-blue, in others they resembled gleaming chalk or, where they had crumbled, gray whalebone. Having touched down near Shackleton's hut, our party headed across the snow toward the rookery on several small hills above the sea. The going was across thick snow until we reached Pony Lake with its treacherously hidden green ice.

The Adélie is about eighteen inches high and weighs some fourteen pounds. (The Emperor is much larger, being about three feet high and weighing about sixty pounds.) Penguins are marvelous navigators. They navigate by the sun, but exactly how is not known. Adélies return to their nest each year. They have been known to attack men (comically) and dogs (tragically), with the manner of a person strong on moral indignation. Everyone has read about their comical behavior, their curiosity about man's doings, their innocence in the presence of huskies, their being preyed upon by leopard seals and skuas.

There were hundreds of them already egg-sitting but there was a great bustle as individuals sought little gray pumice-textured stones for their nest, picking them up earnestly and waddling proudly away, their flippers working like primitive arms. If a nest is temporarily vacant a neighbor doesn't hesitate to steal stones from it. The occupant on returning seems blissfully unaware of the loss. When a bird wanders too close to an occupied nest the nester squawks furiously and makes threatening gestures, causing the trespasser to retreat in haste. There is a great quacking and squawking but with no suggestion of chaos, rather of the patient, endless bustle of a flea market. Their food is in the unfrozen sea miles to the north and they wait unfed until their mate returns from the sea to spell them. We had expected to visit immaculate citizens in formal dress but this was not an immaculate time. The white breasts were stained brown, tan and green and the areas around the nests were colored by guano. We had read in the accounts of the early explorers how strong the guano smell is but it seemed mild today, hardly more pungent than that of cormorants at their hangouts on Point Lobos, California.

Both Scott and Cherry-Garrard have commented on the great beauty of Cape Evans, with its western views of glaciers and snow-capped mountains and with its proximity to the striking snout of the Barne Glacier. On my brief visit, however, I was more impressed by the beauty of Royds. Royds is admittedly less spectacular but its subtle beauty is very rewarding. If the sky had had its usual brilliance the scenes might have been less remarkable. Full of heavy snow clouds yet containing luminous patches, it softened the light majestically. Black pebbly lines flowed like sinuous brush strokes over the virginal white. Black hills blown partially clear of snow stood against a white foreground. A group of birds like round-shouldered tuxedoed men seemed to be conferring at the cape's edge, a mass of blue and green pressure ice behind them.

Shackleton's hut, erected in February 1908, nestles among tiny hills and is small compared with either of Scott's two huts. A group of six men living in this hut had made the first ascent of Erebus. The first book produced on the continent, *Aurora Australis,* was printed here. The first men to reach the South Magnetic Pole were based in it. From this hut Shackleton and three companions began what was up to then the greatest advance toward the Pole, coming to within about a hundred miles of their goal and pioneering the Beardmore route. The hut was abandoned in the lull of a blizzard in 1909. Two years later it looked to visitors as if it had been vacated the day before. The dryness and cold had preserved condensed milk, biscuits, gingerbread, scones. To one visitor, who had been an occupant in 1908 and 1909, the place was eerie because of the feeling of life one felt inside it. When he turned in for the night he imagined hearing shouts. He assumed he was having an attack of nerves until a companion asked him if he too had heard shouting.

WE WANTED TO LINGER but the weather was closing in and the pilot was ready to leave. We were scheduled to tour Williams Field now, and tonight if the weather permitted we would visit a seal station. When we emerged from the heli-copter at the field there was Erebus, unobscured, blue-white, beautiful, a wisp of steam or smoke like a pennant flying from its crest. We waved good-by to the helicopter crew. Four days later the craft's engine failed during level flight. The pilot managed to land the helicopter by autorotation on a slope near a mountain but it slid down and burst into flames, with the two fatalities mentioned earlier.

We had dinner at the field, our last in Antarctica. Shortly after 10 P.M. we left McMurdo in a red USARP tracked vehi-cle for the seal station some miles to the north, sitting on two benches and being flung about as the vehicle went over sas-trugi. When it stopped we crossed the ice to get to a hut near a craggy ice cliff whose colors were startling: aquamarine, turquoise, sapphire, cobalt. Much of the sky was a sheet of grayish lavender but the western ranges were spotlighted by tawny sunlight breaking through.

The hut contained three beds in a tier, a desk and scientific equipment. A TV camera had been lowered through a hole in the ice and could be aimed by remote control. Standing in front of a small TV screen, we observed seals in the water and heard their noises with hydrophones: clucking, whistles, grunts, glottal clicks and pops. These were Weddells. There are several kinds of seals in Antarctica, among them the rare Ross, the vicious leopard, the homely crabeater and the re-markable Weddell. The Weddell can dive two thousand feet in search of food and can stay submerged up to forty minutes. How does it withstand the pressure? How does it detect its prey in the blackness of the depths? How does it find its way back to a hole in the ice? Why doesn't it get the bends on coming up? These are some of the questions scientists are trying to answer. Studies of Weddells may, among other things, reveal how our bodies use oxygen.

Outside, where it was quite cold, some mothers and pups basked on the ice. A large seal lay alone on her back, making coughing noises. Sometimes she blew air hard through her nostrils before closing them tightly with what sounded like a sigh. Or she took a deep, seemingly painful breath and made laughing motions with her throat. But the sounds which issued were comically inappropriate to her mass: they were parakeet whistles. When I drew close she mooed and showed her teeth. At around midnight the sun broke through in a molten white splash in the south, saffron streamers flowing from it. The ice dimples and sastrugi were sharply revealed. A small, gentle white cape lay on the horizon's left side, showing bits of black like ermine tails.

When we returned to the Press Hut we were greeted by five Hawaiian antenna repairmen playing poker in their long johns near the back stove and drinking beer. We had met them—our new hut mates—late one afternoon after a visit to Byrd Station. They were scheduled to work at Byrd and Pole Stations the following week. They had lived in the hut before, so had quickly made themselves at home, depositing a couple of cases of beer in the rear vestibule and lounging in their longjohns around the front stove, where they were drinking Scotch out of paper cups. Although we had never met them they had greeted us warmly and insisted on sharing their bottle.

The Antarctic is an informal place. The waffleweave longjohns are widely used as pajamas not only because the huts can be cold at night but because switching from one to the other is time-consuming and awkward in the extremely narrow, crowded and sometimes dim confines of your cubicle. There are enough chores to do without adding this change to the list. The toilet facilities, at least in the Press Hut, consist of a small metal cone located in the tiny, dark, unheated vestibule between the rear double doors, and the waffleweaves are useful if you must get up at night. Other facilities in the Press Hut are equally simple. There is no water except in a yellowish plastic jug which issues a yellowish liquid to be drunk out of a solitary green ceramic cup.

In the morning you dress fully before venturing out and

you carry your single, small towel, a small bar of yellow soap and your toilet articles up the street to the Officers' Head, where you wrestle with the huge steel door latch both on opening and on shutting the outer door. The head has two rooms, the first of which contains a number of semi-private cubicles. There are no flush toilets. In the inner or basin room you hang your parka, cap and shirt on a high wooden hook, select a basin and set to work. Some men prefer to wash and shave with their shirt on, for despite the oil-fired stove working noisily nearby (the fan is the noisiest part) the room is by no means overheated. One night a ceiling leak put out the stove and flowed onto the floor. By morning the floor was ice-covered.

You use water as sparingly as possible. It's bad form to use it freely. Despite the fact that Antarctica contains some ninety-five percent of the world's permanent ice (if the ice were to melt, the oceans would rise an estimated two hundred to two hundred and fifty feet) there is little natural water during most of the year at McMurdo and none at all at the inland stations. As a consequence fire is probably the greatest single danger on the continent. Potable water is even scarcer than seawater and is expensive to make by the usual method: melting snow. As for showers, everyone is honor-bound not to take more than one a week and a "Navy" shower at that: a quick dousing, a soaping with the water turned off, and a quick rinse. Because of the cold and the extreme dryness one isn't aware of inadequate hygiene.

Having finished with your ablutions, you put on your shirt, parka, cap and gloves and wrestle with the outer latch as you leave. Back at the Press Hut you remove the cap, parka and gloves. At times Antarctic life strikes you as being largely a matter of donning and shedding clothes and opening and shutting double doors, some of the latter heavy enough to remind you of refrigerator doors.

The use of names is also informal. You hear Willy Field or Willy for Williams Field, helo pads for helicopter pads, helo for helicopter, Herc for Hercules, Connie for Constellation,

O Head for Officers' Head, O Club for Officers' Club, Chee-chee for Christchurch, Kiwi for New Zealander, Hono for Honolulu. At first these may seem strange and, in the case of Willy Field, possibly insensitive. (The field is named for Richard T. Williams, who died when his tractor broke through the annual ice and sank in McMurdo Sound.) But in a day or two you become less aware of the strangeness and find yourself slipping into the same usage.

The Navy tends to downgrade formality in such a place, although it continues the tradition of the wardroom and of separate dining quarters for enlisted men, chiefs and officers. But the food and the portions are the same for all ranks in the new, cafeteria-style, steel-frame mess hall at McMurdo, the largest building on the continent and the most obvious sign of the change-over from a temporary residence to an indefinite one. Scientists and most visitors are styled as officers and are requested not to use or visit the dining and bar facilities of the other ranks. In the officers' section of the mess hall one receives a very pleasant impression of diversity within uniformity. People dress alike and eat the same food at the same informal tables but they may be sitting in Navy groups or scientist groups or visitor groups and discussing strikingly dissimilar matters in dissimilar language. But there is a certain formality too, as well as a university air due to the presence of numerous university-affiliated scientists.

Despite its primitive setting and still fairly primitive facilities McMurdo is a sophisticated, intellectual and cosmopolitan outpost, where you see and hear foreigners, for example, as a matter of course in the spring and summer. What everybody seems to have in common are excellent morale and a sense of the ready and rather unreserved acceptance of each other. The latter is probably due to a lively awareness of how hostile the environment can be and of how important therefore free cooperation is. There are endless reasons why men become addicted to Antarctica—the adventure, the unspoiled freshness of it, the beauty, the excitement of scientific research—but ranked high among them, certainly, are the informal way of life, the acceptance of each other and the high morale.

We talked and joked a long time with the Hawaiians before turning in. As I fell off to sleep I could not help but think it had been an all-too-brief stay in a very remarkable world.

PREFATORY NOTE

THE CONTINENT OF ANTARCTICA and its surrounding seas have been the stage of extraordinary adventures during the last two centuries, eliciting remarkable behavior from men in conditions of extreme stress. In a surprising number of instances the men who were the great explorers of Antarctica were also gifted writers. Among them were Cook, Amundsen, Scott, Shackleton and Byrd, whom the reader will encounter in the present volume, the first such Antarctic anthology to be collected.

Renewed interest in Antarctica is timely now for several reasons. 1969 marks the tenth anniversary of the Antarctic Treaty and the fortieth of Byrd's flight over the South Pole; 1971 the sixtieth anniversary of the discovery of the Pole by

Amundsen. The recent discovery of certain fossils on the continent greatly strengthens the theory of continental drift. American women have been introduced into Antarctic life and work and will soon be making valuable contributions in this area. Also, at a time of ecological crisis, the white continent is a model of a still relatively undefiled frontier, and Americans, painfully aware of a bewildering variety of social problems, are perhaps now ready to encounter, if only vicariously, a world of simplicity and purity in which the struggle between man and man must be set aside so that mankind can better understand and endure nature.

JAMES COOK

(*1728–1779*)

REMARKABLE in his time as a navigator, a marine surveyor and an expedition commander, James Cook was also a skilled observer, with an alert prose style. His writing has stood as a model for many of the subsequent British naval explorers, including Robert Falcon Scott, whose works are better known today than those of his predecessor.

Apprenticed at seventeen to a haberdasher, Cook eventually joined the Royal Navy. During the second of three great voyages made in the service of the Royal Navy, he crossed the Antarctic Circle three times, circumnavigated the globe, and reached a farthest south of 71° 10'. He made numerous geographic discoveries. Most important, he disproved the old, persistant reports of the existence of a vast South Pacific continent. At a time when some voyages were losing one-third of their crew to scurvy, he showed the possibility of conquering this vitamin-C-deficiency disease, losing only one man out of a hundred and eighteen during a one-thousand-day voyage at sea. He was greatly admired by his men.

The following selection, taken from the account of his Antarctic voyage, for which he left from England in July 1772, reveals Cook at one of his busiest and most critical times. It is not typical of the writing in the narrative as a whole. Cook is capable of more leisurely observations of men and places than this selection demonstrates. Here, sticking closely to his log and journal, he describes his positions so that they can be plotted and his tracks followed. His concern is that his work be of use to subsequent navigators.

It is interesting to compare the accounts of Cook and Forster where they deal with identical days and events, and to observe how the differences in viewpoint, emphasis and style are, to some extent, due to Cook's responsibilities as the expedition's leader as opposed to the lesser duties of the junior botanist Forster.

In Search of a Continent

1773
Novem-
ber
Friday
26

Decem-
ber
Thurs-
day
2

At eight o'clock in the evening of the 26th, we took our departure from Cape Palliser, and steered to the South, inclining to the East, *having* a favourable gale from the N.W. and S.W. We daily saw some rock-weeds, seals, Port Egmont hens, albatrosses, pintadoes, and other peterels; and on the 2d of December, being in the Latitude of 48° 23′ South, longitude 179° 16′ West, we saw a number of red bill'd penguins, which remained about us for several days. On the 5th, being in the latitude 50° 17′ South, longitude 179° 40′ East, the

variation was 18° 25′ East. At half an hour past
eight o'clock the next evening, we reckoned ourselves antipodes to our friends in London, consequently as far removed from them as possible.

On the 8th, being in latitude 55° 39′, longitude
178° 53′ West, we ceased to see penguins and seals,
and concluded that those we had seen, retired to
the southern parts of New Zealand, whenever it
was necessary for them to be at land. We had now
a strong gale at N.W., and a great swell from S.W.
This swell we got as soon as the South point of New
Zealand came in that direction; and as we had had
no wind from that quarter the six preceding days,
but, on the contrary, it had been at East, North,
and N.W., I conclude there can be no land to the
southward, under the meridian of New Zealand,
but what must lie very far to the South. The two
following days we had very stormy weather, sleet
and snow, winds between the North and South-
west.

The 11th, the storm abated, and the weather
clearing up we found the latitude to be 61° 15′
South, longitude 173° 4′ W. This fine weather was
of short duration: in the evening the wind increased to a strong gale at S.W., blew in squalls
attended with thick snow showers, hail, and sleet.
The mercury in the thermometer fell to thirty-
two; consequently the weather was very cold, and
seemed to indicate that ice was not far off.

At four o'clock the next morning, being in the
latitude of 62° 10′ South, longitude 172° West, we
saw the first ice island,* 11° ½ farther South than
the first ice we saw the preceding year after leaving the Cape of Good Hope. At the time we saw
this ice we also saw an Antarctic peterel, some
grey albatrosses, and our old companions pin-

* An early term for iceberg.

*1773
December
Sunday
5
Monday
6
Wednes.
8*

*Saturday
11*

*Sunday
12*

tadoes and blue peterels. The wind kept veering from S.W. by the N.W. to N.N.E., for the most part a fresh gale, attended with a thick haze and snow; on which account we steered to the S.E. and E., keeping the wind always on the beam, that it might be in our power to return back nearly on the same track, should our course have been interrupted by any danger whatever. For some days we had a great sea from the N.W. and S.W., so that it is not probable there can be any land near, between these two points.

*Tuesday
14*

We fell in with several large islands on the 14th, and, about noon, with a quantity of loose ice, through which we sailed. Latitude 64° 55′ South, longitude 163° 20′ West. Grey albatrosses, blue peterels, pintadoes, and fulmers, were seen. As we advanced to the S.E by E. with a fresh gale at West, we found the number of ice islands increased fast upon us. Between noon and eight in the evening, we saw but two; but before four o'clock in the morning of the 15th, we had passed seventeen, besides a quantity of loose ice which we ran through. At six o'clock, we were obliged to haul to the N.E. in order to clear an immense field which lay to the South and S.E. The ice, in most part of it, lay close packed together; in other places, there appeared partitions in the field, and a clear sea beyond it. However, I did not think it safe to venture through, as the wind would not permit us to return the same way that we must go in. Besides, as it blew strong, and the weather, at times, was exceedingly foggy, it was the more necessary for us to get clear of this loose ice, which is rather more dangerous than the great islands. It was not such ice as is usually found in bays, or rivers, and near shore; but such as breaks off from the islands, and may not improperly be called par-

*Wednes.
15*

ings of the large pieces, or the rubbish or frag- *1773*
ments which fall off when the great islands break *Decem-*
loose from the place where they are formed. *ber*

We had not stood long to the N.E. before we *Wednes.*
found ourselves embayed by the ice, and were *15*
obliged to tack and stretch to the S.W. having the
field, or loose ice, to the South, and many huge
islands to the North. After standing two hours on
this tack, the wind very luckily veering to the
westward, we tacked, stretched to the North, and
soon got clear of all the loose ice; but not before we
had received several hard knocks from the larger
pieces, which, with all our care, we could not
avoid. After clearing one danger we still had another to encounter; the weather remained foggy,
and many large islands lay in our way; so that we
had to luff for one, and bear up for another. One
we were very near falling aboard of; and if it had
happened, this circumstance would never have
been related. These difficulties, together with the
improbability of finding land farther South, and
the impossibility of exploring it, on account of the
ice, if we should find any, determined me to get
more to the North. At the time we last tacked, we
were in the longitude of 159° 20′ West, and in the
latitude of 66° 0′ S. Several penguins were seen on
some of the ice islands, and a few antarctic peterels on the wing.

We continued to stand to the North, with a fresh
gale at West, attended with thick snow showers,
till eight o'clock in the evening, when the wind
abated, the sky began to clear up, and at six o'clock
in the morning of the 16th it fell calm. Four hours *Thurs-*
after, it was succeeded by a breeze at N.E. with *day*
which we stretched to the S.E., having thick hazy *16*
weather, with snow showers, and all our rigging
coated with ice. In the evening we attempted to

take some up out of the sea, but were obliged to desist; the sea running too high, and the pieces being so large, that it was dangerous for the boat to come near them.

The next morning, being the 17th, we succeeded better; for, falling in with a quantity of loose ice, we hoisted out two boats; and, by noon, got on board as much as we could manage. We then made sail for the East, with a gentle breeze northerly, attended with snow and sleet, which froze to the rigging as it fell. At this time we were in the latitude of 64° 41′ South, longitude 155° 44′ West. The ice we took up proved to be none of the best, being chiefly composed of frozen snow; on which account it was porous, and had imbibed a good deal of salt water: but this drained off, after lying a while on deck, and the water then yielded was fresh. We continued to stretch to the East, with a piercing cold northerly wind, attended with a thick fog, snow, and sleet, that decorated all our rigging with icicles. We were hourly meeting with some of the large ice islands, which, in these high latitudes, render navigation so very dangerous: at seven in the evening, falling in with a cluster of them, we narrowly escaped running aboard of one, and, with difficulty, wore clear of the others. We stood back to the West till ten o'clock; at which time the fog cleared away, and we resumed our course to the East. At noon, the next day, we were in the latitude of 64° 49′ S., longitude 149° 19′ West. Some time after, our longitude, by observed distance of the sun and moon, was 149°19′ West; by Mr. Kendal's watch 148° 36′; and, by my reckoning, 148° 43′, latitude 64° 48′ South.

The clear weather, and the wind, veering to N.W., tempted me to steer South; which course we continued till seven in the morning of the 20th,

when the wind changing to N.E. and the sky
becoming clouded, we hauled up S.E. In the afternoon the wind increased to a strong gale, attended
with a thick fog, snow, sleet, and rain, which con-
stitutes the very worst of weather. Our rigging, at
this time, was so loaded with ice, that we had
enough to do to get our topsails down, to double
the reef. At seven o'clock in the evening, in the
longitude of 147° 46', we came, the second time,
within the antarctic or polar circle, continuing our
course to the S.E. till six o'clock the next morning.
At that time, being in the latitude of 67° 5' South,
all at once we got in among a cluster of very large
ice islands, and a vast quantity of loose pieces; and
as the fog was exceedingly thick, it was with the
utmost difficulty we wore clear of them. This done,
we stood to the N.W. till noon, when, the fog being
somewhat dissipated, we resumed our course
again to the S.E. The ice islands we met with in the
morning were very high and rugged, forming at
their tops many peaks; whereas the most of those
we had seen before, were flat at top, and not so
high; though many of them were between two and
three hundred feet in height, and between two
and three miles in circuit, with perpendicular
cliffs or sides, astonishing to behold. Most of our
winged companions had now left us; the grey albatrosses only remained; and, instead of the other
birds, we were visited by a few antarctic peterels.

The 22d we steered E.S.E. with a fresh gale at
North, blowing in squalls, one of which took hold
of the mizzen top-sail, tore it all to rags, and rendered it, for ever after, useless. At six o'clock in the
morning, the wind veering toward the West, our
course was East northerly. At this time we were in
the latitude of 67° 31', the highest we had yet been
in, longitude 142° 54' West.

We continued our course to the E. by N. till noon the 23d, when being in the latitude of 67° 12', longitude 138° 0', we steered S.E.; having then twenty-three ice islands in sight, from off the deck, and twice that number, from the mast-head; and yet we could not see above two or three miles round us. At four o'clock in the afternoon, in the latitude of 67° 20', longitude 137° 12', we fell in with such a quantity of field, or loose ice, as covered the sea in the whole extent from South to East, and was so thick and close as wholly to obstruct our passage. At this time, the wind being pretty moderate, and the sea smooth, we brought to, at the outer edge of the ice, hoisted out two boats and sent them to take some up. In the mean time, we laid hold of several large pieces along-side, and got them on board with our tackle. The taking up ice proved such cold work, that it was eight o'clock by the time the boats had made two trips; when we hoisted them in, and made sail to the West, under double-reefed top-sails and courses, with a strong gale at North, attended with snow and sleet, which froze to the rigging as it fell, making the ropes like wires, and the sails like boards or plates of metal. The shivers also were frozen so fast in the blocks, that it required our utmost efforts to get a top-sail down and up; the cold so intense as hardly to be endured; the whole sea, in a manner, covered with ice; a hard gale, and a thick fog.

Under all these unfavourable circumstances, it was natural for me to think of returning more to the North; seeing no probability of finding any land here, nor a possibility of getting farther South. And to have proceeded to the East in this latitude, must have been wrong, not only on account of the ice, but because we must have left a vast space of sea to the North unexplored; a space of 24° of latitude; in which a large tract of land might have lain. Whether such a supposition was well-grounded, could only be determined by visiting those parts.

1773
Decem-
ber

While we were taking up ice, we got two of the antarctic peterels so often mentioned, by which our conjectures were confirmed of their being of the peterel tribe. They are about the size of a large pigeon; the feathers of the head, back, and part of the upper side of the wings, are of a light brown; the belly, and under side of the wings, white; the tail feathers are also white, but tipped with brown: at the same time, we got another new peterel, smaller than the former, and all of a dark grey plumage. We remarked that these birds were fuller of feathers than any we had hitherto seen; such care has nature taken to cloath them suitably to the climate in which they live. At the same time we saw a few chocolate-coloured albatrosses; these, as well as the peterels above mentioned, we no where saw but among the ice; hence one may, with reason, conjecture that there is land to the South. If not, I must ask where these birds breed? A question which perhaps will never be determined; for hitherto we have found these lands, if any, quite inaccessible. Besides these birds, we saw a very large seal, which kept playing about us some time. One of our people who had been at Greenland, called it a sea-horse; but every one else who saw it, took it for what I have said. Since our first falling in with the ice, the mercury in the thermometer had been from 33 to 31 at noonday.

Thurs-
day
23

On the 24th, the wind abated, veering to the N.W., and the sky cleared up, in the latitude of 67° 0′, longitude 138° 15′. As we advanced to the N. E. with a gentle gale at N.W., the ice islands increased so fast upon us, that this day, at noon, we could see near 100 round us, besides an immense

Friday
24

Saturday
25

number of small pieces. Perceiving that it was likely to be calm, I got the ship into as clear a birth as I could; where she drifted along with the ice, and by taking the advantage of every light air of wind, was kept from falling aboard any of these floating isles. Here it was we spent Christmas day, much in the same manner as we did the preceding one. We were fortunate in having continual daylight, and clear weather; for had it been as foggy as on some of the preceding days, nothing less than a miracle could have saved us from being dashed to pieces.

Sunday 26

In the morning of the 26th, the whole sea was in a manner covered with ice, 200 large islands, and upwards, being seen within the compass of four or five miles, which was the limits of our horizon; besides smaller pieces innumerable. Our latitude at noon was 66° 15'; longitude 134° 22'. By observation we found that the ship had drifted, or gone about 20 miles to the N.E. or E.N.E.; whereas, by the ice islands, it appeared that she had gone little or nothing; from which we concluded that the ice drifted nearly in the same direction, and at the same rate. At four o'clock a breeze sprung up at W.S.W., and enabled us to steer North, the most probable course to extricate ourselves from these dangers.

We continued our course to the North with a gentle breeze at West, attended with clear weather, till four o'clock the next morning, when

Monday 27

meeting with a quantity of loose ice, we brought to, and took on board as much as filled all our empty casks, and for several days present expence. This done, we made sail, and steered N.W. with a gentle breeze at N.E. clear frosty weather. Our latitude at this time was 65° 53' S., longitude 133° 42' West; islands of ice not half so numerous as before.

At four in the morning of the 28th, the wind *1773* having veered more to the East and S.E., in- *Decem-* creased to a fresh gale, and was attended with *ber* snow showers. Our course was North till noon the next day. Being then in the latitude of 62° 24', *Tuesday* longitude 134° 37', we steered N.W. by N. Some *28* hours after, the sky cleared up, and the wind abating, veered more to the South. *Wednes.*

On the 30th, had little wind westerly; dark *29* gloomy weather, with snow and sleet at times; *Thurs-* several whales seen playing about the ship, but *day* very few birds; islands of ice in plenty, and a swell *30* from W.N.W.

On the 31st, little wind from the westward; fair and clear weather, which afforded an opportunity *Friday* to air the spare sails, and to clean and smoke the *31* ship between decks. At noon our latitude was 59° 40' S., longitude 135° 11' West. Our observation to-day gave us reason to conjecture that we had a southerly current. Indeed, this was no more than what might reasonably be supposed, to account for such huge masses of ice being brought from the South. In the afternoon we had a few hours calm, succeeded by a breeze from the East, which enabled us to resume our N.W. by N. course.

January 1st, the wind remained not long at East, *1774* but veered round by the South to West; blew *January* fresh; attended with snow showers. In the eve- *Saturday* ning, being in the latitude of 58° 39' S., we passed *1* two islands of ice; after which we saw no more till we stood again to the South.

At five o'clock in the morning on the 2d, it fell *Sunday* calm: being at this time in the latitude of 58° 2', *2* longitude 137° 12'. The calm being succeeded by a breeze at East, we steered N.W. by W. My reason for steering this course was to explore part of the great space of sea between us and our track to the South.

On the 3d, at noon, being in latitude 56° 46′, longitude 139° 45′, the weather became fair, and the wind veered to S.W. About this time we saw a few small Divers (as we call them) of the peterel tribe, which we judged to be such as are usually seen near land, especially in the bays, and on the coast of New Zealand. I cannot tell what to think of these birds. Had there been more of them, I should have been ready enough to believe that we were, at this time, not very far from land; as I never saw one so far from known land before. Probably these few had been drawn thus far by some shoal of fish; for such were certainly about us, by the vast number of blue peterels, albatrosses, and such other birds as are usually seen in the great ocean; all or most of whom left us before night. Two or three pieces of sea-weed were also seen; but these appeared old and decayed.

At eight o'clock in the evening, being in the latitude of 56° S., longitude 140° 31′ West, the wind fixing in the Western board, obliged us to steer North-Easterly, and laid me under the necessity of leaving unexplored a space of the sea to the West, containing near 40° of longitude, and half that in latitude. Had the wind continued favourable, I intended to have run 15 or 20 degrees of longitude more to the West in the latitude we were then in, and back again to the East in the latitude of 50°. This route would have so intersected the space above mentioned, as hardly to have left room for the bare supposition of any land lying there. Indeed, as it was, we have little reason to believe that there is; but rather the contrary, from the great hollow swell we had had, for several days, from the W. and N.W. though the wind had blown from a contrary direction great part of the time;

which is a great sign we had not been covered by
any land between these two points.

While we were in the high latitudes, many of
our people were attacked with a slight fever, occasioned by colds. It happily yielded to the simplest
remedies; was generally removed in a few days;
and, at this time, we had not above one or two on
the sick list.

We proceeded N.E. by N. till the 6th, at noon. *Thurs-*
Being then in the latitude 52° 0' S., longitude 135° *day*
32' West, and about 200 leagues from our track to *6*
Otaheite, in which space it was not probable, all
circumstances considered, there is any extensive
land; and it being still less probable any lay to the
West, from the great mountainous billows we had
had, and still continued to have, from that quarter,
I, therefore, steered N.E., with a fresh gale at
W.S.W.

At eight o'clock in the morning, on the 7th, be- *Friday*
ing in the latitude of 50° 49' South, we observed *7*
several distances of the sun and moon, which gave
the longitude as follows, viz.

By Mr.	Wales,	133°	24'	West.
	Gilbert,	133	10	
	Clerke,	133	0	
	Smith,	133	37	25″
	Myself,	133	37	
	Mean,	133	21	43
	By the Watch,	133	44	West.
	my reckoning,	133	39	
Variation of the compass,*		6	2	East.
Thermometer,		50		

* The magnetic compass points toward the magnetic pole, not toward the
geographic pole. The discrepancy between the two directions is known as
the variation. This is a simplified explanation. As the magnetic compass nears
the magnetic pole it tends increasingly to point down. This inclination is
known as the dip. At the pole the compass dips 90°.—C. N.

1774
January
Saturday
8

The next morning we observed again; and the results were agreeable to the preceding observations, allowing for the ship's run. I must here take notice that our longitude can never be erroneous, while we have so good a guide as Mr. Kendal's watch. This day, at noon, we steered E.N.E. ½ E. being then in the latitude of 49° 7' South, longitude 131° 2' West.

Sunday
9

On the 9th, in the latitude of 48° 17' S., longitude 127° 10' West, we steered East, with a fine fresh gale at West, attended with clear, pleasant weather, and a great swell from the same direction as the wind.

Monday
10

Tuesday
11

Wednes.
12

In the morning of the 10th, having but little wind, we put a boat in the water, in which some of the officers went and shot several birds. These afforded us a fresh meal: they were of the peterel tribe, and such as are usually seen at any distance from land. Indeed, neither birds, nor any other thing was to be seen, that could give us the least hopes of finding any; and, therefore, at noon the next day, being then in the latitude of 47° 51' S., longitude 122° 12' West, and a little more than 200 leagues from my track to Otaheite in 1769, I altered the course, and steered S.E. with a fresh gale at S.W. by W. In the evening, when our latitude was 48° 22' S. longitude 121° 29' West, we found the variation to be 2° 34' East; which is the least variation we had found without the tropic. In the evening of the next day we found it to be 4° 30' East; our latitude, at that time, was 50° 5' S. longitude 119½° West.

Thurs-
day
13

Our course was now more Southerly, till the evening of the 13th, when we were in the latitude of 53° 0' South, longitude 118° 3' West. The wind being then at N.W. a strong gale, with a thick fog and rain, which made it unsafe to steer large, I

hauled up S.W., and continued this course till noon *1774*
the next day, when our latitude was 56° 4' S., longi- *January*
tude 122° 1' West. The wind having veered to the *Friday*
North, and the fog continuing, I hauled to the *14*
East, under courses and close reefed topsails. But
this sail we could not carry long; for before eight
o'clock in the evening, the wind increased to a *Sunday*
perfect storm, and obliged us to lie to, under the *16*
mizzenstaysail, till the morning of the 16th, when
the wind having a good deal abated, and veered to
West, we set the courses, reefed topsails, and stood
to the South. Soon after, the weather cleared up;
and, in the evening, we found the latitude to be
56° 48' S., longitude 119° 8' West.

We continued to steer to the South, inclining to
the East, till the 18th, when we stood to the S.W. *Tuesday*
with the wind at S.E., being at this time in the *18*
latitude of 61° 9' South, longitude 116° 7' West. At
ten o'clock in the evening, it fell calm, which con- *Wednes.*
tinued till two the next morning, when a breeze *19*
sprung up at North, which soon after increased to
a fresh gale, and fixed at N.E. With this we steered *Thurs-*
South till noon on the 20th, when, being now in *day*
the latitude of 62° 34' South, longitude 116° 24' *20*
West, we were again becalmed.

In this situation we had two ice islands in sight,
one of which seemed to be as large as any we had
seen. It could not be less than two hundred feet in
height, and terminated in a peak not unlike the
cupola of St. Paul's church. At this time we had a
great westerly swell, which made it improbable
that any land should lie between us and the
meridian of 133½°, which was our longitude, under the latitude we were now in, when we stood
to the North. In all this route we had not seen the
least thing that could induce us to think we were
ever in the neighbourhood of any land. We had,

1774
January

indeed, frequently seen pieces of sea-weed; but this, I am well assured, is no sign of the vicinity of land; for weed is seen in every part of the ocean. After a few hours calm, we got a wind from S.E.; but it was very unsettled, and attended with thick snow showers; at length it fixed at S. by E., and we stretched to the East. The wind blew fresh, was piercing cold, and attended with snow and sleet.

Saturday
22

On the 22d, being in the latitude of 62° 5′ South, longitude 112° 24′ West, we saw an ice island, an antarctic peterel, several blue peterels, and some other known birds; but no one thing that gave us the least hopes of finding land.

Sunday
23

On the 23d at noon, we were in the latitude of 62° 22′ S., longitude 110° 24′. In the afternoon, we passed an ice island. The wind, which blew fresh,

Monday
24

continued to veer to the West; and at eight o'clock the next morning, it was to the North of West, when I steered S. by W. and S.S.W. At this time we

Tuesday
25

were in the latitude of 63° 20′ South, longitude 108° 7′ West, and had a great sea from S.W. We continued this course till noon the next day the

Wednes.
26

25th, when we steered due South. Our latitude, at this time, was 65° 24′ South, longitude 109° 31′ West; the wind was at North; the weather mild,

Wednes.
26

and not unpleasant; and not a bit of ice in view. This we thought a little extraordinary; as it was but a month before, and not quite two hundred

Thurs-
day
27

leagues to the East, that we were in a manner blocked up with large islands of ice in this very latitude. Saw a single pintadoe peterel, some blue peterels, and a few brown albatrosses. In the evening, being under the same meridian, and in the latitude of 65° 44′ South, the variation was 19° 27′ East; but the next morning, in the latitude of 66° 20′ South, longitude the same as before, it was

only 18° 20′ East: probably the mean between the
two, is the nearest the truth. At this time, we had
nine small islands in sight; and soon after, we
came, the third time, within the antarctic polar
circle, in the longitude of 109° 31′ West. About
noon, seeing the appearance of land to the S.E.,
we immediately trimmed our sails and stood towards it. Soon after it disappeared, but we did not
give it up till eight o'clock the next morning, when
we were well assured that it was nothing but
clouds, or a fog bank; and then we resumed our
course to the South, with a gentle breeze at N.E.,
attended with a thick fog, snow, and sleet.

We now began to meet with ice islands more
frequently than before; and, in the latitude of
69° 38′ South, longitude 108° 12′ West, we fell in
with a field of loose ice. As we began to be in want
of water, I hoisted out two boats and took up as
much as yielded about ten tons. This was cold
work, but it was now familiar to us. As soon as we
had done, we hoisted in the boats, and afterwards
made short boards over that part of the sea we
had, in some measure, made ourselves acquainted
with. For we had now so thick a fog that we could
not see two hundred yards round us; and as we
knew not the extent of the loose ice, I durst not
steer to the South till we had clear weather. Thus
we spent the night, or rather that part of the
twenty-four hours which answered to night; for
we had no darkness but what was occasioned by
fogs.

At four o'clock in the morning of the 29th, the
fog began to clear away; and the day becoming
clear and serene, we again steered to the South
with a gentle gale at N.E. and N.N.E. The variation was found to be 22° 41′ E. This was in the
latitude of 69° 45′ South, longitude 108° 5′ West;

and, in the afternoon, being in the same longitude, and in the latitude of 70° 23' South, it was 24° 31' East. Soon after, the sky became clouded, and the air very cold. We continued our course to the South, and passed a piece of weed covered with barnacles, which a brown albatross was picking off. At ten o'clock, we passed a very large ice island; it was not less than three or four miles in circuit. Several more being seen ahead, and the weather becoming foggy, we hauled the wind to the Northward; but in less than two hours, the weather cleared up, and we again stood South.

On the 30th, at four o'clock in the morning, we perceived the clouds, over the horizon to the South, to be of an unusual snow-white brightness, which we knew denounced our approach to field-ice. Soon after, it was seen from the top-mast-head; and at eight o'clock, we were close to its edge. It extended East and West, far beyond the reach of our sight. In the situation we were in, just the southern half of our horizon was illuminated, by the rays of light reflected from the ice, to a considerable height. Ninety-seven ice hills were distinctly seen within the field, besides those on the outside; many of them very large, and looking like a ridge of mountains, rising one above another till they were lost in the clouds. The outer, or northern edge of this immense field, was composed of loose or broken ice close packed together; so that it was not possible for any thing to enter it. This was about a mile broad; within which was solid ice in one continued compact body. It was rather low and flat (except the hills), but seemed to increase in height, as you traced it to the South; in which direction it extended beyond our sight. Such mountains of ice as these, were, I believe, never seen in the Greenland Seas; at least, not that

I ever heard or read of; so that we cannot draw a *1774*
comparison between the ice here, and there. It *January*
must be allowed that these prodigious ice mountains must add such additional weight to the ice
fields which inclose them, as cannot but make a
great difference between the navigating this icy
sea and that of Greenland.

I will not say it was impossible any where to get
farther to the South; but the attempting it would
have been a dangerous and rash enterprise, and
what, I believe, no man in my situation would
have thought of. It was, indeed, *my* opinion, as
well as the opinion of most on board, that this ice
extended quite to the pole, or perhaps joined to
some land, to which it had been fixed from the
earliest time; and that it is here, that is to the South
of this parallel, where all the ice we find scattered
up and down to the North, is first formed, and
afterwards broken off by gales of wind, or other
causes, and brought to the North by the currents,
which we always found to set in that direction in
the high latitudes. As we drew near this ice some
penguins were heard, but none seen; and but few
other birds, or any other thing that could induce
us to think any land was near. And yet I think
there must be some to the South behind this ice;
but if there is, it can afford no better retreat for
birds, or any other animals, than the ice itself, with
which it must be wholly covered. I, who had ambition not only to go farther than any one had been
before, but as far as it was possible for man to go,
was not sorry at meeting with this interruption; as
it, in some measure, relieved us; at least, shortened
the dangers and hardships inseparable from the
navigation of the southern polar regions. Since
therefore we could not proceed one inch farther
to the South, no other reason need be assigned for

1774
January

Sunday
30

Monday
31

Febru-
ary
Tuesday
1

Friday
4

Sunday
6

my tacking, and standing back to the North; being at this time in the latitude of 71° 10′ South, longitude 106° 54′ West.

It was happy for us, that the weather was clear when we fell in with this ice, and that we discovered it so soon as we did; for we had no sooner tacked than we were involved in a thick fog. The wind was at East, and blew a fresh breeze; so that we were able to return back over that space we had already made ourselves acquainted with. At noon, the mercury in the thermometer stood at 32½, and we found the air exceedingly cold. The thick fog continuing with showers of snow, gave a coat of ice to our rigging of near an inch thick. In the afternoon of the next day the fog cleared away at intervals; but the weather was cloudy and gloomy, and the air excessively cold; however, the sea within our horizon was clear of ice.

We continued to stand to the North with the wind easterly till the afternoon on the 1st of February, when falling in with some loose ice which had broken from an island to windward, we hoisted out two boats, and having taken some on board, resumed our course to the North and N.E., with gentle breezes from the S.E., attended sometimes with fair weather, and at other times with snow and sleet. On the 4th we were in the latitude of 65° 42′ South, longitude 99° 44′. The next day the wind was very unsettled both in strength and position, and attended with snow and sleet. At length on the 6th, after a few hours calm, we got a breeze at South, which soon after freshened, fixed at W.S.W., and was attended with snow and sleet.

I now came to a resolution to proceed to the North, and to spend the ensuing winter within the Tropic, if I met with no employment before I came there. I was now well satisfied no continent was to be found in this ocean, but what must lie so far to the South as to be wholly inaccessible on account of ice; and that, if one should be found in the Southern Atlantic Ocean, it would be necessary to have the whole summer before us to explore it. On the other hand, upon a supposition that there is no land there, we undoubtedly might have reached the Cape of Good Hope by April, and so have put an end to the expedition, so far as it related to the finding a continent; which indeed was the first object of the voyage. But for me, at this time, to have quitted this Southern Pacific Ocean, with a good ship expressly sent out on discoveries, a healthy crew, and not in want either of stores or of provisions, would have been betraying not only a want of perseverance, but of judgment, in supposing the South Pacific Ocean to have been so well explored, that nothing remained to be done in it. This, however, was not my opinion; for, although I had proved there was no continent but what must lie far to the South, there remained, nevertheless, room for very large islands in places wholly unexamined: and many of those which were formerly discovered, are but imperfectly explored, and their situations as imperfectly known. I was besides of opinion, that my remaining in this sea some time longer, would be productive of improvements in navigation and geography, as well as other sciences. I had several times communicated my thoughts on this subject to Captain Furneaux; but as it then wholly depended on what we might meet with to the South, I could not give it in orders, without running the risque of drawing us from the main object.

Since now nothing had happened to prevent me from carrying these views into execution, my intention was first to go in search of the land, said to

1774
February
Sunday
6

have been discovered by Juan Fernandez, above
a century ago, in about the latitude of 38°; if I
should fail in finding this land, then to go in search
of Easter Island or Davis's Land, whose situation
was known with so little certainty, that the attempts lately made to find it had miscarried. I next
intended to get within the Tropic, and then proceed to the West, touching at, and settling the
situations of such islands as we might meet with till
we arrived at Otaheite, where it was necessary I
should stop to look for the Adventure. I had also
thoughts of running as far West as the Tierra Austral del Espiritu Santo, discovered by Quiros, and
which M. de Bougainville calls the Great Cyclades.
Quiros speaks of this land as being large, or lying
in the neighbourhood of large lands; and as this
was a point which Bougainville had neither
confirmed nor refuted, I thought it was worth
clearing up. From this land my design was to steer
to the South, and so back to the East between the
latitudes of 50° and 60°; intending, if possible, to be
the length of Cape Horn in November next, when
we should have the best part of the summer before
us to explore the southern part of the Atlantic
Ocean. Great as this design appeared to be, I however thought it possible to be executed; and when
I came to communicate it to the officers, I had the
satisfaction to find, that they all heartily concurred
in it. I should not do these gentlemen justice, if I
did not take some opportunity to declare, that
they always shewed the utmost readiness to carry
into execution, in the most effectual manner, every measure I thought proper to take. Under such
circumstances, it is hardly necessary to say, that
the seamen were always obedient and alert; and,
on this occasion, they were so far from wishing the
voyage at an end, that they rejoiced at the pros-

pect of its being prolonged another year, and of
soon enjoying the benefits of a milder climate.
I now steered North, inclining to the East, and
in the evening we were overtaken by a furious
storm at W.S.W., attended with snow and sleet. It
came so suddenly upon us, that before we could
take in our sails, two old top-sails, which we had *Sunday*
bent to the yards, were blown to pieces, and the *6*
other sails much damaged. The gale lasted, without the least intermission, till the next morning,
when it began to abate; it, however, continued to *Monday*
blow very fresh till noon on the 12th, when it *7*
ended in a calm.
At this time we were in the latitude of 50° 14′ *Saturday*
South, longitude 95° 18′ West. Some birds being *12*
about the ship, we took the advantage of the calm
to put a boat in the water, and shot several birds,
on which we feasted the next day. One of these
birds was of that sort, which has been so often
mentioned in this journal, under the name of Port
Egmont hens. They are of the gull kind, about the
size of a raven, with a dark brown plumage, except
the under-side of each wing, where there are some
white feathers. The rest of the birds were albatrosses and sheer-waters.
After a few hours calm, having got a breeze at
N.W., we made a stretch to the S.W. for twenty-
four hours; in which route we saw a piece of wood,
a bunch of weed, and a diving peterel. The wind
having veered more to the West, made us tack and *Monday*
stretch to the North till noon on the 14th, at which *14*
time we were in the latitude of 49° 32′ South, longitude 95° 11′ West. We had now calms and light *Tuesday*
breezes succeeding each other, till the next morn- *15*
ing, when the wind freshened at W.N.W. and was
attended with a thick fog and drizzling rain the
three following days, during which time we

stretched to the North, inclining to the East, and crossed my track to Otaheite in 1769. I did intend to have kept more to the West, but the strong winds from that direction put it out of my power.

On the eighteenth, the wind veered to S.W., and blew very fresh, but was attended with clear weather, which gave us an opportunity to ascertain our longitude by several lunar observations

*Friday
18*

made by Messrs. Wales, Clarke, Gilbert, and Smith. The mean result of all, was 94° 19′ 30″ West; Mr. Kendal's watch, at the same time, gave 94° 46′ West; our latitude was 43° 53′ South. The wind continued not long at S.W. before it veered back to the West and W.N.W.

As we advanced to the North, we felt a most sensible change in the weather. The 20th, at noon,

*Sunday
20*

we were in the latitude of 39° 58′ South, longitude 94° 37′ West. The day was clear and pleasant, and I may say, the only summer's day we had had since we left New Zealand. The mercury in the thermometer rose to 66.

We still continued to steer to the North, as the wind remained in the old quarter; and the next

*Monday
21*

day, at noon, we were in the latitude 37° 54′ South; which was the same that Juan Fernandez's discovery is said to lie in. We, however, had not the least signs of any land lying in our neighbourhood.

*Tuesday
22*

The next day, at noon, we were in latitude 36° 10′ South, longitude 94° 56′ West. Soon after, the wind veered to S.S.E., and enabled us to steer

*Friday
25*

W.S.W., which I thought the most probable direction to find the land of which we were in search; and yet I had no hopes of succeeding, as we had a large hollow swell from the same point. We, however, continued this course till the 25th, when, the wind having veered again round to the westward, I gave it up, and stood away to the

North, in order to get into the latitude of Easter
Island: our latitude, at this time, was 37° 52', longitude 101° 10' West.

I was now well assured that the discovery of
Juan Fernandez, if any such was ever made, can
be nothing but a small island; there being hardly
room for a large land, as will fully appear by the
tracks of Captain Wallis, Bougainville, of the Endeavour, and this of the Resolution. Whoever
wants to see an account of the discovery in question, will meet with it in Mr. Dalrymple's Collection of Voyages to the South Seas. This gentleman
places it under the meridian of 90°, where I think
it cannot be; for M. de Bougainville seems to have
run down under that meridian; and we had now
examined the latitude in which it is said to lie,
from the meridian of 94° to 101'. It is not probable
it can lie to the East of 90°; because if it did, it must
have been seen, at one time or other, by ships
bound from the northern to the southern parts of
America. Mr. Pengré, in a little treatise concerning the Transit of Venus, published in 1768, gives
some account of land having been discovered by
the Spaniards in 1714, in the latitude of 38°, and 550
leagues from the coast of Chili, which is in the
longitude of 110° or 111° West, and within a degree
or two of my track in the Endeavour; so that this
can hardly be its situation. In short, the only probable situation it can have, must be about the
meridian of 106° or 108° West; and then it can only
be a small isle, as I have already observed.

I was now taken ill of the bilious colic, which was
so violent as to confine me to my bed; so that the
management of the ship was left to Mr. Cooper
the first officer, who conducted her very much to
my satisfaction. It was several days before the
most dangerous symptoms of my disorder were

1774
Febru-
ary

removed; during which time Mr. Patten the surgeon was to me, not only a skilful physician, but an
affectionate nurse; and I should ill deserve the
care he bestowed on me, if I did not make this
public acknowledgment. When I began to
recover, a favourite dog belonging to Mr. Forster
fell a sacrifice to my tender stomach. We had no

Friday
25

other fresh meat whatever on board; and I could
eat of this flesh, as well as broth made of it, when
I could taste nothing else. Thus I received nourishment and strength, from food which would have
made most people in Europe sick: so true it is, that
necessity is governed by no law.

Monday
28

On the 28th, in the latitude of 33° 7′ South, longitude 102° 33′ West, we began to see flying-fish,
egg-birds, and nodies, which are said not to go
above sixty or eighty leagues from land; but of this
we have no certainty. No one yet knows to what
distance any of the oceanic birds go to sea; for my
own part, I do not believe there is one in the whole
tribe that can be relied on, in pointing out the
vicinity of land.

In the latitude of 30° 30′ South, longitude 101°
45′ West, we began to see men of war birds. In the
latitude of 29° 44′, longitude 100° 45′ West, we had
a calm for near two days together, during which
time the heat was intolerable; but what ought to
be remarked, was a very great swell from the S.W.

March
Sunday
6

On the 6th of March the calm was succeeded by
an easterly wind, with which we steered N.W. till
noon the 8th, when, being in the latitude of 27°
4′ South, longitude 103° 58′ West, we steered West;

Tuesday
8

meeting every day with great numbers of birds,
such as men of war, tropic, and egg-birds, nodies,
sheer-waters, &c. and once we passed several
pieces of sponge, and a small dried leaf not unlike
a bay one. Soon after, we saw a sea snake, in every

respect like those we had before seen at the Tropi- *1774*
cal Islands. We also saw plenty of fish, but were *March*
such bad fishers that we caught only four al- *Tuesday*
bacores, which were very acceptable, to me espe- *8*
cially, who was just recovering from my late
illness.

GEORGE FORSTER

(*1754–1794*)

IT HAS BEEN SAID that George (Johann George Adam)
Forster had some influence on the subsequent creation by
Goethe, Heine and other German literary masters of a style
of travel literature in which natural scenes and objects are
lovingly presented, yet correctly detailed. His father, Johann
Reinhold Forster, was a clergyman and a talented amateur
scientist. Both father and son were born in Germany and
both emigrated to England in 1766, where George, through
translation work, mastered English prose. The Forsters were
scientific members of Cook's second voyage around the
world, a voyage which was to be the turning point of the son's
life. The son wrote, "On the 11th of June, 1772, my father and
myself were appointed to embark in this expedition, in order

to collect, describe, and draw the objects of natural history which we might expect to meet with in our course." His masterly two-volume description of the voyage, based on his father's journals, made him famous.

He was twelve when he emigrated to England, eighteen when he went on the expedition and twenty-three when his book was published. He died at forty. His interests were wide-ranging and humanitarian, with a modern skeptical cast.

The High Latitudes

1773
November
Saturday
27

December
Monday
6

The morning after we had taken our departure, we had a N.N.W. wind, which raised the thermometer to 64 deg. The two next days it stood at 54 deg. then at 48; and when we were in about 49° of south latitude, at 44½ deg. On the 28th of November, we observed a number of seals, or perhaps sea-lions, passing by us at a distance towards the land which we had left. From that time to the 6th of December we daily saw great flocks of blue and other petrels, together with the different species of albatrosses, the skuas or grey gulls, many penguins, and abundance of sea-weed. About seven in the evening, on that day, we were in the latitude of 51° 33' south, and long. 180°; consequently just at the point of the antipodes of London. The remembrance of domestic felicity, and of the sweets of society, called forth a sigh from every heart which felt the tender ties of filial or parental affection. We are the first Europeans, and I believe I may add, the first human beings, who have reached this point, where it is probable none will come after us.

A common report prevails indeed in England concerning Sir Francis Drake, who is said to have
visited the antipodes, which the legend expresses
by "his having passed under the middle arch of
London-bridge:" but this is a mistake, as his track
lay along the coast of America, and probably origi-
nates from his having passed the *periœci*, or the
point in 180° long. on the same circle of north latitude, on the coast of California.

*1773
Decem-
ber*

In proportion as we advanced to the southward
the thermometer fell; and on the 10th, in the
morning, the wind coming more ahead, it descended to 37°. At noon, we had reached the latitude of 59° south, without having met with any ice,
though we fell in with it the preceding year on the
10th of December, between the 50th and 51st deg.
of south latitude. It is difficult to account for this
difference; perhaps a severe winter preceding our
first course from the Cape of Good Hope, might
accumulate more ice that year than the next,
which is the more probable, as we learnt at the
Cape that the winter had been sharper there than
usual; perhaps a violent storm might break the
polar ice, and drive it so far to the northward as we
found it; and perhaps both these causes might con-
cur, with others, to produce this effect.

*Friday
10*

On the 11th, at night, the cold encreased, the
thermometer standing at 34 deg. and at four
o'clock the next morning a large island of floating
ice was seen ahead, which we passed an hour afterwards. At eight o'clock the thermometer was
already at 31½ deg., the air being probably re-
frigerated by the ice, though we did not see more
than this one piece. At noon we found the latitude
to be 61° 46' south. The next morning the thermometer stood at 31 deg. and we ran to the eastward with a fresh breeze, though we had a

*Sunday
12*

surprising fall of snow, which filled the air to such a degree that we could not see ten yards before us. Our friend Mahine* had already expressed his surprize at several little snow and hail showers on the preceding days, this phænomenon being utterly unknown in his country. The appearance of "white stones," which melted in his hand, was altogether miraculous in his eyes, and though we endeavoured to explain to him that cold was the cause of their formation, yet I believe his ideas on that subject were never very clear. The heavy fall of snow this day surprised him more than what he had seen before, and after a long consideration of its singular qualities, he told us he would call it the *white rain* when he came back to his country. He did not see the first ice on account of the early hour of the morning; but two days after, in about 65 deg. of south latitude, he was struck with astonishment upon seeing one of the largest pieces, and the day following presented him with an extensive field of ice, which blocked up our farther progress to the south, and gave him great pleasure, supposing it to be land. We told him that so far from being land, it was nothing but fresh water, which we found some difficulty to convince him of at first, till we shewed him the ice which was formed in the scuttled cask on the deck. He assured us, however, that he would at all events call this the *white land*, by way of distinguishing it from all the rest. Already, at New Zeeland, he had collected a number of little slender twigs, which he carefully tied in a bundle, and made use of instead of journals. For every island which he had seen and visited, after his departure from the Society Isles, he had selected a little twig; so that his collection amounted at present to nine or ten, of which he

* A native of the Society Islands.

remembered the names perfectly well in the same
order as we had seen them, and the white land, or
whennua tèatèa, was the last. He enquired frequently how many other countries we should
meet with in our way to England, and formed a
separate bundle of them, which he studied every
day with equal care as the first. The tediousness of
this part of our voyage probably made him so eager to know how it would end; and the salt provisions, together with the cold climate, contributed
to disgust him. His usual amusement was to separate the red feathers from the aprons, used in
dancing, which he had purchased at Tonga-Tab-
boo, and to join eight or ten of them together into
a little tuft, by means of coco-nut core. The rest of
his time he passed in walking on deck, visiting the
officers and petty officers, and warming himself by
the fire in the captain's cabin. We took this opportunity to improve in the knowledge of his language, and, by degrees, revised the whole
vocabulary which we had collected at the Society
Isles. By this method we became possessed of a
fund of useful intelligence concerning his country
and the adjacent isles, which led us to make many
enquiries at our subsequent return to those islands.

The ice-fields appeared, in different parts of the
horizon, about us on the 15th in the morning, so
that we were in a manner embayed; and, as we
saw no possibility of advancing to the south, we
ran to the N.N.E. to get clear of them. The
weather, which was already foggy, became
thicker towards noon, and made our situation,
amidst a great number of floating rocks of ice,
extremely dangerous. About one o'clock, whilst
the people were at dinner, we were alarmed by
the sudden appearance of a large island of ice just

ahead of us. It was absolutely impossible either to wear or tack the ship, on account of its proximity, and our only resource was to keep as near the wind as possible, and to try to weather the danger. We were in the most dreadful suspense for a few minutes, and though we fortunately succeeded, yet the ship passed within her own length to wind-ward of it. Notwithstanding the constant perils to which our course exposed us in this unexplored ocean, our ship's company were far from being so uneasy as might have been expected; and, as in battle the sight of death becomes familiar and often unaffecting, so here, by daily experiencing such hair-breadth escapes, we passed uncon-cernedly on, as if the waves, the winds, and rocks of ice had not the power to hurt us. The pieces of ice had a variety of shapes, in the same manner as those which we had observed to the southward of the Indian Ocean; and many pyramids, obelisks, and church-spires appeared from time to time. Their height was not much inferior to that which we had observed among the first islands of ice in 1772; and many likewise resembled them in being of a great extent and perfectly level at top.

The number of birds which we had hitherto met with on our passage, would have persuaded any other voyagers but ourselves of the approach of land. We were, however, so much used to their appearance on the sea at present, as never once to form any expectation of discovering land from that circumstance. Flocks of blue petrels and pin-tadas, many albatrosses, with now and then a soli-tary skua had attended us every day; and to these, since our approach to the ice, we could join the snowy and antarctic petrels and the fulmars. How-ever, pinguins, sea-weed, or seals, had not been observed since the 10th.

The weather, which was extremely moist and *1773* disagreeably cold, proved unfavourable to the *December* doves and pigeons which many people had pur- *ber* chased at the Society and Friendly Islands, and to the singing-birds which they had been at great pains to catch alive at New Zeeland. We had five doves at our departure from this country, all which died one after another before the 16th of December, being much more exposed to the cold in our cabins, than in the sailors' births. The ther- mometer in our cabins was never more than 5 deg. higher than in the open air on deck, and their situation abreast of the main-mast, where the strain of the ship is greatest, exposed them to cur- rents of air, and made them admit water like sieves.

On the 16th, in the afternoon, and on the 17th, *Friday* we hoisted out our boats and collected some loose *17* pieces of ice to fill our empty casks with fresh water. The ice which we picked up was old and spungy, and impregnated with saline particles, from having long been in a state of decay; there- fore did not afford us very good water, but it was drinkable, particularly if we let the pieces of ice lie on deck for some time, by which means the salt- water was almost entirely drained off. From this time till the 20th we saw no birds about us, which disappeared without any visible cause; but on that day some albatrosses appeared again.

Having left the ice behind which obstructed our passage, we had gradually advanced to the south- ward again, that being our principal object, and on the 20th in the afternoon, we crossed the antarctic *Monday* circle the second time during our voyage. The *20* weather was wet and foggy, ice islands were nu- merous around us, and the gale was very brisk. Many antarctic petrels, and a whale which

*1773
December*

spouted up the water near us, seemed to indicate our entrance into the frigid zone. At night two seals appeared, which we had not seen for fourteen days past, and gave some faint hopes of seeing land to several of our shipmates; but our course disappointed their expectations, by continuing within the circle as far as 67° 12′ S. lat. for several days following.

*Thursday
23*

On the 23d in the afternoon, we were surrounded with islands of ice, and the sea was in a manner covered with small fragments. The ship was therefore brought to, the boats hoisted out, and a great quantity of good ice taken on board. The birds were at present very numerous about us again, and some antarctic and other petrels were shot and taken up, which we had an opportunity of drawing and describing. About this time many persons were afflicted with violent rheumatic pains, head-aches, swelled glands, and catarrhal fevers, which some attributed to the use of ice-water. My father, who had complained of a cold for several days past, was obliged to keep his bed today, having a severe rheumatism with a fever. His complaint seemed rather to arise from the wretched accommodations which he had on board, every thing in his cabin rotting in the wet which it admitted, and being mouldy. The cold was so sensible there this day in particular, that he found only a difference of two degrees and a half between the thermometer there, and that upon the deck.

*Saturday
25*

After hoisting in our boats we made sail to the northward, as much as a contrary wind permitted, during all the night and the next day. On the 25th, the weather was clear and fair, but the wind died away to a perfect calm, upwards of ninety large ice-islands being in sight at noon. This being

Christmas-day, the captain according to custom, *1773*
invited the officers and mates to dinner, and one *Decem-*
of the lieutenants entertained the petty-officers. *ber*
The sailors feasted on a double portion of pudding,
regaling themselves with the brandy of their allowance, which they had saved for this occasion
some months before-hand, being sollicitous to
get very drunk, though they are commonly sollicitous about nothing else. The sight of an immense number of icy masses, amongst which we
drifted at the mercy of the current, every moment in danger of being dashed to pieces
against them, could not deter the sailors from
indulging in their favourite amusement. As long
as they had brandy left, they would persist to
keep Christmas "like Christians," though the
elements had conspired together for their destruction. Their long acquaintance with a sea-faring life
had inured them to all kinds of perils, and their
heavy labour, with the inclemencies of weather,
and other hardships, making their muscles rigid
and their nerves obtuse, had communicated insen-
sibility to the mind. It will easily be conceived,
that as they do not feel for themselves sufficiently
to provide for their own safety, they must be incapable of feeling for others. Subjected to a very
strict command, they also exercise a tyrannical
sway over those whom fortune places in their
power. Accustomed to face an enemy, they
breathe nothing but war. By force of habit even
killing is become so much their passion, that we
have seen many instances during our voyage,
where they have expressed a horrid eagerness to
fire upon the natives on the slightest pretences.
Their way of life in general prevents their enjoying domestic comforts; and gross animal appetites
fill the place of purer affections.

At last, extinct each social feeling, fell
And joyless inhumanity pervades
And petrifies the heart.—THOMPSON.

Though they are members of a civilized society,
they may in some measure be looked upon as a
body of uncivilized men, rough, passionate, re-
vengeful, but likewise brave, sincere, and true to
each other.

At noon the observation of the sun's altitude
determined our latitude to be 66° 22′ south, so that
we were just returned out of the antarctic circle.
We had scarcely any night during our stay in the
frigid zone, so that I find several articles in my
father's journal, written by the light of the sun,
within a few minutes before the hour of midnight.
The sun's stay below the horizon was so very short
this night likewise, that we had a very strong twilight all the time. Mahine was struck with the
greatest astonishment at this phænomenon, and
would scarcely believe his senses. All our endeavours to explain it to him miscarried, and he
assured us he despaired of finding belief among his
countrymen, when he should come back to re-
count the wonders of petrified rain, and of perpetual day. The first Venetians who explored the
northern extremes of the European continent,
were equally surprised at the continual appearance of the sun above the horizon, and relate that
they could only distinguish day from night, by the
instinct of the sea-fowl, which went to roost on
shore, for the space of four hours. As we were in
all likelihood far distant from any land, this indication failed us, and we have often observed numerous birds on the wing about us all the night, and
particularly great flocks of different species, so late
as eleven o'clock.

At six in the evening, we counted one hundred and five large masses of ice around us from the deck, the weather continuing very clear, fair, and perfectly calm. Towards noon the next day we were still in the same situation, with a very drunken crew, and from the mast-head observed one hundred and sixty-eight ice-islands, some of which were half a mile long, and none less than the hull of the ship. The whole scene looked like the wrecks of a shattered world, or as the poets describe some regions of hell; an idea which struck us the more forcibly, as execrations, oaths, and curses re-echoed about us on all sides. *1773 December Sunday 26*

A faint breeze sprung up in the afternoon, with which we made slow advances to the northward, the number of ice islands decreasing in proportion as we receded from the antarctic circle. About four the next morning, we hoisted out our boats, and took in a fresh provision of ice. The weather changed soon after, the wind coming about to the north-eastward, which brought on much snow and sleet. My father, and twelve other persons were again much afflicted with rheumatic pains, and confined to their beds. The scurvy did not yet appear under any dangerous form in the ship, and all those who had any slight symptoms of it, amongst whom I was one, drank plentifully of the fresh wort, quite warm, twice a day, and abstained as much as possible from salt-diet. A general languor and sickly look however, manifested itself in almost every person's face, which threatened us with more dangerous consequences. Captain Cook himself was likewise pale and lean, entirely lost his appetite, and laboured under a perpetual costiveness. *Monday 27*

We advanced to the northward as much as the winds would permit us, and lost sight of the ice on

1774
January

Saturday
1
Tuesday
4

*Thurs-
day*
6

the first of January 1774, in 59° 7′ S. latitude. On the 4th, the wind blowing from the westward was very boisterous, and obliged us to keep all our sails double-reefed; the sea ran high, and the ship worked very heavily, rolling violently from side to side. This continued till the 6th at noon, when, having reached 51° of S. latitude, we bore away from the wind, to the N.N.E. We were now within a few degrees of the track which we had made in June and July last, in going from New Zeeland to Taheitee, and had directed our course towards it, in order to leave no considerable part of this great ocean unexplored. As far as we had hitherto advanced, we had found no land, not even indications of land; our first track had crossed the South Sea in the middle latitudes, or between 40 and 50 degrees. In our course till Christmas, we had explored the greatest part of it between 60 degrees and the antarctic circle, and the present course to the northward had crossed the space between the two former runs. If any land has escaped us, it must be an island, whose distance from Europe, and situation in an uncouth climate cannot make it valuable to this country. It is obvious that to search a sea of such extent as the South Sea, in order to be certain of the existence, or non-existence of a small island, would require many voyages in numberless different tracks, and cannot be effected in a single expedition. But it is sufficient for us, to have proved that no large land or continent exists in the South Sea within the temperate zone, and that if it exists at all, we have at least confined it within the antarctic circle.

The long continuance in these cold climates began now to hang heavily on our crew, especially as it banished all hope of returning home this year, which had hitherto supported their spirits. At first a painful despondence, owing to the dreary pros-

pect of another year's cruize to the South, seemed *1774*
painted in every countenance; till by degrees they *January*
resigned themselves to their fate, with a kind of
sullen indifference. It must be owned however,
that nothing could be more dejecting than the
entire ignorance of our future destination, which,
without any apparent reason, was constantly kept
a secret to every person in the ship.

We now stood to the north-eastward for a few
days, till we came so far as 47° 52′ south latitude,
where the thermometer rose to 52 degrees. On
that day, which was the 11th, at noon, the course *Monday*
was directed to the S. E. again, though this fre- *11*
quent and sudden change of climate could not fail
of proving very hurtful to our health in general. *Saturday*
On the 15th the wind encreased very much, and *15*
in a short time blew a tempestuous gale, which
took *Sunday*
16

> ————the ruffian billows by the top
> Curling their monstrous heads and hanging
>   them
> With deaf'ning clamours in the slippery
>   shrouds.
>   —SHAKESPEARE

At nine o'clock a huge mountainous wave struck
the ship on the beam, and filled the decks with a
deluge of water. It poured through the sky-light
over our heads, and extinguished the candle, leaving us for a moment in doubt, whether we were
not entirely overwhelmed and sinking into the
abyss. Every thing was afloat in my father's cabin,
and his bed was thoroughly soaked. His rheumatism, which had now afflicted him above a fortnight, was still so violent as to have almost
deprived him of the use of his legs, and his pains
redoubled in the morning. Our situation at pre-

sent was indeed very dismal, even to those who preserved the blessing of health; to the sick, whose crippled limbs were tortured with excessive pain, it was insupportable. The ocean about us had a furious aspect, and seemed incensed at the presumption of a few intruding mortals. A gloomy melancholy air loured on the brows of our shipmates, and a dreadful silence reigned amongst us. Salt meat, our constant diet, was become loathsome to all, and even to those who had been bred to a nautical life from their tender years; the hour of dinner was hateful to us, for the well known smell of the victuals had no sooner reached our nose, than we found it impossible to partake of them with a hearty appetite.

It will appear from hence that this voyage was not to be compared to any preceding one, for the multitude of hardships and distresses which attended it. Our predecessors in the South Sea had always navigated within the tropic, or at least in the best parts of the temperate zone; they had almost constantly enjoyed mild easy weather, and sailed in sight of lands, which were never so wretchedly destitute as not to afford them refreshments from time to time. Such a voyage would have been merely a party of pleasure to us; continually entertained with new and often agreeable objects, our minds would have been at ease, our conversation cheerful, our bodies healthy, and our whole situation desirable and happy. Ours was just the reverse of this; our southern cruizes were uniform and tedious in the highest degree; the ice, the fogs, the storms and ruffled surface of the sea formed a disagreeable scene, which was seldom cheered by the reviving beams of the sun; the climate was rigorous and our food detestable. In short, we rather vegetated than lived; we withered, and became indifferent to all that animates the soul at other times. We sacrificed our health, our feelings, our enjoyments, to the honour of pursuing a track unattempted before.

The crew were as much distressed as the officers, from another cause. Their biscuit, which had been sorted at New Zeeland, baked over again, and then packed up, was now in the same decayed state as before. This was owing partly to the revisal, which had been so rigorous, that many a bad biscuit was preserved among those that were eatable, and partly to the neglect of the casks, which had not been sufficiently fumigated and dried. Of this rotten bread the people only received two thirds of their usual allowance, from economical principles; but, as that portion is hardly sufficient, supposing it to be all eatable, it was far from being so when nearly one half of it was rotten. However, they continued in that distressful situation till this day when the first mate came to the captain and complained bitterly that he and the people had not wherewith to satisfy the cravings of the stomach, producing, at the same time, the rotten and stinking remains of his biscuit. Upon this the crew were put to full allowance. The captain seemed to recover again as we advanced to the southward, but all those who were afflicted with rheumatisms continued as much indisposed as ever.

The first ice islands which we met with on this run were in 62° 30' south, on the 20th, but they did not accumulate in number in proportion to our progress, so that we crossed the antarctic circle again on the 26th, without seeing more than a few solitary pieces. On that day we were amused with the appearance of land; for after standing on towards it for some hours, it vanished in clouds. The next day, at noon, we were in 67° 52' south; consequently to the southward of any of our former tracks, and met with no ice to stop us. The blue

1774
January

petrels, the little storm petrels, and the pintadas still accompanied us, but albatrosses had left us some time ago. We were now once more in the regions of perpetual day* and had sunshine at the hour of midnight.

Friday
28

On the 28th, in the afternoon, we passed a large bed of broken ice, hoisted out the boats, and took up a great quantity, which afforded a seasonable supply of fresh water. At midnight the thermometer was not lower than 34°, and the next morning we enjoyed the mildest sunshine we had ever experienced in the frigid zone. My father therefore ventured upon deck for the first time after a month's confinement.

We now entertained hopes of penetrating to the south as far as other navigators have done towards the north pole; but on the 30th, about seven o'-clock in the morning, we discovered a solid ice-field of immense extent before us, which bore from E. to W. A bed of fragments floated all round this field, which seemed to be raised several feet high above the level of the water. A vast number of icy masses, some of a very great height, were irregularly piled up upon it, as far as the eye could reach. Our latitude was at this time 71° 10' south, consequently less than 19 deg. from the pole; but as it was impossible to proceed farther, we put the ship about, well satisfied with our perilous expedition, and almost persuaded that no navigator will care to come after, and much less attempt to pass beyond us. Our longitude at this time was nearly 106° W. The thermometer here was at 32°, and a great many pinguins were heard croaking round us, but could not be seen on account of the foggy weather which immediately succeeded.

* In the frozen zone, where the sun remains six months above and six months below the horizon, dividing the year into one long day and night.

As often as we had hitherto penetrated to the southward, we had met with no land, but been stopped sooner or later by a solid ice-field, which extended before us as far as we could see. At the same time we had always found the winds moderate and frequently easterly in these high latitudes, in the same manner as they are said to be in the northern frozen zone. From these circumstances my father has been led to suppose, that all the south pole, to the distance of 20 degrees, more or less, is covered with solid ice, of which only the extremities are annually broken by storms, consumed by the action of the sun, and regenerated in winter. This opinion is the less exceptionable, since there seems to be no absolute necessity for the existence of land towards the formation of ice, and because we have little reason to suppose that there actually is any land of considerable extent in the frigid zone.

1774
February

We ran to the northward with moderate winds till the 5th of February, when we got a fine fresh breeze after a short calm. The day after it shifted to S. E. and freshened so as to blow very hard at night, and split several sails. As it was favourable for the purpose of advancing to the northward, the only circumstance that afforded us comfort, we were far from being concerned at its violence, and in the next twenty-four hours made upwards of three degrees of latitude. The same gale assisted us till the 12th, when we observed the latitude to be 50° 15′ south, our thermometer being once more returned to the milder temperature of 48 degrees. We were now told that we should spend the winter season, which was coming on apace, among the tropical islands of the Pacific Ocean, in the same manner as we had passed that immediately preceding. The prospect of making new dis-

February
Saturday
5

Tuesday
8

coveries, and of enjoying the excellent refreshments which those islands afford, entirely revived our hopes, and made us look on our continuance on the western side of Cape Horne with some degree of satisfaction.

A great number of our people were however afflicted with very severe rheumatic pains, which deprived them of the use of their limbs; but their spirits were so low, that they had no fever. Though the use of that excellent prophylactic the sour krout, prevented the appearance of the scurvy during all the cold weather, yet being made of cabbage, it is not so nutritive that we could live upon it without the assistance of biscuit and salt-beef. But the former of these being rotten, and the other almost consumed by the salt, it is obvious that no wholesome juices could be secreted from thence, which might have kept the body strong and vigorous. Under these difficulties all our patients recovered very slowly, having nothing to restore their strength; and my father, who had been in exquisite torments during the greatest part of our southern cruize, was afflicted with tooth-aches, swelled cheeks, sore-throat, and universal pain till the middle of February, when he ventured on deck perfectly emaciated. The warm weather which was beneficial to him, proved fatal to captain Cook's constitution. The disappearance of his bilious complaint during our last push to the south, had not been so sincere, as to make him recover his appetite. The return to the north therefore brought on a dangerous obstruction, which the captain very unfortunately slighted, and concealed from every person in the ship, at the same time endeavouring to get the better of it by taking hardly any sustenance. This proceeding, instead of removing, encreased the evil, his

stomach being already weak enough before. He 1774
was afflicted with violent pains, which in the space *Febru-*
of a few days confined him to his bed, and forced *ary*
him to have recourse to medicines. He took a
purge, but instead of producing the desired effect,
it caused a violent vomiting, which was assisted
immediately by proper emetics. All attempts however to procure a passage through his bowels were
ineffectual; his food and medicines were thrown
up, and in a few days a most dreadful hiccough
appeared, which lasted for upwards of twenty-
four hours, with such astonishing violence that his
life was entirely despaired of. Opiates and glysters
had no effect, till repeated hot baths, and plasters
of theriaca applied on his stomach, had relaxed his
body and intestines. This however, was not
effected till he had lain above a week in the most
imminent danger. Our servant fell ill about the
same time with the captain, of the same disorder,
and narrowly escaped, but continued weak and
unserviceable the greatest part of our cruize between the tropics.

During this time we advanced to the northward
very fast, so that on the 22d we reached 36° 10′ S. *Tuesday*
latitude, where the albatrosses left us. Our longi- 22
tude being about 94½ degrees west from Greenwich, we steered to the southwestward, in quest of *Friday*
a supposed discovery of Juan Fernandez, which, 25
according to Juan Luis Arias, a Spanish author, is
said to lie in 40° south latitude, and by Mr. Dalrymple's chart in 90° west from London*. We stood on
to the westward till the 25th at noon, where being
in 37° 50′ S. and about 101° W. and seeing no signs
of land, we altered our course something to the
northward. The dangerous situation of captain
Cook, was perhaps the reason, why our track was
* See Mr. Dalrymple's Historical Collection, vol. I. p. 53, and the Chart.

not continued farther to the south so as to put this matter entirely out of doubt for the future. It was indeed of the utmost importance at present, to hasten to a place of refreshment, that being the only chance to preserve his life.

On the 26th, captain Cook felt some relief from the medicines which had been administered to him, and during the three following days, recovered so far as to be able to sit up sometimes, and take a little soup. Next to Providence it was chiefly owing to the skill of our surgeon, Mr. Patton, that he recovered to prosecute the remaining part of our voyage, with the same spirit with which it had hitherto been carried on. The care and assiduity with which this worthy man, watched him during his whole illness, cannot be sufficiently extolled, as all our hopes of future discoveries, as well as union in the ship, depended solely on the preservation of the captain. The surgeon's extreme attention however, had nearly cost him his own life. Having taken no rest for many nights together, and seldom venturing to sleep an hour by day, he was so much exhausted, that we trembled for his life, upon which that of almost every man in the ship in great measure depended. He was taken ill with a bilious disorder, which was dangerous on account of the extreme weakness of his stomach, and it is more than probable, that if we had not speedily fallen in with land, from whence we collected some slight refreshments, he must have fallen a sacrifice to that rigorous perseverance and extreme punctuality with which he discharged the several duties of his profession.

We had easterly winds ever since the 22d of February, which was probably owing to the situation of the sun, still continuing in the southern hemisphere. The weather was warm and comfort-

able again, the thermometer being at 70 degrees; *1774*
and some grey terns were seen from time to time, *March*
which according to our friend Mahine's account, *Tuesday*
never went to a great distance from land. On the *1*
first of March, some bonitos appeared swiftly
swimming past the ship, and the next day, being
in 30½ degrees of latitude, we saw tropic birds
again.

The scurvy now appeared with very strong
symptoms in the ship, and I was particularly
afflicted with it. Excruciating pains, livid blotches,
rotten gums, and swelled legs, brought me extremely low in a few days, almost before I was
aware of the disorder; and my stomach being very
weak, through abstinence from an unwholesome
and loathed diet, I could not take the wort in sufficient quantity to remove my complaint. The same
case existed with regard to a number of other people, who crawled about the decks with the greatest difficulty.

We had almost calm weather from the 3d to the
6th, the sky was clear, and the warmth and
serenity of the weather remarkably pleasing; but
we were impatient to proceed to a place of refreshment, and this delay ill suited with our
wishes.

On the 5th, at night, we saw some towering
clouds and a haze on the horizon to the southward,
from whence we hoped for a fair wind. Already,
during night, we had some smart showers, and at
eight o'clok the next morning we saw the surface
of the sea curled to the south-eastward, upon
which we trimmed our sails, and advanced again
with a fair wind. The next morning four large albecores were caught, the least of which weighed *Monday*
twenty-three pounds. They afforded us a most *7*
delicious repast, it being now an hundred days

1774
March

Tuesday
8

Thurs-
day
10

since we had tasted any fresh fish. Shearwaters, terns, noddies, gannets, and men of war birds appeared numerous about us, hunting the shoals of flying-fish which our ship, the bonitos, albecores, and dolphins had frightened out of the water.

We reached the 27th degree of S. latitude on the 8th at noon, and then shaped our course due west in search of EASTER ISLAND, discovered by Jacob Roggewein in 1722, and since visited by the Spaniards in 1770* who gave it the name of St. Charles's Island. On the 10th, in the morning, the birds of the grey tern-kind were innumerable about us, whilst we advanced at the rate of seven miles an hour. We lay to during night, being apprehensive of falling in with the land, which we actually discovered at five o'clock the next morning. The joy which this fortunate event spread on every countenance is scarcely to be described. We had been a hundred and three days out of sight of land; and the rigorous weather to the south, the fatigues of continual attendance during storms, or amidst dangerous masses of ice, the sudden changes of climate, and the long continuance of a noxious diet, all together had emaciated and worn out our crew. The expectation of a speedy end to their sufferings, and the hope of finding the land stocked with abundance of fowls and planted with fruits, according to the accounts of the Dutch navigator, now filled them with uncommon alacrity and cheerfulness.

We advanced but slowly towards the land by day, to the great disappointment of all on board, who became more eager in proportion as new difficulties arose to prolong their distresses. The land appeared of a moderate height, and divided

* See Mr. Dalrymple's Historical Collection of Voyages, Vol. II, p. 85; also his letter to Dr. Hawkesworth, 1773.

into several hills, which gently sloped from their *1774* summits; its extent did not seem to be consider- *March* able, and we were at too great a distance to be able to form any conjecture as to its productions. The *Saturday* next morning we were becalmed within five *12* leagues of the island, which had then a black and somewhat disagreeable appearance. We amused ourselves with catching sharks, several of which swam about the ship, and eagerly swallowed the hook, which was baited with salt pork or beef. In the afternoon a breeze sprung up, with which we stood towards the shore, in great hopes of reaching an anchoring-place before night. The land did not look very promising as we advanced, there being little verdure, and scarcely any bushes upon it; but to us who had lingered so long under all the distresses of a tedious cruize at sea, the most barren rock would have been a welcome sight. In our way we perceived a great number of black pillars standing upright, near two hummocks, and in different groups. They seemed to be the same which Roggewein's people took for idols*; but we guessed already, at that time, that they were such monuments, in memory of the dead, as the Taheitians and other people in the South Seas erect near their burying-places, and call E-TEE.

The wind, which was contrary and very faint, the approach of night, and the want of an anchoring-place on the east side of the island, disappointed us once more, and forced us to pass another night under sail, during which we saw several fires in the neighbourhood of the pillars above-mentioned. The Dutch, who likewise observed them, called them sacrifices to the idols; but it seems to be more probably that they were only lighted to dress the food of the natives.

* See Mr. Dalrymple's Historical Collection of Voyages, &c. vol. II. p. 91.

We passed the night in making several trips, in order to keep to windward of the island and as near it as possible, resolving to pursue our search of anchorage the next day. In the mean time we reflected on the excellent means of ascertaining the longitude, with which our ship had been furnished, and which had carried us exactly to this island, though several former navigators, such as Byron, Carteret, and Bougainville had missed it, after taking their departure from islands at so short a distance from it as those of Juan Fernandez*. Captain Carteret it seems was only misled by an erroneous latitude in the geographical tables which he consulted; but this could not be the case with the rest. We had the greatest reason to admire the ingenious construction of the two watches which we had on board, one executed by Mr. Kendal, exactly after the model of that made by Mr. Harrison, and the other by Mr. Arnold on his own plan, both which went with great regularity. The last was unfortunately stopped immediately after our departure from New Zeeland in June 1773, but the other went till our return to England, and gave general satisfaction. It appears, however, that in a long run the observations of distances of the moon from the sun or stars, are more to be depended upon, if they be made with good instruments, than the watches or time-keepers, which frequently change their rates of going. The method of deducing the longitude from the distances of the sun and moon, or moon and stars, one of the most valuable acquisitions to the art of navigation, must immortalize its first inventors. TOBIAS MAYER, a German, and professor at Gottingen, was the first who undertook the laborious task of calculating tables for this purpose, for

* Juan Fernandez, properly so called or la de Tierra, and la Mas a fuera.

which his heirs received a parliamentary reward.
Since his death the method was so much facili-
tated by additional calculations, that the longitude
will perhaps never be determined with greater
precision at sea by any other means.

The latitude of Easter Island corresponds within
a minute or two with that which is marked in
admiral Roggewein's own MS. journal*, and his
longitude is only one degree erroneous, our observations having ascertained it in 109° 46′ west from
Greenwich. The Spanish accounts of the latitude
are likewise exact, but they err in longitude about
thirty leagues.

---

* See the Lives of the Governors of Batavia.—It is there expressed 27° 04′
S. latitude, and 265° 42′ E. from Tenerif, or 110° 45′ W. from London.

THADDEUS BELLINGSHAUSEN

(*1779-1852*)

THADDEUS BELLINGSHAUSEN entered the Russian navy at the age of ten. By the age of eighteen he had graduated from the naval academy at Kronstadt to become a naval officer. In 1819 he was given command of two sloops, each of about 500 tons, with the assignment to circumnavigate Antarctica. His primary goal was exploration, his secondary one the gathering of scientific information. The vessels were *Mirnyi*, meaning "peace," and *Vostok*, meaning "east." They are commemorated by two present-day Russian Antarctic stations, Mirnyy on the coast at approximately 90° East Longitude and Vostok on a high inland plateau near the geomagnetic pole. Bellingshausen greatly admired Cook. It was his hope to supplement Cook's findings, not to compete with him. Thus he undertook to sail in seas which Cook had not had the opportunity to explore. He made the first sightings of land within the Antarctic Circle, discovering and naming Peter I Island and Alexander I Island. The Bellingshausen Sea is named for him. Some seven years after the conclusion of the expedition of 1819-21 he distinguished himself in naval operations against the Turks. At his death he was an admiral and the governor of Kronstadt.

Antarctic Seas

1st [January 1820]　On the first day of the New Year we wished each other a happy escape from our dangerous position and a safe return to our dear home on the conclusion of the difficult voyage before us. The thermometer stood at 31.5° F. There was a fresh wind from the north-east by north, and a heavy swell was running from the north. We were just congratulating ourselves that the snowfall had stopped; but our joy did not last long, for at 2 o'clock instead of snow thick fog with wind set in. We found ourselves again amidst a quantity of small ice and the cries of the penguins were to be heard on all sides. Soon after 5.0 A.M. we saw through the fog many icebergs close to us to the north-east. The noise of the waves breaking on the ice and the screaming of the penguins created a most unpleasant feeling. After an exchange of signals the *Vostok* and the *Mirnyi* turned away from the icebergs on a starboard tack, and at the time of turning, when the sails slackened and shook the whole gear, icicles and the frozen snow from the rigging fell on the decks; the frozen ropes looked as if they were threaded through glass beads of a thickness of from 1/20 to ½ an inch. The crew during each watch knocked it off with spikes from the shrouds.

At 6.0 A.M. the thermometer showed 30° F. At 7.0 A.M. on

the *Vostok* a signal was fired and at 8.0 A.M. a fog signal was sounded in order that the *Mirnyi* should reply giving her position; but with the dense fog and the roar of the sea breaking everywhere on the ice, the *Mirnyi* did not hear the signal, whilst we on the *Vostok* did not hear the *Mirnyi's* guns. At 10.0 A.M. the wind was blowing from the east. At midday we passed a number of icebergs and floating ice, to avoid which we were obliged now to keep close to the wind and then bear away. At midday the fog cleared a little, and as we could now see the dangers around us, we were able to avoid them more easily. We also saw the *Mirnyi*, about which we had become very anxious. On sounding we had 120 sazhen (140 fathoms) and no bottom. In spite of the bad weather and our dangerous position amongst unseen ice, all the crew dressed in parade uniform in the morning to celebrate the New Year. In the morning for breakfast we served out tea with rum; for dinner there was good cabbage soup with sauerkraut and pork; after dinner, besides the usual ration, all were given a glass of hot punch and, in the evening, before the rice gruel, a glass of grog. The crews of both vessels were well and cheerful; we only regretted that, owing to the dangerous position and the stormy weather, we were unable to pass the day in the company of Captain Lazarev and the officers of the *Mirnyi*. At midday the temperature was 33° F.; towards 1 P.M., as the *Mirnyi* was near us, we set the main topsail and took a north-north-east course. At 2.0 P.M., in order to equalize the speed of the vessels, we double-reefed the mainsail; until 5.0 P.M. we passed icebergs and floating ice. At 5.0 P.M. we turned on another tack to a west-south-west course. We saw whales playing about in the water, rising perpendicularly about one-third of their whole length out of the water and then diving again, showing their horizontal tails.[1] We again passed through a quantity of ice until 9.0 P.M. when the weather improved a little and we saw

1 These were probably Killer whales (*Orca*) whose habit it is, when in thick pack ice, to rear their heads high out of the water to look over the ice.—F.D. [Frank Debenham, editor of the English version of Bellingshausen's book.]

Cape Bristol S. 58° W. at an estimated distance of about 5½ miles. With the rough weather it was impossible to make any survey of the shore and we therefore stood away from it.

2nd. The wind continued to blow fresh from south-east by east. There was a strong swell from the west and the waves produced a good deal of pitching and rolling. There were 3° of frost. The fog shut out both shore and horizon. Our course took us straight for an iceberg, and at 2.0 A.M. we had to change to another tack, but at 4:30 A.M. we turned back to the former course. At 7.0 A.M. we once more encountered a huge iceberg, and to circumnavigate it had to turn north-wards and then steer north-east by east again. Round this iceberg great numbers of white petrels were circling. At 8.0 A.M. the weather began to clear a little, and we could see the shores of both Cape Montagu and Cape Bristol and were thereby able to fix our positions. We turned towards Cape Bristol under full sail; by 11.0 A.M. we had passed six icebergs. Our course then took us past the eastern extremity of the aforementioned headland and, approaching it about 11.0 A.M., we therefore turned on another tack so as to pass along the eastern side of the Cape, as Captain Cook had not sur-veyed it from that side. After three tacks we rounded the eastern cape on the fourth and observed that the coast, which runs in a north-west by west to south-east by east direction with a circumference of 17 miles, is uneven in height. At the southern extremity there is a pointed moun-tain completely covered with snow and ice, except a few particularly steep dark patches.[1] Proceeding on a S. 14° W. course for 4½ hours, we observed the land extending

1 Captain Bellingshausen is very brief about this island, but nevertheless he manages to mention most of the characteristics which have now been inves-tigated by *Discovery II*. The island rises to 3600 feet in Mount Darnley, which appears to be part of a large extinct crater. The whole of the island is covered with glaciers, including the "pointed mountain" in the south, which is 1900 feet high. This high dome and the large isolated rock of Freezeland Peak (900 feet) are the most striking features of the group.—F.D.

S. 54° W., called Southern Thule by Captain Cook. At 6.0 P.M. we found ourselves in Lat. 59° 13′ S., Long. 26° 13′ W. and observed to port and ahead of us a great deal of pack ice, which we passed through in a direction S. 54° 30′ W. At 10:30 P.M., as the ice was becoming much more frequent, we turned on another tack to pass the night under shortened sail.

3rd. At midnight the thermometer stood at 30.2° F. At 2.0 A.M. we passed one iceberg to starboard and one to port. At 3.0 A.M., at dawn, we turned again S. 40° W. with an east-south-east wind, going 6 knots; in the morning we proceeded under all sail to make the most of the clear weather. We passed through layers of broken ice, not unlike river ice, except that it was much thicker. The officer of the watch was stationed forward and guided the ship by ordering port or starboard helm to avoid the ice; on the port side the ice was quite impenetrable; from the top and the look-out nothing was to be seen but an endless icefield and in the middle of it here and there were icebergs of different shapes and sizes.

The Thule group consists of one high rock and three small islands, of which one is smaller than the other two. These islands are high and inaccessible and lie in Lat. 59° 26′ S., Long. 27° 13′ 30″ W. The middle one, the largest, is about 6 miles long. I called it Cook Island in honour of the great explorer who had been the first to see this shore and who regarded it as the most southern land on the globe. The most westerly island is about 3 miles long and the smallest is about two-thirds of a mile in length. Between the two largest islands lies a rock; all three are covered with snow and ice. Captain Cook, in consequence of the stormy weather, did not approach Thule and Montagu Islands, and therefore the ice between them appeared to him to be land, which he named in honour of the then First Lord of the Admiralty, Lord Sandwich.[1] Captain Cook saw these islands first, and there-

[1] John Montagu, fourth Earl of Sandwich, was born in 1718. Though a man of great talent and activity, he was unprincipled and profligate. On three

fore the names given by him must remain unchanged that the memory of this daring explorer may be handed on to posterity. Consequently I also call them the Sandwich Islands.[1]

We continued on our course S. 40° W., always amidst very thick pack ice, and at 10.0 A.M. we proceeded along the edge of an iceberg about 3 miles square. Its surface was quite level, the sides perpendicular and on the left, that is to the east, of a height of about 30 feet. We saw everywhere uninterrupted ice, formed of flat blocks piled one upon another in different directions; here and there in the middle of the field large icebergs of various forms stood out. Some of these were of a light blue colour; in my opinion, because the iceberg, having lost its balance, had turned upside down and had not yet had time to be bleached by the air.[2] To starboard to the west there appeared to be less broken ice but a great many icebergs. Proceeding from early morning through this ice, we could not avoid several times colliding with it, and, scraping

occasions during his public career he was made First Lord of the Admiralty and once dismissed from that office in disgrace. At this time the British Navy had reached its lowest depths of corruption. Lord Sandwich retired into private life on the fall of the North Administration in 1782.—F.D.

1 These three islands, about which Bellingshausen is tantalizingly brief, are perhaps the most interesting in the whole Sandwich group. They have been fully investigated by *Discovery II*, and Dr. Kemp very appropriately gave the name "Bellingshausen" to the most easterly of the three. This island, though described in the text and figured in the "Atlas", is not shown on the Russian chart, which is additional evidence that the charts were constructed by some one who was not on the expedition and who had not had access to the artist's drawings. As shown in the sketches in the *Discovery* report, the island has a large crater which is in the solfataric stage, but it is only 500 feet high at the highest point. The sketch by the Russian artist is very similar to the modern one from the same point of view, though this can hardly be taken as evidence of no change since that time. The two larger islands, Cook and Thule, were shown by the soundings taken between them to be the remnants of the rim of a very large crater, the cauldron of which now forms a deep basin.—F.D.

2 This ingenious explanation cannot be accepted unfortunately, the true reason being that, in the normal Antarctic iceberg, the upper layers are compressed snow, rather than ice, while towards the bottom the lack of air inclusions gives it the true ice-blue reflection.—F.D.

the whole length of the side of the vessel, it damaged the copper in places and tore away the heads of the copper nails. The damage, however, was slight, as there was no sea on, and the vessels proceeded smoothly.

At midday we fixed our position as in Lat. 59° 57' S., Long. 27° 32' W. The centre of Thule Island bore N. 13° E., 32 miles from us; Cook Island No. 32° E., 32 miles. The mercury stood at only 33.2° F.

At 2.0 P.M. we braced round the mainsails and topsails to give the *Mirnyi*, which had dropped astern, time to come up with us. Meanwhile, in order not to waste time, we sent off two boats to cut some ice and bring it on board. To take it in conveniently, we packed the ice in sugar sacks and then filled all the empty receptacles available, even filling the sacks with it, using them first. No ice was put directly into the barrels down in the hold lest it should cause damp, but the water melted from the ice was run into the barrels. We lay to until 7.0 P.M. By then we had had time to fill ten barrels of medium size, tubs and other vessels with ice. We found ourselves in Lat. 60° 3' 33" S., Long. 27° 39' W., the magnetic variation being 7° 4' E. At 7.0 P.M. the wind veered through south to the south-west quarter. We hoisted sail and, passing through small ice, in a direction S. 40° E., we pushed farther south with the object of circumventing the pack ice, which we had observed to eastward. Snow forced us to shorten sail and to proceed with the greatest caution. In the course of this day, we saw only a few whales, white petrels and penguins. The other sea birds which usually accompanied us daily had disappeared.

4th. At midnight we had 2° F. of frost; below in the crew's quarters it was 51° F. Snow fell until 2.0 A.M., when we hoisted sail and proceeded eastwards with a south wind. A little before 4 o'clock, in Lat. 60° 15' S., Long. 27° 16' W., we encountered impenetrable pack ice, amongst which were many icebergs. This icefield, probably a continuation of the pack ice near which we had found ourselves on the previous day, had

a south-south-east direction. We therefore turned on the port
tack and proceeded among many icebergs. In Lat. 60° 16'
47" S., Long. 27° 24' W., we found the magnetic variation to
be 7° 9' E., with the ship at the time on a west-south-west
course. At 6.30 A.M. we turned on a starboard tack and took
a south-east course with icebergs and broken ice on both
sides. At 9.0 A.M. it was impossible to continue on this course
as we encountered to the east and south an extensive icefield;
from the look-out nothing but unending ice and large icebergs was to be seen; we therefore turned on another tack.
The weather was fine. At midday we were in Lat. 60° 25'
20" S., Long. 27° 38' 30" W., with a view from the look-out
of 40 miles; no continuation of the Sandwich Islands towards
the south could be seen. The icefield lay from south to west.
Finding ourselves among floating ice and not seeing any possibility of passing round it to the southward during the good
season, I considered it desirable to leave this locality betimes
and to circumvent it on the north so as not to lose time
uselessly nor to expose the vessel to damage on the first
approach of stormy weather, a danger which we would certainly have run in that place surrounded by ice. We therefore
turned to west by north past numerous icebergs and a great
deal of broken ice. After 5 miles, we altered course to north
by west with the object of passing round the western side of
Thule, Cook and Bristol Islands. We kept on this course for
22 miles, having on both sides an horizon strewn with icebergs; then snow, hiding the ice from us, made navigation
still more dangerous. At 5.30 we turned north by east, in
order to pass again within sight of Thule and Cook Islands.
Whilst on this course we noted penguins sitting on some of
the icebergs and large blocks of ice. The weather got thicker,
squalls accompanied by snow set in and forced us to shorten
sail; the snow sometimes fell so thickly that, as we approached the ice, the ships scarcely answered the helm in
time to clear it. After proceeding 30 miles, we turned northward and kept on this course for 9 miles up to 11.0 P.M. In
order not to approach too close to Thule Island in the dark-

ness and thick weather, as it was surrounded by icebergs, we turned to about north-east by east at 11.0 P.M. At several points during the day we had seen whales which, as it were, tried to amuse us by spouting water like fountains.

5th. In the course of the night, we proceeded at the rate of 5 to 6 knots; the temperature was 29° F. At 5.0 A.M. we made more sail. When proceeding from the west between the Bristol and Montagu Islands, we found, on a north-east course, a magnetic variation of 5° 52′ E. At 6.0 A.M. we again passed over the meridian of Peak Freezeland, a high pointed rock on the western side of Bristol Island. It was discovered and so named by Captain Cook. Cape Bristol lay from us S. 30° E., and the Peak of the eastern extremity S. 37° E. Passing Peak Freezeland we fixed its longitude at 26° 29′ 06″ W. On the *Mirnyi* the magnetic deviation was found to be 6° 32′ E. on a course north-east by east-half-east. From daybreak until midday we passed many icebergs and much broken ice. Again the officer on watch, stationed on the forecastle, had to exert the greatest care to avoid collision with the ice. At midday we were in Lat. 58° 39′ 09″ S., Long. 25° 51′ 55″ W. Peak Freezeland lay south-east from us, the end of Montagu Island N. 62° 30′ W. distant 20½ miles. Now that we passed in fine weather the place where, on the 1st and 2nd of January, we had been tacking in thick weather and among ice whose proximity we had only discovered by the noise, we were amazed at the great number of icebergs and at our luck in having escaped disaster.

The land discovered by Captain Cook and called by him Sandwich Land, as also the three islands discovered by me and called the Marquis de Traversey Islands, consist, it seems, of the summits of a mountain range, which is connected by the Clerke rocks with South Georgia and by the Aurora Islands with the Falkland Islands.[1] By the volcanic

---

1 More recent soundings have demonstrated the accuracy of this conclusion. The Sandwich group is connected with South Georgia by a low submarine ridge, nowhere more than 1500 fathoms deep, curving round from east to

activity on the Zavodovski and Saunders Islands, the southern hemisphere is relieved in this part of subterranean fire, which does not appear to be very extensive. The northern hemisphere must, it seems, be everywhere warmer than the southern hemisphere, not only with regard to the atmosphere, as is well known, but also in respect of the interior of the earth. This is shown by the many volcanic eruptions at different points in the northern hemisphere, such as Iceland and the coast of Italy, the peninsula of Kamchatka together with the Kurile Islands near the Japanese coast, the Aleutian Islands, etc., compared with which the volcanic activity in the southern hemisphere is small. On Zavodovski Island there was little lava—such as is usually formed by eruptions —to be found, possibly because the substance below the surface of the island does not lend itself to transformation into lava.

At midday we altered course to S. 89° E. in order to get clear of the ice and to make a new attempt to penetrate southward at another more favourable point into high latitudes. By 5 o'clock we had made 32 miles, with icebergs on both sides of us at various distances from the ship. Observing that ice was becoming less frequent, I ordered the ships to turn southward again. In order to reach a higher latitude while at the same time keeping clear of ice, we turned east by south and after 26 miles we took a course south-east by east. At that time the ice had diminished still more and, in the course of 24 hours, we saw few sea birds, except penguins, of which great numbers were sitting on the ice or diving round the ships. To our delight the fine weather made it possible for us to dry and air the crew's clothes and bedding.

6th. With a top-gallant-sail wind, and with a temperature of 30° F., we held the same course for 24 miles until 6.0 A.M. We

south. On the concave side the depths run to over 3000 fathoms, while on the convex side there is a "deep", long and narrow, of over 4000 fathoms.—F.D.

passed a few icebergs and then turned to S. 46° E. and at midday we had proceeded 27 miles in that direction.

For the celebration of the feast of the Epiphany the priest from the *Mirnyi* came aboard at my invitation, and we held a service. At 1.0 P.M. we took him back to the *Mirnyi*. At 2 o'clock we were again under sail when, with the wind, thick weather and snow set in. At 2:30 P.M. we passed a large ice floe on which a great number of white petrels were sitting. The surface of the ice was quite flat. When the *Mirnyi* had come up with us, we set more sail and until midnight held on different tacks, passing ice on both sides of us.

With variable light wind and rather thick weather, the temperature was 30.2° F. We went slowly east and at break of day saw blue petrels. At 4.30 P.M. thick fog set in, and we shortened sail to enable the *Mirnyi* to keep in touch with us. At 6.0 A.M. we had 29° F., and at 10.0 A.M. we observed a whale close to the vessel. In order to indicate our position to the *Mirnyi* we signalled by gunfire, but received no reply. On the gun being fired, the whale immediately dived. At 11.0 A.M., to ascertain the drift, we lowered a boat and kept it stationary by means of a kettle lowered to 50 sazhen (58 fathoms) but no drift was observable. At midday the mist rose and we saw the *Mirnyi*. At 4.0 P.M. a fresh wind blew from south by east with snow, so that we made little headway southward. Until 6.0 P.M. after passing some ice we lay to near a low ice floe on which a great many penguins were sitting. Mr. Simanov and Mr. Demidov started off in a boat to catch some of them; while they caught some with their hands and stowed them in sacks, the others remained sitting; only a few dived into the water, but without waiting till the boat had gone they jumped back on to the floe, helped by the wash of waves. Our booty consisted of thirty penguins. I ordered a few to be sent to the mess, a few to be prepared for stuffing, and the remainder were kept on board and fed on fresh pork, but this appeared to be injurious to them, as they soon sickened, and died after three weeks. The crew skinned them and made caps of the skins, and used the fat for greasing their boots. The penguins were cooked for the officers' mess and we proved that they are good for food, especially if kept for several days in vinegar as is done with certain kinds of game.[1] There was nothing in sight but the unbroken monotony of ice and sea, and the penguin hunt therefore proved a welcome occupation and incidentally provided us with fresh food. We had it stewed together with salt beef and gruel and seasoned with vinegar; the crew liked it, seeing that the officers' mess too pronounced favourably upon it. Fifteen of the penguins were given to the *Mirnyi*.

After the hunt we hoisted the boat and set sail. In the evening when we were in Lat. 59° 49′ 50″ S., Long. 20° 47′ W. the magnetic variation was found to be 2° 34′ W. We saw up to twenty-five icebergs and a good deal of broken ice, whilst blue and white petrels and one albatross flew round us continually.

8th. At midnight we had 3° of frost. We kept to a south-easterly course so as to reach a higher latitude. The wind changed from south by west to south-west and at 3.0 A.M. the horizon was completely invisible. Between daybreak and 10.0 A.M. we passed twenty-two icebergs and a large quantity of small broken ice. We approached one of these icebergs on which we could see a great many penguins. We lay to and lowered the boats to cut the ice and to catch as many penguins as we could. Mr. Simanov, Mr. Lyeskov and Mr. Demidov went for the hunt, taking with them part of a fishing net. By midday they had caught thirty-eight. In the meantime the others were cutting ice with which they were able to fill sixteen barrels and all the tubs and cauldrons. We placed the penguins in the chicken runs and in a bath tub placed on the poop for that purpose.

At midday we were in Lat. 60° 06′ 08″ S., Long. 18° 39′ 51″

[1] Penguin meat is generally regarded as very good and slightly preferable to seal. That it receives only grudging appreciation here is due rather to the natural conservatism of the seaman than to any unusual taste in the meat. —F.D.

W. The set of the stream during three days was S. 89° E. 39 miles. Owing to heavy snow and a great deal of ice we had to proceed on a different tack until 6.0 P.M. At this time by observing eight lunar distances, we fixed the longitude of our position at 18° 12′ 07″ W. The wind had veered to the west. Soon after 6.0 P.M. we saw on the low flat ice a sea animal; we made for it to see what kind it was and with luck to shoot it. Mr. Ignatiev and Mr. Demidov, considering themselves fine shots, loaded their guns. The *Mirnyi*, at the same time, went direct towards this ice floe and, as soon as she came within rifle shot, an attack was made from both vessels. The animal was wounded in the tail and in two places in the head. The ice was covered with blood. The hunters disputed in a friendly way as to whom the booty should fall, but the dispute remained undecided. Mr. Mikhailov drew a sketch of the animal. It was 12 feet long and measured 6 feet round the body; its head somewhat resembled a dog's, the tail was short, the upper part of the body was a greenish-grey colour and the underneath was yellow.[1]

Among the crew of the *Vostok* there was a sailor who came from the town of Archangel. He told us that in that district these animals are called "utlyuga". It seemed to be a species of seal. May one conclude, on encountering such animals in the polar seas, that there is land near or not? This question remains unsolved, all the more as these animals may perfectly well breed, change their coats and rest on these ice floes as we saw them. The nearest land known to us was the Sandwich Islands, which were 270 miles away.

After hoisting the boats, we set all sail and turned east-south-east. At 7.0 P.M. we observed pack ice to the south; at 9.0 P.M. we had sleet. We could see about fifty icebergs besides a great quantity of broken ice which, at 10.0 P.M., in Lat.

---

1 It is curious to find reluctance on the part of the officers to recognize this as a seal. Identification would be easy had the teeth been described but, being too large for a Crab-eater seal, it must have been a Leopard seal *(Stenorhynchus leptonyx)*, especially as it was solitary. It is often found on the pack ice far from land, as too is the Crab-eater seal.—F.D.

60° 22′ S., Long. 17° 18′ 51″ W., obliged us to set our course east and to shorten sail for the night. Up to midnight we passed through a great deal of ice.

9th. With a fresh west wind, fog, sleet and snow, we continued on an easterly course, continually forced to change our course by the great quantity of floating ice. The thermometer stood at 33.5° F. At 12.30 P.M., in order to reduce speed, which had been 6 knots, we took in one reef in the topsails and two reefs in the mizzen topsail. At 1.0 P.M. the thick fog increased the danger of navigating so that the ship scarcely answered the helm in time to clear the ice; but fortunately for us towards 2.0 P.M. the fog lifted and we saw ourselves surrounded by icebergs and floating ice. An icefield extended from north-east to south-south-west, in the midst of which were wedged a number of large flat icebergs. I proceeded to the north by east, the *Mirnyi* following in our wake. I signalled to alter course to port. Although the fog had lifted a little, we were still unable to see much round us; we continued our way until 5.0 P.M. amongst a great quantity of small ice, constantly working the helm from side to side. After proceeding 16 miles in this manner, the weather fortunately cleared, and we observed ahead, from north-north-west to north-east by north, an icefield, surrounded on all sides by small ice. The wind now freshened; it was not possible to turn to the south, nor was there room to turn the vessel to the west. However, from the look-out I saw a narrow passage to the north-east between this field and the other, which we had seen at 2.0 A.M., extending to the point where we now were and surrounded by a large number of icebergs and quantities of small broken ice. I decided, therefore, with the changing wind from south by east, to advance into the ice and we turned to the north-east at 8 knots. To avoid collision with the smaller ice floes, the officer of the watch steered the ship by command, stationing himself on the forecastle. The *Vostok* had the great merit of answering the helm quite well, and thereby several times avoided collision with the floating ice. When we had proceeded 8½ miles to the east, the look-out reported that it was a little clearer to the north-north-east-half-east. After proceeding for 7½ miles through small ice, we found ourselves at 7.30 A.M. out of visible danger. We took another reef in the fore topsail to wait for the *Mirnyi.* During this time we had alternate rain and fitful sunshine.

At 9.0 A.M. in Lat. 59° 47′ 27″ S., Long. 15° 30′ W., we found a magnetic variation of 3° 48′ W. on an east by north course.

We passed near a large iceberg looking like a couch with the back reclining and decorated with carvings. All the ice had a great variety of shapes, though the flat floes were, for the greater part, uniform in appearance.

At 10.0 A.M., with a strong wind, we were obliged to reef again and remain under reefed topsails and strike the top-gallant yards. At midday we found our position by observation to be Lat. 59° 35′ 51″ S., Long. 15° 01′ 35″ W. The wind freshened very much from the south and brought with it high seas; the temperature was 35° F.; the stream set N. 11° W. 7 miles in these 24 hours. We proceeded on an east by north course from 9.0 A.M. to 5.0 P.M. at 7¼ knots, and in order not to get into lower latitudes we kept a course due east.

At 6.0 P.M., passing under the lee of a large iceberg, we noted that the thermometer, which was standing at 31° F., fell to 30° F. but when we had passed the iceberg, the mercury rose again to 31° F.

10th. We continued on the easterly course until 4.0 on the following morning, making 7 knots and passing several large high icebergs with flat surfaces. These icebergs lay in a line south to north. In the morning, in Lat. 59° 15′ S., Long. 11° 19′ W., we found the magnetic deviation to be 4° 8′ W., both ships being then on an east-south-east course. At 4.0 A.M. the wind fell and during the afternoon our speed decreased to 1 knot. At midday we were in Lat. 59° 12′ 46″ S., Long. 10° 41′ 46″ W., the stream setting N. 6° E. 18 miles in 24 hours. At the previous midnight we had a temperature of 30° F., at midday it was 33° F. The weather was fine, and on the horizon we could see, at different points, a number of icebergs and ice floes; but in spite of this, to avail myself of the fine weather, I turned again first to the south-east, shaking out the reefs and setting all sail, later to the south-south-east. A light wind was blowing from the south-east, the swell from the previous high seas continuing from the south, from which we concluded that there was less ice to the south than we had previously encountered. From midday to 6.0 P.M. we passed fifteen icebergs. In the evening, in Lat. 59° 27′ 33″ S., Long. 09° 50′ W., we found a magnetic variation of 7° 06′ W. on a south-south-east course.

At 9.0 P.M. the sky was covered with clouds and mist spread over the horizon. There were many icebergs in sight and the wind blew from the north-west. Towards night we shortened sail and proceeded under topsails only. Soon afterwards we had a snowstorm which prevented our seeing an immense ice floe in the near distance, though we knew it was near by the noise of the swell breaking over it. At 10.0 P.M. the snow stopped. At 11.0 P.M., in order to reduce speed, we took in another reef in the fore topsail.

11th. Very soon we had snow again and 3° F. of frost. At 1.0 A.M., owing to darkness caused by the heavy snow, I ordered the ships to turn on the port tack to the north-east. At 2.30 A.M., when it got lighter, we saw that there was no ice in our neighbourhood, but a good deal to the south-east of us. We turned to an easterly course for 27 miles, passing a few icebergs with small ice falling from them, and noted that the swell, which had come from the north-west, was now setting in from the south-east. Thick weather with sleet continued from 9.0 to 10.0 A.M. We steered one point more into the wind to pass to the south of five large icebergs lying in our route. At 10.0 A.M., having passed these, we turned south-east under all sail; the existence of a swell from that point suggested that there was little, if any, ice in that direction.

At midday we were in Lat. 59° 43′ 55″ S., Long. 8° 11′ 24″

W.; the stream set N. 82° E. 5 miles in 24 hours. The temperature was 35° F. The wind shifted to the south-west and we set our course south-east by south. About 4.30 P.M. we were in Lat. 60° 07′ 07″ S., Long. 7° 18′ W., the magnetic variation being 9° 12′ W. From midday to midnight, we made 6 to 7 knots under a fresh south-west wind. The weather continued overcast and from time to time snow fell.

12th. The wind dropped a little, there was a swell from the south-west, and the temperature was 35° F. We proceeded on a south-south-east course. Towards 5.0 A.M. we were in Lat. 60° 50′ S., Long. 5° 52′ W., magnetic variation 10° 37′ W. From morning until midday in Lat. 61° 21′ S., we passed eight icebergs; the wind freshened a little. The horizon was still hidden by the haze and the temperature was 36° F. At 5.0 P.M. we passed an iceberg with a steeply rising top and at 6.0 P.M. we had rain but it was not for long. At 9.0 P.M., on account of the darkness and thick weather, we shortened sail so that the *Mirnyi* should be able to come up with us.

13th. At midnight the mercury stood at freezing point, but below, where the crew slept, it was at 50° F. There was a fresh wind from the west, the horizon was hazy, and at 3.0 A.M. and at 7.0 A.M. we passed icebergs on a south by west course. In Lat. 63° 18′ S., Long. 3° 53′ W., we found a magnetic variation of 9° 55′ W. We proceeded at the rate of 8 knots and at midday we were in Lat. 63° 49′ 21″ S., Long. 2° 36′ 42″ W. We continued on a south by west course until 5.30 of the following morning—14th January—when, with a change of the wind to the north, the whole horizon was covered with a haze and snow and rain were falling. Fearing still worse weather, I ordered the main topsails to be close-reefed and turned the ship on the starboard tack. At 8.30, on account of the high wind and considerable pitching and rolling, we struck the topyards.

15th. At 7.0 A.M. on the following morning, although the weather remained unchanged, I did not hope for any improvement, and therefore proceeded again on a south by west course. Up to midday, we passed three icebergs; we were then in Lat. 66° 53' 42" S., Long. 3° 03' 54" W.[1] At 4.0 P.M. we saw three blue petrels.

16th. The thick weather, with snow and ice and high north-west wind, continued through the night. At 4.0 A.M. we saw a grey (smoke-coloured) albatross flying near the ship. At 7.0 A.M. the wind changed to the north, the snow ceased for a time and the blessed sun now and then broke through the clouds.

At 9.0 A.M., in Lat. 69° 17' 26" S., Long. 2° 45' 46" W., we found a magnetic variation of 8° 48' W. Proceeding south, at midday, in Lat. 69° 21' 28" S., Long. 2° 14' 50" W., we encountered icebergs, which came in sight through the falling snow looking like white clouds. We had a moderate north-east wind with a heavy swell from the north-west and, in consequence of the snow, we could see for but a short distance. We hauled close to the wind on a south-east course and had made 2 miles in this direction when we observed that there was a solid stretch of ice running from east through south to west. Our course was leading us straight in to this field, which was covered with ice hillocks. The barometer fell from 20.50 to 29, warning us of bad weather. We had 2° F. of frost. We turned north-west by west in the hope that in this direction we should find no ice.[2] During the last 24 hours we had

[1] It is to be noted as curious that no mention is made of this, their first, crossing of the Antarctic Circle, usually a great event in polar expeditions. —F.D.

[2] This day must be accounted an unfortunate one for the Russian expedition for we know now that they must have been within a few miles, not more than twenty at most, of the coast of what is now called Princess Martha Land, discovered in 1929–30 by the Norvegia expedition. It is even possible that the "solid stretch of ice running from east through south to west" was indeed the land ice which, everywhere along this coast, marks the edge of the continent. In any case, a few hours of clear weather on this day would have certainly antedated the discovery of land here by 110 years.—F.D.

observed snow-white and blue petrels and heard the cries of penguins.

17th. The thick weather and snow continued through the night. At 2.0 A.M. both ships put about on the port tack. At 6.0 A.M. we observed right ahead of us an iceberg which we only just succeeded in avoiding. The thermometer stood at freezing point; at the same time the wind began to freshen and we were forced to double-reef the topsails. At 8.0 A.M. the *Vostok,* turning to the wind, joined up with the *Mirnyi.* Towards midday the sky cleared a little of snow clouds and the sun appeared. We were able to take midday observations and found our position to be Lat. 68° 51′ 51″ S., Long. 3° 07′ 06″ W., the stream having set N. 20° W. 13 miles. We did not, however, enjoy the sun for long; in these latitudes it is so rarely visible. Fog and snow, the travelling companions of the navigator in the Antarctic, again overtook us.

In these high latitudes, into which we extended our voyage, the sea is a most beautiful blue colour, which in some measure serves to indicate the great distance of land. The penguins, whose cries we heard, are in no need of land. They live just as comfortably, and indeed seem to prefer living, on the flat ice, far more so than other birds do on land. When we caught penguins on the ice, many dived into the water but, without even waiting till the hunters had gone, they returned to their former places with the help of the waves.[1] Judging by the form of their bodies and their air of repose, one may conclude that it is merely the stimulus of seeking food that drives them from the ice into the water. They are very tame. When Mr. Lyeskov threw a net over a number of

1 In several places Bellingshausen refers to the waves assisting the penguins to jump out on to the floes, a misconception due to the extraordinary suddenness of a penguin's leap out of the water so that it appears to be propelled. The bird swims under water at a fast rate and at the appropriate distance elevates its tail sharply which causes it to rise steeply out of the water with a shower of spray. Usually it allows a large margin for the height of the ice above water level and therefore jumps much higher than is really necessary to clear the edge of the floe.—F.D.

them, the others, not caught by the net, remained quite quiet and indifferent to the fate of their unhappy fellows who, before their eyes, were put into sacks. The suffocating air in these sacks and careless handling while catching, transferring and taking the penguins on board the vessels, produced a sickness amongst them, and in a short time they threw up a great quantity of shrimps, which evidently form their food.[1] At this point I may add that we had so far not found any sort of fish in the high southern latitudes, excepting the different species of whale.

At 8 o'clock the *Vostok* waited for the *Mirnyi* and, joining her, we passed to windward on a starboard tack so as to draw away from the ice and lie to during the foggy weather. The wind blew steadily from the north with occasional snow. The whole horizon was in a haze. Since our arrival in these higher latitudes we had always the same sort of bad weather with north winds, but with the wind from the south we had dry weather with a clear horizon.

18th. At midnight we turned on to the port tack. The thermometer in the open air showed a temperature of 33° F.; below deck where the crew slept 53° F. At midday the wind fell almost completely, but continued from the north. The weather cleared, but the horizon still remained hazy. There was no ice in sight. We were in Lat. 68° 35' 28" S., Long. 2° 33' 51" W. The barometer stood at 29.13.

Profiting by the calm and clear weather, we invited in the morning, by signal, Mr. Lazarev and all the officers of the *Mirnyi* who were not on duty, to dinner. They arrived at 1.0 P.M. and did not return to the *Mirnyi* until 11.0 P.M. The weather was clear and calm with a light north wind. This day corresponded exactly to the 18th July in the northern hemisphere;[2] the thermometer showed 33° F.

---

1 Practically the only food of the smaller types of penguins is a small reddish crustacean, *Euphausia*, which is also the food of whales in the Antarctic seas. —F.D.

2 The meaning here is somewhat obscure but apparently refers to the fact that they were almost on the Greenwich meridian.—F.D.

Mr. Lazarev, amongst other things, reported to me that on the 9th instant at 2.30 A.M., when passing through a narrow passage between icefields and floating ice, the *Mirnyi* struck against a fairly large flat ice floe with such force that everybody rushed on deck. The result of the collision was that a timber, about 4 feet long and 1 foot wide, below the water level was forced out of the stern. Such a shock probably startled even the bravest. The watch was at that time being taken by Lieutenant Obernibessov. He was on the forecastle, and from there gave orders for the helm.

We passed the day in friendly conversation, talking over the dangers and adventures we had encountered since our last meeting, and quite forgetting for a time that we were in a region uninhabited save for whales, penguins and other birds, and where thick fogs and frequent snow prevailed.

19th. It remained calm until 3.0 A.M., and then a light wind with snow blew up from the south-east by east. We steered on a starboard tack in a north-easterly direction. It was my intention to work a little to the east and then to return southward to push at a new point into the higher latitudes. At 6.0 A.M. the wind from east-north-east freshened. We reefed the top-gallant sail and took in a reef in the topsail. At 8.30 A.M. we turned to port and set the mainsail. At midday we found ourselves in Lat. 68° 36′ 36″ S., Long. 1° 43′ 59″ W., with the temperature 1° F. above freezing point. On sounding, we had 100 sazhen (116 fathoms), still no bottom. The snow continued to fall during a contrary east wind. We endeavoured to proceed on our course on short tacks and encountered no ice. On that day for the first time we succeeded in bringing down a "polar bird", so named by Captain Cook. It was the size of a hen, the feathers on the back, wings and top of the head were brown, the neck and breast much lighter in colour, tail and under part of the body white. The upper tail feathers were brown at the top; the colour of these tail feathers was regularly divided, i.e. the underside of each feather was brown and the upper part of it white. The eyes were dark with black pupils, the beak and feet were dark, the membrane between the claws being a muddy dark colour, the legs still darker. This bird resembles in all particulars the other petrels and therefore I shall call it the "polar petrel".[1]

20th. At 4.30 a.m., after tacking to the eastward for 30 miles and seeing the persistence of contrary winds from that quarter, I was convinced of the truth of Captain Cook's observation that in the higher southern latitudes there are always easterly winds. I therefore decided to make straight for the south, until it should be quite impossible to continue navigating farther, and then to return to lower latitudes. From there we should get farther to the east under the prevailing west winds and then turn again to higher latitudes. And so I turned southward, in thick weather, snow falling steadily until 3.0 P.M. At 7.0 P.M. we observed an iceberg of about ¾ mile circumference and up to 70 feet high, the sides perpendicular. There was a heavy swell from the east, with wind, all of which were indications to us that there was probably little ice in our neighbourhood towards the east. A few snow-white and polar petrels, also some storm petrels, flew near the ship. These latter we found in all latitudes from the equator to the ice regions and called them, during the voyage, "Jews of the Sea", because, like the Jews on land, these birds have no abiding place but roam over the ocean in all latitudes.

21st. We still continued southward with a light wind from the south-east by south and clear weather. Whales spouted and polar and snow-white petrels—a warning of the vicinity of ice—flew round the ships. Towards the south it became lighter from hour to hour. At 1.0A.M. we saw ice ahead and, farther south at 2.0 A.M., found ourselves among broken ice; farther to the south there were about fifty icebergs of various sizes enclosed in the middle of the field. As we surveyed the

1 Antarctic petrel *(Thalassoica antarctica)*. This bird is plentiful in the pack ice in summer and ranges farther north in the winter. It was not until 1912 that their nests and young were first discovered, by the expedition under Sir Douglas Mawson, on rocky islets close to the mainland.—F.D.

extent of the icefield around us to the east, south and west, we were unable to see its limits; it was precisely an extension of that which we had seen in thick weather on the 16th, but had been unable to examine properly on account of the mist and snow.[1]

At this point we found it impossible to proceed farther south. We were then in Lat. 69° 25′ S., Long. 1° 11′ W.; the air was dry and we had 6° F. of frost. On sounding we found 100 sazhen (116 fathoms), no bottom. Turning on another tack to north-east by north, we much regretted that the wind did not allow us to pass along the ice, or at least to go parallel with it to the eastward, in order to penetrate at another point into higher latitudes.

1 The ships were again probably within 30 miles of the continent.—F.D.

JAMES WEDDELL

(*1787–1834*)

JAMES WEDDELL was one of the rare early British sealers to write an account of his explorations. His style is unpolished and nautical, his observations wry.

His father, an upholsterer, died when Weddell was very young. The young Weddell educated himself by reading. At an early age, with only a meager schooling, Weddell was bound to the master of a coastal vessel. He made several voyages to the West Indies and became a capable navigator. In 1819 he was given command of the sealing brig *Jane of Leith*, in which he made three voyages to the Antarctic. During the last of these (1822–24) he, with the cutter *Beaufoy*, while persistently searching for a large tract of land in very high latitudes, penetrated pack ice until he broke out and discovered the large sea named in his honor. In this sea he reached a new farthest south of 74° 15'. The Weddell seal is also named after him.

Towards the Pole

On the 17th of September 1822, I gave Mr. Matthew Brisbane his instructions, and at five o'clock in the afternoon both vessels weighed, and made sail out of the Downs.

We had the wind blowing fresh from E.N.E., which by the 18th, in the afternoon, brought us off Portland. At 4^h P.M. with the Bill N. ¼ E. by compass, distant fourteen miles, I took sights of the sun for chronometers, and departure for dead reckoning. The breeze continued to blow from the eastward, and steering a channel course, darkness soon closed from our contemplations the view of our beloved country.

As I had directed Mr. Brisbane to separate, when below the Bill of Portland, and to proceed direct to the Island of Bona Vista, while I was to touch at Madeira, by the way, we allowed the *Beaufoy* to pass out of sight about midnight.

Nothing worthy of remark occurred during our passage to Madeira, except that in making Porto Santo, I found that we had experienced an easterly current of 85 miles in ten days.

It was Friday the 4th of October before we arrived in Funchal Roads, and at half after seven in the morning I took sights for chronometers. The longitude deduced, placed Funchal centre in 16° 52' 28".

By the 5th in the evening, having (by the kind assistance of John Blandy, Esq. to whom I had letters of introduction), completed my business on shore, I returned on board, and at nine o'clock made all sail for the island of Bona Vista, one of the Cape de Verdes. We took the trade wind at N.E. after clearing Funchal Bay, and carried it, blowing steadily, to Bona Vista, where we arrived on Monday the 14th, and found the *Beaufoy*, with several small American and Portuguese vessels, at anchor.

Having to take in a quantity of salt, it was immediately set about, and by the 19th having received 36 tons, divided in the two vessels, and being in all other respects supplied and ready for sea, on the evening of the 20th both vessels weighed, and made sail to the southward.

While at Bona Vista, I dined several times in company with the Bishop of the Cape de Verdes, who usually resides at St. Iago. He was at this period making his triennial visit, and with his retinue of priests, lived at the house of Senhor Manoel Martins, who was absent on a mission to the Cortes, as representative of the Cape de Verdes. I found the Bishop a man of agreeable address, and by his winning manner calculated to make proselytes; indeed he attempted the conversion of an inmate of the house, an American lady, whose child he had baptized. She, however, with the common attachment that people have towards the faith in which they have been bred, repulsed all his endeavours.

The greatest respect was paid to this holy person by the principal inhabitants of the island; and great deference by the commonalty. Forbearance, suavity of manners, and rigid clerical discipline, appeared conspicuously in his character. When he rose from table he immediately withdrew to his room to study, and was seldom seen, except at table or taking a short evening walk, during which he was usually accompanied by a few of the chief people of the Island. Some of his priestly retinue were not quite so precise; for I could discover that when from under the eye of the Bishop, they were, like the laity, fond of the society of ladies, and open to their attractions.

The common people of these islands, are for the most part, intolerably indolent, and hence proceeds their miserable way of living. Their slaves, of whom they have many, are made to work hard, under the fear of the whip; for although, amongst all other nations, the Africans now enjoy a share of freedom, here no such blessing is afforded them.

Their principal occupation is making salt, and carrying on a small trade with the neighbouring islands, and with the ships that call here. The town of English Roads, which is generally called Bonavista, contains from forty to fifty houses; which, excepting about half a dozen, are rudely constructed of wood and clay, and mostly of negro-architecture. The colour of the inhabitants is from white to negro jet, comprehending all the intermediate shades; and they are so intermarried, slaves excepted, that they may be said to be but one family.

About three miles east of Bonavista, lies a town, called Nova Cidade, or New City, where the governor used to reside. It contains a neat church, and about 100 buildings, the most of which are huts. The Governor, whom I found here on a former voyage, spoke good English, and was extremely polite and communicative. He was an European, and a colonel in the Portuguese regular army; his age might be about 65, and he had been 42 years governor of Bonavista.

He informed me that the population of the island was about 3000, and that nearly 300 of these were regular troops. The soil, he said, was very prolific, when the rains fell at the usual seasons and were copious; but that they frequently suffered much from want of rain, and indeed sometimes of good drinking water: hence no vessel touching here can expect to procure that invaluable article. The mean of chronometers gave 22° 0′ 59″ for the longitude of the anchorage.

Sea stock of pigs, goats, sheep, and poultry may be had here, but all are lean and of an inferior breed: perhaps the best place for stock is St. Iago, where it is better fed, although somewhat dearer. I called at the latter on my last voyage, and waited on the Governor, who was on board a schooner of war, at anchor in the Bay. He was dressed in a general's uniform, and rather a good looking man. On my telling him that my object was to procure a supply of stock, and that the vessels should not anchor, he immediately granted permis-

sion to land, at the same time, recommending to my consideration the poultry yard of his lady, who, he assured me,
would furnish me very reasonably. I was a good deal surprised to hear that a governor's lady should condescend to
such a traffic, but immediately went on shore and proceeded
to the palace. The door was guarded by a soldier, who refused
me admittance; but on my business being announced, I was
allowed to pass by this sentinel and two others, and at length
arrived in the presence of the lady. I found her employed in
getting out the stock, consisting of pigs, turkeys, and fowls,
into the middle of the yard for inspection. According to the
usual practice, she represented them as being fat and cheap,
and I chose a number of turkies, &c. which were sent down
to the boat. Our bargain was concluded in the house, over a
glass of wine, and she politely desired her son, a youth of
about fourteen, to play me a tune on the guitar, which he did
with peculiar sweetness; after he had finished I settled for my
purchase, and bade her ladyship good day.

Having mentioned this circumstance as exhibiting a singular union of rank and occupation, if not of pomp and avarice,
I now return to my narrative by observing, that having
weighed anchor at Bonavista, we carried all possible sail to
the southward.

We had nothing remarkable until the 21st of October,
when being in latitude north 14 degrees, we were not a little
surprised to find the water up to the cabin deck; the cause
was soon discovered to be a leak somewhere in the counter;
and in consequence of coals being stowed in the after-hold,
the water could not find its way forward. We immediately
hove the ship to, brought her by the head, and finding the
leak in the counter ends, succeeded in stopping it in a temporary manner.

An account of common occurrences on board a merchant
vessel, and the ship's place in latitude or longitude over so
obvious a track, can convey no useful or interesting information. I shall therefore hurry on to regions less frequented.

On the 23d of October, in the latitude of eight degrees

north, the wind became light and variable, and continued so till we reached the latitude of five degrees north, when we took the S.E. trade wind. On the 7th November in the longitude of 30° we crossed the equator. The trade wind being far southerly we passed Cape St. Augustine, on the coast of Brazil, within 100 miles.

On the 14th, in latitude 14° S., we closed with a Portuguese schooner, having a cargo of slaves, bound to Bahia, and I boarded her. My officers were seriously impressed with the idea of making her a prize; but I was aware that we could not legally do so. This inability I much regretted, as we were of sufficient force to have relieved 250 fellow creatures from a cruel bondage. The men slaves were stowed in the hold, and almost suffocated by the smallness of the place; the women and children were seated on the lee-side of the deck, many of them shackled by the feet. As it was out of my power to render them any assistance, much as I deplored their miserable situation, I returned on board and the vessels separated.

This nefarious traffic is still carried on by the Portuguese, to a considerable extent to the southward of the Equator, in spite of all the humane efforts of Great Britain to put an end to it.

As far as the latitude of 24 degrees south, we had the wind frequently from N.W. to N.N.E. blowing in heavy squalls, with thunder and heavy rain.

At this season, the route we took may be recommended for a quick passage, but, for the health of a crew entering upon a long voyage, the coasting passage is highly injurious. I had one man at the point of death by an attack of tetanus, brought on by his exposure to heavy rains.

We continued standing to the southward with the *Beaufoy* in company, till we reached the latitude of 40°; we then steered to the westward to make the land of Patagonia.

On the 10th of December we arrived off Port Valdees lying in latitude 42° 32″. I sent the chief mate to sound the passage into the harbour; but finding by his report, that there was only two and a half fathoms at low water in mid-channel, and that the tide ran rapidly across the entrance, I did not attempt going in with the vessels.

On the 11th in the morning, we made sail along the coast to the southward, touching at several places for furs.

On the 19th, we put into Port St. Elena. Our principal business here was to stop the leak in the brigs' counter; in doing which, in order to secure the counter ends, we were obliged to unship the rudder and bring the vessel two feet down by the head.

The following day I sent Mr. Brisbane with the *Beaufoy* to examine St. George's Bay; and to meet me on the 28th, off Penguin Island. On the 26th, our business being completed, about noon we put to sea.

Port St. Elena lies in latitude 44° 34' 16" and longitude, (by mean of chronometers, compared with four sets of lunar observations taken eight days previous,) 65° 16' 52".

The bay affords good shelter from S. by E. via west, to E. by S.; and, as the heavy and prevailing winds are between these points, this place may well be recommended to stop at for a few days. The winds are seldom from South East and generally light; and, the tide running strong across the entrance of the bay, the sea, during strong S.E. winds, is a good deal cut off.

As this anchorage is the most easy of access of any on the coast, I shall annex a plan of it; for which I ran a base line of 400 fathoms, and took angles. In the valley marked A, I observed two holes which had been dug for obtaining fresh water, but what they now contained was quite brackish; farther up this valley, about half a mile, I found very sweet water, but not in quantity sufficient to supply a vessel without a considerable expense of time and labour.

Guanacoes are here very numerous, but not easily approached: they much resemble deer; their flesh is well tasted, and they are large enough to make them an object of consideration to ships touching on this coast in want of refreshments. We caught one which when cleaned weighed 120 lb. and was, to my taste, very like well fed mutton. The difficulty of procuring these animals from their fleetness and watchfulness is such, however, that they cannot be taken hastily; but must be entrapped by lurking behind bushes about their watering places at the dawn of the morning. Hares, which are also numerous here, are much larger than in other countries. The tide flows at the full and change at 3° 30', and rises about 22 feet.

On the 30th of December, in latitude 47° 54' and off Penguin Island, in the afternoon, amidst several water-spouts, which are so dreaded by many, we rejoined the *Beaufoy,* and made sail to the southward.

We had now decidedly taken our departure for a voyage of investigation to the southward, and though we were a month later than I had intended, I was happy that we had made the brig comparatively effective; and was determined, should I not be successful at the South Orkneys, to prosecute a search beyond the tracks of former navigators.

I had given Mr. Brisbane my instructions how to act in the event of separation, and we now proceeded to the southward in company.

At noon of the 2d of January 1823, we were in the latitude of 51° 55', and longitude 65° 7' 15", and this being the latitude assigned to the L'aigle shoal, discovered in 1817 by a Captain Bristow, I hauled up N.E. by E. ½ E. in order to obtain a sight of it; but with a run of 14 miles, and a view of 10 from the mast head, I saw nothing. Had it been accurately laid down I ought to have found it. This shoal must be very dangerous, as it lies in midchannel between the Falkland Islands and the coast of Patagonia; but as I have never seen it I cannot describe it. It is reported to be a patch of breakers about 300 yards in extent. Mr. Poole places it in latitude 51° 51', and longitude 64° 50', which, in my opinion, is not to be depended on; and therefore ships must be much delayed here in waiting, with a fair wind, for daylight.

At 8 o'clock in the morning of the 3d, the wind shifted suddenly from W.N.W. to south, and in less than half an hour we were brought to under a close-reefed main-topsail. The gale continued with great violence, and with a most irregular sea till the evening of the 4th, when it moderated, and we made more sail. The temperature of the elements during the gale was of air 39° 30′, and that of water 49° 30′. This was surprisingly low for midsummer, and the latitude of 53 degrees; but when we consider that a south wind blows over the frozen land of Shetland, the temperature of the air must of consequence be much reduced in the neighbourhood of Cape Horn.

On the 6th in the morning the wind again freshened at S. by E. to a gale, with a high and irregular sea, which, in the afternoon, stove two boats, washed away part of the bulwarks, and carried several things off the deck. This distressing sea was no doubt produced by a tide or current, as we were not more than 100 miles S.E. of the Falkland Islands. At midnight the weather moderated suddenly, and left us scarce wind sufficient to keep the ship steady.

The 7th being fine I communicated with the *Beaufoy*, and was happy to hear they were all well, and had met with no accident.

The wind continued blowing moderately from S. by E. to S.S.W. with passing snow squalls; and on the 10th, in latitude 58°, we saw five ice islands and an appearance of land in the N.E.; but as I had cruised over that spot on a former voyage I gave it no credit.

On the 11th at noon our latitude by observation was 59° 37′, and longitude by chronometers 46° 1′. The temperature of the air was 38°, and that of water 33°. Many ice islands were in sight which accounted for the temperature of the water being reduced.

At daylight in the morning of the 12th we saw some pigeons, and at 6 o'clock perceived the east end of the islands of South Orkneys*, bearing W. by S., distant about 11 leagues. We carried all possible sail to get under the land, but the wind soon became light and left us almost at the mercy of a

* Reported by me to the Commissioners of His Majesty's Navy, on my arrival in England, in 1822.

heavy swell, in the midst of ice islands, which made our navigation truly hazardous. At 8 o'clock one of the eastern islands, which from its figure we named Saddle Island, bore S. 10 W., distant about 11 leagues.

During the 13th, the wind was light, and from the N.N.W., which in this region generally brings fog, and now obliged us to keep an offing. At 10 o'clock the wind shifted to S.E. with clear weather. The temperature of air was 34°, that of water 33°. At daylight of the 14th we saw the land in the S.W., distant about 10 leagues; and by 7 o'clock we were within one mile of the shore.

I had landed on these islands the year before; but having a loaded ship, and no second vessel, I was obliged to relinquish a deliberate examination of their shores for that season.

Being now close under the land, I sent a boat from each vessel to explore them. We continued to tack the vessels about in a bay, which from Saddle Island forming part of it, we called Saddle Island Bay. The ice bergs, which form in the bays in winter, and break away in the summer, now produced so much drift ice, that we had frequently to work ship to avoid striking it. This coast is, if possible, more terrific in appearance than South Shetland. The tops of the islands, for the most part, terminate in craggy towering peaks, and look not unlike the mountaintops of a sunken land. The loftiest of these summits, towering up to a point, I denominated Noble's Peak, in honour of an esteemed friend, Mr. James Noble, orientalist, Edinburgh. This Peak, in a clear day, may be seen at the distance of fifteen leagues.

On the 14th I made observations for settling the latitude and longitude of Saddle Island. The latitude of its centre was found to be 60° 37′ 50″, and longitude by means of three chronometers 44° 52′ 45″ west of Greenwich. Two of these chronometers on the 12th agreed to the same second, and the third differed but 12″; hence it may be presumed that the situation of the island is correctly determined.

On the 15th in the afternoon, the vessel being close in shore and the weather settled, I landed on the south side of the Bay, and having climbed a mountain, was employed in taking a bird's-eye view of the country, when a dense fog set in, which in a few minutes shut the vessels from observation. I hurried down to the boat, and put off, hoping to get sight of the vessels before losing the land; but I was mistaken, for we soon lost the one without obtaining the other. My anxiety for the safety of the vessel lying among islands, in a thick fog, was great; but I was fortunately soon relieved by its clearing up, and allowing me to get on board.

Having seen some sea-leopards* on shore, I sent the second mate to take them, who soon returned with six which he had captured.

This creature resembles the quadruped of the same name in being spotted. The drawing of one deposited in the Edinburgh Museum is annexed; and Professor Jamieson has kindly communicated to me a description of the animal. He considers it to be a new species of phoca, and gives it the following distinguishing characters:—Leopardine seal, the neck long and tapering; the head small; the body pale-greyish above, yellowish below, and back spotted with pale white. This species to be referred to the division Stenorhinque, of F. Cuvier; the teeth, however, do not quite agree with those of his Phoque Septonyx, nor with those of Sir E. Home, figured in Pl. xxix of the Philosophical Transactions for 1822.

In the evening the boats returned, having coasted these islands for fifty miles. They had found but one fur-seal, and some sea-leopards, the skins of which they brought on board. This examination, though unsuccessful, afforded some hope, as the seal was an earnest of our falling in with more: I therefore hauled off the shore, to go round the west end of the islands for a further search.

On the 17th the wind freshened to a gale from the N.N.E., and at 4 o'clock in the afternoon we saw the land under our lee, distant but about five miles. I made the signal of our situation to the *Beaufoy*, and carried an oppressive quantity

* Now called leopard seals.—C.N.

of sail to keep off the land: about midnight, however, it fortunately moderated, and the wind shifted to the S.S.W. We
continued plying to the westward, examining the shores as
we passed; and at 9 in the morning of the 19th we saw the
west end, bearing S.W. ½ W., and straits running to the
southward, which I called Spencer Straits, in honour of the
Right Honourable C. Spencer; at the same time bore S.E. by
S. ½ S.

The weather being frequently foggy and the winds light,
we did not get off the western point till noon of the 20th, and
at 3 o'clock I settled the latitude of this Cape to be 60° 42′ S.,
and longitude 46° 23′ 52″ W.

Not finding any animals in this quarter, I bore up to the
east, to examine the other parts of the islands. On the 22d in
the morning we were within six miles off the east point,
which I called Cape Dundas, in honour of the illustrious
family of that name. I presently despatched two boats to
explore the shores, and in the meantime made observations
for determining the position of this end of the Archipelago.

By a good meridian altitude I found Cape Dundas to lie in
latitude 60° 46′ 30″, and, by chronometers, in longtidue 44°
35′ 45″ west of Greenwich. Two miles from the shore, we
sounded on a bottom of dark-coloured sand, with 58 fathoms
water. About the Cape, where a little soil remained, there
was a patch of short grass, and many birds assembled round
it.

In the evening the boats returned with two seals and ten
leopards' skins. They had investigated this eastern island
thoroughly, and as we had now explored the whole of the
group without attaining our object, I concluded that the seals
we had found had migrated from some land, probably not
very distant. My officers had besides ascended a hill, from
which they said they had seen a range of land lying in the S.E.
As I thought it probable it might be so, we stood in that
direction, but on the 23d, in the morning, we were undeceived, for the supposed land was discovered to be a chain
of immense ice islands, lying E.N.E. and W.S.W. We made

various courses to the southward, and presently arrived at comparatively clear water. At noon our latitude by account was 61° 50′, and longitude 43°. The wind had shifted into the N.W. with a thick fog, on which we hauled to the wind to the N.E. under easy sail. In the afternoon the wind shifted to the W.S.W. and blew a gale, with strong snow squalls. We stood to the southward with little sail, and about midnight passed through a cluster of ice islands. In the morning of the 24th the wind moderated, and it became foggy, and we hove to. In order to avoid separation, the two vessels of necessity sailed very closely, our consort keeping constantly on our weather quarter. Our latitude at noon, by account, was 62° 35′: the weather continued foggy, with short intervals of comparatively clear weather, during which we always bore up to the southward. This very slow manner of sailing was teasing and unprofitable, but in these fogs it was risk enough to drift to the southward, lying to. In the evening, indeed, whilst enveloped in fog, the second mate called to me in the cabin, that breakers were close under our lee. I immediately prepared ship to ply to windward, but not seeing the broken water again, I concluded that what the officer saw was the breathing of whales; which must, indeed, have been the case, as when the fog cleared away nothing like breakers was visible.

On 27th at noon we had reached the latitude of 64° 58′, our longitude by mean of chronometers was 39° 40′ 30″. The variation of the compass at 10 o'clock in the forenoon, by azimuth, was 10° 37′ east. The temperature of air in the shade was 37°, that of water 34°; but in the rays of the sun, when clouded, the thermometer rose to 48 degrees. The weather being here so much more settled than in the lower latitudes of 60 and 61 degrees, could we but find land with produce, I had little doubt, but that in three or four weeks both vessels might have had their cargoes on board. As, however, we were to the southward of South Shetland, I stood back to the northward, considering it probable that land might be found between the South Orkneys and Sandwich Land; and as the summer season was now far advanced, it was advisable to examine those lower latitudes while the nights were yet but short,—since darkness added to fog makes navigation in an icy sea still more dangerous.

We stood to the northward with the wind between S.E. and S.W., and on the 29th at noon our latitude at observation was 61° 18′, and longitude by chronometers 40° 32′ 15″. The temperature of air was 34°, that of water 34°. Ice islands were our constant companions, and indeed they had become so familiar that they were little dreaded.

At 11 o'clock at night we passed within two ships' length of an object, which had the appearance of a rock. The lead was immediately thrown out, but finding no bottom, we continued lying to, till the chief mate ascertained it to be a dead whale very much swollen: such objects, seen imperfectly in the night are often alarming.

We carried easy sail to the northward with the wind westerly, much fog and falls of snow. On the 1st of February, at noon, our latitude was 58° 50′, longitude 38° 51′. As there was no sign of land in this situation, we stood to the south-east, making an angle with our course, coming northward, which would enable us to see land midway.

I had offered a gratuity of 10 *l.* to the man who should first discover land. This proved the cause of many a sore disappointment; for many of the seamen, of lively and sanguine imaginations, were never at a loss for an island. In short, fog banks out of number were reported for land; and many, in fact, had so much that appearance, that nothing short of standing towards them till they vanished could satisfy us as to their real nature.

In the morning of the 2d the wind freshened W.S.W. to a gale, which obliged us to lie to; snow qualls were frequent, and having many ice-islands to pass, we had to make various courses, and changes in the quantity of sail on the vessels. I carefully avoided the tracks of Captains Cook and Furneaux: and I may here remark how narrowly Captain Furneaux in the *Adventure*, in December 1773 and January 1774, escaped seeing South Shetland and the South Orkneys. He passed within 45 miles of the east end of Shetland and 75 miles of the South Orkneys: hence 20 miles, we may presume, of a more southerly course, would have given us a knowledge of South Shetland 50 years ago.

Running east in this latitude of from 60° to 61° we were constantly accompanied by all the birds common in these latitudes. Great numbers of finned and hump-backed whales were also seen; and penguins in large shoals, having for their resting-place some ice island.

Being determined to examine these latitudes thoroughly, we constantly hauled to the wind under close-reefed topsails during fogs and the darkest part of the night, bearing up to the eastward when daylight appeared. On the 4th in the morning land was believed to be seen in the N.E., resembling an island. The signal to that effect was made to our consort, and we carried all sail to ascertain the fact; but our pleasing hopes were again speedily dispelled by our illusive island sinking below the horizon. We returned to our former easterly course, and passed several ice islands, lying east and west. In fact, we found all the clusters to lie in that direction, which is caused, no doubt, by the prevalent westerly winds carrying them along to the eastward, and spreading them in proportion to their hold of the water and the surface they present above.

By the evening of the 4th we were within 100 miles of Sandwich Land, and within such a distance of the track of Captain Cook, as convinced me that no land lay between.

Our pursuit of land here, therefore, was now at an end, but I conceived it probable that a large tract might be found a little farther south than we had yet been. I accordingly informed Mr. Brisbane of my intention of standing to the southward, and he, with a boldness which greatly enhanced the respect I bore him, expressed his willingness to push our research in that direction, though we had been hitherto so unsuccessful.

The weather being dark and foggy we stood to the southward under close-reefed topsails only. At 10 o'clock the following morning the temperature of air was 37, that of water 36 degrees; our latitude at noon, by observation, was 61° 44', and longitude, by chronometers, 31° 13' 15".

From having had a long course of dense fogs and fresh gales, the decks of our vessels were constantly wet, which produced amongst our seamen colds, agues, and rheumatisms. To remedy this in some measure, I had the ship's cooking stove moved below for their comfort, and good fires kept for drying their clothes; and by attending to these matters, and administering a little medicine, their complaints were soon removed.

I had allowed them three wine-glasses of rum a day per man, since we were in these seas; and their allowance of beef and pork was one pound and a quarter a man per day; five pounds of bread, two pints of flour, three of peas, and two of barley, a man per week. These allowances in a cold climate were rather scanty, but the uncertainty of the length of our voyage required the strictest economy.

During the 6th and 7th we passed many ice islands, one of which I estimated to be two miles in length, and 250 feet high. The wind prevailed between W.S.W. and W.N.W. with foggy and clear weather alternately. At noon we observed in latitude 64° 15', and our longitude by chronometers was 30° 46'. The variation by azimuth in the forenoon was 8° 19' easterly.

At 10 o'clock at night, the weather being foggy, we narrowly escaped striking an ice island in passing. We hailed our consort, but she was so close to our stern that she passed also very near to it. The temperature of air at 8 o'clock in the evening was 34°, that of water 36°. In the afternoon of the 9th, the fog clearing away, we saw an appearance of land in the N.W.; but, after the usual practice of pursuing all such appearances, we discovered it to be one of our delusive attendants, the fog banks. The wind now shifted to south and blew strong, accompanied by snow squalls.

At daylight in the morning of the 10th the chief mate re-

ported land within sight, in the shape of a sugar loaf; as soon
as I saw it I believed it to be a rock, and fully expected to find
terra firma a short distance to the southward.

It was 2 o'clock in the afternoon before we reached it; and
not till then, when passing within 300 yards, could we satisfy
ourselves that it was not land, but black ice. We found an
island of clear ice lying close, and detached above water,
though connected below, which made a contrast of colour
that had favoured or rather completed the deception. In
short, its north side was so thickly incorporated with black
earth, that hardly any person at a distance would have hesi-
tated to pronounce it a rock. This was a new disappointment,
and seriously felt by several of our crew, whose hopes of
having an immediate reward for their patience and perseverance were again frustrated.

The wind was at south and blowing a fresh gale, with which
we might have gone rapidly to the northward; but the circumstance of having seen this ice island so loaded with earth,
encouraged me to expect that it had disengaged itself from
land possessing a considerable quantity of soil; and that our
arrival at that very desirable object might, perhaps, not be
very distant. These impressions induced me to keep our
wind, and we stood to the S.W.

I may here remark that many of the doubtful rocks laid
down in the chart of the North Atlantic have been probably
objects similar to what I have described; and still remain
unascertained, to the great annoyance of all cautious navigators. Our latitude at noon was by account 66° 26′, and our
longitude by chronometers 32° 32′. The temperature of air
was 35° 30′, that of water 34°.

On the 11th in the morning the wind shifted to S.W. by S.,
and we stood to the S.E. At noon our latitude by observation
was 65° 32′, that of account 65° 53′; and the chronometers
giving 44 miles more westing than the log. We had in 3 days
experienced a current running N. 64° W. 48 miles: the difficulty, however, of keeping a correct reckoning, from the
many changes made in the course and quantity of sail, must

subject the error to a suspicion of arising more from bad observation than from real current. We had evidently been set to the northward and westward, which is contrary to what is generally the case, as the current almost constantly sets to the eastward. In the afternoon I found the variation by azimuth 12° 2′ east.

During the 12th and 13th we had the wind from S.S.W., and we stood to the S.E. Ice islands were numerous, and on the 14th at noon our latitude by account was 68° 28′, and longitude by chronometers 29° 43′ 15″. In the afternoon, with the ship's head S.S.W. the variation by azimuth was 8° 5′ east. At 4 o'clock ice islands were so numerous as almost to prevent our passing; sixty-six were counted around us, and for about 50 miles to the south we had seldom fewer in sight.

On the 15th at noon our latitude observed was 68° 44′, by account 69°; this difference of 16 miles in the latitude with easting given by chronometers, makes a current in 4 days of N. 53° E. 27 miles. In the forenoon, with the ship's head S. by W., I took a set of azimuths, which to my great astonishment gave the variation but 1° 20′ east; in the afternoon I took a second set, which gave 4° 58′. As I had taken great pains in making the observations, and the instruments were good, however unaccountable this great difference was, I could not do otherwise than abide by the result.

On the 16th at noon our latitude by account was 70° 26′, and longitude by chronometers 29° 58′; the wind was moderate from the westward, and the sea tolerably smooth. Ice islands had almost disappeared, and the weather became very pleasant. Through the afternoon we had the wind fresh from the N.E., and we steered S.W. by W.

In the morning of the 17th the water appearing discoloured, we hove a cast of the lead, but found no bottom. A great number of birds of the blue peterel kind were about us, and many hump and finned back whales.

In the morning I took an amplitude, which gave variation 12° 24′ east. The wind had shifted to the S.E. and became light. Our latitude at noon by account was 71° 34′, and longitude by chronometers 30° 12'. As the weather was now more settled, our consort sailed wide, in order to extend our view.

On the 18th the weather was remarkably fine, and the wind in the S.E. Having unfortunately broken my two thermometers, I could not exactly ascertain the temperature, but it was certainly not colder than we had found it in December (summer) in the latitude of 61°. With the ship's head S.W. by S. at about 8ʰ 30' in the morning I took a set of azimuths, which gave variation 13° 23' east. At noon our latitude by observation was 72° 38', by account 72° 24'; hence, with chronometer difference of longitude, we had been set in three days S. 62° W., distance 30 miles. In the afternoon I took a long set of azimuths, which gave variation 19° 58'. This increase in so short a distance seemed unsatisfactory; on which account I neglected no opportunity of making observations in order to reconcile these irregularities. I had all the compasses brought upon deck, and I found them to agree, but rather inactive in traversing.

In the evening we had many whales about the ship, and the sea was literally covered with birds of the blue peterel kind. NOT A PARTICLE OF ICE OF ANY DESCRIPTION WAS TO BE SEEN. The evening was mild and serene, and had it not been for the reflection that probably we should have obstacles to contend with in our passage northward, through the ice, our situation might have been envied. The wind was light and easterly during the night, and we carried all sail. The sun's amplitude in the morning of the 19th when the ship's head was S. by E. gave variation 15° 10' east.

The weather being pleasant, our carpenter was employed in repairing a boat, and we were enabled to make several repairs on the sails and rigging. At noon our latitude by observation was 73° 17', an longitude by chronometers 35° 54' 45". In the evening, by several sets of amplitudes, I found the variation to be but 5° 35' east. About midnight it fell calm, but presently a breeze sprang up from the S.W. by W., and we hauled on a wind S. by E.

In the morning of the 20th the wind shifted to S. by W. and

blew a fresh breeze, and seeing a clouded horizon, and a great number of birds in the S.E., we stood in that direction. At 10 o'clock in the forenoon, when the ship's head was E.S.E., I took a set of azimuths, which gave variation 11° 20′ east. The atmosphere now became very clear, and nothing like land was to be seen. Three ice islands were in sight from the deck, and one other from the mast-head. On one we perceived a great number of penguins roosted. Our latitude at this time, 20th February, 1822, was 74° 15′, and longitude 34° 16′ 45″; the wind blowing fresh at south, prevented, what I most desired, our making farther progress in that direction. I would willingly have explored the S.W. quarter, but taking into consideration the lateness of the season, and that we had to pass homewards through 1000 miles of sea strewed with ice islands, with long nights, and probably attended with fogs, I could not determine otherwise than to take advantage of this favourable wind for returning.

I much regretted that circumstances had not allowed me to proceed to the southward, when in the latitude of 65°, on the 27th of January, as I should then have had sufficient time to examine this sea to my satisfaction.

Situated however as I actually was, my attention was naturally roused to observe any phenomena which might be considered interesting to science. I was well aware that the making of scientific observations in this unfrequented part of the globe was a very desirable object, and consequently the more lamented my not being well supplied with the instruments with which ships fitted out for discovery are generally provided.

As the exact longitude of the ship and of harbours, &c. is of the first consideration, I had expended 240*l.* in the purchase of three chronometers; all of these performed remarkably well, and, in particular, one of eight days, (No. 820.) Murry, London, continued regular in its daily rate of gaining through an unparalleled trial by repeated shocks, which the vessel (but slightly built) sustained during a month among field ice. Such perfection in this most useful machine, cannot be too much appreciated by commanders of ships, who, by assistance of so precise a nature, can easily avoid embarrassment in critical situations, where many lives and much valuable property frequently depend on a true knowledge of the ship's place.

The laws to which the compass seems to be subject in regard to its variation have lately undergone such accurate investigation by eminent individuals, that the phenomena attending it are now, in a great degree, ascertained.

My own actual observations with regard to the variation, are inserted at the end of the volume.

Those which I made about the latitude of 60 degrees, are corrected for local attraction from the table of experiments made with Mr. Barlow's plate, in H.M.S. Conway, by Captain Basil Hall, and by Mr. Forster; but the observations arrived at about the latitude of 70 degrees cannot be reconciled, as to quantity of local attraction, with the theory adopted on the subject; I therefore let them remain at the observed results. I found a difference of from 3 to 5 degrees between the variation taken at the binnacle and that on the main hatches; and I have found as great a difference when the observations were made, even on the same spot, an hour apart. In fact, it appeared evident that the magnetic energy of the earth upon the needle was much diminished when far to the southward; partly arising, no doubt, from the increased dip or diminution of horizontal action on the needle, which must be attracted in an increased degree by objects immediately about it. This, however, cannot be altogether decided till a more satisfactory theory in respect to the emanation of the magnetic influence has been demonstrated.

The Aurora Australis, which Mr. Forster saw in his voyage round the world with Captain Cook in the year 1773, I particularly looked for during the time the sun was beneath the horizon, which was more than six hours, but nothing of the kind was observable. As the twilight, however, was never out of the sky, that might be the cause of its not being visible.

The remarkable and distorted appearances which objects

and the horizon itself assume by refraction in high northern latitudes, occurred here but little more than in an ordinary way. The water spouted by whales half an hour after sunrise in the morning of the 19th exhibited an increased refraction, but it soon disappeared.

The reason of this phenomenon not existing as singularly in the south as it does in corresponding northern latitudes, may be attributed to this sea being clear of field ice.

It distinctly appears to me, that the conjecture of Captain Cook, that field ice is formed and proceeds from land, and is not formed in the open sea, is true. He latterly, however, changes his opinion from having found ice solid in field in the latitude of 70 degrees to the northward of Bhering's Straits. But I think it likely that the ice he fell in with there proceeded from land in the north, not more distant, perhaps, than 150 miles. No person can doubt the probability of my conjecture, when it is remembered, that in the latitude of 74° 15' south, (which, according to the received opinion of former navigators that the southern hemisphere is proportionably colder by 10 degrees of latitude than the northern, would be equal to 84° 15' north) I found a sea perfectly clear of field ice; whereas in the latitude of 61° 30', about 100 miles from the land, I was beset in heavy packed ice. As in that situation we could not see the land, had I not known of the existence of South Shetland, I might have fallen into the commonly received error, that this ice proceeded continuously from the South Pole. If, therefore, no land exist to the south of the latitude at which I arrived, *viz.* seventy-four degrees, fifteen minutes,—being three degrees and five minutes, or 214 geographical miles farther south than Captain Cook, or any preceding navigator reached, how is it possible that the South Pole should not be more attainable than the North, about which we know there lies a great deal of land?

The excessive cold of the southern hemisphere has been variously accounted for, every philosopher adopting that theory which best suited his own hydrographical system. Saint Pierre supposes it to proceed from a cupola of ice surrounding the South Pole, and stretching far northward. We have now better data to go upon; for though great exertions were used in the years 1773 and 1774 to discover the *terra australis incognita* without success, yet we find there is a range of land lying as far north as the latitude of 61 degrees. We may also conjecture, without much fear of being in the wrong, that the land with which we are acquainted, lying in latitude of 61 degrees, and in longitude 54° 30′, namely, the east end of South Shetland, stretches to the W.S.W., beyond the longitude in which Captain Cook penetrated to the latitude of 71° 10′. It is this land which, no doubt, ought to be looked upon as the source from which proceeds the excessive cold of these regions. The temperature of air and water in the latitude of 60 and 61 degrees, I have mentioned to be but little above the freezing point. The cold earthless land, and its immense ice islands, which are continually separating in the summer, and are made, by prevailing westerly winds, almost to girdle the earth, is evidently the cause of the very low temperature which prevails.

The part of the country which I have seen is without soil, reared in columns of impenetrable rock, inclosing and producing large masses of ice, even in the low latitude of 60° 45′.

It is certain that ice islands are formed only in openings or recesses of land; and field ice, I think, is not readily formed in a deep sea.

On soundings, the water is soon cooled down to the freezing point; hence field ice is found at the distance of many miles from any shore. These considerations induce me to conclude, that from having but three ice islands in sight, in latitude 74° degrees, the range of land, of which I have spoken, does not extend more southerly than the 73d degree. If this be true, and if there be no more land to the southward, the antarctic polar sea may be found less icy than is imagined, and a clear field of discovery, even to the South Pole, may therefore be anticipated.

CHARLES WILKES

(1798-1877)

IN THE FOLLOWING SELECTION the United States explorer
Charles Wilkes defends his claimed discovery of Antarctica
as indeed a land mass of continental proportions. Posterity
has proved him correct. A vast part of Antarctica south of
Australia, from approximately 100° to 140° Longitude East and
including Knox Coast, Budd Coast, Sabrina Coast, Banzare
Coast, Clarie Coast and Adélie Coast, is now known as Wilkes
Land.

Wilkes's father, a successful businessman, provided Wilkes
with a good education, a fact which comes through in
Wilkes's narrative. Wilkes entered the United States Navy as
a midshipman in 1818. In 1826 he became a lieutenant. He
was chosen to command a wide-ranging United States ex-

ploring expedition, proposed by the Navy as early as 1828, although he was still only a lieutenant. The expedition, consisting of the flagship, the *Vincennes,* and five other vessels, left the United States in August 1838 and returned in July 1842. Prominent among its several goals was the exploration of the high southern latitudes. After the return of the expedition Wilkes was court-martialed for excessive strictness with his men but the charges against him did not stand.

His narrative is written with intelligence, vividness, simplicity and sensitivity. The present selection illustrates with much suspense the dangers of cruising in Antarctic waters in sailing vessels. Wilkes recounts his farthest southern penetration as well as his sightings of what he judged to be a continental mass.

Antarctic Cruise

The subjects of which I am about to treat in the following chapters are exclusively nautical. I shall therefore adopt in treating them more of the form of a log-book, and follow the daily order of their occurrence with more strictness than I have hitherto considered necessary. This will be done in order to illustrate more fully the nature of remote regions we traversed, and for the purpose of giving a more exact relation of the incidents of this part of our cruise,—incidents that I cannot but hope have made this part of our labours particularly interesting to all of our countrymen who possess a feeling of national pride.

The credit of these discoveries has been claimed on the part of one foreign nation, and their extent, nay, actual existence, called into question by another; both having rival expeditions abroad, one at the same time, the other the year succeeding.

Each of these nations, with what intent I shall not stop to inquire, has seemed disposed to rob us of the honour by underrating the importance of their own researches, and would restrict the Antarctic land to the small parts they respectively saw. However willing I might be in a private capacity to avoid contesting their statements, and let truth make its own way, I feel it due to the honour of our flag to make a proper assertion of the priority of the claim of the American Expedition, and of the greater extent of its discoveries and researches.

That land does exist within the Antarctic Circle is now confirmed by the united testimony of both French and English navigators. D'Urville, the celebrated French navigator, within a few days after land was seen by the three vessels of our squadron, reports that his boats landed on a small point of rocks, at the place (as I suppose) which appeared accessible to us in Piner's Bay, whence the *Vincennes* was driven by a violent gale; this he called Clarie Land, and testifies to his belief of the existence of a vast tract of land, where our view of it has left no doubt of its existence. Ross, on the other hand, penetrated to the latitude of 79° S. * in the succeeding year, coasted for some distance along a lofty country connected with our Antarctic Continent, and establishes beyond all cavil the correctness of our assertion, that we have discovered, not a range of detached islands, but a vast Antarctic Continent. How far Captain Ross was guided in his search by our previous discoveries, will best appear by reference to the chart, with a full account of the proceedings of the squadron, which I sent to him, and which I have inserted in Appendix XXIV and Atlas. Although I have never received any acknowledgment of their receipt from him personally, yet I have heard of their having reached his hands a few months prior to his Antarctic cruise. Of this, however, I do not complain, and feel only the justifiable desire to maintain the truth in relation to a claim that is indisputable. The following nar-

* Ross reported that his farthest south was 78° 4'—C.N.

rative must, I feel satisfied, leave no doubt in any unprejudiced mind of the correctness of the assertion that we have discovered a vast continent; but I would ask in advance, who was there prior to 1840, either in this country or in Europe, that had the least idea that any large body of land existed to the south of New Holland? † and who is there that now doubts the fact, whether he admits it to be a vast continent, or contends that it is only a collection of islands?

Examine all the maps and charts published up to that time, and upon them will any traces of such land be found? They will not, and for the very best of reasons—none was known or even suspected to exist. We ourselves anticipated no such discovery; the indications of it were received with doubt and hesitation; I myself did not venture to record in my private journal the certainty of land, until three days after those best acquainted with its appearance in these high latitudes were assured of the fact; and finally, to remove all possibility of doubt, and to prove conclusively that there was no deception in the case, views of the same land were taken from the vessels in three different positions, with the bearings of its peaks and promontories, by whose intersection their position is nearly as well established as the peaks of any of the islands we surveyed from the sea.

All doubt in relation to the reality of our discovery gradually wore away, and towards the close of the cruise of the *Vincennes* along the icy barrier, the mountains of the Antarctic Continent became familiar and of daily appearance, insomuch that the log-book, which is guardedly silent as to the time and date of its being first observed, now speaks throughout of "the land."

After leaving Sydney we had, until the 31st December,* fine weather and favourable winds. We took advantage of these, and all sail was crowded on the vessels of the squadron. At the above date we had reached the latitude of 43° S.

† An early name for Australia—C.N.
* During the 29th, 30th, and 31st December, the sea was very phosphorescent; temperature 50°.

Under such circumstances, the usual order of sailing, in a line abreast, was easily maintained, and the communications between the vessels were frequent. On the 31st of December, I issued the sailing instructions for the cruise, which will be found in Appendix XXV.

During this favourable weather, all hands were employed in tightening the ports, in order to secure the interior of the vessels as much as possible from the cold and wet, which were to be apprehended in the region to which we were bound. For this purpose, after calking all the openings, the seams were covered with tarred canvass, over which strips of sheet-lead were nailed. The sailors exhibited great interest in these preparations, and studiously sought to make everything snug; all useless articles were stowed away in the hold, for we were in truth full to overflowing, and places at other times sacred were now crowded.

It was fortunate that the weather for the first few days was so favourable; for so full was every place, that we had been compelled to stow bread in the launch and cutter, and this in bulk; for the quantity was so much beyond that which had been carried on any former occasion, that a sufficient number of bags were not to be had, and in the hurry of its reception on board, time had not been found to provide them. Every ounce of bread thus exposed was looked to with solicitude, for there was a chance that all of it might be needed.

Among other preparations, rough casings of boards were built around all the hatches, having doors furnished with weights and pulleys, in order to insure that they should not be left open. Having thus provided for the exclusion of cold air, I contented myself with preparations for keeping the interior of the vessel at a temperature no higher than 50°. I deemed this preferable to a higher temperature, in order to prevent the injurious effects which might be produced by passing suddenly from below to the deck. I conceived it far more important to keep the air dry than warm, particularly as a lower temperature would have the effect of inducing the men to take exercise for the purpose of exciting their animal heat.

Aware that warm and dry clothing was an object of the first importance, inspections of the men's feet and dress were held morning and evening, in which the wearing of a suitable number of garments was insisted upon, as well as the greatest personal cleanliness. With the same views, the drying-stoves were particularly attended to; and that every part under deck might be effectually and quickly freed of moisture, additional stoves had been procured at Sydney. Thermometers were hung up in proper places, and frequently consulted, in order by following their indications to secure an equable temperature, and at the time to ascertain when the use of stoves might be dispensed with, in whole or in part. The latter was an important consideration, for we were under the necessity of husbanding our stock of fuel, by expending it only when absolutely necessary.

We also took advantage of the fine weather to bend all our best sails, and to shift our top-gallant masts.

The 1st January [1840] was one of those days, which are termed, both at sea and on shore, a weather-breeder. The sea was smooth and placid, but the sky was in places lowering, and had a wintry cast, to which we had long been strangers; the temperature shortly began to fall, the breeze to increase, and the weather to become misty. In a few hours we were sailing rapidly through the water, with a rising sea, and by midnight it was reported that the tender *Flying-Fish* was barely visible. I shortened sail, but it was difficult to stop our way; and on the morning of the 2d of January, the fog was dense, and the *Peacock* and *Porpoise* only were in sight; we hove-to, and the *Peacock* and *Porpoise* were ordered to stand east and west, in order to intercept the tender, but they returned without success; we also fired guns in hopes of being heard. In the afternoon, I deemed it useless to wait any longer for her, and that I must take the chance of falling in with her at Macquarie Island, our first appointed place of rendezvous,—a visit to which I had flattered myself might have been avoided, but which it became necessary now to make. We accordingly proceeded on our course for that island, with all sail set. This separation of the tender took place in the latitude of 48° S., and she was not again seen until our return. The officers and crew were not slow in assigning to the *Flying-Fish* a similar fate with her unfortunate mate, the *Sea-Gull*. Men-of-war's men are prone to prognosticate evil, and on this occasion they were not wanting in various surmises. Woeful accounts were soon afloat of the distress the schooner was in when last seen,—and this in quite a moderate sea.

The barometer now began to assume a lower range, and the temperature to fall below 50°. On the 3d, the fog continuing very thick, the *Peacock* got beyond hearing of our horns, bells, drums, and guns, and was parted with. This, however, I did not now regret so much, as it was of little consequence whether we sought one or two vessels at our rendezvous, although it might cause a longer detention there.

The wind was now (5th January) veering rapidly to the northwest, with some thunder and lightning, and we in consequence expected the wind to haul to the southwest, but to my surprise, it went back to the northeast, with thick rainy weather. This return of the wind to its old quarter followed a fall of the barometer to 29.60 in., and in a few hours afterwards to 29.30 in., while the weather continued moderate; a large number of albatrosses, Port Egmont hens, and petrels, were seen.

For the last few days we were unable to get any observations, but on the 6th we were favoured with a sight of the sun, and found ourselves in the latitude of 53° 30′ S., and longitude 157° 35′ E. Our variation had increased to fifteen and a half degrees easterly. This being a fine day, we completed our calking, and the more effectual securing of the ship. At midnight we were about fifty miles from Macquarie Island.

The morning of the 7th was misty, with squally weather. A heavy sea rising, and a strong gale setting in, we lost sight of the *Porpoise* for a few hours. Being unable to see beyond an eighth of a mile, it was thought imprudent to run, for fear of passing the island, and we hove-to to await its moderating. It cleared at noon, and we obtained an observation, by which we found ourselves in latitude 54° 20′ S., and longitude 160° 47′ E. I found that we had been carried to the eastward upwards of twenty miles in less than eighteen hours; this, with the wind hauling to the southwest, brought us to leeward of the island, and the sea and wind increasing, I saw it was useless to attempt to reach it without great loss of time. I therefore bore off to the southward for our second rendezvous, Emerald Island, or its supposed locality.

On the morning of the 8th, the wind, which continued from the same quarter, with heavy cumulous clouds, began to moderate, and we were enabled to make more sail. By our observations, we found a current setting to the southeast, of one mile an hour. Our longitude was 162° 13′ E., latitude 55° 38′ S. The barometer stood at 30.00 in.; the temperature had fallen to 38°; and this change, on account of the rawness of the air, was much felt by the crew.

During the 9th we passed the site of Emerald Isle, situate, as has been stated, in latitude 57° 15′ S., and longitude 162° 30′ E., but saw nothing of it, nor any indications of land, which I therefore infer does not exist in the locality where it is laid down. We again experienced the southeast current of twenty miles a day. Our variation had increased to twenty-two degrees easterly. Making our course with all sail set, the *Porpoise* in company, we passed to-day some pieces of kelp. The temperature continued at 38°. Numerous flocks of gray petrels around us.

The 10th we encountered the first iceberg, and the temperature of the water fell to 32°. We passed close to it, and found it a mile long, and one hundred and eighty feet in height. We had now reached the latitude of 61° 08′ S., and longitude 162° 32′ E. The current to-day set in the same direction as before, about half a mile per hour. The second iceberg seen was thirty miles, and the third about fifty-five miles south of the first. These ice-islands were apparently much worn by the sea into cavities, exhibiting fissures as though they were

ready to be rent asunder, and showed an apparent stratifica-
tion, much inclined to the horizon. The weather now became
misty, and we had occasionally a little snow. I congratulated
myself that we had but few on the sick-list, and all were in
high spirits at the novelty of the cruise. We continued to
meet icebergs of different heights, some of which, though
inclined to the horizon, had a plane upper surface.

11th. The fair wind from the northwest, (accompanied with
a light mist, rendering objects on the horizon indistinct,) still
enabled us to pursue our course southerly. Icebergs became
so numerous as to compel us occasionally to change our
course. They continued of the same character, with caverns
worn in their perpendicular sides, and with flat tops, but the
latter were now on a line with the horizon. Towards 6 P.M.,
we began to perceive smaller pieces of ice, some of which
were not more than an eighth of a mile in length, floating as
it were in small patches. As the icebergs increased in number, the sea became smoother, and there was no apparent
motion. Between 8 and 9 P.M., a low point of ice was perceived ahead, and in a short time we passed within it. There
was now a large bay before us. As the vessels moved rapidly,
at 10½ P.M. we had reached its extreme limits, and found our
further progress entirely stopped by a compact barrier of ice,
enclosing large square icebergs. The barrier consisted of
masses closely packed, and of every variety of shape and size.
We hove-to until full daylight. The night was beautiful, and
every thing seemed sunk in sleep, except the sound of the
distant and low rustling of the ice, that now and then met the
ear. We had now reached the latitude of 64° 11′ S., longitude
164° 30′ E., and found our variation twenty-two degrees easterly. One and all felt disappointed, for we had flattered ourselves that the way was open for further progress to the
southward, and had imbibed the impression (from the extraordinary weather we had had at Sydney, and the reports
of icebergs having been seen farther to the northward than
usual, by all the vessels arriving) that the season would be an
open one. What surprised me most was a change in the col-

our of the water to an olive-green, and some faint appearances resembling distant land; but as it was twilight, and I did
not believe the thing credible, I put no faith in these indications, although some of the officers were confident they were
not occasioned by icebergs. The barometer stood at 29.20 in.;
the temperature of the air 33°, water 32°. We lay-to until four
o'clock. As it grew light, on the 12th, a fog set in so thick that
we lost sight of the *Porpoise*, and could not hear any answer
to our signals. I therefore determined to work along the
barrier to the westward.

We were all day beating in a thick fog, with the barrier of
ice close to us, and occasionally in tacking brought it under
our bow; at other times we were almost in contact with
icebergs. During the whole day we could not see at any time
further than a quarter of a mile, and seldom more than the
ship's length. The fog, or rather thick mist, was forming in ice
on our rigging. From the novelty of our situation, and the
excitement produced by it, we did not think of the danger.

I shall now leave the *Vincennes* and *Porpoise* pursuing
their course to the westward with a head wind, and bring the
Peacock up to the barrier.

Previously to parting company on the 3rd of January, the
crew of that ship had also been engaged in building hurri-
cane-houses, calking, and chintzing, to secure them from the
wet and cold. After parting company, Captain Hudson immediately steered for the first rendezvous, Macquarie Island,
and was more fortunate than we were in reaching it, although the *Peacock* had experienced the same kind of
weather that we had, and currents setting to the eastward.

On approaching the island, they discovered large patches
of kelp, and saw numerous procellaria and albatrosses about
the ship. On the 10th of January they made the island, and
observed a reef of rocks extending three quarters of a mile
off its south end. Passing within a short distance of it, they did
not observe any of the signals of the squadron flying as they
had anticipated. They, notwithstanding, stood in, lowered a
boat, and despatched several officers to put up the signal,

make experiments, and collect specimens. The boat approached an indentation on the west side, too open to be called a bay, and found that the surf was running high, and beating with great violence against the rocks, which, together with the kelp, rendered it dangerous to attempt landing. They made for several other places which looked favourable at a distance, but on approaching them, they were found even less accessible. The boat then returned to the first place to make another attempt, which was attended with great difficulty. The boat's anchor was dropped, and she was backed in with great caution to the edge of the rollers; the surf was very high, and rolled in with a noise like thunder, breaking furiously upon the rocks, so as to make the boat fairly tremble, and threatening every moment to overwhelm her; once or twice she was prevented from getting broadside-to by hauling out towards her anchor. At length, after a dozen fruitless attempts, and awaiting a favourable opportunity, Mr. Eld and a quarter-master succeeded in getting ashore, but not without being immersed up to their breasts. It was found impossible to land any instruments; and the quarter-master was despatched to erect the necessary signals, while Mr. Eld proceeded to visit the penguin-rookery not far distant. On approaching the island, it had appeared to be covered with white spots: these excited conjecture; but after landing, the exhalations rendered it not long doubtful that it was birdlime.

Mr. Eld, in his journal, gives the following account of his visit: "Although I had heard so often of the great quantity of birds on the uninhabited islands, I was not prepared to see them in such myriads as here. The whole sides of the rugged hills were literally covered with them. Having passed a deep fissure in the rocks, I ascended a crag that led to what I thought was their principal roost, and at every step my astonishment increased. Such a din of squeaking, squalling, and gabbling, I never before heard or dreamed could be made by any of the feathered tribe. It was impossible to hear one's self speak. It appeared as if every one was vying with his neighbour to make the greatest possible noise. I soon found my presence particularly displeased them, for they snapped at me in all directions, catching hold of my trousers, shaking and pinching my flesh so violently as to make me flinch and stand upon the defensive. As we wanted a number of specimens, I commenced kicking them down the precipice, and knocked on the head those which had the temerity to attack me. After having collected a number, and a few eggs, I laid them aside, whilst I ascended higher on the hill. I had not left them more than eighteen feet, before two albatrosses came down, and commenced picking at the dead birds I had just killed, but not being able to make any impression upon them, deliberately picked up two of the eggs with their beaks, and in spite of my efforts to prevent it, flew away with them. The eggs were about the size of a goose's; the original color seemed to have been white, but they were so dirty that it was difficult to say with certainty. They were no doubt the eggs of the penguin, as I took them out of their nest, which was only a small place scratched in the earth, just big enough to hold one or two eggs, with little or no grass, sticks, or any thing else to form a nest of. I afterwards picked up a number of these eggs, and another was found, of the size of a hen's egg, white, with a slight tinge of green. On mounting the hill still higher, which was very steep, and composed of volcanic rock, loose stones, and a little soil mixed with birdlime, I found that there were more of these birds than I anticipated. The nests were within two feet of each other, with one or two young ones in each; one of the old ones watching and sitting on the nest, whilst the young were trying ineffectually to nestle themselves under the small wings of the old ones. The appearance of the young was not unlike that of goslings, being covered with a dark thick down.

"These penguins are the Eudyptes chrysocome; they are from sixteen to twenty inches in height, with white breast and nearly black back, the rest being of a dark dove-colour, with the exception of the head, which is adorned on each side with four or five yellow feathers, three or four inches long, looking like graceful plumes. The birds stand erect in rows, which gives them the appearance of Lilliputian soldiers. The sight was novel and beautiful, and had it not been for the gabble,—enough to deafen me,—I could have stayed much longer. It was now time to return to the boat, when it occurred to me that live birds would be preferable to the dead; so throwing the latter down, I seized one old and a couple of young ones, and with three or four eggs in my cap, made the best of my way to the boat. It was now found impossible to hand them on board, and not willing to surrender my prize, a lead-line was thrown me from the boat, but did not come near enough, and in my attempts to get it, I was overtaken by a sea, and was thrown violently against the rocks among the kelp, and just made out to crawl on hands and knees beyond the reach of the returning sea, somewhat bruised, wet, and benumbed with the cold."

At this juncture, the quarter-master returned with a large species of penguin over his shoulders, but without the crown of feathers on his head. He described a similar rookery, and also saw some green paroquets with a small red spot on the head, and an oblong slaty or purple spot at the root of the bill, and with straight beaks. Mr. Eld was too much exhausted to return with him to get specimens, and the hour being late, it was necessary to return to the boat, which had been waiting for some time for them. The quarter-master succeeded in getting his penguins to the boat, but Mr. Eld's began floundering about, and although their legs were tied, managed to get into the water, where they were at home, and were soon out of reach. The tying of the legs did not seem any impediment to their exertions in the water, and thus several interesting specimens of natural history were lost, the trouble that it cost making them doubly valuable. With great difficulty Mr. Eld reached the boat; for, having again missed his foothold, he fell among the kelp, but by the timely aid of those on board he was rescued. After an hour's tug at their oars, they reached the ship in safety. During their absence the ship sounded with a line of three hundred fathoms, two and a half miles from the shore; but no bottom was found. The temperature of the water at the surface was 43°, and at three hundred fathoms deep 39°. The current was tried, but none found.

The south end of Macquarie Island lies in latitude 54° 44′ S., and longitude 159° 49′ E. The island is high and much broken; it is apparently covered with verdure, although a long tufted rank grass was the only plant seen by those who landed.

The highest peak on the island is from twelve to fifteen hundred feet high, and as far as our observations extended, it had neither tree nor shrub on it. At 6 P.M. the ship filled away, and at eight was abreast of the *Bishop* and *Clerk*. Macquarie Island affords no inducement for a visit, and as far as our examination went, has no suitable place for landing with a boat. The only thing I had to regret was not being able to make it a magnetic station.

On the 11th and 12th nothing particular occurred on board the *Peacock*. All sail was set, and running to the southward on the 13th, in latitude 61° 30′ S., longitude 161° 05′ E., the first ice-islands were seen. The dip was observed with Lloyd's and Dolland's needles, which made it 86° 53′.

There was no occasion on the night of the 13th to light the binnacle-lamps, as newspaper print could be read with ease at midnight. On the 14th, while still making much progress to the south, and passing occasionally icebergs and brash ice, the water appeared somewhat discoloured. Robinson's, Lloyd's, and Dolland's needles, gave, the same day, in the cabin, 86° 37′ for the dip, and in the ward-room, 86° 46′. Albatrosses, Cape pigeons, and other birds about.

On the 15th, they passed many ice-islands. The weather was thick, and snow fell at intervals; the wind continued from the westward. Many whales were seen; albatrosses, petrels, and Cape pigeons were frequent about the ship. At 4 P.M., the mist raised a little, and to their surprise they saw a perfect barrier of ice, extending to the southwest, with several large icebergs enclosed within it. Shortly after, they discovered a sail, which proved to be the *Porpoise.*

The *Vincennes* and *Porpoise* were left in our narrative near the icy barrier, separated by the fogs and mists that prevailed at times. The *Porpoise,* on the 13th, in latitude 65° 08' S., longitude 163° E., discovered several sea-elephants on the ice, and sent a boat to capture them, but without success. The current was tried, and found to set west one-fifth of a mile per hour. Some time afterwards, seeing some sea-elephants near the edge of the ice, a boat was sent, and succeeded in capturing a female. From the numerous sea-elephants, and the discoloration of the water and ice, they were strongly impressed with the idea of land being in the vicinity, but on sounding with one hundred fathoms, no bottom was found; Lieutenant-Commandant Ringgold felt convinced, from the above circumstances, and the report that penguins were heard, that land was near, and thought he could discern to the southeast something like distant mountains. A nearer approach was impossible, as they were then in actual contact with the icy barrier.

On the 14th, at 3 P.M., the water being still discoloured, tried soundings, but found no bottom.

Two sea-elephants were seen lying motionless on the ice. On being shot at, the animal would raise its head and look around for an instant, and then resume its former posture. Boats were lowered, when they were captured and brought on board: they proved to be the Phoca proboscidea. Dr. Holmes examined their stomachs, and found nothing but well-digested food. Their dimensions were as follows:

Total length	10	feet,	9 inches.
Length of posterior flipper	1	"	9 "
Breadth	2	"	4 "
Circumference of largest part of body	6	"	3 "

This was a young female. The other was taken afterwards; he measured—

In length	8	feet,	6	inches.
Greatest circumference behind anterior flipper	5	"	0	"
Length of flippers	1	"	5	"
Breadth "	1	"	5	"

On the 15th the *Peacock* and *Porpoise* were in company: the specimens of sea-elephants were put on board the *Peacock;* and, after having had communication with each other, the vessels again separated, standing on opposite tacks.

On the 16th the three vessels were in longitude 157° 46′ E., and all within a short distance of each other. The water was much discoloured, and many albatrosses, Cape pigeons, and petrels were seen about the ships. On board the *Vincennes,* we sounded with two hundred and thirty fathoms, and found no bottom; the water had the appearance of an olive-green colour, as if but forty and fifty fathoms deep. At the surface, its temperature was 32°, at the depth sounded, 31°. I should have tried for a deeper cast, but the line was seen to be stranded, when we were obliged to stop; we fortunately saved our apparatus, with Six's thermometers.

On this day (16th January) appearances believed at the time to be land were visible from all the three vessels, and the comparison of the three observations, when taken in connexion with the more positive proofs of its existence afterwards obtained, has left no doubt that the appearance was not deceptive. From this day, therefore, we date the discovery which is claimed for the squadron.

On board the *Peacock,* it appears that Passed Midshipmen Eld and Reynolds both saw the land from the masthead, and reported it to Captain Hudson: he was well satisfied on examination that the appearance was totally distinct from that of ice-islands, and a majority of the officers and men were also satisfied that if land could exist, that was it.

I mention particularly the names of these two gentlemen, because they have stated the same fact under oath, before the court-martial, after our return.

On board the *Porpoise*, Lieutenant-Commandant Ringgold states, that "he went aloft in the afternoon, the weather being clear and fine, the horizon good, and clouds lofty; that he saw over the field-ice an object, large, dark, and rounding, resembling a mountain in the distance; the icebergs were all light and brilliant, and in great contrast." He goes on to say, in his report, "I watched for an hour to see if the sun in his decline would change the colour of the object: it remained the same, with a white cloud above, similar to that hovering over high land. At sunset the appearance remained the same. I took the bearings accurately, intending to examine it closely as soon as we got a breeze. I am thoroughly of opinion it is an island surrounded by immense fields of ice. The *Peacock* in sight to the southward and eastward over the ice; the sun set at a few minutes before ten; soon after, a light air from the southward, with a fog-bank arising, which quickly shut out the field-ice."

In Passed Midshipman Eld's journal, he asserts that he had been several times to the masthead during the day, to view the barrier; that it was not only a barrier of ice, but one of terra firma. Passed Midshipman Reynolds and himself exclaimed, with one accord, that it was land. Not trusting to the naked eye, they descended for spyglasses, which confirmed, beyond a doubt, their first impressions. The mountains could be distinctly seen, over the field-ice and bergs, stretching to the southwest as far as any thing could be discerned. Two peaks, in particular, were very distinct, (which I have named after those two officers,) rising in a conical form; and others, the lower parts of which were quite as distinct, but whose summits were lost in light fleecy clouds. Few clouds were to be seen in any other direction, for the weather was remarkably clear. The sun shone brightly on ridge after ridge, whose sides were partially bare; these connected the eminences I have just spoken of, which must be from one to two thousand feet high. Mr. Eld further states, that on reporting the discovery to Captain Hudson, the latter replied that there was no doubt of it, and that he believed that most of the icebergs then in sight were aground. At this time they were close in with the barrier, and could approach no nearer. On this day, the *Peacock* got a cast of the deep-sea lead, with Six's thermometer attached, to the depth of eight hundred and fifty fathoms, only a short distance from the barrier: the temperature of the surface was 31°, and at the depth sounded, 31½°; current one-fourth of a mile, north-by-east.

The log-book of the *Porpoise* has also this notice in it: "From six to eight, calm and pleasant,—took in studding-sails; at seven set maintopgallant-studding-sail; discovered what we took to be an island, bearing south-by-east,—a great deal of field-ice in sight; noticed penguins around the brig. (Signed) J. H. North." Dr. Holmes, on the same evening, noted in his journal, a marked appearance of land.

On board the *Vincennes* there was on the same day much excitement among the crew. All eagerly watched the flight of birds, together with the whales and penguins, and spoke of the proximity of land, which, from the appearance of never-failing signs, could scarcely be doubted. The following is a sketch which I made of what I myself saw, and have called Ringgold's Knoll on the chart, and which at the same time will show the field-ice* as it appeared.

This night we were beating with frequent tacks, in order to gain as much southing as possible. Previous to its becoming broad daylight, the fog rendered every thing obscure, even

---

* The field-ice is composed of a vast number of pieces, varying in size, and separated from one another, the long swell keeping the outer ones always in motion. The smallest pieces were about six feet in diameter, while the largest sometimes exceeded five or six hundred feet. Their depth below the surface varies still more, and some appear to be soft, whilst others were hard and compact. The depth of these does not probably in any case exceed twenty feet. Most of them, and particularly the larger ones, had a covering of about eighteen inches of snow. The whole at a distance appeared like a vast level field, broken up as it were by the plough, and presenting shapeless angular masses of every possible figure, while here and there a table-topped iceberg was enclosed.

at a short distance from the ship. I knew that we were in close proximity to icebergs and field-ice, but, from the report of the look-out at sunset, believed that there was an opening or large bay leading to the southward. The ship had rapid way on her, and was much tossed about, when in an instant all was perfectly still and quiet; the transition was so sudden that many were awakened by it from sound sleep, and all well knew, from the short experience we had had, that the cessation of the sound and motion usual at sea, was a proof that we had run within a line of ice,—an occurrence from which the feeling of great danger is inseparable. The watch was called by the officer of the deck, to be in readiness to execute such orders as might be necessary for the safety of the ship. Many of those from below were seen hurrying up the hatches, and those on deck straining their eyes to discover the barrier in time to avoid accident. The ship still moving rapidly along, some faint hope remained that the bay might prove a deep one, and enable me to satisfy my sanguine hopes and belief relative to the land.

The feeling is awful and the uncertainty most trying thus to enter within the icy barrier blindfolded as it were by an impenetrable fog, and the thought constantly recurring that both ship and crew were in imminent danger; yet I was satisfied that nothing could be gained but by pursuing this course. On we kept, until it was reported to me, by attentive listeners, that they heard the low and distant rustling of the ice: suddenly a dozen voices proclaimed the barrier to be in sight, just ahead. The ship, which a moment before seemed as if unpeopled, from the stillness of all on board, was instantly alive with the bustle of performing the evolutions necessary to bring her to the wind, which was unfavourable to a return on the same track by which we had entered. After a quarter of an hour, the ice was again made ahead, and the full danger of our situation was realized. The ship was certainly embayed; and although the extent of sea-room to which we were limited, was rendered invisible by the dark and murky weather, yet that we were closely circumscribed was evident from having made the ice so soon on either tack, and from the audible rustling around us. It required several hours to extricate the ship from this bay.

Few are able to estimate the feelings that such an occasion causes to a commander, who has the responsibility of the safety of ship and crew operating as a heavy weight upon his heart, and producing a feeling as if on the verge of some overwhelming calamity. All tends to satisfy him that nothing could guide him in safety through, or shield from destruction those who have been entrusted to his charge, but the hand of an all-wise Providence.

17th. In the morning we discovered a ship apparently within a mile of us, to which we made signal and fired a gun, but she was shortly after lost sight of. We also saw the brig to the eastward, close to the barrier of ice. In the afternoon we spoke to the *Peacock:* she had not seen us in the morning; and I should be disposed to believe that the cause of her image appearing so close to us in the morning was produced by refraction above a low fog-bank; but the usual accompaniment of such phenomena, a difference of temperature below and aloft, did not exist.

I now desired Captain Hudson to make the best use of his time in exploring, as to attempt to keep company would only impede our progress, and, without adding to our safety, might prevent the opportunity of examining the barrier for an opening. I was also satisfied that the separation would be a strong incentive to exertion, by exciting rivalry among the officers and crews of the different vessels. This day at noon we were in latitude 66° 20′ S., longitude 156° 02′ E. Many petrels, albatrosses, a few whales, and a seal, were seen from the ship; and the water was quite green.

18th. The weather this day was variable, with light westerly winds; the temperature of air and water 32°. Occasional squalls of snow and mist occurred, but it was at times clear. The water was still olive-green; and the other vessels occasionally in sight, beating to windward.

On the morning of the 19th, we found ourselves in a deep bay, and discovered the *Peacock* standing to the southwest.

Until eight o'clock, A.M., we had a moderate breeze. The water was of a darker olive-green, and had a muddy appearance. Land was now certainly visible from the *Vincennes*, both to the south-southeast and southwest, in the former direction most distinctly. Both appeared high. It was between eight and nine in the morning when I was fully satisfied that it was certainly land, and my own opinion was confirmed by that of some of the oldest and most experienced seamen on board. The officer of the morning watch, Lieutenant Alden, sent twice, and called my attention to it. We were at this time in longitude 154° 30' E., latitude 66° 20' S.; the day was fine, and at times quite clear, with light winds. After divine service, I still saw the outline of the land, unchanged in form but not so distinct as in the morning. By noon, I found we were sagging on to the barrier; the boats were lowered in consequence, and the ship towed off. The report from aloft, was, "A continued barrier of ice around the bay, and no opening to be seen, having the western point of it bearing to the northward of west of us." I stood to the westward to pass around it, fully assured that the *Peacock* would explore all the outline of the bay.

The *Peacock*, at 3^h 30^m, according to Captain Hudson's journal, having got into the drift-ice, with a barrier still ahead to the west, tacked to the southeast to work up for an immense mass, which had every appearance of land, and which was believed to be such by all on board. It was seen far beyond and towering above an ice-island that was from one hundred and fifty to two hundred feet in height. It bore from them about southwest, and had the appearance of being three thousand feet in height, forming a sort of amphitheatre, looking gray and dark, and divided into two distinct ridges or elevations throughout its entire extent, the whole being covered with snow. As there was no probability of getting nearer to it in this quarter, they stood out of the bay, which was about twenty miles deep, to proceed to the westward, hoping to get an opportunity to approach the object more closely on the other side.

We had a beautiful and unusual sight presented to us this

night: the sun and moon both appeared above the horizon at the same time, and each throwing its light abroad. The latter was nearly full. The former illuminated the icebergs and distant continent with his deep golden rays; while the latter, in the opposite horizon, tinged with silvery light the clouds in its immediate neighbourhood. There now being no doubt in any mind of the discovery of land, it gave an exciting interest to the cruise, that appeared to set aside all thought of fatigue, and to make every one willing to encounter any difficulty to effect a landing.

20th. This day, on board the *Peacock* they witnessed a sea-fight between a whale and one of its many enemies. The sea was quite smooth, and offered the best possible view of the whole combat. First, at a distance from the ship, a whale was seen floundering in a most extraordinary way, lashing the smooth sea into a perfect foam, and endeavouring apparently to extricate himself from some annoyance. As he approached the ship, the struggle continuing and becoming more violent, it was perceived that a fish, apparently about twenty feet long, held him by the jaw, his contortions, spouting, and throes all betokening the agony of the huge monster. The whale now threw himself at full length from the water with open mouth, his pursuer still hanging to the jaw, the blood issuing from the wound and dyeing the sea to a distance around; but all his flounderings were of no avail; his pertinacious enemy still maintained his hold, and was evidently getting the advantage of him. Much alarm seemed to be felt by the many other whales around. These "killers," as they are called, are of a brownish colour on the back, and white on the belly, with a long dorsal fin. Such was the turbulence with which they passed, that a good view could not be had of them to make out more nearly the description. These fish attack a whale in the same way as dogs bait a bull, and worry him to death. They are armed with strong sharp teeth, and generally seize the whale by the lower jaw. It is said that the only part of them they eat is the tongue. The whalers give some marvellous accounts of these killers and of their immense strength; among them, that they have been known to drag a whale away from several boats which were towing it to the ship.

There was a great quantity of animalcula in the water, and some large squids (Medusæ) and quantities of shrimp were frequently seen about the icebergs; these are no doubt the attractions which bring whales to frequent these seas.

The last two days we had very many beautiful snow-white petrels about. The character of the ice had now become entirely changed. The tabular-formed icebergs prevailed, and there was comparatively little field-ice. Some of the bergs were of magnificent dimensions, one-third of a mile in length, and from one hundred and fifty to two hundred feet in height, with sides perfectly smooth, as though they had been chiselled. Others, again, exhibited lofty arches of many-coloured tints, leading into deep caverns, open to the swell of the sea, which rushing in, produced loud and distant thunderings. The flight of birds passing in and out of these caverns, recalled the recollection of ruined abbeys, castles, and caves, while here and there a bold projecting bluff, crowned with pinnacles and turrets, resembled some Gothic keep. A little farther onwards would be seen a vast fissure, as if some powerful force had rent in twain these mighty masses. Every noise on board, even our own voices, reverberated from the massive and pure white walls. These tabular bergs are like masses of beautiful alabaster: a verbal description of them can do little to convey the reality to the imagination of one who has not been among them. If an immense city of ruined alabaster palaces can be imagined, of every variety of shape and tint, and composed of huge piles of buildings grouped together, with long lanes or streets winding irregularly through them, some faint idea may be formed of the grandeur and beauty of the spectacle. The time and circumstances under which we were viewing them, threading our way through these vast bergs, we knew not to what end, left an impression upon me of these icy and desolate regions that can never be forgotten.

22d. It was now, during fine weather, one continued day; but we had occasional snow-squalls that produced an obscurity that was tantalizing. The bergs were so vast and inaccessible, that there was no possibility of landing upon them.

The *Peacock* and *Porpoise* were in sight of each other this day. A large number of whales, albatrosses, petrels, penguins, &c., were seen around, and a flock of ducks was also reported as having been seen from the *Vincennes*, as well as several seals. The effect of sunrise, at a little after 2 A.M., on the 23d, was glorious.

As the events which occurred on board the *Peacock* during the next few days are particularly interesting, I shall proceed to narrate them in detail, leaving the *Vincennes* and *Porpoise* to pursue their route along their dangerous and novel pathway, and would particularly refer the reader to the actual condition of the *Peacock,* a statement of which has been heretofore given, that it may be borne in mind that our vessels had no planking, extra fastening, or other preparations for these icy regions, beyond those of the vessels of war in our service.

The *Peacock* stood into the bay which the *Vincennes* had found closed the day before, and saw the same appearance of high land in the distance. The water was much discoloured, and of a dark dirty green. They hove-to, for the double purpose of getting a cast of the lead, and of lowering the boats to carry the instruments to a small iceberg, on which it was possible to land, for the purpose of making magnetic observations. A line of one thousand four hundred fathoms was prepared to sound, and to the lead was attached the cylinder with Six's thermometer. The wind being fresh, several leads at different distances were attached to the line. They were not aware that the leadline had touched bottom, until they began to haul in, when it was found that the lead bent on at five hundred fathoms was filled with blue and slate-coloured mud. Attached to the lead also was a piece of stone, and a fresh bruise on it, as though the lead had struck heavily on rock.

The remainder of the line had evidently lain on the bottom, as the copper cylinder was covered with mud, and the water inside of it was quite muddy. They then beat up a short distance to windward, and again sounded, when, with the line hanging vertically, bottom was reached at three hundred and twenty fathoms; the matter brought up was slate-coloured mud. The temperature of the water at the surface was 32°, and at the above depth 27½°, being a decrease of 4½°.

The boats now returned, and on approaching the ship the persons in them were much startled by hearing the crew cheer ship in consequence of finding soundings. This was a natural burst of joy, on obtaining this unquestionable proof that what they saw was indeed the land; a circumstance that, while it left no doubt, if any had existed, in the mind of any one on board the *Peacock*, that what they had previously seen was truly terra firma, furnished a proof that cannot be gainsaid, even by those disposed to dispute the evidence of sight, unsupported by so decisive a fact. Mr. Eld and Mr. Stuart, in the boats, succeeded in getting observations, and the mean dip by the needles was 86° 16′.

Mr. Eld's boat succeeded in taking a king-penguin of enormous size, viz.: from tip of tail to the bill, forty-five inches; across the flippers, thirty-seven inches; and the circumference of the body, thirty-three inches. He was taken after a truly sailor-like fashion, by knocking him down. The bird remained quite unmoved on their approach, or rather showed a disposition to come forward to greet them. A blow with the boat-hook, however, stunned him, and before his recovery he was well secured. He showed, on coming to himself, much resentment at the treatment he had received, not only by fighting, but by an inordinate noise. He was in due time preserved as a specimen, and now graces the collection at Washington. In his craw were found thirty-two pebbles, from the size of a pea to that of a hazel-nut.

24th. Bergs and field-ice were in various directions around. They had light baffling winds, clear and pleasant weather, with a smooth sea. The water was of a dark green colour. Standing into the bay for the purpose of approaching the land, they at 5 A.M. passed through drift-ice into an open space, and when they had again approached the field, hove-to for the purpose of sounding. Here bottom was found at the depth of eight hundred fathoms; and the matter brought up was similar to that obtained the day before. The distance between the points where these two soundings were obtained, was but short.

At 8^h 30^m A.M., while attempting to box off the ship from some ice under the bow, she made a stern-board, which brought the stern so forcibly in contact with another mass of ice, that it seemed from the shock, as if it were entirely stove in; the rudder was so much canted from its position, as to carry away the starboard wheel-rope, and to wrench the neck of the rudder itself in such a manner as to render it unserviceable, or even worse than useless. In hopes of lessening the difficulty, relieving-tackles were applied to the tiller, but without effect, for it was discovered that the rudder had been so far twisted as to make a considerable angle with the keel, and every exertion to move it proved ineffectual.

All hands were now called, and every officer and man was speedily at his station. The ship was found to be rapidly entering the ice, and every effort to direct her course by the management of the sails proved fruitless. In this helpless condition scarcely a moment passed without a new shock in some quarter or other from the ice, and every blow threatened instant destruction. The hope was not yet abandoned, that some temporary expedient might be found to bring the rudder again into use, until they should be extricated from this perilous situation. A stage was, therefore, rigged over the stern, for the purpose of examining into its state, but it was found to be so much injured that it was impossible to remedy its defects while in its place, and preparations were forthwith made for unshipping it. In the mean time the position of the vessel was every instant growing worse, surrounded as she was by masses of floe-ice, and driving further and further into it, towards an immense wall-sided iceberg. All attempts to get the vessel on the other tack failed, in consequence of her being so closely encompassed, and it was therefore thought expedient to attempt to bring her head round, by hanging her to an iceberg by the ice-anchors, and thus complete what had been partially effected by the sails. The anchor was attached, but just at the moment the hawser was passed on board, the ship took a start so suddenly astern, that the rope was literally dragged out of the men's hands before they could get a turn around the bits.

The ship now drove stern foremost into the midst of the huge masses of ice, striking the rudder a second time. This blow gave it the finishing stroke, by nearly wringing off the head, breaking two of the pintles, and the upper and lower brace.

The wind now began to freshen, and the floe-ice to set upon the ship. The sails were furled, and spars rigged up and down the ship's sides as fenders. Attempts were again made to plant the ice-anchors, for which purpose the boats were lowered; but the confined space, and the force with which the pieces of ice ground against each other was so great, that the boats proved nearly as unmanageable as the ship. After much exertion, however, the ice-anchors were planted, and the hawser hauled taut. Here they for a time enjoyed comparative security, as the vessel hung by the anchors, which were planted in a large floe. The ice continued to close in rapidly upon them, grinding, crushing, and carrying away the fenders; and the wind, that had changed to seaward, rose with appearances that foreboded bad weather.

At 10^h 30^m this security was at an end; for the anchors, in spite of the exertions of the officers and men who were near them, broke loose, and the ship was again at the mercy of huge floating masses. A rapid stern-board was the consequence; and a contact with an ice-island, vast, perpendicular, and as high as the mastheads, appeared inevitable.

Every possible preparation was made to meet the expected shock. There was no noise or confusion, and the self-possession and admirable conduct of the commander in-spired courage and confidence in all. Preparations were made to cockbill the yards, and spars were got out.

While these preparations were going forward, the immi-nence of the danger lessened for a while: the anchors again held, and there was a hope that they might bring the vessel up before she struck. This hope, however, endured but for a moment; for the anchors, with the whole body of ice to which they were attached, came in, and the ship going astern, struck quartering upon a piece of ice which lay between her and the great ice-island. This afforded the last hope of pre-venting her from coming in contact with it; and this hope failed also; for, grinding along the ice, she went nearly stern foremost, and struck with her larboard quarter upon the ice-island with a tremendous crash.

The first effect of this blow was to carry away the spanker-boom, the larboard stern-davit, and to crush the stern-boat. The starboard stern-davit was the next to receive the shock, and as this is connected with the spar-deck bulwarks, the whole of them were started; the knee, a rotten one, which bound the davit to the taffrail, was broken off, and with it all the stanchions to the plank-sheer, as far as the gangway.

Severe as was this shock, it happened fortunately that it was followed by as great a rebound. This gave the vessel a cant to star-board, and by the timely aid of the jib and other sails, carried her clear of the ice-island, and forced her into a small opening. While doing this, and before the vessel had moved half her length, an impending mass of ice and snow fell in her wake. Had this fallen only a few seconds earlier, it must have crushed the vessel to atoms.

It was also fortunate that the place where she struck the ice-island was near its southern end, so that there was but a short distance to be passed before she was entirely clear of it. This gave more room for the drifting ice, and permitted the vessel to be worked by her sails.

The relief from this pressing danger, however gratifying, gave no assurance of ultimate safety. The weather had an unusually stormy appearance; and the destruction of the vessel seemed almost inevitable, with the loss of every life on board. They had the melancholy alternative in prospect of being frozen to death one after the other, or perishing in a body by the dissolving of the iceberg on which they should take refuge, should the vessel sink.

When the dinner hour arrived the vessel was again fast in the ice, and nothing could for a time be done: it was therefore piped as usual. This served to divert the minds of the men from the dangers around them.

When the meal was over, the former manoeuvring was resorted to, the yards being kept swinging to and fro, in order to keep the ship's head in the required direction. She was labouring in the swell, with ice grinding and thumping against her on all sides; every moment something either fore or aft was carried away—chains, bolts, bobstays, bowsprit, shrouds; even the anchors were lifted, coming down with a surge that carried away the eyebolts and lashings, and left them to hang by the stoppers. The cut-water also was injured, and every timber seemed to groan.

Similar dangers attended those in the boats. Passed Midshipman Eld was sent to plant the ice-anchors: there was no room for the use of oars; the grinding and grating of the ice, as it rose and fell with the swell, rendered great precaution necessary to prevent the boat from being swamped or crushed; and when it is stated that two hours of hard exertion were required to plant the ice-anchors, some idea of the difficulty attending this service will be had. But this was not all; the difficulty of returning was equally great, and no possible way of effecting it seemed to suggest itself. The sides of the icebergs could not be ascended, and to approach the berg on the side next the ship was certain destruction to the boat and crew, for the ice and water were foaming like a cauldron; and to abandon the former was equally out of the question. At last a chance offered, although almost a hopeless one, by passing between two of these bergs, that appeared on the other side of a small clear space. The boat was upon a small piece of ice, from which, by great exertions, she was launched; a few pulls at the oars brought them to the passage; the bergs were closing fast, and agitated by the swell; no time, therefore, was to be lost: the danger was already great, and in a few seconds it would be impossible to pass. They entered; their oars caught, and they got but half-way through when the icebergs closed in upon them, and pressed the gunwales together, so as almost to crush the boat; the water entered her, and she was near sinking, when the berg stopped, retreated, and by another hard shove they went through, and were soon alongside the ship.

Every exertion was now made to work the ship and avoid heavy thumps from the ice. The mode resorted to, to get the ship about, was a novel one, namely, by urging her lee bow against a piece of ice, which had the same effect as giving her a lee helm; but this was found rather too expensive a mode of effecting the object, and on the pumps showing an increase of water, it was discontinued. The ice had been rapidly accumulating around the ship, contracting still more narrowly the space or area in which they were, and rendering their situation more hazardous.

At 4 P.M., they clewed up the topsails, the ship being fast in the ice, with the wind directly in from the seaward. The ice-anchors were now again run out, in hopes of relieving her from some of the strain. A short time afterwards the ice clearing from the stern enabled them to unship the rudder, which was taken on board in two pieces: it was immediately placed on the quarter-deck, and all the carpenters employed on it.

It soon began to snow violently, and no clear sea could be seen from the ship in any direction. It becoming obscure, the chance was that they would have to take up their last abode there. About six o'clock the weather cleared a little, and the wind freshened; they parted the hawser attached to the ice-anchor, and made sail again for the clear sea, which could now be seen from the masthead. Towards 8 P.M., as if to blast the little hope that the continuance of clear weather inspired, the ship took a wrong cant, and was forced into a small opening leading farther into the ice to leeward, and towards the massive walls of the berg. Great exertions were made, and fortunately, by the aid of the ice-anchors and sails, they succeeded in getting her round, and her head again pointed towards the clear sea; but they were shortly afterwards wedged in between two large masses of ice. At midnight the sea was observed to rise, although the wind had not increased, causing much motion among the ice; and the stormy appearance of the sky continued, and gave promise of a gale. The only hope left was to force the ship through, and every means were employed to effect this object. The ice they had now to contend with was of larger dimensions, and the increased sea rendered it doubly dangerous. Some of the shocks against it were so heavy as to excite fears that the ship's bow would be driven in, and on one occasion three of the chronometers were thrown out of their beds of sawdust upon their sides. They continued to make but little headway, and the grinding and thumping on the ship was most painful. The hope of extricating her lessened every moment; for the quanity of ice between them and the sea was increasing, and the ship evidently moved with it to leeward. Few situations could be more trying, but the emergency was met by Captain Hudson with a coolness, perseverance, and presence of mind, which secured the admiration of all who were present, and inspired full confidence and a firm reliance in his ability to overcome every difficulty that lay within the power of human means.

In the afternoon of the 25th, the sea continued to increase, and the ship frequently struck against the masses of ice, while every foot they forged ahead carried them seemingly into a more precarious situation. At about 3 A.M., they found that the gripe had been beaten off, and they were now bruising up the stem and grinding away the bows. There appeared no other course but to drive her out, which was deemed the only chance of saving the ship and crew. All the canvas that would draw was therefore set to force her through; and the wind

favouring them, they had by four o'clock succeeded in passing the thick and solid ice, and shortly afterwards found
themselves in clear water, without a rudder, the gripe gone,
and, as was afterwards found, the stem ground down to
within an inch and a half of the wood-ends.

The carpenters were still employed on the rudder, and had
succeeded in removing the broken pieces of the pintles from
the second and third braces on the stern-post; the upper and
lower pintles were broken, leaving only two to hang the
rudder by. The weather seemed now to favour them, and
about ten o'clock they had finished the rudder, which had
been repaired in the best possible manner. Great credit is
due to Mr. Dibble, the carpenter, (who left his sick bed on
the occasion,) for his exertions, attention, and perseverance.
He and the carpenter's crew worked twenty-four hours without intermission. The ship was now hove-to, for it was apprehended that her rolling would render the task of shipping
the rudder troublesome. By meridian they were again in a
situation to make sail to extricate themselves from a bay
some thirty miles in extent, which, with the exception of the
small opening by which they had entered, was apparently
closed by the barrier.

Shortly afterwards, the wind becoming fair, they made all
sail for the outlet. The weather proved fine, and the winds
moderate. At midnight they found the only opening left,
which was not more than a quarter of a mile wide; they
succeeded in passing through this, by 2 A.M., in a snow-storm,
and felt grateful to God for their providential escape.

Captain Hudson now came to the conclusion of returning
north. "After," as he says, "thoroughly turning over in my
own mind the state of the ship,—with the head of the rudder
gone, hanging by two braces, and in such a state that we
could hardly hope to make it answer its purposes again, in
encountering the boisterous weather we should have to pass
through before reaching the first port,—the ship considerably strained; her starboard spar-deck bulwarks gone as far
forward as the gangway; the gripe off, and the stern muti-

lated;—fully satisfied from this state of things that she was perfectly useless for cruising among icebergs, and the accompanying dangers, in thick foggy weather, to which, in these latitudes, we should be more or less subject, and where rapid evolutions were often necessary, in which the rudder must perform its part; and that the ship would require extensive repairs before being employed in surveying operations; and feeling that the season was rapidly coming round when our services would be required in that duty, I held a council of the ward-room officers, and required their opinions as to making any further attempts to cruise in these latitudes.

"There was but one opinion as to the necessity of the ship's returning north, with the exception of Mr. Emmons and Mr. Baldwin, who thought the rudder might stand, provided we did not get near the ice or fall in with icebergs. This of course would be to effect little or nothing, and result only in a loss of time. I accordingly put the ship's head north, determined to proceed at once to Sydney, to effect the necessary repairs, so as to be ready at the earliest possible day to join the squadron."

Such were the dangers and difficulties from which the *Peacock*, by the admirable conduct of her officers and crew, directed by the consummate seamanship of her commander, was enabled at this time to escape. There still, however, remained thousands of miles of a stormy ocean to be encountered, with a ship so crippled as to be hardly capable of working, and injured to such an extent in her hull as to be kept afloat with difficulty.

JAMES CLARK ROSS

(*1800–1862*)

JAMES CLARK ROSS was a British explorer who discovered the Ross Sea, the Ross Ice Shelf and Ross Island and who named many of the most conspicuous features of Ross Island and its vicinity: Mount Erebus, Mount Terror, Cape Crozier, Cape Bird, McMurdo Bay (now called McMurdo Sound), Victoria Land, Beaufort Island and Franklin Island. The rare Ross Seal is named after him.

Ross entered the Royal Navy at the age of twelve. He was a member of several important Arctic expeditions. At the age of thirty-one he discovered the north magnetic pole. He commanded the *Erebus* and the *Terror* during the Antarctic expedition of 1839–43. On this voyage he conducted experiments in terrestrial magnetism and gathered important data on the behavior of magnetic compasses in the high southern latitudes. Also, he attempted to reach the south magnetic pole. His hope of being the discoverer of both magnetic poles was frustrated by the fact that the south magnetic pole was not attainable by sea, being located in Victoria Land, and by the dangerous lateness of the season, which made it imperative that he return north without an attempt to winter over on the continent. It was while intrepidly drawing ever closer to the pole that he broke through a wide belt of pack ice into the unknown, large and clear sea that was to bear his name. Like Wilkes he is a precise, detailed and vivid writer, sensitive to the seductive beauty of Antarctica. In the following selection he describes the discovery of Franklin, Ross and Beaufort Islands; describes an eruption of Mount Erebus; details his eastward exploration of the cliffs of the Ross Ice Shelf; and reports on the first entry into McMurdo Sound.

Farthest South

1841
Jan.
22

Again a southerly breeze came on at 4 A.M.; we continued beating to windward under all sail, and thus regained some of the lost ground; but at noon we were still four miles to the northward of our yesterday's latitude. As the breeze freshened and the motion of the ship increased, the compasses became very uncertain in their indications; but the weather was beautifully clear, the sun shining in great splendour; and although the barometer was already above the mean pressure of the atmosphere of these latitudes, it continued to rise (the second instance of the kind we have observed) as the wind increased to a moderate gale about midnight, which prevailed the whole of the next day, accompanied by sharp squalls and con- *1841* tinuous showers of snow. By our reckoning we *Jan.* made some southing, being at noon in lat. 74° *22* 20′ S.; and by 7 P.M., having good grounds for believing that we had reached a higher southern latitude than that attained by our enterprising countryman, the late Captain James Weddell, and therefore beyond all our predecessors, an extra allowance of grog was issued to our very deserving crews; and, being Saturday night, the seaman's favourite toast of "Sweethearts and wives" was not forgotten in the general rejoicing on the occasion.

The gale, which rather freshened during the *Jan.* night, gradually veered more to the eastward; we *23* therefore wore round and stood towards the land on the port tack; but, owing to the continuance of *Jan.* thick and snowy weather during the whole of Sun- *24* day, we did not get sight of it until 7 P.M., when it was indistinctly seen ahead of the ship. At mid- *Jan.* night we were in lat. 74° 29′ by observation. We *25* carried all sail, and both wind and sea abating, we approached the land rapidly; the barometer which had been rising throughout the gale, reached the unusual height of 29.33 at 4 A.M. the next morning; the line of coast was at this time distinctly seen, but at a great distance: a heavy pack extended at least forty or fifty miles from the shore, into which we stood amongst the loose ice as far as we could without getting beset; this I did not think proper to hazard, as it would assuredly have occasioned considerable loss of time without any equivalent advantage, and every hour at this period of the season was of much importance to us. I have no doubt that, had it been our object, we might have penetrated it several miles further, for although heavy-looking ice, it was not very densely packed, nor any thing like the solid land-

ice we had seen further to the northward, and we
·should certainly have made the attempt, had not
the land imposed an insuperable barrier to our
reaching the Pole,* which we still hoped to accomplish by a more circuitous route; and we were not
then in a condition to be content with anything
short of complete success. Observations at noon
placed us in lat. 74° 44′, long. 169° 30′, dip 87°
54′ S., var. 67° 13′, from which we deduced the
place of the magnetic pole to be distant two hundred and forty-nine miles. We had penetrated the
pack as far as the ice admitted to the westward by
half-past eight in the evening, when we tacked
and obtained observations by which we found we
had approached so much nearer the Pole that the
dip had increased to 88° 10′. We tried for soundings
with three hundred fathoms line, but it did not
reach the bottom. Mount Melbourne and Mount
Monteagle were here seen to great advantage; the
immense crater of the former, and the more
pointed summit of the latter, rose high above the
contiguous mountains; and they form two of the
more remarkable objects of this most wonderful
and magnificent mass of volcanic land.

Whilst struggling to get through the pack, we
found it drifting, under the influence of the wind
and current, rapidly to the northward, which
seemed to encourage a hope, that, if defeated in
our attempt to pass round its southern extremity,
we might be able, at a later period of the season
when more of the land-ice should have drifted
away, to penetrate to the shore, and find some
place wherein to secure the ships for the winter.
For several days past we had seen very few
whales, which was the more remarkable on account of the very great numbers we met with not

* Ross is referring here to the magnetic pole.—C.N.

more than sixty or seventy miles to the northward.
There must be doubtless some cause for their absence from this spot, which perhaps future observation may supply; for it is desirable to know
where they are not to be found as well as where
they are, that valuable time may not be thrown
away by those who go in pursuit of them.

On reaching the clear water, we found a short
irregular sea, in which the ships pitched heavily
under the easiest sail we could prevail on ourselves to carry, which seemed to indicate a change
of tide to windward. As we pursued our way along
the pack edge to the southward, we saw a great
many of the beautiful snowy petrel, and some penguins. The temperature of the air varied only one
degree during the twenty-four hours, from 25° to
26°, which was sufficiently low to freeze into ice
the sprays that fell on board the ship, and soon
accumulated such a load about our bows as to keep
the watch continually at work clearing it away,
and beating it off the running ropes. At noon we
had increased the dip to 88° 33', so that the magnetic pole was now only one hundred and seventy-
four miles from us in a W. by S. (true) bearing.
Mount Melbourne bore W. by N. eighty miles.

In the afternoon, as we got further from the
pack, the uneasy irregular sea subsided, and the
wind becoming more westerly enabled us to stand
direct for the east extreme of the "land blink,"
which bore S.W. by S. (true) from us; and at this
time some strong indications of land appeared,
which we all hoped would prove a "Cape Flya-
way," as many others had done before. As we increased our distance from the pack, the
temperature of the sea at its surface gradually rose
from 28° to 31°, at about twelve miles off, although
the air was at the time at 25.5°.

Light baffling winds, which prevailed for two or three hours, were succeeded by a moderate breeze from the eastward; all sail that the ships could spread was immediately set; and although the fog and rain came on so thick as to prevent our seeing more than half a mile before us, we continued to run with studding-sails on both sides set to the south-westward until nearly eight o'clock, when we were suddenly taken aback by the wind shifting to that quarter, and on the fog clearing away, we found that we had been steering into a deep bight of the main ice, which we now saw stretching across from the extreme point of the main land to an island bearing (true) south of us, and thus preventing our proceeding any further to the westward in this part; after closely examining the pack, in which no opening was to be seen, we stood away to the southward to endeavour to land on the island.

At noon we were in lat. 75° 48', S. long. 168° 33' E., dip 88° 25', variation 80° 50' E. At 3 P.M. we sounded in 200 fathoms, on fine black sand and small black stones, about twelve miles north of the island. At five o'clock when we were within two or three miles of it, I left the ship, accompanied by several officers, and soon afterwards followed by Commander Crozier, and a party from the *Terror*, we pulled towards the shore. A high southerly swell broke so heavily against the cliffs, and on the only piece of beach we could see as we rowed from one end of the island to the other, as almost to forbid our landing; a mortification not to be endured if possible to be avoided: the *Terror*'s whale boat being more fit for encountering such a surf than the heavy cutter of the *Erebus*, I got into her, and by the great skill and management of the officers and crew I succeeded, by watching the oppor-

tunity when the boat was on the crest of the breakers, in jumping on to the rocks. By means of a rope,
some of the officers landed with more facility, but
not without getting thoroughly wetted; and one
having nearly lost his life in this difficult affair, I
was obliged to forbid any more attempting to land,
to their very great disappointment. The thermometer being at 22°, every part of the rocks which
were washed by the waves was covered with a
coating of ice, so that in jumping from the boat, he
slipped from them into the water, between her
stern and the almost perpendicular rock on which
we had landed, and but for the promptitude of
those in the boat, in instantly pulling off, he must
have been crushed between it and the rocks. It
was most mercifully ordered otherwise, and he
was taken into the boat without having suffered
any other injury than being benumbed with the
cold. We proceeded at once therefore to take
possession of the island in due form; and to the
great satisfaction of every individual in the expedition, I named it "Franklin Island;" in compliment
of His Excellency Captain Sir John Franklin of the
Royal Navy, to whom, and his amiable lady, I have
already had occasion to express the gratitude we
all felt for the great kindness we received at their
hands, and the deep interest they manifested in all
the objects of the expedition. Having procured
numerous specimens of the rocks of the island, we
hastened our departure, in consequence of the
perishing condition of our unlucky companion,
and succeeded in embarking without any further
accident; we gained the ships before nine o'clock,
all of us thoroughly drenched to the skin, and painfully cold.

Franklin Island is situate in lat. 76° 8' S., long. 168°
12' E. It is about twelve miles long and six broad,

and is composed wholly of igneous rocks; the northern side presents a line of dark precipitous cliffs, between five and six hundred feet high, exposing several longitudinal broad white, probably aluminous, bands of several feet thickness; two or three of them were of a red ochre colour, and gave a most strange appearance to the cliffs. We could not perceive the smallest trace of vegetation, not even a lichen or piece of sea-weed growing on the rocks; and I have no doubt from the total absence of it at both the places we have landed, that the vegetable kingdom has no representative in antarctic lands. We observed that the white petrel had its nests on the ledges of the cliffs, as had also the rapacious skua gull; several seals were seen, and it is by no means improbable that the beach on which we in vain attempted to land may, at the proper season, be one of their places of resort, or *"rookeries"* as they are termed by the seal fishers.

At between two and three miles distance from the land, the soundings were regular, in thirty-eight to forty-one fathoms, on a bed of fine sand and black stones, and probably good anchorage might be found near the shore with southerly winds. A high cliff of ice projects into the sea from the south and south-west sides, rendering it there quite inaccessible, and a dangerous reef of rocks extends from its southern cape at least four or five miles, with apparently a deep water passage between them and the cape; several icebergs of moderate size were aground on the banks to the northward and westward of the island. At midnight the bearings of eight separate islands are given in the log of the *Erebus;* but as these afterwards proved to be the summits of mountains, at a great distance, belonging to the mainland, they do not appear upon the chart as islands. With a favourable breeze, and very clear weather, we

stood to the southward, close to some land which 1841
had been in sight since the preceding noon, and *Jan.*
which we then called the "High Island;"* it 28
proved to be a mountain twelve thousand four
hundred feet of elevation above the level of the
sea, emitting flame and smoke in great profusion;
at first the smoke appeared like snow drift, but as
we drew nearer, its true character became manifest.

The discovery of an active volcano in so high a
southern latitude cannot but be esteemed a circumstance of high geological importance and interest, and contribute to throw some further light
on the physical construction of our globe. I named
it "Mount Erebus," and an extinct volcano to the
eastward, little inferior in height, being by mea-
surement ten thousand nine hundred feet high,
was called "Mount Terror."

A small high round island, which had been in
sight all the morning, was named "Beaufort Island," in compliment to Captain Francis Beaufort,
of the Royal Navy, Hydrographer to the Admiralty, who was not only mainly instrumental in
promoting the sending forth our expedition, but
afforded me much assistance, during its equipment, by his opinion and advice; and it is very
gratifying to me to pay this tribute of respect and
gratitude to him for the many acts of kindness and
personal friendship I have received at his hands.
At 4 P.M. we were in lat. 76° 6′ S., long. 168° 11′ E.
The magnetic dip 88° 27′ S., and the variation
95° 11′ E. The magnetic dip 88° 27′ S., and the
variation 95° 31′ E.; we were therefore considerably to the southward of the magnetic pole, without
any appearance of being able to approach it on
account of the land-ice, at a short distance to the
westward, uniting with the western point of the

* Later called Ross Island in honor of Ross.—C.N.

"High Island," which, however, afterwards proved to be part of the main land,* and of which Mount Erebus forms the most conspicuous object. As we approached the land under all studding-sails, we preceived a low white line extending from its eastern extreme point as far as the eye could discern to the eastward. It presented an extraordinary appearance, gradually increasing in height, as we got nearer to it, and proving at length to be a perpendicular cliff of ice, between one hundred and fifty and two hundred feet above the level of the sea, perfectly flat and level at the top, and without any fissures or promontories on its even seaward face.† What was beyond it we could not imagine; for being much higher than our mast-head, we could not see any thing except the summit of a lofty range of mountains extending to the southward as far as the seventy-ninth degree of latitude. These mountains, being the southernmost land hitherto discovered, I felt great satisfaction in naming after Captain Sir William Edward Parry, R.N., in grateful remembrance of the honour he conferred on me, by calling the northernmost known land on the globe by my name‡; and more especially for the encouragement, assistance, and friendship which he bestowed on me during the many years I had the honour and happiness to serve under his distinguished command, on four successive voyages to the arctic seas; and to which I mainly attribute the opportunity now afforded me of thus expressing how deeply I feel myself indebted to his assistance and example. Whether "Parry Mountains" again take an east-

* Ross was in error in thinking that the island was connected to the mainland.
† This was his first view of what was later to be called the Ross Ice Shelf.
‡ Parry's *Polar Voyage*, p. 121.

erly trending, and form the base to which this
extraordinary mass of ice is attached, must be left
for future navigators to determine.* If there be
land to the southward, it must be very remote, or
of much less elevation than any other part of the
coast we have seen, or it would have appeared
above the barrier. Meeting with such an obstruction was a great disappointment to us all, for we
had already, in expectation, passed far beyond the
eightieth degree, and had even appointed a
rendezvous there, in case of the ships accidentally
separating. It was, however, an obstruction of such
a character as to leave no doubt upon my mind as
to our future proceedings, for we might with equal
chance of success try to sail through the Cliffs of
Dover, as penetrate such a mass. When within
three or four miles of this most remarkable object,
we altered our course to the eastward, for the purpose of determining its extent, and not without
the hope that it might still lead us much further to
the southward. The whole coast here from the
western extreme point, now presented a similar
vertical cliff of ice, about two or three hundred
feet high. The eastern cape at the foot of Mount
Terror was named after my friend and colleague
Commander Francis Rawdon Moira Crozier, of
the *Terror*, to whose zeal and cordial co-operation
is mainly to be ascribed, under God's blessing, the
happiness as well as success of the expedition: under the circumstances we were placed in, it is impossible for others fully to understand the value of
having so tried a friend, of now more than twenty
years' standing, as commander of the second ship,
upon whom the harmony and right feeling between the two vessels so greatly depends. I consid-

* Scott's first expedition discovered, some sixty years later, that
the Parry Mountains are nonexistent.—C.N.

ered myself equally fortunate in having for the senior lieutenant of the *Erebus*, one whose worth was so well known to me, and who, as well as Commander Crozier, had ever shown so much firmness and prudence during the arduous voyages to the arctic regions, in which we sailed together as messmates, under the most successful arctic navigator; in compliment to him, I named the western promontory at the foot of Mount Erebus, "Cape Bird." These two points form the only conspicuous headlands of the coast, the bay between them being of inconsiderable depth. At 4 P.M. Mount Erebus was observed to emit smoke and flame in unusual quantities, producing a most grand spectacle. A volume of dense smoke was projected at each successive jet with great force, in a vertical column, to the height of between fifteen hundred and two thousand feet above the mouth of the crater, when condensing first at its upper part, it descended in mist or snow, and gradually dispersed, to be succeeded by another splendid exhibition of the same kind in about half an hour afterwards, although the intervals between the eruptions were by no means regular. The diameter of the columns of smoke was between two and three hundred feet, as near as we could measure it; whenever the smoke cleared away, the bright red flame that filled the mouth of the crater was clearly perceptible; and some of the officers believed they could see streams of lava pouring down its sides until lost beneath the snow which descended from a few hundred feet below the crater, and projected its perpendicular icy cliff several miles into the ocean. Mount Terror was much more free from snow, especially on its eastern side, where were numerous little conical crater-like hillocks, each of which had probably been, at some period, an active volcano; two very con-

spicuous hills of this kind were observed close to
Cape Crozier. The land upon which Mount
Erebus and Terror stand comprised between
Cape Crozier and Cape Bird, had the appearance
of an island from our present position; but the
fixed ice, not admitting of our getting to the westward of Cape Bird, prevented our ascertaining
whether it was so or not at this time.

The day was remarkably fine; and favoured by
a fresh north-westerly breeze, we made good progress to the E.S.E., close along the lofty perpendicular cliffs of the icy barrier. It is impossible to
conceive a more solid-looking mass of ice; not the
smallest appearance of any rent or fissure could
we discover throughout its whole extent, and the
intensely bright sky beyond it but too plainly indicated the great distance to which it reached to
the southward. Many small fragments lay at the
foot of the cliffs, broken away by the force of the
waves, which dashed their spray high up the face
of them.

Having sailed along this curious wall of ice in
perfectly clear water a distance of upwards of one
hundred miles, by noon we found it still stretching
to an indefinite extent in an E.S.E. direction. We
were at this time in lat. 77° 47' S., long. 176° 43' E.
The magnetic dip had diminished to 87° 22' S., and
the variation amounted to 104° 25' E. The wind fell
light shortly before noon, but we fortunately had
time to increase our distance from the barrier
before it fell calm; for the northerly swell, though
by no means of any great height, drifted us gradually towards it without our being able to make any
effort to avoid the serious consequences that must
have resulted had we been carried against it. We
had gained a distance of twelve or fourteen miles
from it, and as the *Terror* was getting short of
water, I made the signal to Commander Crozier to

collect some of the numerous fragments of the barrier that were about us; whilst in the *Erebus* we were engaged making observations on the depth and temperature of the sea. We sounded in four hundred and ten fathoms, the leads having sunk fully two feet into a soft green mud, of which a considerable quantity still adhered to them. The temperature of three hundred fathoms was 34° 2', and at one hundred and fifty fathoms, 33°; that of the surface being 31°, and the air 28°.* So great a depth of water seemed to remove the supposition that had been suggested, of this great mass of ice being formed upon a ledge of rock, and to show that its outer edge at any rate could not be resting on the ground.

We had closed it several miles during the calm, but all our anxiety on that account was removed on a breeze springing up from the south-east. I went on board the *Terror* for a short time, this afternoon, to consult with Commander Crozier, and compare our chronometers and barometers†, and on my return at half-past four, we made all sail on the starboard tack to the eastward; but not being able to fetch along the barrier, and the weather becoming thick with snow, we lost sight of it before nine o'clock in the evening. Several gigantic petrel were seen, and one that was badly wounded by Mr. Abernethy falling at too great a distance for us to send a boat after it, was immediately attacked by two others of the same kind, and torn to pieces. Many white petrel, stormy petrel, small penguins, and some of the Skua gull were

* Current S. by E. twelve miles per diem.

† After an absence now of nearly three months from Van Diemen's Land, the chronometers of the two ships were found to differ only 4″ of time, equal to a mile of longitude, or in this latitude less than a quarter of a mile of distance; a sufficient proof of the excellence of the instruments with which we were furnished:—the agreement of the barometers was perfect.

also seen. The breeze freshened very much, and
drew more round to the eastward. The barrier was
occasionally seen between the frequent snow-
showers; and as we made but slow progress along
it, we could quite clearly determine its continuity.
At midnight we had gained the lat. of 78° S., in
180° of E. long. At this time the wind was blowing
fresh from E.S.E., bringing a considerable swell
along the face of the barrier, to which our ships
pitched heavily, and greatly retarded our progress; but it was a gratifying evidence to us that
there was still much clear water in that direction.

The wind and sea had increased so much that
our dull-sailing ships could no longer gain any
ground by beating to windward; making two
points of leeway, they could only sail again and
again over the same space upon each successive
tack. I thought it therefore advisable to make a
long board under all sail to the north-east, so as to
pass over as great an extent of unknown space as
possible during the continuance of the adverse
wind, and resume the examination of the barrier
from the point we had last seen whenever the
circumstances of wind and weather became
favourable for doing so. The whole aspect of the
sky indicated a very unsettled state of the atmosphere, whilst heavy clouds of snow drifting frequently over us obscured every thing from our
sight. I therefore considered it desirable at any
rate to get a greater distance from the barrier, in
case of a change of wind making it a lee shore to
us of the most dangerous character. The intervals
of clear weather between the showers afforded us
opportunities of seeing sufficiently far ahead to
prevent our running into any very serious difficulty, so that we could venture to proceed with
confidence. Several heavy pieces of ice were

passed, evidently the fragments of the barrier or broken-up bergs, of which it was very remarkable we had not seen one during a run of one hundred and sixty miles along the barrier; from which, no doubt, some must occasionally break away. But a little reflection soon furnished an explanation: in summer the temperature of the atmosphere and of the ocean seldom differ more than three or four degrees, the air being generally the colder, but never more than eight or ten degrees: it is therefore probably of rare occurrence that any great disruption should occur at that season of the year, the whole mass being then of so uniform a temperature. But in the winter, when the air is probably forty or fifty degrees below zero, and the sea from twenty-eight to thirty degrees above, the unequal expansion of those parts of the mass exposed to so great a difference of temperature could not fail to produce the separation of large portions. These, impelled by the prevailing southerly winds, drift to the north as soon as the winter breaks up, and are met with abundantly in the lower latitudes, where they rapidly melt away and break in pieces. We have often in the arctic regions witnessed the astonishing effects of a sudden change of temperature during the winter season, causing great rents and fissures of many miles extent; especially on the fresh-water lakes of those regions, where the ice being perfectly transparent, affords better means of observing the effects produced: a fall of thirty or forty degrees of the thermometer immediately occasions large cracks, traversing the whole extent of the lake in every variety of direction, and attended with frequent, loud explosions; some of the cracks opening in places several inches by the contraction of the upper surface in contact with the extreme cold of the atmosphere. In those regions we have also witnessed the almost magical power of the sea in breaking up land-ice or extensive floes *1841* of from twenty to thirty feet thick, which have in *Jan.* a few minutes after the swell reached them, been *30* broken up into small fragments by the power of the waves.

But this extraordinary barrier of ice, of probably more than a thousand feet in thickness, crushes the undulations of the waves, and disregards their violence: it is a mighty and wonderful object, far beyond any thing we could have thought or conceived.

Thick squally weather, with constant snow prevailing, we stood away to the E.N.E. all day, without meeting either land or ice until 8 P.M., when, the snow clearing off, we could discover the strong iceblink of the barrier to the southward, and soon afterwards several icebergs were seen ahead of us: they were chiefly of the tabular form, perfectly flat on the top, precipitous in every part, and from 150 to 200 feet high: they had evidently at one time formed a part of the barrier, and I felt convinced, from finding them at this season so near the point of their formation, that they were resting on the ground. The lines were immediately prepared, *Jan.* and when we got amongst them at 3 A.M. the next *31* morning we hove to, and obtained soundings in two hundred and sixty fathoms, on a bottom of stiff green mud, leaving no doubt on our minds that all the bergs about us, after having broken away from the barrier, had grounded on this curious bank, which being two hundred miles from Cape Crozier, the nearest known land, and about sixty from the edge of the barrier, was of itself a discovery of considerable interest.

We continued our course to the eastward, sailing amongst many large bergs and much loose ice. Whales were again seen during the day, but in no great numbers; white petrels were very numerous, and a king penguin of unusual size was seen on a piece of ice. At noon we were in lat. 77° 6', long. 189° 6'. The dip had diminished to 86° 23'; and although the compasses again began to act with more precision, we here observed an unaccountable decrease of variation from 96 E. to 77 E., and then again an increase of sixteen degrees. The observations were numerous and very satisfactory, so that I have no doubt we had passed one of those extraordinary magnetic points first observed during Sir Edward Parry's second voyage to the Arctic Seas, near the eastern entrance of the Hecla and Fury Straits, but either of much less power or at a greater distance. These observations should not be employed in determining the position of the magnetic pole, as they would tend to throw it very considerably to the southward of the truth. At 1 P.M. we sounded in three hundred fathoms; but here there were no bergs in sight even from the mast-head. A strong ice-blink to the eastward led us to expect to find the barrier in that direction, but it proved to be occasioned by a heavy loose pack, which we entered at half-past four o'clock, and penetrated about twelve or thirteen miles, when it became too close for us to venture further. We were at this time in 192° east longitude, when we tacked to get back into the open water; this, however, we found more difficult, for the ice had closed so much since we entered the pack that it was not without receiving many severe blows, and losing some of our copper, as we bored through the heavier streams, that we regained a more open space. A boat was sent after a small seal that was seen asleep on the ice, and brought it on board; it was of the common kind, and very prettily marked with dark spots: its stomach was full of small red shrimps. Several whales

were also seen at the edge of the pack; young ice *1841*
was observed to be forming in every sheltered *Jan.*
situation under the lee of the larger pieces of ice, *31*
the temperature of the air being 19°. The wind
continued too strong from the southward for us to
make any way by beating to windward; we therefore stood back to the westward during the night
upon nearly the same line as we had sailed during
the day, but in the opposite direction.

A calm of three hours' duration was followed at
9 A.M. by a gentle breeze from the north-west-
ward, which again enabled us to stand towards the
barrier. At noon, in lat. 77° 5′ S., long. 188° 27′ E.,
we obtained soundings in two hundred and fifty *Feb.*
fathoms, on soft green mud and small stones. We *1*
also found the temperature of the sea at that depth
33° 2′, and at one hundred and fifty fathoms 33°,
the surface being 32°; the current was setting to
the northward at the rate of three quarters of a
mile per hour, its strength being greater no doubt
over the shallow bank than in the deeper water. In
the evening, whilst running with all studding sails
set, the wind suddenly shifted to the south-eastward, and the *Terror* being between two and
three miles astern, we shortened sail to wait for
her.

During a snow shower of four or five hours' con- *Feb.*
tinuance, and variable winds and squalls, we kept *2*
company by firing muskets every quarter of an
hour, the ships not being more than an eighth of
a mile from each other, but perfectly concealed by
fog and snow. These cleared off at 5 A.M., but the
whole morning was lost to us by alternate calms
and light baffling winds. At noon, in lat. 77° 46′ S.,
long. 187° E., we got soundings with two hundred
and eighty fathoms, greenish mud and clay. The
top of the barrier at the time was distinctly visible

from the deck, just rising above the horizon. We now made all sail to a light breeze from the northeast directly towards it; the loose ice became closer as we proceeded to the southward, and at a quarter past nine stopped our further progress. We were about ten or twelve miles from the barrier, but the whole of the intervening space was filled with packed heavy ice; we therefore wore round, hove to, and sounded in two hundred and sixty fathoms. I made the signal for Captain Crozier to come on board, who concurring in opinion with me of the utter impracticability of penetrating the dense pack between us and the barrier, I determined to devote a few more days to tracing its extent to the eastward; for although we could not hope to be able to get much further to the southward so late in the season, yet we knew the land-ice must still be clearing away from the shores at the most probable place of our being able to approach most nearly to the magnetic pole. Our dead reckoning since noon placed us in latitude 78° 3′, the *Terror's* 78° 5′; we therefore assumed 78° 4′ as the true latitude, which proved to be the highest attained this season; the face of the barrier at this part was therefore in 78 ¼° S.; it was about one hundred and sixty feet high, and extended as far to the east and west as the eye could discern, continuing in one unbroken line from Cape Crozier, a distance of two hundred and fifty miles.

At 10 P.M. we made sail to the northwest, to get clear of the pack, and by midnight were again in open water. I obtained an observation of the sun at 28 minutes after midnight, which gave the latitude 77° 56′ S., agreeing with the reckoning of the preceding and subsequent noon in placing our point of furthest south in latitude 78° 4′; at the same time an observation was made in the *Terror,* which, also, when reduced back to our position at 9:15 P.M., agreed exactly with the former determination.

With a moderate breeze from the north-eastward, we stood to the N.N.W. to gain an offing, as we were prevented by the pack making any way to the eastward, and the barometer falling gradually seemed to indicate the approach of unfavourable weather. But the wind veering to the south-east in the afternoon, and late in the evening to south, the weather, contrary to our expectations, continued clear, and the breeze freshening we made way to the eastward, having got to the northward of the pack, and having the barrier still in sight to the southward. We passed through several streams of loose ice, and saw a great many whales of small size; several of them marked with large white patches. In the evening a cask was put overboard in lat. 77° S. and long. 187° 24' E., containing a brief account of our proceedings, and with a request that whoever might find it would forward the paper to the Secretary of the Admiralty. It was my practice to throw a bottle over almost every day containing a paper with our latitude and longitude marked on it, for the purpose of gaining information respecting the joint effects of the prevailing winds and currents in these parts; but amongst ice, and in so turbulent an ocean, I fear but few of them will ever be found to subserve the intended purpose.

The next day we had a strong breeze from the southward, and pushed our way through loose ice and amongst numerous bergs to the eastward; at noon we were in lat. 77° S., and long. 192° 15' E., when the ice appearing more open, with smooth water, we began to beat up to the southward to endeavour to close the barrier; many seals and penguins were seen on the ice. At 8 P.M. we had

1841
Feb.
2

Feb.
3

Feb.
4

reached lat. 77° 18′ and long. 193°, where we found the ice so close in every direction that we were unable to proceed any further, and were obliged to dodge about in a hole of water two or three miles in diameter to wait for a favourable change. We obtained soundings in two hundred and seventy fathoms, muddy bottom, at four o'clock the next morning. The ice was so closely packed to the eastward and southward that we could make no way in either direction, so we continued beating about in the small hole of water in which we were shut up by the closing of the ice. We saw several of the large penguins, and three were brought on board: they were very powerful birds, and we had some difficulty in killing them: each of the two larger weighed sixty-six pounds, and the smallest fifty-seven pounds: their flesh is very dark, and of a rank fishy flavour. In the evening we made fast with warps to a heavy floe piece, and employed all hands in collecting ice to replenish our water, which was now getting rather short. Two seals were also captured to furnish us with oil for the winter. We cast off again at 10 P.M., having taken on board a sufficient quantity of ice, and stood out through a narrow opening we had watched forming to the westward. We passed through much closely packed ice to gain the clear water, which was seen from the mast-head early in the morning, and which we succeeded in accomplishing by noon, in lat. 77° 1′ S., long. 188° 26′ E.; the remainder of the day was spent in beating to the southwest to get away from the pack edge, on which the wind was blowing, and threatening to drive us down upon it.

It moderated during the next morning, and the wind getting to the westward enabled us to steer a more southerly course amongst loose ice, passing

only a few bergs, and occasionally through a sheet
of newly-formed ice: it fell calm at midnight, and
continued so for several hours.

At 1 A.M. sounded in two hundred and eighty-
eight fathoms, muddy bottom. We passed a berg
which had a large rock upon it. At 8 A.M. a steady
breeze sprung up from the northward, when we
made all sail before it, running along the pack
edge in clear water: at noon we were in lat. 77°
39′, and long. 187° 5′ E. After passing through several streams of young ice the barrier was seen
right ahead of us at 5 P.M. The main pack now
trending more to the south-eastward, we hauled
up along its edge, to run between it and the barrier, the whole of the surface of the sea being
covered with "pancake" ice. At midnight, when
about seven miles from the barrier, we obtained
soundings in two hundred and seventy-five fathoms.

The low temperature of the air and the smooth-
ness of the water combined to favour the rapid
formation of young ice, which greatly retarded us,
and rendered the attainment of our purpose of
more than ordinary difficulty; although the heavy
pack to the north of us was fast closing the barrier,
it was still fourteen or fifteen miles distant, and
favoured with a commanding breeze, we stood on
between the pack and barrier towards a remarkable looking bay, the only indentation we had perceived throughout its whole extent; and as clear
water was observed even to the foot of the barrier,
I could not permit myself to relinquish so favourable an opportunity of getting quite close to it, although I must confess the hazard was greater than
a due degree of prudence would have ventured to
encounter. At 5.40 A.M., being within a quarter of
a mile of its Icy Cliffs, we tacked and sounded in

1841
Feb.
7
Feb.
8

Feb.
9

three hundred and thirty fathoms, green muddy bottom. We had now a better opportunity of measuring the elevation of this perpendicular barrier, which, far overtopping our mast-heads, of course limited our view to the cliffs themselves, and these we considered to be much lower than at other points of it which we had previously approached: our angles gave them an elevation of one hundred and fifty feet. The bay we had entered was formed by a projecting peninsula of ice, terminated by a cape one hundred and seventy feet high; but at the narrow isthmus which connected it to the great barrier it was not more than fifty feet high, affording us the only opportunity we had of seeing its upper surface from our mast-heads: it appeared to be quite smooth, and conveyed to the mind the idea of an immense plain of frosted silver. Gigantic icicles depended from every projecting point of its perpendicular cliffs, proving that it sometimes thaws, which otherwise we could not have believed; for at a season of the year equivalent to August in England we had the thermometer at 12°, and at noon not rising above 14°; this severity of temperature is remarkable also when compared with our former experience in the northern seas, where from every iceberg you meet with, streams of water are constantly pouring off during the summer.

Young ice formed so quickly in this sheltered position, and the whole space between the barrier and the main pack which was driving down upon us being occupied by pancake ice, we found ourselves in a situation of much difficulty, the ice becoming so thick from being pressed fold over fold, as to render it for some hours a question of doubt whether we should be able to force our way through it to the open water which we could not

at this time see from the mast-head; but fortunately for us the breeze maintained sufficient
strength to enable us, with the assistance of great
exertions of the crews in breaking up the ice
before the ships, to regain a clearer space; and
then, when we required its aid no longer, the wind
came directly against us from the westward, so
that had we lingered longer near the barrier, or
had the wind shifted half an hour sooner, we
should certainly have been frozen up in a most
dangerous situation between the barrier and the
pack; and had we eventually escaped without
more serious consequences, we should at any rate
have lost some of the few remaining days of the
navigable season. A thick fog which prevailed for
several hours added to the embarrassment of our
situation, and rendered it the more difficult to
keep the ships together, by obliging us to carry
more moderate sail whilst amongst so much heavy
ice and so many bergs.

At noon we were in lat. 77° 56′ S., long. 190°
15′ E. At 4 P.M. the fog cleared away, and we were
again enabled to press all sail on the ships, running
to the westward close along the edge of the main
pack; the wind freshening from the northward
drove it quickly down upon the barrier; and soon
the channel by which we had escaped was filled by
heavy ice closely pressed together, so that not the
smallest hole of water could be seen amongst it. I
was most anxious to examine as great an extent of
the barrier to the eastward as possible, in order to
leave less to be accomplished the following year;
but the season was now fast drawing to a close, and
the present state of the pack rendered any attempt to penetrate it quite hopeless. I determined, however, to devote two or three days to
seeking a passage through it further to the north-

ward, and accordingly the whole of the tenth and eleventh was passed examining the pack edge, but without our being able to get so far to the eastward as we had been on the fourth and fifth by seventy or eighty miles.

At noon we were in lat. 76° 11' S., long. 187° 53' E., and were very much hampered by the newly formed ice, which was so thick, and extended so far from the main pack, as to render our efforts to examine it quite fruitless, and the fatigue and labour excessive. We continued, however, to coast along its western edge seeking for an opening; but the severe cold of the last few days had completely cemented it together, and the thick covering of snow that had fallen had united it, to appearance, into a solid unbroken mass: although we knew quite well that it consisted entirely of loose pieces, through which only a few days before we had sailed upwards of fifty miles, yet we could find no part of it now in which we could have forced the ships their own length.

We had further evidence of the approach of winter in the very great thickness of young ice we had to pass through as we ran along the pack edge, in many places between three and four inches thick, and entirely covering the surface of the sea for many miles around us: had we not been favoured with a strong breeze of very precarious duration, which enabled us to force our ships through it, we should certainly have been frozen in; and I could not but feel that the object we were pursuing was by no means of sufficient importance to justify the hazard of thus sacrificing the accomplishment of far more important purposes.

In the afternoon, whilst running before this favouring breeze, the main pack was reported in every direction of us except directly to windward;

and we soon found that during the thick weather *1841*
we had run down into a deep bight of it. The ships *Feb.*
were instantly hauled to the wind, and it was with *13*
the greatest difficulty they were extricated from
their dangerous situation before the wind increased to a violent gale that reduced us before
midnight to a close-reefed main-topsail and storm
stay-sails, under which we barely weathered a
great number of very large bergs clustered together under our lee, and most probably aground;
but we could not venture to try for soundings,
being uncertain whether we might not be driven
down amongst them: it was no doubt this chain of
bergs that had arrested the main pack in its northerly course and spread it out so far to the westward. One of the bergs was nearly four miles long,
though not more than one hundred and fifty feet
high. For some hours we were in a state of considerable anxiety, not knowing how far to the westward the chain of bergs might extend, the thick
falling snow preventing our seeing to any distance
before us; the waves, as they broke over the ships,
froze as they fell on the decks and rigging, and
covered our clothes with a thick coating of ice, so
that our people suffered severely during the continuance of the gale. We passed many bergs and
loose pieces of ice during the early part of the next
day, and were frequently obliged to bear away to
clear them. In the afternoon the storm began to
abate, and on the weather clearing up for a short
time, we found ourselves in a more open space.

I now became convinced of the necessity of at
once relinquishing any attempt to penetrate to
the eastward, and of deferring the further examination of the barrier to the following season; and
the wind having shifted to the eastward, we bore
away before it for the purpose of making another

attempt to reach the magnetic pole, and of seeking a harbour in its vicinity in which we might pass the winter.

Thick fog and constant snow, which prevailed during the remainder of this and greater part of the following day, obliged us to run under moderate sail, to prevent the ships separating, and to be in readiness to avoid any danger that might suddenly arise; we, however, were in a perfectly clear

sea, not a single piece of ice to be seen during the whole time, and the temperature of the air had risen to the freezing point.

At noon we were in lat. 76° 22′ S., long. 178° 16′ E.; the dip had again increased to 87° as we approached the pole, now distant from us about three hundred and sixty miles, and the variation being 91°, showed us we were very nearly in its latitude: we continued, therefore, to steer direct south by compass. The mildness of the day, notwithstanding the constant snow, was much enjoyed by us, as it allowed us to open the hatches, which had been closely battened down during the late gale of three days' continuance. The condensation of vapour between decks had been so great as to run down the ship's sides in small streams. I therefore directed the warm-air stove to be put into operation, which speedily and effectually removed every appearance of damp, driving the vapours up the hatchways, and circulating in its place a dry, pure air. The admirable performance of this most invaluable invention of Mr. Sylvester cannot be mentioned in adequate terms of praise.

Towards evening the swell had greatly subsided, but there was still a strong wind blowing, and the snow falling so thick, that we could seldom see a mile before us: running down upon a lee shore under such circumstances was a measure of some anxiety, but the barometer was rising fast *1841* from its very low state, and promised an improvement of the weather.

We were still a hundred miles from Franklin Island, for which we were steering, and I was unwilling to lose the advantage of the favourable breeze, even at some degree of hazard; for I felt we had but a few days to do much that we still hoped to accomplish.

On the 27th of January we had not been able to approach the pole nearer than about eighty leagues, but during the time we had spent in examining the barrier, a period of nearly three weeks, we could not but hope that so much more of the land ice would have broken away as to admit of our getting very close to, perhaps even complete the attainment of the pole.

The wind veered to the southward, and the snow ceased; several pieces of ice with rock on them were passed, and at 11 A.M. Franklin Island *Feb.* was seen at a distance of seven leagues ahead of us. *15* We ran to leeward of it at 3 P.M., and when five miles N. N. W. from it we sounded in fifty fathoms, rocky bottom. Some streams of ice appearing soon afterwards, we hauled more to the southward to avoid them; and as we closed the main land we got in amongst a great quantity of brash ice of a brownish yellow colour; some of it was collected and placed under a powerful microscope, but we were unable to ascertain the true nature of the colouring matter; by most of us it was believed to be the fine ashes from Mount Erebus, not more than eighty miles south of us.

At 11 P.M., being nearly calm, we sounded in three hundred and eighty fathoms, greenish-coloured mud and clay: Beaufort Island at the time bearing true south.

The wind was so light and variable, and the

sludge and pancake ice so thick, we could scarcely get the ships through it. Mount Erebus was seen at 2.30 A.M., and the weather becoming very clear, we had a splendid view of the whole line of coast, to all appearance connecting it with the main land, which we had not before suspected to be the case. A very deep bight was observed to extend far to the south-west from Cape Bird, in which a line of low land might be seen; but its determination was too uncertain to be left unexplored; and as the wind, blowing feebly from the west, prevented our making any way in that direction through the young ice that now covered the surface of the ocean in every part, as far as we could see from the mast-head, I determined to steer towards the bight, to give it a closer examination, and to learn with more certainty its continuity or otherwise. At noon we were in lat. 76° 32' S., long. 166° 12' E., dip 88° 24', and variation 107° 18' E.

During the afternoon we were nearly becalmed, and witnessed some magnificent eruptions of Mount Erebus, the flame and smoke being projected to a great height; but we could not, as on a former occasion, discover any lava issuing from the crater; although the exhibitions of to-day were upon a much grander scale.

A great number of whales of two different kinds were seen, the larger kind having an extremely long, erect back-fin, whilst that of the smaller species was scarcely discernible. The Skua gull, white petrel, penguins, and seals were also about us in considerable numbers.

At 10 P.M. we sounded in three hundred and sixty fathoms, green mud. Soon after midnight a breeze sprang up from the eastward, and we made all sail to the southward until 4 A.M., although we had an hour before distinctly traced the land en-

tirely round the bay connecting Mount Erebus *1841*
with the main land. I named it McMurdo Bay,*
after the senior Lieutenant of the *Terror*, a compliment that his zeal and skill well merited. The wind
having shifted to the southward enabled us to
resume our endeavours to approach the magnetic
pole, and we accordingly stood away to the north-
west, sailing through quantities of tough newly
formed ice perfectly covered with the colouring
matter I have before noticed. When the melted
ice was filtered through bibulous paper, it left a
very thin sediment, which on being dried became
an impalpable powder, seeming to confirm our
belief of its volcanic origin.

At 2 P.M. we had penetrated the pack so far as
to have got within ten or twelve miles of the low
coast line, when our further progress was stopped
by heavy closely packed ice. To the north-west-
ward we observed a low point of land with a small
islet off it, which we hoped might afford us a place
of refuge during the winter, and accordingly endeavoured to struggle through the ice towards it,
until 4 P.M., when the utter hopelessness of being
able to approach it was manifest to all; the space
of fifteen or sixteen miles between it and the ships
being now filled by a solid mass of land ice. We
therefore wore round and hove to for Commander Crozier to come on board; and as he quite
concurred with me in thinking it impossible to get
any nearer to the pole, I determined at once to
relinquish the attempt, as we could not hope at so
late a period of the season that any more of the
land ice would break away. The cape with the islet
off it was named after Professor Gauss, the great
mathematician of Göttingen, who has done more

* Now known as McMurdo Sound. McMurdo Station (on Ross
Island) is also named after McMurdo.—C.N.

than any other philosopher of the present day to advance the science of terrestrial magnetism.

We were at this time in latitude 76° 12′ S., longitude 164° E.; the magnetic dip 88° 40′, and the variation 109° 24′ E. We were therefore only one hundred and sixty miles from the pole.

Had it been possible to have found a place of security upon any part of this coast where we might have wintered, in sight of the brilliant burning mountain, and at so short a distance from the magnetic pole, both of those interesting spots might easily have been reached by travelling parties in the following spring; but all our efforts to effect that object proved quite unsuccessful; and although our hopes of complete attainment were not realised, yet it was some satisfaction to know that we had approached the pole some hundreds of miles nearer than any of our predecessors; and from the multitude of observations that were made in so many different directions from it, its position may be determined with nearly as much accuracy as if we had actually reached the spot itself.

ROALD AMUNDSEN

(*1872–1928*)

AMUNDSEN'S EXPEDITION of 1910–12, originally intended as a North Polar voyage, dramatically changed character when Amundsen reversed course at sea and sailed to Madeira, from which he cabled Scott in Melbourne, Australia the terse news that he was heading south. This could mean only one thing to Scott: Amundsen intended to be first at the Pole. Thus the race between the Norwegian and the English parties began.

Amundsen sailed from Madeira to the Ross Sea without calling at any port, and established a base at the Bay of Whales on the Ross Ice Shelf, a place which Ernest Shackleton a few years earlier had rejected as too hazardous because it was in danger of calving off from the shelf and floating out to sea as a tabular berg. The advantage, however, of this position was that it placed Amundsen approximately sixty miles closer to the Pole than Scott, who was based at Cape Evans on Ross Island. In later years Cherry-Garrard, a member of Scott's expedition, wrote that the Scott party had badly underestimated Amundsen's abilities.

By 1910 Amundsen had had considerable polar experience. He was not a newcomer to the Antarctic. He had been a mate on the *Belgica* expedition of 1897, which was the first to winter over on the continent. He knew skiing, sledging and huskies well and was able to make brilliant decisions based on limited information. Instead of depending, as Scott did, on the Beardmore Glacier route over the Transantarctic Mountains, a route that had been pioneered by Shackleton, he used the still unexplored Axel Heiberg Glacier, and the glacier served him well. Amundsen relied heavily on dogs. He did not mistrust them in polar work as Scott did, and he did not believe in the value of manhauling sledges, in which Scott seemed at times to have an almost mystical faith. Amundsen landed on the ice shelf with 116 dogs and erected a hut some two miles inland. He started for the Pole October 20, 1911 with four companions, four sledges and fifty-two dogs and reached the Pole December 14, 1911, beating the Scott party by a little more than a month. He remained at the Pole two days to fix his position. His journey to the Pole was fast and easy in contrast with that of the ill-fated Scott.

Amundsen and the Italian explorer, Umberto Nobile, crossed the North Pole by dirigible in 1926. In 1928, when Nobile's airship, *Italia*, was wrecked on its return from the North Pole, Amundsen went to search for him. He was lost over the Arctic seas and no trace of him was found.

The present selection, in which he recounts what it was like to ascend the Heiberg Glacier and to reach the Pole, exemplifies the vividness, modesty and admirable simplicity of his narrative as a whole.

At the Pole

We had difficulty in finding a place for the tent that evening; the surface was equally hard everywhere, and at last we had to set it on the bare ice. Luckily for our tent-pegs, this ice was not of the bright, steely variety; it was more milky in appearance and not so hard, and we were thus able to knock in the pegs with the axe. When the tent was up, Hassel went out as usual to fetch snow for the cooker. As a rule he performed this task with a big knife, specially made for snow; but this evening he went out armed with an axe. He was very pleased with the abundant and excellent material that lay to his hand; there was no need to go far. Just outside the tent door, two feet away, stood a fine little haycock, that looked as if it would serve the purpose well. Hassel raised his axe and gave a good sound blow; the axe met with no resistance, and went in up to the haft. The haycock was hollow. As the axe was pulled out the surrounding part gave way, and one could hear the pieces of ice falling down through the dark hole. It appeared, then, that two feet from our door we had a most convenient way down into the cellar. Hassel looked as if he enjoyed the situation. "Black as a sack," he smiled; "couldn't see any bottom." Hanssen was beaming; no doubt he would have liked the tent a little nearer. The material provided by the haycock was of the best quality, and well adapted for cooking purposes.

The next day, December 1, was a very fatiguing one for us all. From early morning a blinding blizzard raged from the south-east, with a heavy fall of snow. The going was of the very worst kind—polished ice. I stumbled forward on ski, and had comparatively easy work. The drivers had been obliged to take off their ski and put them on the loads, so as to walk by the side, support the sledges, and give the dogs help when they came to a difficult place; and that was pretty often, for on this smooth ice surface there were a number of small scattered *sastrugi,* and these consisted of a kind of snow that reminded one more of fish-glue than of anything else when the sledges came in contact with it. The dogs could get no hold with their claws on the smooth ice, and when the sledge came on to one of these tough little waves, they could not manage to haul it over, try as they might. The driver then had to put all his strength into it to prevent the sledge stopping. Thus in most cases the combined efforts of men and dogs carried the sledge on.

In the course of the afternoon the surface again began to be more disturbed, and great crevasses crossed our path time after time. These crevasses were really rather dangerous; they looked very innocent, as they were quite filled up with snow, but on a nearer acquaintance with them we came to understand that they were far more hazardous than we dreamed of at first. It turned out that between the loose snow-filling and the firm ice edges there was a fairly broad, open space, leading straight down into the depths. The layer of snow which covered it over was in most cases quite thin. In driving out into one of these snow-filled crevasses nothing happened as a rule; but it was in getting off on the other side that the critical moment arrived. For here the dogs came up on to the smooth ice surface, and could get no hold for their claws, with the result that it was left entirely to the driver to haul the sledge up. The strong pull he then had to give sent him through the thin layer of snow. Under these circumstances he took a good, firm hold of the sledge-lashing, or of a special strap that had been made with a view to these accidents. But familiarity breeds contempt, even with the most cautious, and some of the drivers were often within an ace of going down into "the cellar."

If this part of the journey was trying for the dogs, it was certainly no less so for the men. If the weather had even been fine, so that we could have looked about us, we should not have minded it so much, but in this vile weather it was, indeed, no pleasure. Our time was also a good deal taken up with thawing noses and cheeks as they froze—not that we stopped; we had no time for that. We simply took off a mit, and laid the warm hand on the frozen spot as we went; when we thought we had restored sensation, we put the hand back into the mit. By this time it would want warming. One does not keep one's hands bare for long with the thermometer several degrees below zero and a storm blowing. In spite of the unfavourable conditions we had been working in, the sledge-meters that evening showed a distance of fifteen and a half miles. We were well satisfied with the day's work when we camped.

Let us cast a glance into the tent this evening. It looks cosy enough. The inner half of the tent is occupied by three sleeping-bags, whose respective owners have found it both comfortable and expedient to turn in, and may now be seen engaged with their diaries. The outer half—that nearest the door—has only two sleeping-bags, but the rest of the space is taken up with the whole cooking apparatus of the expedition. The owners of these two bags are still sitting up. Hanssen is cook, and will not turn in until the food is ready and served. Wisting is his sworn comrade and assistant, and is ready to lend him any aid that may be required. Hanssen appears to be a careful cook; he evidently does not like to burn the food, and his spoon stirs the contents of the pot incessantly. "Soup!" The effect of the word is instantaneous. Everyone sits up at once with a cup in one hand and a spoon in the other. Each one in his turn has his cup filled with what looks like the most tasty vegetable soup. Scalding hot it is, as one can see by the faces, but for all that it disappears with surprising rapidity. Again the cups are filled, this time with more solid stuff—pemmican. With praiseworthy despatch their contents are once more demolished, and they are filled for the third time. There is nothing the matter with these men's appetites. The cups are carefully scraped, and the enjoyment of bread and water begins. It is easy to see, too, that it is an enjoyment—greater, to judge by the pleasure on their faces, than the most skilfully devised menu could afford. They positively caress the biscuits before they eat them. And the water—ice-cold water they all call for—this also disappears in great quantities, and procures, I feel certain from their expression, a far greater pleasure and satisfaction than the finest wine that was ever produced. The Primus hums softly during the whole meal, and the temperature in the tent is quite pleasant.

When the meal is over, one of them calls for scissors and looking-glass, and then one may see the Polar explorers dressing their hair for the approaching Sunday. The beard is cut quite short with the clipper every Saturday evening; this is done not so much from motives of vanity as from considerations of utility and comfort. The beard invites an accumulation of ice, which may often be very embarrassing. A beard in the Polar regions seems to me to be just as awkward and unpractical as—well, let us say, walking with a tall hat on each foot. As the beard-clipper and the mirror make their round, one after the other disappears into his bag, and with five "Good-nights," silence falls upon the tent. The regular breathing soon announces that the day's work demands its tribute. Meanwhile the south-easter howls, and the snow beats against the tent. The dogs have curled themselves up, and do not seem to trouble themselves about the weather.

The storm continued unabated on the following day, and on account of the dangerous nature of the ground we decided to wait awhile. In the course of the morning—towards noon, perhaps—the wind dropped a little, and out we went. The sun peeped through at times, and we took the welcome opportunity of getting an altitude—86° 47' S. was the result.

At this camp we left behind all our delightful reindeer-skin clothing, as we could see that we should have no use for it, the temperature being far too high. We kept the hoods of our reindeer coats, however; we might be glad of them in going against the wind. Our day's march was not to be a long one; the little slackening of the wind about midday was only a joke. It soon came on again in earnest, with a sweeping blizzard from the same quarter—the south-east. If we had known the ground, we should possibly have gone on; but in this storm and driving snow, which prevented our keeping our eyes open, it was no use. A serious accident might happen and ruin all. Two and half miles was therefore our whole distance. The temperature when we camped was −5.8° F. Height above the sea, 9,780 feet.

In the course of the night the wind veered from south-east to north, falling light, and the weather cleared. This was a good chance for us, and we were not slow to avail ourselves of it. A gradually rising ice surface lay before us, bright as a mirror. As on the preceding days, I stumbled along in front on ski, while the others, without their ski, had to follow and support the sledges. The surface still offered filled crevasses, though perhaps less frequently than before. Meanwhile small patches of snow began to show themselves on the polished surface, and soon increased in number and size, until before very long they united and covered the unpleasant ice with a good and even layer of snow. Then ski were put on again, and we continued our way to the south with satisfaction.

We were all rejoicing that we had now conquered this treacherous glacier,[1] and congratulating ourselves on having at last arrived on the actual plateau.[2] As we were going along, feeling pleased about this, a ridge suddenly appeared right ahead, telling us plainly that perhaps all our sorrows were not yet ended. The ground had begun to sink a little, and as we came nearer we could see that we had to cross a rather wide, but not deep, valley before we arrived under the ridge. Great lines of hummocks and haycock-shaped pieces of ice came in view on every side; we could see that we should have to keep our eyes open.

And now we came to the formation in the glacier that we called the Devil's Ballroom. Little by little the covering of snow that we had praised in such high terms disappeared,

1 The Axel Heiberg Glacier.—C.N.
2 That is, the polar plateau, on which the Pole is situated.—C.N.

and before us lay this wide valley, bare and gleaming. At first it went well enough; as it was downhill, we were going at a good pace on the smooth ice. Suddenly Wisting's sledge cut into the surface, and turned over on its side. We all knew what had happened—one of the runners was in a crevasse. Wisting set to work, with the assistance of Hassel, to raise the sledge, and take it out of its dangerous position; meanwhile Bjaaland had got out his camera and was setting it up. Accustomed as we were to such incidents, Hanssen and I were watching the scene from a point a little way in advance, where we had arrived when it happened. As the photography took rather a long time, I assumed that the crevasse was one of the filled ones and presented no particular danger, but that Bjaaland wanted to have a souvenir among his photographs of the numerous crevasses and ticklish situations we had been exposed to. As to the crack being filled up, there was of course no need to inquire. I hailed them, and asked how they were getting on. "Oh, all right," was the answer; "we've just finished."—"What does the crevasse look like?" —"Oh, as usual," they shouted back; "no bottom." I mention this little incident just to show how one can grow accustomed to anything in this world. There were these two—Wisting and Hassel—lying over a yawning, bottomless abyss, and having their photograph taken; neither of them gave a thought to the serious side of the situation. To judge from the laughter and jokes we heard, one would have thought their position was something quite different.

When the photographer had quietly and leisurely finished his work—he got a remarkably good picture of the scene— the other two together raised the sledge, and the journey was continued. It was at this crevasse that we entered his Majesty's Ballroom. The surface did not really look bad. True, the snow was blown away, which made it difficult to advance, but we did not see many cracks. There were a good many pressure-masses, as already mentioned, but even in the neighbourhood of these we could not see any marked disturbance. The first sign that the surface was more treacherous than it appeared to be was when Hanssen's leading dogs went right through the apparently solid floor. They remained hanging by their harness, and were easily pulled up again. When we looked through the hole they had made in the crust, it did not give us the impression of being very dangerous, as 2 or 3 feet below the outer crust, there lay another surface, which appeared to consist of pulverized ice. We assumed that this lower surface was the solid one, and that therefore there was no danger in falling through the upper one. But Bjaaland was able to tell us a different story. He had, in fact, fallen through the outer crust, and was well on his way through the inner one as well, when he got hold of a loop of rope on his sledge and saved himself in the nick of time. Time after time the dogs now fell through, and time after time the men went in. The effect of the open space between the two crusts was that the ground under our feet sounded unpleasantly hollow as we went over it. The drivers whipped up their dogs as much as they could, and with shouts and brisk encouragement they went rapidly over the treacherous floor. Fortunately this curious formation was not of great extent, and we soon began to observe a change for the better as we came up the ridge. It soon appeared that the Ballroom was the glacier's last farewell to us. With it all irregularities ceased, and both surface and going improved by leaps and bounds, so that before very long we had the satisfaction of seeing that at last we had really conquered all these unpleasant difficulties. The surface at once became fine and even, with a splendid covering of snow everywhere, and we went rapidly on our way to the south with a feeling of security and safety.

In lat. 87° S.—according to dead reckoning—we saw the last of the land to the northeast. The atmosphere was then apparently as clear as could be, and we felt certain that our view covered all the land there was to be seen from that spot. We were deceived again on this occasion, as will be seen later. Our distance that day (December 4) was close upon twenty-five miles; height above the sea, 10,100 feet.

The weather did not continue fine for long. Next day

(December 5) there was a gale from the north, and once more the whole plain was a mass of drifting snow. In addition to this there was thick falling snow, which blinded us and made things worse, but a feeling of security had come over us and helped us to advance rapidly and without hesitation, although we could see nothing. That day we encountered new surface conditions—big, hard snow waves (*sastrugi*). These were anything but pleasant to work among, especially when one could not see them. It was of no use for us "fore-runners" to think of going in advance under these circumstances, as it was impossible to keep on one's feet. Three or four paces was often the most we managed to do before falling down. The *sastrugi* were very high, and often abrupt; if one came on them unexpectedly, one required to be more than an acrobat to keep on one's feet. The plan we found to work best in these conditions was to let Hanssen's dogs go first; this was an unpleasant job for Hanssen, and for his dogs too, but it succeeded, and succeeded well. An upset here and there was, of course, unavoidable, but with a little patience the sledge was always righted again. The drivers had as much as they could do to support their sledges among the *sastrugi*, but while supporting the sledges, they had at the same time a support for themselves. It was worse for us who had no sledges, but by keeping in the wake of them we could see where the irregularities lay, and thus get over them. Hanssen deserves a special word of praise for his driving on this surface in such weather. It is a difficult matter to drive Eskimo dogs forward when they cannot see; but Hanssen managed it well, both getting the dogs on and steering his course by compass. One would not think it possible to keep an approximately right course when the uneven ground gives such violent shocks that the needle flies several times round the compass, and is no sooner still again than it recommences the same dance; but when at last we got an observation, it turned out that Hanssen had steered to a hair, for the observations and dead reckoning agreed to a mile. In spite of all hindrances, and of being able to see nothing, the sledge meters showed nearly twenty-five miles. The hypsometer showed 11,070 feet above the sea; we had therefore reached a greater altitude than the Butcher's.

December 6 brought the same weather: thick snow, sky and plain all one, nothing to be seen. Nevertheless we made splendid progress. The *sastrugi* gradually became leveled out, until the surface was perfectly smooth; it was a relief to have even ground to go upon once more. These irregularities that one was constantly falling over were a nuisance; if we had met with them in our usual surroundings it would not have mattered so much; but up here on the high ground, where we had to stand and gasp for breath every time we rolled over, it was certainly not pleasant.

That day we passed 88° S., and camped in 88° 9' S. A great surprise awaited us in the tent that evening. I expected to find, as on the previous evening, that the boiling point had fallen somewhat; in other words, that it would show a continued rise of the ground, but to our astonishment this was not so. The water boiled at exactly the same temperature as on the preceding day. I tried it several times, to convince myself that there was nothing wrong, each time with the same result. There was great rejoicing among us all when I was able to announce that we had arrived on the top of the plateau.

December 7 began like the 6th, with absolutely thick weather, but, as they say, you never know what the day is like before sunset. Possibly I might have chosen a better expression than this last—one more in agreement with the natural conditions—but I will let it stand. Though for several weeks now the sun had not set, my readers will not be so critical as to reproach me with inaccuracy. With a light wind from the northeast, we now went southward at a good speed over the perfectly level plain, with excellent going. The uphill work had taken it out of our dogs, though not to any serious extent. They had turned greedy—there is no denying that—and the half kilo of pemmican they got each day was not enough to fill their stomachs. Early and late they were looking for something—no matter what—to devour. To begin with they contented themselves with such loose objects as ski bindings, whips, boots, and the like; but as we came to know their proclivities, we took such care of everything that they found no extra meals lying about. But that was not the end of the matter. They then went for the fixed lashings of the sledges, and—if we had allowed it—would very quickly have resolved the various sledges into their component parts. But we found a way of stopping that: every evening, on halting, the sledges were buried in the snow, so as to hide all the lashings. That was successful; curiously enough, they never tried to force the "snow rampart."

I may mention as a curious thing that these ravenous animals, that devoured everything they came across, even to the ebonite points of our ski sticks, never made any attempt to break into the provision cases. They lay there and went about among the sledges with their noses just on a level with the split cases, seeing and scenting the pemmican, without once making a sign of taking any. But if one raised a lid, they were not long in showing themselves. Then they all came in a great hurry and flocked about the sledges in the hope of getting a little extra bit. I am at a loss to explain this behavior; that bashfulness was not at the root of it, I am tolerably certain.

During the forenoon the thick, gray curtain of cloud began to grow thinner on the horizon, and for the first time for three days we could see a few miles about us. The feeling was something like that one has on waking from a good nap, rubbing one's eyes and looking around. We had become so accustomed to the gray twilight that this positively dazzled us. Meanwhile, the upper layer of air seemed obstinately to remain the same and to be doing its best to prevent the sun from showing itself. We badly wanted to get a meridian altitude, so that we could determine our latitude. Since 86° 47′ S. we had had no observation, and it was not easy to say when we should get one. Hitherto, the weather conditions on the high ground had not been particularly favorable. Although the prospects were not very promising, we halted at 11 A.M. and made ready to catch the sun if it should be kind enough to look out. Hassel and Wisting used one sextant and artificial horizon, Hanssen and I the other set.

I don't know that I have ever stood and absolutely pulled at the sun to get it out as I did that time. If we got an observation here which agreed with our reckoning, then it would be possible, if the worst came to the worst, to go to the Pole on dead reckoning; but if we got none now, it was a question whether our claim to the Pole would be admitted on the dead reckoning we should be able to produce. Whether my pulling helped or not, it is certain that the sun appeared. It was not very brilliant to begin with, but, practiced as we now were in availing ourselves of even the poorest chances, it was good enough. Down it came, was checked by all, and the altitude written down. The curtain of cloud was rent more and more, and before we had finished our work—that is to say, caught the sun at its highest, and convinced ourselves that it was descending again—it was shining in all its glory. We had put away our instruments and were sitting on the sledges, engaged in the calculations. I can safely say that we were excited. What would the result be, after marching blindly for so long and over such impossible ground, as we had been doing? We added and subtracted, and at last there was the result. We looked at each other in sheer incredulity: the result was as astonishing as the most consummate conjuring trick—88° 16′ S., precisely to a minute the same as our reckoning, 88° 16′ S. If we were forced to go to the Pole on dead reckoning, then surely the most exacting would admit our right to do so. We put away our observation books, ate one or two biscuits, and went at it again.

We had a great piece of work before us that day: nothing less than carrying our flag farther south than the foot of man had trod. We had our silk flag ready; it was made fast to two ski sticks and laid on Hanssen's sledge. I had given him orders that as soon as we had covered the distance to 88° 23′ S., which was Shackleton's farthest south, the flag was to be hoisted on his sledge. It was my turn as forerunner, and I pushed on. There was no longer any difficulty in holding one's course; I had the grandest cloud formations to steer by, and everything now went like a machine. First came the forerunner for the time being, then Hanssen, then Wisting, and finally Bjaaland. The forerunner who was not on duty went where he liked; as a rule he accompanied one or other of the sledges. I had long ago fallen into a reverie—far removed from the scene in which I was moving; what I thought about I do not remember now, but I was so preoccupied that I had entirely forgotten my surroundings. Then suddenly I was roused from my dreaming by a jubilant shout, followed by ringing cheers. I turned round quickly to discover the reason of this unwonted occurrence, and stood speechless and overcome.

I find it impossible to express the feelings that possessed me at this moment. All the sledges had stopped, and from the foremost of them the Norwegian flag was flying. It shook itself out, waved and flapped so that the silk rustled; it looked wonderfully well in the pure, clear air and the shining white surroundings. 88° 23' was past; we were farther south than any human being had been. No other moment of the whole trip affected me like this. The tears forced their way to my eyes; by no effort of will could I keep them back. It was the flag yonder that conquered me and my will. Luckily I was some way in advance of the others, so that I had time to pull myself together and master my feelings before reaching my comrades. We all shook hands, with mutual congratulations; we had won our way far by holding together, and we would go farther yet—to the end.

We did not pass that spot without according our highest tribute of admiration to the man who—together with his gallant companions—had planted his country's flag so infinitely nearer to the goal than any of his precursors. Sir Ernest Shackleton's name will always be written in the annals of Antarctic exploration in letters of fire. Pluck and grit can work wonders, and I know of no better example of this than what that man has accomplished.

The cameras of course had to come out, and we got an excellent photograph of the scene which none of us will ever forget. We went on a couple of miles more, to 88° 25', and then camped. The weather had improved, and kept on improving all the time. It was now almost perfectly calm, radiantly clear, and, under the circumstances, quite summerlike: −0.4° F. Inside the tent it was quite sultry. This was more than we had expected.

After much consideration and discussion we had come to the conclusion that we ought to lay down a depot—the last one—at this spot. The advantages of lightening our sledges were so great that we should have to risk it. Nor would there be any great risk attached to it, after all, since we should adopt a system of marks that would lead even a blind man back to the place. We had determined to mark it not only at right angles to our course—that is, from east to west—but by snow beacons at every two geographical miles to the south.

We stayed here on the following day to arrange this depot. Hanssen's dogs were real marvels, all of them; nothing seemed to have any effect on them. They had grown rather thinner, of course, but they were still as strong as ever. It was therefore decided not to lighten Hanssen's sledge, but only the two others; both Wisting's and Bjaaland's teams had suffered, especially the latter's. The reduction in weight that was effected was considerable—nearly 110 pounds on each of the two sledges; there was thus about 220 pounds in the depot. The snow here was ill-adapted for building, but we put up quite a respectable monument all the same. It was dogs' pemmican and biscuits that were left behind; we carried with us on the sledges provisions for about a month. If, therefore, contrary to expectation, we should be so unlucky as to miss this depot, we should nevertheless be fairly sure of reaching our depot in 86° 21' before supplies ran short. The cross-marking of the depot was done with sixty splinters of black packing case on each side, with 100 paces between each. Every other one had a shred of black cloth on the top. The splinters on the east side were all marked, so that on seeing them we should know instantly that we were to the east of the depot. Those on the west had no marks.

The warmth of the past few days seemed to have matured our frost sores, and we presented an awful appearance. It was Wisting, Hanssen, and I who had suffered the worst damage in the last southeast blizzard; the left side of our faces was one mass of sore, bathed in matter and serum. We looked like the worst type of tramps and ruffians, and would probably not have been recognized by our nearest relations. These sores were a great trouble to us during the latter part of the journey. The slightest gust of wind produced a sensation as if one's face were being cut backward and forward with a blunt knife. They lasted a long time, too; I can remember Hanssen removing the last scab when we were coming into Hobart— three months later. We were very lucky in the weather during this depot work; the sun came out all at once, and we had an excellent opportunity of taking some good azimuth observations, the last of any use that we got on the journey.

December 9 arrived with the same fine weather and sunshine. True, we felt our frost sores rather sharply that day, with −18.4° F. and a little breeze dead against us, but that could not be helped. We at once began to put up beacons— a work which was continued with great regularity right up to the Pole. These beacons were not so big as those we had built down on the Barrier;[1] we could see that they would be quite large enough with a height of about 3 feet, as it was very easy to see the slightest irregularity on this perfectly flat surface. While thus engaged we had an opportunity of becoming thoroughly acquainted with the nature of the snow. Often—very often indeed—on this part of the plateau, to the south of 88° 25′, we had difficulty in getting snow good enough—that is, solid enough for cutting blocks. The snow up here seemed to have fallen very quietly, in light breezes or calms. We could thrust the tent pole, which was 6 feet long, right down without meeting resistance, which showed

---

1 That is, on the Ross Ice Shelf.—C.N.

that there was no hard layer of snow. The surface was also perfectly level; there was not a sign of *sastrugi* in any direction.

Every step we now took in advance brought us rapidly nearer the goal; we could feel fairly certain of reaching it on the afternoon of the 14th. It was very natural that our conversation should be chiefly concerned with the time of arrival. None of us would admit that he was nervous, but I am inclined to think that we all had a little touch of that malady. What should we see when we got there? A vast, endless plain, that no eye had yet seen and no foot yet trodden; or—— No, it was an impossibility; with the speed at which we had traveled, we must reach the goal first, there could be no doubt about that. And yet—and yet——Wherever there is the smallest loophole, doubt creeps in and gnaws and gnaws and never leaves a poor wretch in peace. "What on earth is Uroa scenting?" It was Bjaaland who made this remark, on one of these last days, when I was going by the side of his sledge and talking to him. "And the strange thing is that he's scenting to the south. It can never be——" Myliuns, Ring, and Suggen showed the same interest in the southerly direction; it was quite extraordinary to see how they raised their heads, with every sign of curiosity, put their noses in the air, and sniffed due south. One would really have thought there was something remarkable to be found there.

From 88° 25′ S. the barometer and hypsometer indicated slowly but surely that the plateau was beginning to descend toward the other side. This was a pleasant surprise to us; we had thus not only found the very summit of the plateau, but also the slope down on the far side. This would have a very important bearing for obtaining an idea of the construction of the whole plateau. On December 9 observations and dead reckoning agreed within a mile. The same result again on the 10th: observation 2 kilometers behind reckoning. The weather and going remained about the same as on the preceding days: light southeasterly breeze, temperature −18.4° F. The snow surface was loose, but ski and sledges glided over it well. On the 11th, the same weather conditions.

Temperature −13° F. Observation and reckoning again agreed exactly. Our latitude was 89° 15′ S. On the 12th we reached 89° 30′, reckoning 1 kilometer behind observation. Going and surface as good as ever. Weather splendid—calm with sunshine. The noon observation on the 13th gave 89° 37′ S. Reckoning 89° 38.5′ S. We halted in the afternoon, after going eight geographical miles, and camped in 89° 45′, according to reckoning.

The weather during the forenoon had been just as fine as before; in the afternoon we had some snow showers from the southeast. It was like the eve of some great festival that night in the tent. One could feel that a great event was at hand. Our flag was taken out again and lashed to the same two ski sticks as before. Then it was rolled up and laid aside, to be ready when the time came. I was awake several times during the night, and had the same feeling that I can remember as a little boy on the night before Christmas Eve—an intense expectation of what was going to happen. Otherwise I think we slept just as well that night as any other.

On the morning of December 14 the weather was of the finest, just as if it had been made for arriving at the Pole. I am not quite sure, but I believe we dispatched our breakfast rather more quickly than usual and were out of the tent sooner, though I must admit that we always accomplished this with all reasonable haste. We went in the usual order— the forerunner, Hanssen, Wisting, Bjaaland, and the reserve forerunner. By noon we had reached 89° 53′ by dead reckoning, and made ready to take the rest in one stage. At 10 A.M. a light breeze had sprung up from the southeast, and it had clouded over, so that we got no noon altitude; but the clouds were not thick, and from time to time we had a glimpse of the sun through them. The going on that day was rather different from what it had been; sometimes the ski went over it well, but at others it was pretty bad. We advanced that day in the same mechanical way as before; not much was said, but eyes were used all the more. Hanssen's neck grew twice as long as before in his endeavor to see a few inches farther. I had asked him before we started to spy out ahead for all he was worth, and he did so with a vengeance. But, however keenly he stared, he could not descry anything but the end-less flat plain ahead of us. The dogs had dropped their scent-ing, and appeared to have lost their interest in the regions about the earth's axis.

At three in the afternoon a simultaneous "Halt" rang out from the drivers. They had carefully examined their sledge meters, and they all showed the full distance—our Pole by reckoning. The goal was reached, the journey ended. I can-not say—though I know it would sound much more effective —that the object of my life was attained. That would be romancing rather too barefacedly. I had better be honest and admit straight out that I have never known any man to be placed in such a diametrically opposite position to the goal of his desires as I was at that moment. The regions around the North Pole—well, yes, the North Pole itself—had attracted me from childhood, and here I was at the South Pole. Can anything more topsy-turvy be imagined?

We reckoned now that we were at the Pole. Of course, every one of us knew that we were not standing on the absolute spot; it would be an impossibility with the time and the instruments at our disposal to ascertain that exact spot. But we were so near it that the few miles which possibly separated us from it could not be of the slightest importance. It was our intention to make a circle round this camp, with a radius of twelve and a half miles, and to be satisfied with that. After we had halted we collected and congratulated each other. We had good grounds for mutual respect in what had been achieved, and I think that was just the feeling that was expressed in the firm and powerful grasps of the fist that were exchanged. After this we proceeded to the greatest and most solemn act of the whole journey—the planting of our flag. Pride and affection shone in the five pairs of eyes that gazed upon the flag, as it unfurled itself with a sharp crack, and waved over the Pole. I had determined that the act of planting it—the historic event—should be equally divided among us all. It was not for one man to do this; it was for *all* who had staked their lives in the struggle, and held together through thick and thin. This was the only way in which I could show my gratitude to my comrades in this desolate spot. I could see that they understood and accepted it in the spirit in which it was offered. Five weatherbeaten, frostbitten fists they were that grasped the pole, raised the waving flag in the air, and planted it as the first at the geographical South Pole. "Thus we plant thee, beloved flag, at the South Pole, and give to the plain on which it lies the name of King Haakon VII's Plateau." That moment will certainly be remembered by all of us who stood there.

One gets out of the way of protracted ceremonies in those regions—the shorter they are the better. Everyday life began again at once. When we had got the tent up, Hanssen set about slaughtering Helge, and it was hard for him to have to part from his best friend. Helge had been an uncommonly useful and good-natured dog; without making any fuss he had pulled from morning to night, and had been a shining example to the team. But during the last week he had quite fallen away, and on our arrival at the Pole there was only a shadow of the old Helge left. He was only a drag on the others, and did absolutely no work. One blow on the skull, and Helge had ceased to live. "What is death to one is food to another," is a saying that can scarcely find a better application than these dog meals. Helge was portioned out on the spot, and within a couple of hours there was nothing left of him but his teeth and the tuft at the end of his tail. This was the second of our eighteen dogs that we had lost. The Major, one of Wisting's fine dogs, left us in 88° 25' S., and never returned. He was fearfully worn out, and must have gone away to die. We now had sixteen dogs left, and these we intended to divide into two equal teams, leaving Bjaaland's sledge behind.

Of course, there was a festivity in the tent that evening—not that champagne corks were popping and wine flowing—no, we contented ourselves with a little piece of seal meat each, and it tasted well and did us good. There was no other sign of festival indoors. Outside we heard the flag flapping in the breeze. Conversation was lively in the tent that evening, and we talked of many things. Perhaps, too, our thoughts sent messages home of what we had done.

Everything we had with us had now to be marked with the words "South Pole" and the date, to serve afterward as souvenirs. Wisting proved to be a firstclass engraver, and many were the articles he had to mark. Tobacco—in the form of smoke—had hitherto never made its appearance in the tent. From time to time I had seen one or two of the others take a quid, but now these things were to be altered. I had brought with me an old briar pipe, which bore inscriptions from many places in the Arctic regions, and now I wanted it marked "South Pole." When I produced my pipe and was about to mark it, I received an unexpected gift: Wisting offered me tobacco for the rest of the journey. He had some cakes of plug in his kit bag, which he would prefer to see me smoke. Can anyone grasp what such an offer meant at such a spot, made to a man who, to tell the truth, is very fond of a smoke after meals? There are not many who can understand it fully. I accepted the offer, jumping with joy, and on the way home I had a pipe of fresh, fine-cut plug every evening. Ah! that Wisting, he spoiled me entirely. Not only did he give me tobacco, but every evening—and I must confess I yielded to the temptation after a while, and had a morning smoke as well—he undertook the disagreeable work of cutting the plug and filling my pipe in all kinds of weather.

But we did not let our talk make us forget other things. As we had got no noon altitude, we should have to try and take one at midnight. The weather had brightened again, and it looked as if midnight would be a good time for the observation. We therefore crept into our bags to get a little nap in the intervening hours. In good time—soon after 11 P.M.—we were out again, and ready to catch the sun; the weather was of the best, and the opportunity excellent. We four navigators all had a share in it, as usual, and stood watching the course of the sun. This was a labor of patience, as the difference of altitude was now very slight. The result at which we finally arrived was of great interest, as it clearly shows how unreliable and valueless a single observation like this is in these regions. At 12.30 A.M. we put our instruments away, well satisfied with our work, and quite convinced that it was the midnight altitude that we had observed. The calculations which were carried out immediately afterward gave us 89° 56′ S. We were all well pleased with this result.

The arrangement now was that we should encircle this camp with a radius of about twelve and a half miles. By encircling I do not, of course, mean that we should go round in a circle with this radius; that would have taken us days, and was not to be thought of. The encircling was accomplished in this way: Three men went out in three different directions, two at right angles to the course we had been steering, and one in continuation of that course. To carry out this work I had chosen Wisting, Hassel, and Bjaaland. Having concluded our observations, we put the kettle on to give ourselves a drop of chocolate; the pleasure of standing out there in rather light attire had not exactly put warmth into our bodies. As we were engaged in swallowing the scalding drink, Bjaaland suddenly observed: "I'd like to tackle this encircling straight away. We shall have lots of time to sleep when we get back." Hassel and Wisting were quite of the same opinion, and it was agreed that they should start the work immediately. Here we have yet another example of the good spirit that prevailed in our little community. We had only lately come in from our day's work—a march of about eighteen and a half miles—and now they were asking to be allowed to go on another twenty-five miles. It seemed as if these fellows could never be tired. We therefore turned this meal into a little breakfast—that is to say, each man ate what he wanted of his bread ration, and then they began to get ready for the work. First, three small bags of light windproof stuff were made, and in each of these was placed a paper, giving the position of our camp. In addition, each of them carried a large square flag of the same dark brown material, which could be easily seen at a distance. As flagpoles we elected to use our spare sledge runners, which were both long—12 feet—and strong, and which we were going to take off here in any case, to lighten the sledges as much as possible for the return journey.

Thus equipped, and with thirty biscuits as an extra ration, the three men started off in the directions laid down. Their march was by no means free from danger, and does great honor to those who undertook it, not merely without raising the smallest objection, but with the greatest keenness. Let us consider for a moment the risk they ran. Our tent on the boundless plain, without marks of any kind, may very well be compared with a needle in a haystack. From this the three men were to steer out for a distance of twelve and a half miles. Compasses would have been good things to take on such a walk, but our sledge compasses were too heavy and unsuitable for carrying. They therefore had to go without. They had the sun to go by, certainly, when they started, but who could say how long it would last? The weather was then fine enough, but it was impossible to guarantee that no sudden change would take place. If by bad luck the sun should be hidden, then their own tracks might help them. But to trust to tracks in these regions is a dangerous thing. Before you know where you are the whole plain may be one mass of driving snow, obliterating all tracks as soon as they are made. With the rapid changes of weather we had so often experienced, such a thing was not impossible. That these three risked their lives that morning, when they left the tent at 2.30, there can be no doubt at all, and they all three knew it very well. But if anyone thinks that on this account they took a solemn farewell of us who stayed behind, he is much mistaken. Not a bit; they all vanished in their different directions amid laughter and chaff.

The first thing we did—Hanssen and I—was to set about arranging a lot of trifling matters; there was something to be done here, something there, and above all we had to be ready for the series of observations we were to carry out together, so as to get as accurate a determination of our position as possible. The first observation told us at once how necessary this was. For it turned out that this, instead of giving us a greater altitude than the midnight observation, gave us a smaller one, and it was then clear that we had gone out of the meridian we thought we were following. Now the first thing to be done was to get our north and south line and latitude determined, so that we could find our position once more. Luckily for us, the weather looked as if it would hold. We measured the sun's altitude at every hour from 6 A.M. to 7 P.M., and from these observations found, with some degree of certainty, our latitude and the direction of the meridian.

By nine in the morning we began to expect the return of our comrades; according to our calculation they should then have covered the distance—twenty-five miles. It was not till ten o'clock that Hanssen made out the first black dot on the horizon, and not long after the second and third appeared. We both gave a sigh of relief as they came on; almost simultaneously the three arrived at the tent. We told them the result of our observations up to that time; it looked as if our camp was in about 89° 54′ 30″ S., and that with our encircling we had therefore included the actual Pole. With this result we might very well have been content, but as the weather was so good and gave the impression that it would continue so, and our store of provisions proved on examination to be very ample, we decided to go on for the remaining ten kilometers (five and a half geographical miles), and get our position determined as near to the Pole as possible. Meanwhile the three wanderers turned in—not so much because they were tired, as because it was the right thing to do—and Hanssen and I continued the series of observations.

In the afternoon we again went very carefully through our provision supply before discussing the future. The result was that we had food enough for ourselves and the dogs for eighteen days. The surviving sixteen dogs were divided into two teams of eight each, and the contents of Bjaaland's sledge were shared between Hanssen's and Wisting's. The abandoned sledge was set upright in the snow, and proved to be a splendid mark. The sledge meter was screwed to the sledge, and we left it there; our other two were quite sufficient for the return journey; they had all shown themselves very accurate. A couple of empty provision cases were also left behind. I wrote in pencil on a piece of case the information that our tent—"Polheim"—would be found five and a half geographical miles northwest quarter west by compass from the sledge. Having put all these things in order the same day, we turned in, very well satisfied.

Early next morning, December 16, we were on our feet again. Bjaaland, who had now left the company of the drivers and been received with jubilation into that of the forerunners, was immediately entrusted with the honorable task of leading the expedition forward to the Pole itself. I assigned this duty, which we all regarded as a distinction, to him as a mark of gratitude to the gallant Telemarkers for their preeminent work in the advancement of ski sport. The leader that day had to keep as straight as a line, and if possible to follow the direction of our meridian. A little way after Bjaaland came Hassel, then Hanssen, then Wisting, and I followed a good way behind. I could thus check the direction of the march very accurately, and see that no great deviation was made. Bjaaland on this occasion showed himself a matchless forerunner; he went perfectly straight the whole time. Not once did he incline to one side or the other, and when we arrived at the end of the distance, we could still clearly see the sledge we had set up and take its bearing. This showed it to be absolutely in the right direction.

It was 11 A.M. when we reached our destination. While some of us were putting up the tent, others began to get everything ready for the coming observations. A solid snow pedestal was put up, on which the artificial horizon was to be placed, and a smaller one to rest the sextant on when it was not in use. At 11:30 A.M. the first observation was taken. We divided ourselves into two parties—Hanssen and I in one, Hassel and Wisting in the other. While one party slept, the other took the observations, and the watches were of six hours each. The weather was altogether grand, though the sky was not perfectly bright the whole time. A very light, fine, vaporous curtain would spread across the sky from time to time, and then quickly disappear again. This film of cloud was not thick enough to hide the sun, which we could see the whole time, but the atmosphere seemed to be disturbed. The effect of this was that the sun appeared not to change its altitude for several hours, until it suddenly made a jump.

Observations were now taken every hour through the whole twenty-four. It was very strange to turn in at 6 P.M., and then on turning out again at midnight to find the sun apparently still at the same altitude, and then once more at 6 A.M. to see it still no higher. The altitude had changed, of course, but so slightly that it was imperceptible with the naked eye. To us it appeared as though the sun made the circuit of the heavens at exactly the same altitude. The times of day that I have given here are calculated according to the meridian of Framheim; we continued to reckon our time from this. The observations soon told us that we were not on the absolute Pole, but as close to it as we could hope to get with our instruments.

On December 17 at noon we had completed our observations, and it is certain that we had done all that could be done. In order if possible to come a few inches nearer to the actual Pole, Hanssen and Bjaaland went out four geographical miles (seven kilometers) in the direction of the newly found meridian.

Bjaaland astonished me at dinner that day. Speeches had not hitherto been a feature of this journey, but now Bjaaland evidently thought the time had come, and surprised us all with a really fine oration. My amazement reached its culmination when, at the conclusion of his speech, he produced a cigar case full of cigars and offered it round. A cigar at the Pole! What do you say to that? But it did not end there. When the cigars had gone round, there were still four left. I was quite touched when he handed the case and cigars to me with the words: "Keep this to remind you of the Pole." I have taken good care of the case, and shall preserve it as one of the many happy signs of my comrades' devotion on this journey. The cigars I shared out afterward, on Christmas Eve, and they gave us a visible mark of that occasion.

When this festival dinner at the Pole was ended, we began our preparations for departure. First we set up the little tent we had brought with us in case we should be compelled to divide into two parties. It had been made by our able sail-maker, Rönne, and was of very thin windproof gabardine. Its drab color made it easily visible against the white surface. Another pole was lashed to the tent pole, making its total height about 13 feet. On the top of this a little Norwegian flag was lashed fast, and underneath it a pennant, on which "Fram" was painted. The tent was well secured with guy ropes on all sides. Inside the tent, in a little bag, I left a letter, addressed to H.M. the King, giving information of what we had accomplished. The way home was a long one, and so many things might happen to make it impossible for us to give an account of our expedition. Besides this letter, I wrote a short epistle to Captain Scott, who, I assumed, would be the first to find the tent. Other things we left there were a sextant with a glass horizon, a hypsometer case, three reindeerskin foot bags, some kamiks and mitts.

When everything had been laid inside, we went into the tent, one by one, to write our names on a tablet we had fastened to the tent pole. On this occasion we received the congratulations of our companions on the successful result, for the following messages were written on a couple of strips of leather, sewed to the tent: "Good luck," and "Welcome to 90°." These good wishes, which we suddenly discovered, put us in very good spirits. They were signed by Beck and Rönne. They had good faith in us. When we had finished this we came out, and the tent door was securely laced together, so that there was no danger of the wind getting a hold on that side.

And so good-by to Polheim. It was a solemn moment when

we bared our heads and bade farewell to our home and our flag. And then the traveling tent was taken down and the sledges packed. Now the homeward journey was to begin—homeward, step by step, mile after mile, until the whole distance was accomplished. We drove at once into our old tracks and followed them. Many were the times we turned to send a last look to Polheim. The vaporous, white air set in again, and it was not long before the last of Polheim, our little flag, disappeared from view.

ROBERT FALCON SCOTT

(*1868–1912*)

THE GREAT BRITISH EXPLORER Robert Falcon Scott devoted most of his life to the service of the Royal Navy. He became a naval cadet at thirteen, a midshipman at fifteen and a full lieutenant at twenty-three. He was recognized as a man of high intelligence, whose admirable personal style made him a natural leader. He was reticent, sensitive and moody. He was a naval commander at the time he was chosen to lead his first Antarctic expedition, formally known as the National Antarctic Expedition (1901–04), but sometimes referred to as the *Discovery* expedition after the ship in which the exploration was made. The *Discovery*, of about 700 tons, was specially built for Antarctic work.

Scott based himself on one of the southernmost points of

Ross Island: Hut Point, in what is now McMurdo Station. From the beginning he was intent on starting as close to the Pole as he could. Ross Island, as has been mentioned earlier, is the point farthest south that is accessible by ship.

Scott's was the first party since Ross's in 1841 to enter McMurdo Sound, to see Ross Island and to study the Ross Ice Shelf. On this expedition Scott introduced a number of Nansen's Arctic techniques into Antarctic work and opened the era of full-scale land exploration of the continent, using sledging traverses. He made numerous geographical discoveries, among them Edward VII Land, which much later was found to be a peninsula and was renamed accordingly. He, Shackleton and Wilson reached a new farthest south of 82° 17' on December 30, 1902.

Scott's second and last expedition left England in June 1910 on the *Terra Nova*. Because of ice conditions that year Scott was unable to base himself again at Hut Point. He chose Cape Evans instead, some fifteen miles to the north, and built the second of his now famous huts there. Like Cook, he was greatly interested in the scientific work of his expeditions, to such an extent that he often tempered the fevers of geographical exploration in order to gather and retain the materials for scientific investigation. His expeditions, like Cook's and Ross's, were assigned both geographic and scientific goals. But always, Scott's and the British nation's prime hope was the discovery of the Pole.

Scott and four companions—Wilson, Bowers, Oates and Evans— left their last polar support party in November 1911 and reached the Pole January 18, 1912, only to find they had been bested by Amundsen. Their return journey was beset by illness, hunger and blizzards. Evans died February 17. On March 17 Oates walked out of the tent into a blizzard in the hope of saving those more physically fit. Scott, Wilson and Bowers pitched their final cámp only some eleven miles from One Ton Depot on the Ross Ice Shelf but were hopelessly blizzarded in. Scott, in a great naval tradition of keeping logs even under the most adverse circumstances, kept writing his journal until close to the end. When he realized that the end was imminent, he wrote several letters to friends and colleagues detailing what had gone wrong and crediting his companions with noble behavior under heart-breaking conditions. In these letters he referred to himself and his companions as dead men. But there is no self-pity and not much self-concern in either the journals or the letters. His outlook remained broad to the end, even though he probably made no assumption that his journals and letters would be found.

On November 12, 1912 a search party discovered his tent, containing his body and those of Wilson and Bowers, as well as his records, letters and journals. On the sledge were thirty-five pounds of geological specimens, gathered on the Beardmore Glacier, which the party had declined to abandon despite the fact that for a long time they had been exhausting themselves in manhauling this material.

The Last March

Tuesday, January 16. Camp 68. Height 9760. T. −23.5°. The worst has happened, or nearly the worst. We marched well in the morning and covered 7½ miles. Noon sight showed us in Lat. 89° 42′ S., and we started off in high spirits in the afternoon, feeling that to-morrow would see us at our destination. About the second hour of the march Bowers' sharp eyes detected what he thought was a cairn; he was uneasy about it, but argued that it must be a sastrugus. Half an hour later he detected a black speck ahead. Soon we knew that this could not be a natural snow feature. We marched on, found that it was a black flag tied to a sledge bearer; near by the remains of a camp; sledge tracks and ski tracks going and coming and the clear trace of dogs' paws—many dogs. This told us the whole story. The Norwegians have forestalled us and are first at the Pole. It is a terrible disappointment, and I am very sorry for my loyal companions. Many thoughts come and much discussion have we had. To-morrow we must march on to the Pole and then hasten home with all the speed we can compass. All the daydreams must go; it will be a wearisome return. We are descending in altitude—certainly also the Norwegians found an easy way up.

Wednesday, January 17. Camp 69. T. −22° at start. Night −21°. The Pole. Yes, but under very different circumstances from those expected. We have had a horrible day—add to our disappointment a head wind 4 to 5, with a temperature −22°, and companions labouring on with cold feet and hands.

We started at 7.30, none of us having slept much after the shock of our discovery. We followed the Norwegian sledge tracks for some way; as far as we make out there are only two men. In about three miles we passed two small cairns. Then the weather overcast, and the tracks being increasingly drifted up and obviously going too far to the west, we decided to make straight for the Pole according to our calculations. At 12.30 Evans had such cold hands we camped for lunch—an excellent 'week-end one.' We had marched 7.4 miles. Lat. sight. gave 89° 53′ 37″. We started out and did 6½ miles due south. To-night little Bowers is laying himself out to get sights in terrible difficult circumstances; the wind is blowing hard, T. −21°, and there is that curious damp, cold feeling in the air which chills one to the bone in no time. We have been descending again, I think, but there looks to be a rise ahead; otherwise there is very little that is different from the awful monotony of past days. Great God! this is an awful place and terrible enough for us to have laboured to it without the reward of priority. Well, it is something to have got here, and the wind may be our friend to-morrow. We have had a fat Polar hoosh in spite of our chagrin, and feel comfortable inside—added a small stick of chocolate and the queer taste of a cigarette brought by Wilson. Now for the run home and a desperate struggle. I wonder if we can do it.

Thursday morning, January 18. Decided after summing up all observations that we were 3.5 miles away from the Pole

—one mile beyond it and 3 to the right. More or less in this direction Bowers saw a cairn or tent.

We have just arrived at this tent, 2 miles from our camp, therefore about 1½ miles from the Pole. In the tent we find a record of five Norwegians having been here, as follows:

Roald Amundsen
Olav Olavson Bjaaland
Hilmer Hanssen
Sverre H. Hassel
Oscar Wisting.   16 Dec. 1911.

The tent is fine—a small compact affair supported by a single bamboo. A note from Amundsen, which I keep, asks me to forward a letter to King Haakon!

The following articles have been left in the tent: 3 half bags of reindeer containing a miscellaneous assortment of mits and sleeping socks, very various in description, a sextant, a Norwegian artificial horizon and a hypsometer without boiling-point thermometers, a sextant and hypsometer of English make.

Left a note to say I had visited the tent with companions. Bowers photographing and Wilson sketching. Since lunch we have marched 6.2 miles S.S.E. by compass (i.e. northwards). Sights at lunch gave us ½ to ¾ of a mile from the Pole, so we call it the Pole Camp. (Temp. Lunch −21°.) We built a cairn, put up our poor slighted Union Jack, and photographed ourselves—mighty cold work all of it—less than ½ a mile south we saw stuck up an old underrunner of a sledge. This we commandeered as a yard for a floorcloth sail. I imagine it was intended to mark the exact spot of the Pole as near as the Norwegians could fix it. (Height 9500.) A note attached talked of the tent as being 2 miles from the Pole. Wilson keeps the note. There is no doubt that our predecessors have made thoroughly sure of their mark and fully carried out their programme. I think the Pole is about 9500 feet in height; this is remarkable, considering that in Lat. 88° we were about 10,500.

We carried the Union Jack about ¾ of a mile north with us and left it on a piece of stick as near as we could fix it. I fancy the Norwegians arrived at the pole on the 15th Dec. and left on the 17th, ahead of a date quoted by me in London as ideal, viz. Dec. 22. It looks as though the Norwegian party expected colder weather on the summit than they got; it could scarcely be otherwise from Shackleton's account. Well, we have turned our back now on the goal of our ambition and must face our 800 miles of solid dragging—and good-bye to most of the day-dreams!

Friday, January 19. Lunch 8.1, T. −22.6°. Early in the march we picked up a Norwegian cairn and our outward tracks. We followed these to the ominous black flag which has first apprised us of our predecessors' success. We have picked this flag up, using the staff for our sail, and are now camped about 1½ miles further back on our tracks. So that is the last of the Norwegians for the present. The surface undulates considerably about this latitude; it was more evident to-day than when we were outward bound.

Night camp R. 2.* Height 9700. T. −18.5°, Minimum −25.6°. Came along well this afternoon for three hours, then a rather dreary finish for the last 1½. Weather very curious, snow clouds, looking very dense and spoiling the light, pass overhead from the S., dropping very minute crystals; between showers the sun shows and the wind goes to the S.W. The fine crystals absolutely spoil the surface; we had heavy dragging during the last hour in spite of the light load and a full sail. Our old tracks are drifted up, deep in places, and toothed sastrugi have formed over them. It looks as though this sandy snow was drifted about like sand from place to place. How account for the present state of our three day old tracks and the month old ones of the Norwegians?

It is warmer and pleasanter marching with the wind, but

---

* A number preceded by R. marks the camps on the return journey.—L.H. [Leonard Huxley, the editor of *Scott's Last Expedition.*]

I'm not sure we don't feel the cold more when we stop and camp than we did on the outward march. We pick up our cairns easily, and ought to do so right through, I think; but, of course, one will be a bit anxious till the Three Degree Depôt is reached.* I'm afraid the return journey is going to be dreadfully tiring and monotonous.

Saturday, January 20. Lunch camp, 9810. We have come along very well this morning, although the surface was terrible bad—9.3 miles in 5 hours 20 m. This has brought us to our Southern Depôt, and we pick up 4 days' food. We carry on 7 days from to-night with 55 miles to go to the Half Degree Depôt made on January 10. The same sort of weather and a little more wind, sail drawing well.

Night Camp R. 3. 9860. Temp. —18°. It was blowing quite hard and drifting when we started our afternoon march. At first with full sail we went along at a great rate; then we got on to an extraordinary surface, the drifting snow lying in heaps; it clung to the ski, which could only be pushed forward with an effort. The pulling was really awful, but we went steadily on and camped a short way beyond our cairn of the 14th. I'm afraid we are in for a bad pull again to-morrow, luckily the wind holds. I shall be very glad when Bowers gets his ski; I'm afraid he must find these long marches very trying with short legs, but he is an undefeated little sportsman. I think Oates is feeling the cold and fatigue more than most of us. It is blowing pretty hard to-night, but with a good march we have earned one good hoosh and are very comfortable in the tent. It is everything now to keep up a good marching pace; I trust we shall be able to do so and catch the ship. Total march, 18½ miles.

Sunday, January 21. R. 4. 10,010. Temp. blizzard, —18° to —11°, to —14° now. Awoke to a stiff blizzard; air very thick with snow and sun very dim. We decided not to march owing

* Still over 150 miles away. They had marched 7 miles on the homeward track the first afternoon, 18½ the second day.—L.H.

to likelihood of losing track; expected at least a day of lay up, but whilst at lunch there was a sudden clearance and wind dropped to light breeze. We got ready to march, but gear was so iced up we did not get away till 3.45. Marched till 7.40— a terribly weary four-hour drag; even with helping wind we only did 5½ miles (6¼ statute). The surface bad, horribly bad on new sastrugi, and decidedly rising again in elevation.

We are going to have a pretty hard time this next 100 miles I expect. If it was difficult to drag downhill over this belt, it will probably be a good deal more difficult to drag up. Luckily the cracks are fairly distinct, though we only see our cairns when less than a mile away; 45 miles to the next depôt and 6 days' food in hand—then pick up 7 days' food (T. −22°) and 90 miles to go to the 'Three Degree' Depôt. Once there we ought to be safe, but we ought to have a day or two in hand on arrival and may have difficulty with following the tracks. However, if we can get a rating sight for our watches to-morrow we shall be independent of the tracks at a pinch.

Monday, January 22. 10,000. Temp. −21°. I think about the most tiring march we have had; solid pulling the whole way, in spite of the light sledge and some little helping wind at first. Then in the last part of the afternoon the sun came out, and almost immediately we had the whole surface covered with soft snow.

We got away sharp at 8 and marched a solid 9 hours, and thus we have covered 14.5 miles (geo.) but, by Jove! it has been a grind. We are just about on the 89th parallel. To-night Bowers got a rating sight. I'm afraid we have passed out of the wind area. We are within 2½ miles of the 64th camp cairn, 30 miles from our depôt, and with 5 days' food in hand. Ski boots are beginning to show signs of wear; I trust we shall have no giving out of ski or boots, since there are yet so many miles to go. I thought we were climbing to-day, but the barometer gives no change.

Tuesday, January 23. Lowest Minimum last night −30°, Temp. at start −28°. Lunch height 10,100. Temp, with wind 6 to 7, −19°. Little wind and heavy marching at start. Then wind increased and we did 8.7 miles by lunch, when it was practically blowing a blizzard. The old tracks show so remarkably well that we can follow them without much difficulty—a great piece of luck.

In the afternoon we had to reorganise. Could carry a whole sail. Bowers hung on to the sledge, Evans and Oates had to lengthen out. We came along at a great rate and should have got within an easy march of our depôt had not Wilson suddenly discovered that Evans' nose was frostbitten—it was white and hard. We thought it best to camp at 6.45. Got the tent up with some difficulty, and now pretty cosy after good hoosh.

There is no doubt Evans is a good deal run down—his fingers are badly blistered and his nose is rather seriously congested with frequent frost bites. He is very much annoyed with himself, which is not a good sign. I think Wilson, Bowers and I are as fit as possible under the circumstances. Oates gets cold feet. One way and another, I shall be glad to get off the summit! We are only about 13 miles from our 'Degree and half' Depôt and should get there to-morrow. The weather seems to be breaking up. Pray God we have something of a track to follow to the Three Degree Depôt—once we pick that up we ought to be right.

Wednesday, January 24. Lunch Temp. −8°. Things beginning to look a little serious. A strong wind at the start has developed into a full blizzard at lunch, and we have had to get into our sleeping-bags. It was a bad march, but we covered 7 miles. At first Evans, and then Wilson went ahead to scout for tracks. Bowers guided the sledge alone for the first hour, then both Oates and he remained alongside it; they had a fearful time trying to make the pace between the soft patches. At 12.30 the sun coming ahead made it impossible to see the tracks further, and we had to stop. By this time the gale was at its height and we had the dickens of a time getting up the tent, cold fingers all round. We are only 7 miles from our depôt, but I made sure we should be there to-night. This is the second full gale since we left the Pole. I don't like the look of it. Is the weather breaking up? If so, God help us, with the tremendous summit journey and scant food. Wilson and Bowers are my standby. I don't like the easy way in which Oates and Evans get frostbitten.

Thursday, January 25. Temp. Lunch —11°, Temp. night —16°. Thank God we found our Half Degree Depôt. After lying in our bags yesterday afternoon and all night, we debated breakfast; decided to have it later and go without lunch. At the time the gale seemed as bad as ever, but during breakfast the sun showed and there was light enough to see the old track. It was a long and terribly cold job digging out our sledge and breaking camp, but we got through and on the march without sail, all pulling. This was about 11, and at about 2.30, to our joy, we saw the red depôt flag. We had lunch and left with 9½ days' provisions, still following the track—marched till 8 and covered over 5 miles, over 12 in the day. Only 89 miles (geogr.) to the next depôt, but it's time we cleared off this plateau. We are not without ailments: Oates suffers from a very cold foot; Evans' fingers and nose are in a bad state, and to-night Wilson is suffering tortures from his eyes. Bowers and I are the only members of the party without troubles just at present. The weather still looks unsettled, and I fear a succession of blizzards at this time of year; the wind is strong from the south, and this afternoon has been very helpful with the full sail. Needless to say I shall sleep much better with our provision bag full again. The only real anxiety now is the finding of the Three Degree Depôt. The tracks seem as good as ever so far; sometimes for 30 or 40 yards we lose them under drifts, but then they reappear quite clearly raised above the surface. If the light is good there is not the least difficulty in following. Blizzards are our bugbear, not only stopping our marches, but the cold damp air takes it out of us. Bowers got another rating sight to-night —it was wonderful how he managed to observe in such a horribly cold wind. He has been on ski to-day whilst Wilson walked by the sledge or pulled ahead of it.

Friday, January 26. Temp. −17°. Height 9700, must be high barometer. Started late, 8.50—for no reason, as I called the hands rather early. We must have fewer delays. There was a good stiff breeze and plenty of drift, but the tracks held. To our old blizzard camp of the 7th we got on well, 7 miles. But beyond the camp we found the tracks completely wiped out. We searched for some time, then marched on a short way and lunched, the weather gradually clearing, though the wind holding. Knowing there were two cairns at four mile intervals, we had little anxiety till we picked up the first far on our right, then steering right by a stroke of fortune, and Bowers' sharp eyes caught a glimpse of the second far on the left. Evidently we made a bad course outward at this part. There is not a sign of our tracks between these cairns, but the last, marking our night camp of the 6th, No. 59, is in the belt of hard sastrugi, and I was comforted to see signs of the track reappearing as we camped. I hope to goodness we can follow it to-morrow. We marched 16 miles (geo.) to-day, but made good only 15.4.

Saturday, January 27. R. 10. Temp. −16° (lunch), −14.3° (evening). Minimum −19°. Height 9900. Barometer low? Called the hands half an hour late, but we got away in good time. The forenoon march was over the belt of storm-tossed sastrugi; it looked like a rough sea. Wilson and I pulled in front on ski, the remainder on foot. It was very tricky work following the track, which pretty constantly disappeared, and in fact only showed itself by faint signs anywhere—a foot or two of raised sledge-track, a dozen yards of the trail of the sledgemeter wheel, or a spatter of hard snow-flicks where feet had trodden. Sometimes none of these were distinct, but one got an impression of lines which guided. The trouble was that on the outward track one had to shape course constantly to avoid the heaviest mounds, and consequently there were many zig-zags. We lost a good deal over a mile by these halts, in which we unharnessed and went on the search for signs. However, by hook or crook, we managed to stick on the old track. Came on the cairn quite suddenly, marched past it, and camped for lunch at 7 miles. In the afternoon the sastrugi gradually diminished in size and now we are on fairly level ground to-day, the obstruction practically at an end, and, to our joy, the tracks showing up much plainer again. For the last two hours we had no difficulty at all in following them. There has been a nice helpful southerly breeze all day, a clear sky and comparatively warm temperature. The air is dry again, so that tents and equipment are gradually losing their icy condition imposed by the blizzard conditions of the past week.

Our sleeping-bags are slowly but surely getting wetter and I'm afraid it will take a lot of this weather to put them right. However, we all sleep well enough in them, the hours allowed being now on the short side. We are slowly getting more hungry, and it would be an advantage to have a little more food, especially for lunch. If we get to the next depôt in a few marches (it is now less than 60 miles and we have a full week's food) we ought to be able to open out a little, but we can't look for a real feed till we get to the pony food depôt. A long way to go, and, by Jove, this is tremendous labour.

Sunday, January 28. Lunch, −20°. Height, night, 10,130. R. 11. Supper Temp. −18°. Little wind and heavy going in forenoon. We just ran out 8 miles in 5 hours and added another 8 in 3 hours 40 mins. in the afternoon with a good wind and better surface. It is very difficult to say if we are going up or down hill; the barometer is quite different from outward readings. We are 43 miles from the depôt, with six days' food in hand. We are camped opposite our lunch cairn of the 4th, only half a day's march from the point at which the last supporting party left us.

Three articles were dropped on our outward march—Oates' pipe, Bowers' fur mits, and Evans' night boots. We picked up the boots and mits on the track, and to-night we found the pipe lying placidly in sight on the snow. The sledge tracks were very easy to follow to-day; they are becoming more and more raised, giving a good line shadow often visible half a mile ahead. If this goes on and the weather holds we shall get our depôt without trouble. I shall indeed be glad to get it on the sledge. We are getting more hungry, there is no doubt. The lunch meal is beginning to seem inadequate. We are pretty thin, especially Evans, but none of us are feeling worked out. I doubt if we could drag heavy loads, but we can keep going well with our light one. We talk of food a good deal more, and shall be glad to open out on it.

Monday, January 29. R. 12. Lunch Temp. −23°. Supper Temp. −25°. Height 10,000. Excellent march of 19½ miles, 10.5 before lunch. Wind helping greatly, considerable drift; tracks for the most part very plain. Some time before lunch we picked up the return track of the supporting party, so that there are now three distinct sledge impressions. We are only 24 miles from our depôt—an easy day and a half. Given a fine day to-morrow we ought to get it without difficulty. The wind and sastrugi are S.S.E. and S.E. If the weather holds we ought to do the rest of the inland ice journey in little over a week. The surface is very much altered since we passed out. The loose snow has been swept into heaps, hard and wind-tossed. The rest has a glazed appearance, the loose drifting snow no doubt acting on it, polishing it like a sand blast. The sledge with our good wind behind runs splendidly on it; it is all soft and sandy beneath the glaze. We are certainly getting hungrier every day. The day after to-morrow we should be able to increase allowances. It is monotonous work, but, thank God, the miles are coming fast at last. We ought not to be delayed much now with the down-grade in front of us.

Tuesday, January 30. R. 13. 9860. Lunch Temp. −25°, Supper Temp. −24.5°. Thank the Lord, another fine march—19 miles. We have passed the last cairn before the depôt, the track is clear ahead, the weather fair, the wind helpful, the gradient down—with any luck we should pick up our depôt in the middle of the morning march. This is the bright side; the reverse of the medal is serious. Wilson has strained a tendon in his leg; it has given pain all day and is swollen to-night. Of course, he is full of pluck over it, but I don't like the idea of such an accident here. To add to the trouble Evans has dislodged two finger-nails to-night; his hands are really bad, and to my surprise he shows signs of losing heart over it. He hasn't been cheerful since the accident. The wind shifted from S.E. to S. and back again all day, but luckily it keeps strong. We can get along with bad fingers, but it [will be] a mighty serious thing if Wilson's leg doesn't improve.

Wednesday, January 31. 9800. Lunch Temp. −20°, Supper Temp. −20°. The day opened fine with a fair breeze; we marched on the depôt,* picked it up, and lunched an hour later. In the afternoon the surface became fearfully bad, the wind dropped to light southerly air. Ill luck that this should happen just when we have only four men to pull. Wilson rested his leg as much as possible by walking quietly beside the sledge; the result has been good, and to-night there is much less inflammation. I hope he will be all right again soon, but it is trying to have an injured limb in the party. I see we had a very heavy surface here on our outward march. There is no doubt we are travelling over undulations, but the inequality of level does not make a great difference to our pace; it is the sandy crystals that hold us up. There has been very great alteration of the surface since we were last here—the sledge tracks stand high. This afternoon we picked up Bowers' ski†—the last thing we have to find on the summit, thank

* Three Degree Depôt.—L.H.
† Left on December 31.—L.H.

Heaven! Now we have only to go north and so shall welcome strong winds.

Thursday, February 1. R. 15. 9778. Lunch Temp. −20°, Supper Temp. −19.8°. Heavy collar work most of the day. Wind light. Did 8 miles, 4¾ hours. Started well in the afternoon and came down a steep slope in quick time; then the surface turned real bad—sandy drifts—very heavy pulling. Working on past 8 P.M. we just fetched a lunch cairn of December 29, when we were only a week out from the depôt.* It ought to be easy to get in with a margin, having 8 days' food in hand (full feeding). We have opened out on the 1/7th increase and it makes a lot of difference. Wilson's leg much better. Evans' fingers now very bad, two nails coming off, blisters burst.

Friday, February 2. 9340. R. 16. Temp.: Lunch −19°, Supper −17°. We started well on a strong southerly wind. Soon got to a steep grade, when the sledge overran and upset us one after another. We got off our ski, and pulling on foot reeled off 9 miles by lunch at 1.30. Started in the afternoon on foot, going very strong. We noticed a curious circumstance towards the end of the forenoon. The tracks were drifted over, but the drifts formed a sort of causeway along which we pulled. In the afternoon we soon came to a steep slope—the same on which we exchanged sledges on December 28. All went well till, in trying to keep the track at the same time as my feet, on a very slippery surface, I came an awful 'purler' on my shoulder. It is horribly sore to-night and another sick person added to our tent—three out of five injured, and the most troublesome surfaces to come. We shall be lucky if we get through without serious injury. Wilson's leg is better, but might easily get bad again, and Evans' fingers.

At the bottom of the slope this afternoon we came on a

* The Upper Glacier Depôt, under Mount Darwin, where the first supporting party turned back.—L.H.

confused sea of sastrugi. We lost the track. Later, on soft snow, we picked up E. Evans' return track, which we are now following. We have managed to get off 17 miles. The extra food is certainly helping us, but we are getting pretty hungry. The weather is already a trifle warmer and the altitude lower, and only 80 miles or so to Mount Darwin. It is time we were off the summit—Pray God another four days will see us pretty well clear of it. Our bags are getting very wet and we ought to have more sleep.

Saturday, February 3. R. 17. Temp.: Lunch −20°; Supper −20°. Height 9040 feet. Started pretty well on foot; came to steep slope with crevasses (few). I went on ski to avoid another fall, and we took the slope gently with our sail, constantly losing the track, but picked up a much weathered cairn on our right. Vexatious delays, searching for tracks, &c., reduced morning march to 8.1 miles. Afternoon, came along a little better, but again lost tracks on hard slope. To-night we are near camp of December 26, but cannot see cairn. Have decided it is waste of time looking for tracks and cairn, and shall push on due north as fast as we can.

The surface is greatly changed since we passed outward, in most places polished smooth, but with heaps of new toothed sastrugi which are disagreeable obstacles. Evans' fingers are going on as well as can be expected, but it will be long before he will be able to help properly with the work. Wilson's leg *much* better, and my shoulder also, though it gives bad twinges. The extra food is doing us all good, but we ought to have more sleep. Very few more days on the Plateau I hope.

Sunday, February 4. R.18. 8620 feet. Temp.: Lunch −22°; Supper −23°. Pulled on foot in the morning over good hard surface and covered 9.7 miles. Just before lunch unexpectedly fell into crevasses, Evans and I together—a second fall for Evans, and I camped. After lunch saw disturbance ahead, and what I took for disturbance (land) to the right. We went on ski over hard shiny descending surface. Did very well, especially towards end of march, covering in all 18.1. We have come down some hundreds of feet. Half way in the march the land showed up splendidly, and I decided to make straight for Mt. Darwin, which we are rounding. Every sign points to getting away off this plateau. The temperature is 20° lower than when we were here before; the party is not improving in condition, especially Evans, who is becoming rather dull and incapable.* Thank the Lord we have good food at each meal, but we get hungrier in spite of it. Bowers is splendid, full of energy and bustle all the time. I hope we are not going to have trouble with ice-falls.

Monday, February 5. R. 19. Lunch, 8320 ft., Temp. −17°; Supper, 8120 ft., Temp. −17.2°. A good forenoon, few crevasses; we covered 10.2 miles. In the afternoon we soon got into difficulties. We saw the land very clearly, but the difficulty is to get at it. An hour after starting we came on huge pressures and great street crevasses partly open. We had to steer more and more to the west, so that our course was very erratic. Late in the march we turned more to the north and again encountered open crevasses across our track. It is very difficult manoeuvring amongst these and I should not like to do it without ski.

We are camped in a very disturbed region, but the wind has fallen very light here, and our camp is comfortable for the first time for many weeks. We may be anything from 25 to 30 miles from our depôt, but I wish to goodness we could see a way through the disturbances ahead. Our faces are much cut up by all the winds we have had, mine least of all; the others tell me they feel their noses more going with than against wind. Evans' nose is almost as bad as his fingers. He is a good deal crocked up.

Tuesday, February 6. Lunch 7900; Supper 7210. Temp. −15°. We've had a horrid day and not covered good mileage. On turning out found sky overcast; a beastly position amidst

---

* The result of concussion in the morning's fall.—L.H.

crevasses. Luckily it cleared just before we started. We went straight for Mt. Darwin, but in half an hour found ourselves amongst huge open chasms, unbridged, but not very deep, I think. We turned to the north between two, but to our chagrin they converged into chaotic disturbance. We had to retrace our steps for a mile or so, then struck to the west and got on to a confused sea of sastrugi, pulling very hard; we put up the sail, Evans' nose suffered, Wilson very cold, everything horrid. Camped for lunch in the sastrugi; the only comfort, things looked clearer to the west and we were obviously going downhill. In the afternoon we struggled on, got out of sastrugi and turned over on glazed surface, crossing many crevasses—very easy work on ski. Towards the end of the march we realised the certainty of maintaining a more or less straight course to the depôt, and estimate distance 10 to 15 miles.

Food is low and weather uncertain, so that many hours of the day were anxious; but this evening, though we are not as far advanced as I expected, the outlook is much more promising. Evans is the chief anxiety now; his cuts and wounds suppurate, his nose looks very bad, and altogether he shows considerable signs of being played out. Things may mend for him on the glacier, and his wounds get some respite under warmer conditions. I am indeed glad to think we shall so soon have done with plateau conditions. It took us 27 days to reach the Pole and 21 days back—in all 48 days—nearly 7 weeks in low temperature with almost incessant wind.

END OF THE SUMMIT JOURNEY

Wednesday, February 7. Mount Darwin [or Upper Glacier] Depôt, R. 21. Height 7100. Lunch Temp. −9°; Supper Temp. [a blank here]. A wretched day with satisfactory ending. First panic, certainty that biscuit-box was short. Great doubt as to how this has come about, as we certainly haven't over-issued allowances. Bowers is dreadfully disturbed about it. The shortage is a full day's allowance. We started our march at 8.30, and travelled down slopes and over terraces covered with hard sastrugi—very tiresome work—and the land didn't seem to come any nearer. At lunch the wind increased, and what with hot tea and good food, we started the afternoon in a better frame of mind, and it soon became obvious we were nearing our mark. Soon after 6.30 we saw our depôt easily and camped next it at 7.30.

Found note from E. Evans to say the second return party passed through safely at 2.30 on January 14—half a day longer between depôts than we have been. The temperature is higher, but there is a cold wind to-night.

Well, we have come through our 7 weeks' ice camp journey and most of us are fit, but I think another week might have had a very bad effect on P.O. Evans, who is going steadily downhill.

It is satisfactory to recall that these facts give absolute proof of both expeditions having reached the Pole and placed the question of priority beyond discussion.

Thursday, February 8. R. 22. Height 6260. Start Temp. −11°; Lunch Temp. −5°; Supper, zero. 9.2 miles. Started from the depôt rather late owing to weighing biscuit, &c., and rearranging matters. Had a beastly morning. Wind very strong and cold. Steered in for Mt. Darwin to visit rock. Sent Bowers on, on ski, as Wilson can't wear his at present. He obtained several specimens, all of much the same type, a close-grained granite rock which weathers red. Hence the pink limestone. After he rejoined we skidded downhill pretty fast, leaders on ski, Oates and Wilson on foot alongside sledge —Evans detached. We lunched at 2 well down towards Mt. Buckley, the wind half a gale and everybody very cold and cheerless. However, better things were to follow. We decided to steer for the moraine under Mt. Buckley and, pulling with crampons, we crossed some very irregular steep slopes with big crevasses and slid down towards the rocks. The moraine was obviously so interesting that when we had advanced some miles and got out of the wind, I decided to camp and spend the rest of the day geologising. It has been extremely interesting. We found ourselves under perpendicular cliffs of Beacon sandstone, weathering rapidly and carrying veritable coal seams. From the last Wilson, with his sharp eyes, has picked several plant impressions, the last a piece of coal with beautifully traced leaves in layers, also some excellently preserved impressions of thick stems, showing cellular structure. In one place we saw the cast of small waves on the sand. To-night Bill has got a specimen of limestone with archeo-cyathus—the trouble is one cannot imagine where the stone comes from; it is evidently rare, as few specimens occur in the moraine. There is a good deal of pure white quartz. Altogether we have had a most interesting afternoon, and the relief of being out of the wind and in a warmer temperature is inexpressible. I hope and trust we shall all buck up again now that the conditions are more favourable. We have been in shadow all the afternoon, but the sun has just reached us, a little obscured by night haze. A lot could be written on the delight of setting foot on rock after 14 weeks of snow and ice and nearly 7 out of sight of aught else. It is like going ashore after a sea voyage. We deserve a little good bright weather after all our trials, and hope to get a chance to dry our sleeping-bags and generally make our gear more comfortable.

Friday, February 9. R. 23. Height 5,210 ft. Lunch Temp. +10°; Supper Temp. +12.5°. About 13 miles. Kept along the edge of moraine to the end of Mt. Buckley. Stopped and geologised. Wilson got great find of vegetable impression in piece of limestone. Too tired to write geological notes. We all felt very slack this morning, partly rise of temperature, partly reaction, no doubt. Ought to have kept close in to glacier north of Mt. Buckley, but in bad light the descent looked steep and we kept out. Evidently we got amongst bad ice pressure and had to come down over an ice-fall. The crevasses were much firmer than expected and we got down with some difficulty, found our night camp of December 20, and lunched an hour after. Did pretty well in the afternoon, marching 3¾ hours; the sledgemeter is unshipped, so cannot tell distance traversed. Very warm on march and we are all pretty tired. To-night it is wonderfully calm and warm, though it has been overcast all the afternoon. It is remarkable to be able to stand outside the tent and sun oneself. Our food satisfies now, but we must march to keep in the full ration, and we want rest, yet we shall pull through all right, D.V. We are by no means worn out.

Saturday, February 10. R. 24. Lunch Temp. $+12°$; Supper Temp. $+10°$. Got off a good morning march in spite of keeping too far east and getting in rough, cracked ice. Had a splendid night sleep, showing great change in all faces, so didn't get away till 10 A.M. Lunched just before 3. After lunch the land began to be obscured. We held a course for 2½ hours with difficulty, then the sun disappeared, and snow drove in our faces with northerly wind—very warm and impossible to steer, so camped. After supper, still very thick all round, but sun showing and less snow falling. The fallen snow crystals are quite feathery like thistledown. We have two full days' food left, and though our position is uncertain, we are certainly within two outward marches from the middle glacier depôt. However, if the weather doesn't clear by to-morrow, we must either march blindly on or reduce food. It is very trying. Another night to make up arrears of sleep. The ice crystals that first fell this afternoon were very large. Now the sky is clearer overhead, the temperature has fallen slightly, and the crystals are minute.

Sunday, February 11. R. 25. Lunch Temp. $-6.5°$; Supper $-3.5°$. The worst day we have had during the trip and greatly owing to our own fault. We started on a wretched surface with light S.W. wind, sail set, and pulling on ski—horrible light, which made everything look fantastic. As we went on light got worse, and suddenly we found ourselves in pressure.

Then came the fatal decision to steer east. We went on for 6 hours, hoping to do a good distance, which in fact I suppose we did, but for the last hour or two we pressed on into a regular trap. Getting on to a good surface we did not reduce our lunch meal, and thought all going well, but half an hour after lunch we got into the worst ice mess I have ever been in. For three hours we plunged on on ski, first thinking we were too much to the right, then too much to the left; meanwhile the disturbance got worse and my spirits received a very rude shock. There were times when it seemed almost impossible to find a way out of the awful turmoil in which we found ourselves. At length, arguing that there must be a way on our left, we plunged in that direction. It got worse, harder, more icy and crevassed. We could not manage our ski and pulled on foot, falling into crevasses every minute—most luckily no bad accident. At length we saw a smoother slope towards the land, pushed for it, but knew it was a woefully long way from us. The turmoil changed in character, irregular crevassed surface giving way to huge chasms, closely packed and most difficult to cross. It was very heavy work, but we had grown desperate. We won through at 10 P.M. and I write after 12 hours on the march. I *think* we are on or about the right track now, but we are still a good number of miles from the depôt, so we reduced rations to-night. We had three pemmican meals left and decided to make them into four. To-morrow's lunch must serve for two if we do not make big progress. It was a test of our endurance on the march and our fitness with small supper. We have come through well. A good wind has come down the glacier which is clearing the sky and surface. Pray God the wind holds to-morrow. Short sleep to-night and off first thing, I hope.

Monday, February 12. R. 26. In a very critical situation. All went well in the forenoon, and we did a good long march over a fair surface. Two hours before lunch we were cheered by the sight of our night camp of the 18th December, the day after we made our depôt—this showed we were on the right track. In the afternoon, refreshed by tea, we went forward, confident of covering the remaining distance, but by a fatal chance we kept too far to the left, and then we struck uphill and, tired and despondent, arrived in a horrid maze of crevasses and fissures. Divided councils caused our course to be erratic after this, and finally, at 9 P.M. we landed in the worst place of all. After discussion we decided to camp, and here we are, after a very short supper and one meal only remaining in the food bag; the depôt doubtful in locality. We *must* get there to-morrow. Meanwhile we are cheerful with an effort. It's a tight place, but luckily we've been well fed up to the present. Pray God we have fine weather to-morrow.

[At this point the bearings of the mid-glacier depôt are given, but need not be quoted.]

Tuesday, February 13. Camp R. 27, beside Cloudmaker. Temp. −10°. Last night we all slept well in spite of our grave anxieties. For my part these were increased by my visits outside the tent, when I saw the sky gradually closing over and snow beginning to fall. By our ordinary time for getting up it was dense all around us. We could see nothing, and we could only remain in our sleeping-bags. At 8.30 I dimly made out the land of the Cloudmaker. At 9 we got up, deciding to have tea, and with one biscuit, no pemmican, so as to leave our scanty remaining meal for eventualities. We started marching, and at first had to wind our way through an awful turmoil of broken ice, but in about an hour we hit an old moraine track, brown with dirt. Here the surface was much smoother and improved rapidly. The fog still hung over all and we went on for an hour, checking our bearings. Then the whole place got smoother and we turned outward a little. Evans raised our hopes with a shout of depôt ahead, but it proved to be a shadow on the ice. Then suddenly Wilson saw the actual depôt flag. It was an immense relief, and we were soon in possession of our 3½ days' food. The relief to all is inexpressible; needless to say, we camped and had a meal.

Marching in the afternoon, I kept more to the left, and

closed the mountain till we fell on the stone moraines. Here Wilson detached himself and made a collection, whilst we pulled the sledge on. We camped late, abreast the lower end of the mountain, and had nearly our usual satisfying supper. Yesterday was the worst experience of the trip and gave a horrid feeling of insecurity. Now we are right up, we must march. In future food must be worked so that we do not run so short if the weather fails us. We mustn't get into a hole like this again. Greatly relieved to find that both the other parties got through safely. Evans seems to have got mixed up with pressures like ourselves. It promises to be a very fine day to-morrow. The valley is gradually clearing. Bowers has had a very bad attack of snow blindness, and Wilson another almost as bad. Evans has no power to assist with camping work.

Wednesday, February 14. Lunch Temp. 0°; Supper Temp. −1°. A fine day with wind on and off down the glacier, and we have done a fairly good march. We started a little late and pulled on down the moraine. At first I thought of going right, but soon, luckily, changed my mind and decided to follow the curving lines of the moraines. This course has brought us well out on the glacier. Started on crampons; one hour after, hoisted sail; the combined efforts produced only slow speed, partly due to the sandy snowdrifts similar to those on summit, partly to our torn sledge runners. At lunch these were scraped and sand-papered. After lunch we got on snow, with ice only occasionally showing through. A poor start, but the gradient and wind improving, we did 6½ miles before night camp.

There is no getting away from the fact that we are not going strong. Probably none of us: Wilson's leg still troubles him and he doesn't like to trust himself on ski; but the worst case is Evans, who is giving us serious anxiety. This morning he suddenly disclosed a huge blister on his foot. It delayed us on the march, when he had to have his crampon readjusted.

Sometimes I fear he is going from bad to worse, but I trust he will pick up again when we come to steady work on ski like this afternoon. He is hungry and so is Wilson. We can't risk opening out our food again, and as cook at present I am serving something under full allowance. We are inclined to get slack and slow with our camping arrangements, and small delays increase. I have talked of the matter to-night and hope for improvement. We cannot do distance without the ponies. The next depôt* some 30 miles away and nearly 3 days' food in hand.

Thursday, February 15. R. 29. Lunch Temp. −10°; Supper Temp. −4°. 13.5 miles. Again we are running short of provision. We don't know our distance from the depôt, but imagine about 20 miles. Heavy march—did 13¾ (geo.). We are pulling for food and not very strong evidently. In the afternoon it was overcast; land blotted out for a considrable interval. We have reduced food, also sleep; feeling rather done. Trust 1½ days or 2 at most will see us at depôt.

Friday, February 16. 12.5 m. Lunch Temp. −6.1°; Supper Temp. −7°. A rather trying position. Evans has nearly broken down in brain, we think. He is absolutely changed from his normal self-reliant self. This morning and this afternoon he stopped the march on some trivial excuse. We are on short rations with not very short food; spin out till to-morrow night. We cannot be more than 10 or 12 miles from the depôt, but the weather is all against us. After lunch we were enveloped in a snow sheet, land just looming. Memory should hold the events of a very troublesome march with more troubles ahead. Perhaps all will be well if we can get to our depôt to-morrow fairly early, but it is anxious work with the sick man. But it's no use meeting troubles half way, and our sleep is all too short to write more.

* The Lower Glacier Depôt.—L.H.

Saturday, February 17. A very terrible day. Evans looked a little better after a good sleep, and declared, as he always did, that he was quite well. He started in his place on the traces, but half an hour later worked his ski shoes adrift, and had to leave the sledge. The surface was awful, the soft recently fallen snow clogging the ski and runners at every step, the sledge groaning, the sky overcast, and the land hazy. We stopped after about one hour, and Evans came up again, but very slowly. Half an hour later he dropped out again on the same plea. He asked Bowers to lend him a piece of string. I cautioned him to come on as quickly as he could, and he answered cheerfully as I thought. We had to push on, and the remainder of us were forced to pull very hard, sweating heavily. Abreast the Monument Rock we stopped, and seeing Evans a long way astern, I camped for lunch. There was no alarm at first, and we prepared tea and our own meal, consuming the latter. After lunch, and Evans still not appearing, we looked out, to see him still afar off. By this time we were alarmed, and all four started back on ski. I was first to reach the poor man and shocked at his appearance; he was on his knees with clothing disarranged, hands uncovered and frost-bitten, and a wild look in his eyes. Asked what was the matter, he replied with a slow speech that he didn't know, but thought he must have fainted. We got him on his feet, but after two or three steps he sank down again. He showed every sign of complete collapse. Wilson, Bowers, and I went back for the sledge, whilst Oates remained with him. When we returned he was practically unconscious, and when we got him into the tent quite comatose. He died quietly at 12.30 A.M. On discussing the symptoms we think he began to get weaker just before we reached the Pole, and that his downward path was accelerated first by the shock of his frostbitten fingers, and later by falls during rough travelling on the glacier, further by his loss of all confidence in himself. Wilson thinks it certain he must have injured his brain by a fall. It is a terrible thing to lose a companion in this way, but calm reflection shows that there could not have been a better ending to the terrible anxieties of the past week. Discussion of the situation at lunch yesterday shows us what a desperate pass we were in with a sick man on our hands at such a distance from home.

At 1 A.M. we packed up and came down over the pressure ridges, finding our depôt easily.

Sunday, February 18. R. 32. Temp. −5.5°. at Shambles Camp. We gave ourselves 5 hours' sleep at the lower glacier depôt after the horrible night, and came on at about 3 today to this camp, coming fairly easily over the divide. Here with plenty of horsemeat we have had a fine supper, to be followed by others such, and so continue a more plentiful era if we can keep good marches up. New life seems to come with greater food almost immediately, but I am anxious about the Barrier surfaces.

Monday, February 19. Lunch T. −16°. It was late (past noon) before we got away today, as I gave nearly 8 hours sleep, and much camp work was done shifting sledges and fitting up new one with mast, &c., packing horsemeat and personal effects. The surface was every bit as bad as I expected, the sun shining brightly on it and its covering of soft loose sandy snow. We have come out about 2′ on the old tracks. Perhaps lucky to have a fine day for this and our camp work, but we shall want wind or change of sliding conditions to do anything on such a surface as we have got. I fear there will not be much change for the next 3 or 4 days.

R. 33. Temp. −17°. We have struggled out 4.6 miles in a short day over a really terrible surface—it has been like pulling over desert sand, not the least glide in the world. If this goes on we shall have a bad time, but I sincerely trust it is only the result of this windless area close to the coast and that, as we are making steadily outward, we shall shortly escape it. It is perhaps premature to be anxious about covering distance. In all other respects things are improving. We have our sleeping bags spread on the sledge and they are drying, but, above all, we have out full measure of food again. To-night we had a sort of stew fry of pemmican and horseflesh, and voted it the best hoosh we had ever had on a sledge journey. The absence of poor Evans is a help to the commissariat, but if he had been here in a fit state we might have got along faster. I wonder what is in store for us, with some little alarm at the lateness of the season.

Monday, February 20. R. 34. Lunch Temp. −13°; Supper Temp. −15°. Same terrible surface; four hours' hard plodding in morning brought us to our Desolation Camp, where we had the four-day blizzard. We looked for more pony meat, but found none. After lunch we took to ski with some improvement of comfort. Total mileage for day 7—the ski tracks pretty plain and easily followed this afternoon. We have left another cairn behind. Terribly slow progress, but we hope for better things as we clear the land. There is a tendency to cloud over in the SE tonight, which may turn to our advantage. At present our sledge and ski leave deeply ploughed tracks which can be seen winding for miles behind. It is distressing, but as usual trials are forgotten when we camp, and good food is our lot. Pray God we get better traveling as we are not so fit as we were, and the season is advancing apace.

Tuesday, February 21. R. 35. Lunch Temp. −9½°; Supper Temp. −11°. Gloomy and overcast when we started; a good deal warmer. The marching almost as bad as yesterday. Heavy toiling all day, inspiring gloomiest thoughts at times. Rays of comfort when we picked up tracks and cairns. At lunch we seemed to have missed the way, but an hour or two after we passed the last pony walls, and since, we struck a tent ring, ending the march actually on our old pony tracks. There is a critical spot here with a long stretch between cairns. If we can tide that over we get on the regular cairn route, and with luck should stick to it; but everything de-

pends on the weather. We never won a march of 8½ miles
with greater difficulty, but we can't go on like this. We are
drawing away from the land and perhaps may get better
things in a day or two. I devoutly hope so.

Wednesday, February 22. R. 36. Supper Temp. −2°. There
is little doubt we are in for a rotten critical time going home,
and the lateness of the season may make it really serious.
Shortly after starting today the wind grew very fresh from
the SE with strong surface drift. We lost the faint track immediately, though covering ground fairly rapidly. Lunch
came without sight of the cairn we had hoped to pass. In the
afternoon, Bowers being sure we were too far to the west,
steered out. Result, we have passed another pony camp without seeing it. Looking at the map tonight there is no doubt
we are too far to the east. With clear weather we ought to be
able to correct the mistake, but will the weather get clear?
It's a gloomy position, more especially as one sees the same
difficulty returning even when we have corrected this error.
The wind is dying down tonight and the sky clearing in the
south, which is hopeful. Meanwhile it is satisfactory to note
that such untoward events fail to damp the spirit of the party.
Tonight we had a pony hoosh so excellent and filling that one
feels really strong and vigorous again.

Thursday, February 23. R. 37. Lunch Temp. −9.8°; Supper
Temp. −12°. Started in sunshine, wind almost dropped.
Luckily Bowers took a round of angles and with help of the
chart we fogged out that we must be inside rather than
outside tracks. The data were so meager that it seemed a
great responsibility to march out and we were none of us
happy about it. But just as we decided to lunch, Bowers'
wonderful sharp eyes detected an old double lunch cairn, the
theodolite telescope confirmed it, and our spirits rose accordingly. This afternoon we marched on and picked up another
cairn; then on and camped only 2½ miles from the depôt. We

cannot see it, but given fine weather, we cannot miss it. We are, therefore, extraordinarily relieved. Covered 8.2 miles in 7 hours, showing we can do 10 to 12 on this surface. Things are again looking up, as we are on the regular line of cairns, with no gaps right home, I hope.

Friday, February 24. Lunch. Beautiful day—too beautiful— an hour after starting loose ice crystals spoiling surface. Saw depôt and reached it middle forenoon. Found store in order except shortage oil—shall have to be *very* saving with fuel— otherwise have ten full days' provision from tonight and shall have less than 70 miles to go. Note from Meares who passed through December 15, saying surface bad; from Atkinson, after fine marching (2¼ days from pony depôt), reporting Keohane better after sickness. Short note from Evans, not very cheerful, saying surface bad, temperature high. Think he must have been a little anxious. It is an immense relief to have picked up this depôt and, for the time, anxieties are thrust aside. There is no doubt we have been rising steadily since leaving the Shambles Camp. The coastal Barrier descends except where glaciers press out. Undulation still, but flattening out. Surface soft on top, curiously hard below. Great difference now between night and day temperatures. Quite warm as I write in tent. We are on tracks with half-march cairn ahead; have covered 4¼ miles. Poor Wilson has a fearful attack snow blindness consequent on yesterday's efforts. Wish we had more fuel.

Night camp R. 38. Temp −17°. A little despondent again. We had a really terrible surface this afternoon and only covered 4 miles. We are on the track just beyond a lunch cairn. It really will be a bad business if we are to have this pulling all through. I don't know what to think, but the rapid closing of the season is ominous. It is great luck having the horsemeat to add to our ration. To-night we have had a real fine hoosh. It is a race between the season and hard conditions and our fitness and good food.

Saturday, February 25. Lunch Temp. −12°. Managed just 6 miles this morning. Started somewhat despondent; not relieved when pulling seemed to show no improvement. Bit by bit surface grew better, less sastrugi, more glide, slight following wind for a time. Then we began to travel a little faster. But the pulling is still *very* hard; undulations disappearing but inequalities remain.

Twenty-six Camp walls about 2 miles ahead, all tracks in sight—Evans' track very conspicuous. This is something in favour, but the pulling is tiring us, though we are getting into better ski drawing again. Bowers hasn't quite the trick and is a little hurt at my criticisms, but I never doubted his heart. Very much easier—write diary at lunch—excellent meal— now one pannikin very strong tea—four biscuits and butter.

Hope for better things this afternoon, but no improvement apparent. Oh! for a little wind—E. Evans evidently had plenty.

R. 39. Temp. −20°. Better march in afternoon. Day yields 11.4 miles—the first double figure of steady dragging for a long time, but it meant and will mean hard work if we can't get a wind to help us. Evans evidently had a strong wind here, SE I should think. The temperature goes very low at night now when the sky is clear as at present. As a matter of fact this is wonderfully fair weather—the only drawback the spoiling of the surface and absence of wind. We see all tracks very plain, but the pony walls have evidently been badly drifted up. Some kind people had substituted a cairn at last camp 27. The old cairns do not seem to have suffered much.

Sunday, February 26. Lunch Temp. −17°. Sky overcast at start, but able see tracks and cairn distinct at long distance. Did a little better, 6½ miles to date. Bowers and Wilson now in front. Find great relief pulling behind with no necessity to keep attention on track. Very cold nights now and cold feet starting march, as day footgear doesn't dry at all. We are doing well on our food, but we ought to have yet more. I hope the next depôt, now only 50 miles, will find us with enough surplus to open out. The fuel shortage still an anxiety. R. 40. Temp. −21°. Nine hours' solid marching has given us 11½ miles. Only 43 miles from the next depôt. Wonderfully fine weather but cold, very cold. Nothing dries and we get our feet cold too often. We want more food yet and especially more fat. Fuel is woefully short. We can scarcely hope to get a better surface at this season, but I wish we could have some help from the wind, though it might shake us up badly if the temp. didn't rise.

Monday, February 27. Desperately cold last night: −33° when we got up, with −37° minimum. Some suffering from cold feet, but all got good rest. We *must* open out on food soon. But we have done 7 miles this morning and hope for some 5 this afternoon. Overcast sky and good surface till now, when sun shows again. It is good to be marching the cairns up, but there is still much to be anxious about. We talk of little but food, except after meals. Land disappearing in satisfactory manner. Pray God we have no further setbacks. We are naturally always discussing possibility of meeting dogs, where and when, &c. It is a critical position. We may find ourselves in safety at next depôt, but there is a horrid element of doubt.

Camp R. 41. Temp. −32°. Still fine clear weather but very cold—absolutely calm tonight. We have got off an excellent march for these days (12.2) and are much earlier than usual in our bags. 31 miles to depot, 3 days' fuel at a pinch, and 6 days' food. Things began to look a little better; we can open out a little on food from tomorrow night, I think.

Very curious surface—soft recent sastrugi which sink underfoot, and between, a sort of flaky crust with large crystals beneath.

Tuesday, February 28. Lunch. Thermometer went below −40° last night; it was desperately cold for us, but we had a fair night. I decided to slightly increase food; the effect is undoubtedly good. Started marching in −32° with a slight northwesterly breeze—blighting. Many cold feet this morning; long time over footgear, but we are earlier. Shall camp earlier and get the chance of a good night, if not the reality. Things must be critical till we reach the depôt, and the more I think of matters, the more I anticipate their remaining so after that event. Only 24½ miles from the depôt. The sun shines brightly, but there is little warmth in it. There is no doubt the middle of the Barrier is a pretty awful locality.

Camp 42. Splendid pony hoosh sent us to bed and sleep happily after a horrid day, wind continuing; did 11½ miles. Temp. not quite so low, but expect we are in for cold night (Temp. −27°).

Wednesday, February 29. Lunch. Cold night. Minimum Temp. −37.5°; −30° with northwest wind, force 4, when we got up. Frightfully cold starting; luckily Bowers and Oates in their last new finnesko; keeping my old ones for present. Expected awful march and for first hour got it. Then things improved and we camped after 5½ hours marching close to lunch camp—22½. Next camp is our depôt and it is exactly 13 miles. It ought not to take more than 1½ days; we pray for another fine one. The oil will just about spin out in that event, and we arrive 3 clear days' food in hand. The increase of ration has had an enormously beneficial result. Mountains now looking small. Wind still very light from west—cannot understand this wind.

Thursday, March 1. Lunch. Very cold last night—minimum −41.5°. Cold start to march, too, as usual now. Got away at 8 and have marched within sight of depôt; flag something under 3 miles away. We did 11½ yesterday and marched 6 this morning. Apart from sledging considerations the weather is wonderful. Cloudless days and nights and the wind trifling. Worse luck, the light airs come from the north and keep us horribly cold. For this lunch hour the exception has come. There is a bright and comparatively warm sun. All our gear is out drying.

Friday, March 2. Lunch. Misfortunes rarely come singly. We marched to the depôt fairly easily yesterday afternoon, and since that have suffered three distinct blows which have placed us in a bad position. First we found a shortage of oil; with most rigid economy it can scarce carry us to the next depôt on this surface. Second, Titus Oates disclosed his feet, the toes showing very bad indeed, evidently bitten by the late temperatures. The third blow came in the night, when the wind, which we had hailed with some joy, brought dark overcast weather. It fell below −40° in the night, and this morning it took 1½ hours to get our footgear on, but we got away before night. We lost cairn and tracks together and made as steady as we could N by W, but have seen nothing. Worse was to come—the surface is simply awful. In spite of strong wind and full sail we have only done 5½ miles. We are in a very queer street since there is no doubt we cannot do the extra marches and feel the cold horribly.

Saturday, March 3. Lunch. We picked up the track again yesterday, finding ourselves to the eastward. Did close on 10 miles and things looked a trifle better; but this morning the outlook is blacker than ever. Started well and with good breeze; for an hour made good headway; then the surface grew awful beyond words. The wind drew forward; every circumstance was against us. After 4½ hours things so bad that we camped, having covered 4½ miles. One cannot consider this a fault of our own—certainly we were pulling hard this morning—it was more than three parts surface which held us back—the wind at strongest, powerless to move the sledge. When the light is good it is easy to see the reason. The surface, lately a very good hard one, is coated with a thin layer of woolly crystals, formed by radiation no doubt. These are too firmly fixed to be removed by the wind and cause impossible friction on the runners. God help us, we can't keep up this pulling, that is certain. Amongst ourselves we are unendingly cheerful, but what each man feels in his heart I can only guess. Pulling on footgear in the morning is getting slower and slower, therefore every day more dangerous.

Sunday, March 4. Lunch. Things looking *very* black indeed. As usual we forgot our trouble last night, got into our bags, slept splendidly on good hoosh, woke and had another, and started marching. Sun shining brightly, tracks clear, but surface covered with sandy frost rime. All the morning we had to pull with all our strength, and in 4½ hours we covered 3½ miles. Last night it was overcast and thick, surface bad; this morning sun shining and surface as bad as ever. One has little to hope for except perhaps strong dry wind—an unlikely contingency at this time of year. Under the immediate surface crystals is a hard sastrugi surface, which must have been excellent for pulling a week or two ago. We are about 42 miles from the next depôt and have a week's food, but only about 3 to 4 days' fuel—we are as economical of the latter as one can possibly be, and we cannot afford to save food and pull as we are pulling. We are in a very tight place indeed, but none of us despondent *yet*, or as least we preserve every semblance of good cheer, but one's heart sinks as the sledge stops dead at some sastrugi behind which the surface sand lies thickly heaped. For the moment the temperature is on the −20°—an improvement which makes us much more comfortable, but a colder snap is bound to come again soon. I fear that Oates at least will weather such an event very poorly. Providence to our aid! We can expect little from man now except the possibility of extra food at the next depôt. It will be real bad if we get there and find the same shortage of oil. Shall we get there? Such a short distance it would have appeared to us on the summit! I don't know what I should do if Wilson and Bowers weren't so determinedly cheerful over things.

Monday, March 5. Lunch. Regret to say going from bad to worse. We got a slant of wind yesterday afternoon, and going on 5 hours we converted our wretched morning run of 3½ miles into something over 9. We went to bed on a cup of cocoa and pemmican solid with the chill off. (R. 47.) The result is telling on all, but mainly on Oates, whose feet are in a wretched condition. One swelled up tremendously last night and he is very lame this morning. We started march on tea and pemmican as last night—we pretend to prefer the pemmican this way. Marched for 5 hours this morning over a slightly better surface covered with high moundy sastrugi. Sledge capsized twice; we pulled on foot, covering about 5½ miles. We are two pony marches and 4 miles about from our depôt. Our fuel dreadfully low and the poor Soldier nearly done. It is pathetic enough because we can do nothing for him; more hot food might do a little, but only a little, I fear. We none of us expected these terrible low temperatures, and of the rest of us Wilson is feeling them most; mainly, I fear, from his self-sacrificing devotion in doctoring Oates' feet. We cannot help each other, each has enough to do to take care of himself. We get cold on the march when the trudging is heavy, and the wind pierces our warm garments. The others, all of them, are unendingly cheerful when in the tent. We mean to see the game through with a proper spirit, but it's tough work to be pulling harder than we ever pulled in our lives for long hours, and to feel that the progress is so slow. One can only say "God help us!" and plod on our weary way, cold and very miserable, though outwardly cheerful. We talk of all sorts of subjects in the tent, not much of food now, since we decided to take the risk of running a full ration. We simply couldn't go hungry at this time.

Tuesday, March 6. Lunch. We did a little better with help of wind yesterday afternoon, finishing 9½ miles for the day, and 27 miles from depôt. (R. 48.) But this morning things have been awful. It was warm in the night and for the first time during the journey I overslept myself by more than an hour; then we were slow with footgear; then, pulling with all our might (for our lives) we could scarcely advance at rate of a mile an hour; then it grew thick and three times we had to get out of harness to search for tracks. The result is something

less than 3½ miles for the forenoon. The sun is shining now
and the wind gone. Poor Oates is unable to pull, sits on the
sledge when we are track-searching—he is wonderfully
plucky, as his feet must be giving him great pain. He makes
no complaint, but his spirits only come up in spurts now, and
he grows more silent in the tent. We are making a spirit lamp
to try and replace the primus when our oil is exhausted. It
will be a very poor substitute and we've not got much spirit.
If we could have kept up our 9-mile days we might have got
within reasonable distance of the depôt before running out,
but nothing but a strong wind and good surface can help us
now, and though we had quite a good breeze this morning,
the sledge came as heavy as lead. If we were all fit I should
have hopes of getting through, but the poor Soldier has become a terrible hindrance, though he does his utmost and
suffers much I fear.

Wednesday, March 7. A little worse I fear. One of Oates'
feet *very* bad this morning; he is wonderfully brave. We still
talk of what we will do together at home.

We only made 6½ miles yesterday. (R. 49.) This morning
in 4½ hours we did just over 4 miles. We are 16 from our
depôt. If we only find the correct proportion of food there
and this surface continues, we may get to the next depôt but
not to One Ton Camp. We hope against hope that the dogs
have been to Mt. Hooper; then we might pull through. If
there is a shortage of oil again we can have little hope. One
feels that for poor Oates the crisis is near, but none of us are
improving, though we are wonderfully fit considering the
really excessive work we are doing. We are only kept going
by good food. No wind this morning till a chill northerly air
came ahead. Sun bright and cairns showing up well. I should
like to keep the track to the end.

Thursday, March 8. Lunch. Worse and worse in morning;
poor Oates' left foot can never last out, and time over foot-
gear something awful. Have to wait in night footgear for

nearly an hour before I start changing, and then am generally first to be ready. Wilson's feet giving trouble now, but
this mainly because he gives so much help to others. We did
4½ miles this morning and are now 8½ miles from the depôt
—a ridiculously small distance to feel in difficulties, yet on
this surface we know we cannot equal half our old marches,
and that for that effort we expend nearly double the energy.
The great question is, What shall we find at the depôt? If the
dogs have visited it we may get along a good distance, but if
there is another short allowance of fuel, God help us indeed.
We are in a very bad way, I fear, in any case.

Saturday, March 10. Things steadily downhill. Oates' foot
worse. He has rare pluck and must know that he can never
get through. He asked Wilson if he had a chance this morning, and of course Bill had to say he didn't know. In point of
fact he has none. Apart from him, if he went under now, I
doubt whether we could get through. With great care we
might have a dog's chance, but no more. The weather conditions are awful, and our gear gets steadily more icy and difficult to manage. At the same time of course poor Titus is the
greatest handicap. He keeps us waiting in the morning until
we have partly lost the warming effect of our good breakfast,
when the only wise policy is to be up and away at once; again
at lunch. Poor chap! it is too pathetic to watch him; one
cannot but try to cheer him up.

Yesterday we marched up the depôt, Mt. Hooper. Cold
comfort. Shortage on our allowance all round. I don't know
that anyone is to blame. The dogs which would have been
our salvation have evidently failed. Meares had a bad trip
home I suppose.

This morning it was calm when we breakfasted, but the
wind came from the WNW as we broke camp. It rapidly grew
in strength. After traveling for half an hour I saw that none
of us could go on facing such conditions. We were forced to
camp and are spending the rest of the day in a comfortless
blizzard camp, wind quite foul. (R. 52.)

Sunday, March 11. Titus Oates is very near the end, one feels. What we or he will do, God only knows. We discussed the matter after breakfast; he is a brave fine fellow and understands the situation, but he practically asked for advice. Nothing could be said but to urge him to march as long as he could. One satisfactory result to the discussion; I practically ordered Wilson to hand over the means of ending our troubles to us, so that any one of us may know how to do so. Wilson had no choice between doing so and our ransacking the medicine case. We have 30 opium tabloids apiece and he is left with a tube of morphine. So far the tragical side of our story. (R. 53.)

The sky completely overcast when we started this morning. We could see nothing, lost the tracks, and doubtless have been swaying a good deal since—3.1 miles for the forenoon —terribly heavy dragging—expected it. Know that 6 miles is about the limit of our endurance now, if we get no help from wind or surfaces. We have 7 days' food and should be about 55 miles from One Ton Camp tonight, $6 \times 7 = 42$, leaving us 13 miles short of our distance, even if things get no worse. Meanwhile the season rapidly advances.

Monday, March 12. We did 6.9 miles yesterday, under our necessary average. Things are left much the same, Oates not pulling much, and now with hands as well as feet pretty well useless. We did 4 miles this morning in 4 hours 20 min.—we may hope for 3 this afternoon, $7 \times 6 = 42$. We shall be 47 miles from the depôt. I doubt if we can possibly do it. The surface remains awful, the cold intense, and our physical condition running down. God help us! Not a breath of favourable wind for more than a week, and apparently liable to head winds at any moment.

Wednesday, March 14. No doubt about the going downhill, but everything going wrong for us. Yesterday we woke to a strong northerly wind with temp. $-37°$. Couldn't face it, so remained in camp (R. 54.) till 2, then did 5¼ miles. Wanted to march later, but party feeling the cold badly as the breeze (N) never took off entirely, and as the sun sank the temp. fell. Long time getting supper in dark. (R. 55.)

This morning started with southerly breeze, set sail and passed another cairn at good speed; halfway, however, the wind shifted to W by S or WSW, blew through our wind clothes and into our mits. Poor Wilson horribly cold, could not get off ski for some time. Bowers and I practically made camp, and when we got into the tent at last we were all deadly cold. Then temp. now midday down −43° and the wind strong. We *must* go on, but now the making of every camp must be more difficult and dangerous. It must be near the end, but a pretty merciful end. Poor Oates got it again in the foot. I shudder to think what it will be like to-morrow. It is only with greatest pains rest of us keep off frostbites. No idea there could be temperatures like this at this time of year with such winds. Truly awful outside the tent. Must fight it out to the last biscuit, but can't reduce rations.

Friday, March 16 or Saturday 17. Lost track of dates, but think the last correct. Tragedy all along the line. At lunch, the day before yesterday, poor Titus Oates said he couldn't go on; he proposed we should leave him in his sleeping bag. That we could not do, and we induced him to come on, on the afternoon march. In spite of its awful nature for him he struggled on and we made a few miles. At night he was worse and we knew the end had come.

Should this be found I want these facts recorded. Oates' last thoughts were of his mother, but immediately before he took pride in thinking that his regiment would be pleased with the bold way in which he met his death. We can testify to his bravery. He has borne intense suffering for weeks without complaint, and to the very last was able and willing to discuss outside subjects. He did not—would not—give up hope till the very end. He was a brave soul. This was the end. He slept through the night before last, hoping not to wake; but he woke in the morning—yesterday. It was blowing a blizzard. He said, "I am just going outside and may be some time." He went out into the blizzard and we have not seen him since.

I take this opportunity of saying that we have stuck to our sick companions to the last. In case of Edgar Evans, when absolutely out of food and he lay insensible, the safety of the remainder seemed to demand his abandonment, but Providence mercifully removed him at this critical moment. He died a natural death, and we did not leave him till two hours after his death. We knew that poor Oates was walking to his death, but though we tried to dissuade him, we knew it was the act of a brave man and an English gentleman. We all hope to meet the end with a similar spirit, and assuredly the end is not far.

I can only write at lunch and then only occasionally. The cold is intense, −40° at midday. My companions are unendingly cheerful, but we are all on the verge of serious frostbites, and though we constantly talk of fetching through I don't think any one of us believes it in his heart.

We are cold on the march now, and at all times except meals. Yesterday we had to lay up for a blizzard and today we move dreadfully slowly. We are at No. 14 pony camp, only two pony marches from One Ton Depôt. We leave here our theodolite, a camera, and Oates' sleeping bags. Diaries, &c., and geological specimens carried at Wilson's special request, will be found with us or on our sledge.

Sunday, March 18. Today, lunch, we are 21 miles from the depôt. Ill fortune presses, but better may come. We have had more wind and drift from ahead yesterday; had to stop marching; wind NW, force 4, temp. −35°. No human being could face it, and we are worn out *nearly*.

My right foot has gone, nearly all the toes—two days ago I was proud possessor of best feet. These are the steps of my downfall. Like an ass I mixed a small spoonful of curry pow-

der with my melted pemmican—it gave me violent indiges-
tion. I lay awake and in pain all night; woke and felt done on
the march; foot went and I didn't know it. A very small
measure of neglect and have a foot which is not pleasant to
contemplate. Bowers takes first place in condition, but there
is not much to choose after all. The others are still confident
of getting through—or pretend to be—I don't know! We
have the last *half* fill of oil in our primus and a very small
quantity of spirit—this alone between us and thirst. The wind
is fair for the moment, and that is perhaps a fact to help. The
mileage would have seemed ridiculously small on our outward journey.

Monday, March 19. Lunch. We camped with difficulty last
night, and were dreadfully cold till after our supper of cold
pemmican and biscuit and a half a pannikin of cocoa cooked
over the spirit. Then, contrary to expectation, we got warm
and slept well. To-day we started in the usual dragging manner. Sledge dreadfully heavy. We are 15½ miles from the
depôt and ought to get there in three days. What progress!
We have two days' food but barely a day's fuel. All our feet
are getting bad—Wilson's best, my right foot worst, left all
right. There is no chance to nurse one's feet till we can get
hot food into us. Amputation is the least I can hope for now,
but will the trouble spread? That is the serious question. The
weather doesn't give us a chance—the wind from N to NW
and −40° temp. today.

Wednesday, March 21. Got within 11 miles of depôt Monday
night; had to lay up all yesterday in severe blizzard. To-day
forlorn hope, Wilson and Bowers going to depôt for fuel.

Thursday, March 22 and 23. Blizzard bad as ever—Wilson
and Bowers unable to start—to-morrow last chance—no fuel
and only one or two of food left—must be near the end. Have
decided it shall be natural—we shall march for the depôt
with or without our effects and die in our tracks.

Thursday, March 29. Since the 21st we have had a continuous gale from WSW and SW. We had fuel to make two cups of tea apiece and bare food for two days on the 20th. Every day we have been ready to start for our depôt 11 *miles* away, but outside the door of the tent it remains a scene of whirling drift. I do not think we can hope for any better things now. We shall stick it out to the end, but we are getting weaker, of course, and the end cannot be far.

It seems a pity, but I do not think I can write more.

R. SCOTT.

Last entry.
For God's sake look after our people.

ERNEST SHACKLETON

(*1874–1922*)

THE BRITISH EXPLORER Ernest Shackleton made four voyages to Antarctica, the first as a lieutenant on Scott's *Discovery* expedition, during which, with Scott and Edward Wilson, he reached a farthest south of 82° 17′. On the return trip he came down with scurvy complicated by the coughing of blood, and Wilson, a doctor, had serious fears for his life. Scott seemed to feel that Shackleton had let the party down, even though he recognized that Shackleton's illness was as disappointing and as disagreeable to Shackleton as to himself. Shackleton was invalided home in March 1903 with a taint of disgrace, as if he had not been fit for the rigors of a polar traverse. After his recovery he mounted his own Antarctic expedition but had considerable difficulty financing it. When he asked Scott if he could use the latter's *Discovery* hut on Ross Island, Scott declined with the explanation that he hoped to return to the continent later and use the hut himself.

Shackleton's *Nimrod* expedition left England in 1907. He planned to base himself on the Ross Ice Shelf off the Bay of Whales, but on examining the ice decided it was too unstable there and therefore dangerous. He settled on Cape Royds, Ross Island, where he built his now famous hut. During this expedition he made a southing to within ninety-seven miles of the Pole, in the process pioneering the Beardmore Glacier route over the Transantarctic Mountains. He barely made it back to Ross Island.

Some years later, after Amundsen had reached the Pole, Shackleton concluded that "there remained but one great main object of Antarctic journeyings—the crossing of the South Polar continent from sea to sea." The route he chose was from the Weddell Sea to McMurdo Sound. In 1914 he commanded the British Imperial Trans-Antarctic Expedition with the hope of achieving this goal. He failed, but as with Scott, the failure was in some respects a glorious one, a triumph of the human spirit over great adversities. His ship *Endurance* was trapped by ice in the Weddell Sea, where it drifted for ten months, then was slowly crushed. The crew thereupon lived on an ice floe for almost five months, drifting northward. Finally, escaping by whaleboats which they had saved from the *Endurance,* they reached deserted Elephant Island. Shackleton and five companions then set out in an open boat to seek help, crossing 800 miles of Antarctic waters to South Georgia, where they became the first men to traverse the island's high, dangerous mountains in their journey to the Norwegian whaling station on the opposite side of the island. The men stranded on Elephant Island were rescued but only on the fourth attempt. One of the extraordinary facts of the Weddell Sea part of the expedition is that not one life was lost. The McMurdo Sound section, however, lost three men, including its leader.

Shackleton died at the early age of forty-eight in South Georgia, at the beginning of his fourth Antarctic expedition.

His is one of the most celebrated open-boat voyages ever made. He describes it in detail in the following pages.

Boat Journey

The increasing sea made it necessary for us to drag the boats farther up the beach. This was a task for all hands, and after much labor we got the boats into safe positions among the rocks and made fast the painters to big boulders. Then I discussed with Wild and Worsley the chances of reaching South Georgia before the winter locked the seas against us. Some effort had to be made to secure relief. Privation and exposure had left their mark on the party, and the health and mental condition of several men were causing me serious anxiety. Blackborrow's feet, which had been frostbitten during the boat journey, were in a bad way, and the two doctors feared that an operation would be necessary. They told me that the toes would have to be amputated unless animation could be restored within a short period. Then the food supply was a vital consideration. We had left ten cases of provisions in the crevice of the rocks at our first camping place on the island. An examination of our stores showed that we had full rations for the whole party for a period of five weeks. The rations could be spread over three months on a reduced allowance and probably would be supplemented by seals and sea elephants to some extent. I did not dare to count with full confidence on supplies of meat and blubber, for the animals seemed to have deserted the beach and the winter was near.

Our stocks included three seals and two and a half skins (with blubber attached). We were mainly dependent on the blubber for fuel, and, after making a preliminary survey of the situation, I decided that the party must be limited to one hot meal a day.

A boat journey in search of relief was necessary and must not be delayed. That conclusion was forced upon me. The nearest port where assistance could certainly be secured was Port Stanley, in the Falkland Islands, 540 miles away, but we could scarcely hope to beat up against the prevailing north-westerly wind in a frail and weakened boat with a small sail area. South Georgia was over 800 miles away, but lay in the area of the west winds, and I could count upon finding whalers at any of the whaling stations on the east coast. A boat party might make the voyage and be back with relief within a month. provided that the sea was clear of ice and the boat survive the great seas. It was not difficult to decide that South Georgia must be the objective, and I proceeded to plan ways and means. The hazards of a boat journey across 800 miles of stormy subantarctic ocean were obvious, but I calculated that at worst the venture would add nothing to the risks of the men left on the island. There would be fewer mouths to feed during the winter and the boat would not require to take more than one month's provisions for six men, for if we did not make South Georgia in that time we were sure to go under. A consideration that had weight with me was that there was no chance at all of any search being made for us on Elephant Island.

The case required to be argued in some detail, since all hands knew that the perils of the proposed journey were extreme. The risk was justified solely by our urgent need of assistance. The ocean south of Cape Horn in the middle of May is known to be the most tempestuous storm-swept area of water in the world. The weather then is unsettled, the skies are dull and overcast, and the gales are almost unceasing. We had to face these conditions in a small and weather-beaten boat, already strained by the work of the months that had passed. Worsley and Wild realized that the attempt must be made, and they both asked to be allowed to accompany me on the voyage. I told Wild at once that he would have to stay behind. I relied upon him to hold the party together while I was away and to make the best of his way to Deception Island with the men in the spring in the event of our failure to bring help. Worsley I would take with me, for I had a very high opinion of his accuracy and quickness as a navigator, and especially in the mapping and working out of positions in difficult circumstances—an opinion that was only enhanced during the actual journey. Four other men would be required, and I decided to call for volunteers, although, as a matter of fact, I pretty well knew which of the people I would select. Crean I proposed to leave on the island as a right-hand man for Wild, but he begged so hard to be allowed to come in the boat that, after consultation with Wild, I promised to take him. I called the men together, explained my plan, and asked for volunteers. Many came forward at once. Some were not fit enough for the work that would have to be done, and others would not have been much use in the boat since they were not seasoned sailors, though the experiences of recent months entitled them to some consideration as seafaring men. McIlroy and Macklin were both anxious to go but realized that their duty lay on the island with the sick men. They suggested that I should take Blackborrow in order that he might have shelter and warmth as quickly as possible, but I had to veto this idea. It would be hard enough for fit men to live in the boat. Indeed, I did not see how a sick man, lying helpless in the bottom of the boat, could possibly survive in the heavy weather we were sure to encounter. I finally selected McNeish, McCarthy, and Vincent in addition to Worsley and Crean. The crew seemed a strong one, and as I looked at the men I felt confidence increasing.

The decision made, I walked through the blizzard with Worsley and Wild to examine the *James Caird*. The 20-ft. boat had never looked big; she appeared to have shrunk in some mysterious way when I viewed her in the light of our new undertaking. She was an ordinary ship's whaler, fairly strong, but showing signs of the strains she had endured since the crushing of the *Endurance*. Where she was holed in leaving the pack was, fortunately, about the water line and easily patched. Standing beside her, we glanced at the fringe of the storm-swept, tumultuous sea that formed our path. Clearly, our voyage would be a big adventure. I called the carpenter and asked him if he could do anything to make the boat more seaworthy. He first inquired if he was to go with me, and seemed quite pleased when I said "Yes." He was over fifty years of age and not altogether fit, but he had a good knowledge of sailing boats and was very quick. McCarthy said that he could contrive some sort of covering for the *James Caird* if he might use the lids of the cases and the four sledge runners that we had lashed inside the boat for use in the event of a landing on Graham Land at Wilhelmina Bay. This bay, at one time the goal of our desire, had been left behind in the course of our drift, but we had retained the runners. The carpenter proposed to complete the covering with some of our canvas, and he set about making his plans at once.

Noon had passed and the gale was more severe than ever. We could not proceed with our preparations that day. The tents were suffering in the wind and the sea was rising. We made our way to the snow slope at the shoreward end of the spit, with the intention of digging a hole in the snow large enough to provide shelter for the party. I had an idea that Wild and his men might camp there during my absence, since it seemed impossible that the tents could hold together for many more days against the attacks of the wind; but an examination of the spot indicated that any hole we could dig probably would be filled quickly by the drift. At dark, about 5 P.M., we all turned in, after a supper consisting of a pannikin of hot milk, one of our precious biscuits, and a cold penguin leg each.

The gale was stronger than ever on the following morning (April 20). No work could be done. Blizzard and snow, snow and blizzard, sudden lulls and fierce returns. During the lulls we could see on the far horizon to the northeast bergs of all shapes and sizes driving along before the gale, and the sinister appearance of the swift-moving masses made us thankful indeed that, instead of battling with the storm amid the ice, we were required only to face the drift from the glaciers and the inland heights. The gusts might throw us off our feet, but at least we fell on solid ground and not on the rocking floes. Two seals came up on the beach that day, one of them within ten yards of my tent. So urgent was our need of food and blubber that I called all hands and organized a line of beaters instead of simply walking up to the seal and hitting it on the nose. We were prepared to fall upon this seal *en masse* if it attempted to escape. The kill was made with a pick handle, and in a few minutes five days' food and six days' fuel were stowed in a place of safety among the boulders above highwater mark. During this day the cook, who had worked well on the floe and throughout the boat journey, suddenly collapsed. I happened to be at the galley at the moment and saw him fall. I pulled him down the slope to his tent and pushed him into its shelter with orders to his tent mates to keep him in his sleeping bag until I allowed him to come out or the doctors said he was fit enough. Then I took out to replace the cook one of the men who had expressed a desire to lie down and die. The task of keeping the galley fire alight was both difficult and strenuous, and it took his thoughts away from the chances of immediate dissolution. In fact, I found him a little later gravely concerned over the drying of a naturally not overclean pair of socks which were hung up in close proximity to our evening milk. Occupation had brought his thoughts back to the ordinary cares of life.

There was a lull in the bad weather on April 21, and the carpenter started to collect material for the decking of the *James Caird*. He fitted the mast of the *Stancomb Wills* fore and aft inside the *James Caird* as a hogback and thus strengthened the keel with the object of preventing our boat "hogging"—that is, buckling in heavy seas. He had not sufficient wood to provide a deck, but by using the sledge runners and box lids he made a framework extending from the forecastle aft to a well. It was a patched-up affair, but it provided a base for a canvas covering. We had a bolt of canvas frozen stiff, and this material had to be cut and then thawed out over the blubber stove, foot by foot, in order that it might be sewn into the form of a cover. When it had been nailed and screwed into position it certainly gave an appearance of safety to the boat, though I had an uneasy feeling that it bore a strong likeness to stage scenery, which may look like a granite wall and is in fact nothing better than canvas and lath. As events proved, the covering served its purpose well. We certainly could not have lived through the voyage without it.

Another fierce gale was blowing on April 22, interfering with our preparations for the voyage. The cooker from No. 5 tent came adrift in a gust, and, although it was chased to the water's edge, it disappeared for good. Blackborrow's feet were giving him much pain, and McIlroy and Macklin thought it would be necessary for them to operate soon. They were under the impression then that they had no chloroform, but they found some subsequently in the medicine chest after we had left. Some cases of stores left on a rock off the spit on the day of our arrival were retrieved during this day. We were setting aside stores for the boat journey and choosing the essential equipment from the scanty stock at our disposal. Two ten-gallon casks had to be filled with water melted down from ice collected at the foot of the glacier. This was a rather slow business. The blubber stove was kept going all night, and the watchmen emptied the water into the casks from the pot in which the ice was melted. A working party started to dig a hole in the snow slope about forty feet above sea level with the object of providing a site for a camp. They made fairly good progress at first, but the snow drifted down unceasingly from the inland ice, and in the end the party had to give up the project.

The weather was fine on April 23, and we hurried forward

our preparations. It was on this day I decided finally that the crew for the *James Caird* should consist of Worsley, Crean, McNeish, McCarthy, Vincent, and myself. A storm came on about noon, with driving snow and heavy squalls. Occasionally the air would clear for a few minutes, and we could see a line of pack ice, five miles out, driving across from west to east. This sight increased my anxiety to get away quickly. Winter was advancing, and soon the pack might close completely round the island and stay our departure for days or even for weeks. I did not think that ice would remain around Elephant Island continuously during the winter, since the strong winds and fast currents would keep it in motion. We had noticed ice and bergs going past at the rate of four or five knots. A certain amount of ice was held up about the end of our spit, but the sea was clear where the boat would have to be launched.

Worsley, Wild, and I climbed to the summit of the seaward rocks and examined the ice from a better vantage point than the beach offered. The belt of pack outside appeared to be sufficiently broken for our purposes, and I decided that, unless the conditions forbade it, we would make a start in the *James Caird* on the following morning. Obviously the pack might close at any time. This decision made, I spent the rest of the day looking over the boat, gear, and stores, and discussing plans with Worsley and Wild.

Our last night on the solid ground of Elephant Island was cold and uncomfortable. We turned out at dawn and had breakfast. Then we launched the *Stancomb Wills* and loaded her with stores, gear, and ballast, which would be transferred to the *James Caird* when the heavier boat had been launched. The ballast consisted of bags made from blankets and filled with sand, making a total weight of about 1000 lb. In addition we had gathered a number of round boulders and about 250 lb. of ice, which would supplement our two casks of water.

The stores taken in the *James Caird*, which would last six men for one month, were as follows:

30 boxes of matches.
6½ gallons paraffin.
1 tin methylated spirit.
10 boxes of flamers.
1 box of blue lights.
2 Primus stoves with spare parts and prickers.
1 Nansen aluminum cooker.
6 sleeping bags.
A few spare socks.
A few candles and some blubber oil in an oil bag.

Food:

3 cases sledging rations = 300 rations.
2 cases nut food   = 200   "
2 cases biscuits   = 600 biscuits.
1 case lump sugar.
30 packets of Trumilk.
1 tin of Bovril cubes.
1 tin of Cerebos salt.
36 gallons of water.
112 lb. of ice.

Instruments:

Sextant.	Sea anchor.
Binoculars.	Charts.
Prismatic compass.	Aneroid.

The swell was slight when the *Stancomb Wills* was launched and the boat got under way without any difficulty; but half an hour later, when we were pulling down the *James Caird*, the swell increased suddenly. Apparently the movement of the ice outside had made an opening and allowed the sea to run in without being blanketed by the line of pack. The swell made things difficult. Many of us got wet to the waist while dragging the boat out—a serious matter in that climate. When the *James Caird* was afloat in the surf she nearly capsized among the rocks before we could get her clear, and Vincent and the carpenter, who were on the deck, were thrown into the water. This was really bad luck, for the two men would have small chance of drying their clothes after we had got under way. Hurley, who had the eye of the professional photographer for "incidents," secured a picture of the upset, and I firmly believe that he would have liked the two unfortunate men to remain in the water until he could get a "snap" at close quarters; but we hauled them out immediately, regardless of his feelings.

The *James Caird* was soon clear of the breakers. We used all the available ropes as a long painter to prevent her drifting away to the northeast, and then the *Stancomb Wills* came alongside, transferred her load, and went back to the shore for more. As she was being beached this time the sea took her stern and half filled her with water. She had to be turned over and emptied before the return journey could be made. Every member of the crew of the *Stancomb Wills* was wet to the skin. The water casks were towed behind the *Stancomb Wills* on this second journey, and the swell, which was increasing rapidly, drove the boat on to the rocks, where one of the casks was slightly stove in. This accident proved later to be a serious one, since some sea water had entered the cask and the contents were now brackish.

By midday the *James Caird* was ready for the voyage. Vincent and the carpenter had secured some dry clothes by exchange with members of the shore party (I heard afterward that it was a full fortnight beofre the soaked garments were finally dried), and the boat's crew was standing by waiting for the order to cast off. A moderate westerly breeze was blowing. I went ashore in the *Stancomb Wills* and had a last word with Wild, who was remaining in full command, with directions as to his course of action in the event of our failure to bring relief, but I practically left the whole situation and scope of action and decision to his own judgment, secure in the knowledge that he would act wisely. I told him that I trusted the party to him and said good-by to the men. Then we pushed off for the last time, and within a few minutes I was aboard the *James Caird.* The crew of the *Stancomb Wills* shook hands with us as the boats bumped together and offered us the last good wishes. Then, setting our jib, we cut the painter and moved away to the northeast. The men who were staying behind made a pathetic little group on the beach, with the grim heights of the island behind them and the sea seething at their feet, but they waved to us and gave three hearty cheers. There was hope in their hearts and they trusted us to bring the help that they needed.

I had all sails set, and the *James Caird* quickly dipped the beach and its line of dark figures. The westerly wind took us rapidly to the line of pack, and as we entered it I stood up with my arm around the mast, directing the steering, so as to avoid the great lumps of ice that were flung about in the heave of the sea. The pack thickened and we were forced to turn almost due east, running before the wind toward a gap I had seen in the morning from the high ground. I could not see the gap now, but we had come out on its bearing and I was prepared to find that it had been influenced by the easterly drift. At four o'clock in the afternoon we found the channel, much narrower than it had seemed in the morning but still navigable. Dropping sail, we rowed through without touching the ice anywhere, and by 5:30 P.M. we were clear of the pack with open water before us. We passed one more piece of ice in the darkness an hour later, but the pack lay behind, and with a fair wind swelling the sails we steered our little craft through the night, our hopes centered on our distant goal. The swell was very heavy now, and when the time came for our first evening meal we found great difficulty in keeping the Primus lamp alight and preventing the hoosh splashing out of the pot. Three men were needed to attend to the cooking, one man holding the lamp and two men guarding the aluminum cooking pot, which had to be lifted clear of the Primus whenever the movement of the boat threatened to cause a disaster. Then the lamp had to be protected from water, for sprays were coming over the bows and our flimsy decking was by no means watertight. All these operations were conducted in the confined space under the decking, where the men lay or knelt and adjusted themselves as best they could to the angles of our cases and ballast. It was uncomfortable, but we found consolation in the reflection that without the decking we could not have used the cooker at all.

The tale of the next sixteen days is one of supreme strife amid heaving waters. The subantarctic Ocean lived up to its evil winter reputation. I decided to run north for at least two days while the wind held and so get into warmer weather before turning to the east and laying a course for South Georgia. We took two-hourly spells at the tiller. The men who were not on watch crawled into the sodden sleeping bags and tried to forget their troubles for a period; but there was no comfort in the boat. The bags and cases seemed to be alive in the unfailing knack of presenting their most uncomfortable angles to our rest-seeking bodies. A man might imagine for a moment that he had found a position of ease, but always discovered quickly that some unyielding point was impinging on muscle or bone. The first night aboard the boat was one of acute discomfort for us all, and we were heartily glad when the dawn came and we could set about the preparation of a hot breakfast.

This record of the voyage to South Georgia is based upon scanty notes made day by day. The notes dealt usually with the bare facts of distances, positions, and weather, but our memories retained the incidents of the passing days in a period never to be forgotten. By running north for the first two days I hoped to get warmer weather and also to avoid lines of pack that might be extending beyond the main body. We needed all the advantage that we could obtain from the higher latitude for sailing on the great circle, but we had to be cautious regarding possible ice streams. Cramped in our narrow quarters and continually wet by the spray, we suffered severely from cold throughout the journey. We fought the seas and the winds and at the same time had a daily struggle to keep ourselves alive. At times we were in dire peril. Generally we were upheld by the knowledge that we were making progress toward the land where we would be, but there were days and nights when we lay hove to, drifting across the storm-whitened seas and watching, with eyes interested rather than apprehensive, the uprearing masses of water, flung to and fro by Nature in the pride of her strength. Deep seemed the valleys when we lay between the reeling seas. High were the hills when we perched momentarily on the tops of giant combers. Nearly always there were gales. So small was our boat and so great were the seas that often our sail flapped idly in the calm between the crests of two waves. Then we would climb the next slope and catch the full fury of the gale where the wool-like whiteness of the breaking water surged around us. We had our moments of laughter— rare, it is true, but hearty enough. Even when cracked lips and swollen mouths checked the outward and visible signs of amusement we could see a joke of the primitive kind. Man's sense of humor is always most easily stirred by the petty misfortunes of his neighbors, and I shall never forget Worsley's efforts on one occasion to place the hot aluminum stand on top of the Primus stove after it had fallen off in an extra heavy roll. With his frostbitten fingers he picked it up, dropped it, picked it up again, and toyed with it gingerly as though it were some fragile article of lady's wear. We laughed, or rather gurgled with laughter.

The wind came up strong and worked into a gale from the northwest on the third day out. We stood away to the east. The increasing seas discovered the weaknesses of our decking. The continuous blows shifted to box lids and sledge runners so that the canvas sagged down and accumulated water. Then icy trickles, distinct from the driving sprays, poured fore and aft into the boat. The nails that the carpenter had extracted from cases at Elephant Island and used to fasten down the battens were too short to make firm the decking. We did what we could to secure it, but our means were very limited, and the water continued to enter the boat at a dozen points. Much baling was necessary, and nothing that we could do prevented our gear from becoming sodden. The searching runnels from the canvas were really more unpleasant than the sudden definite douches of the sprays. Lying under the thwarts during watches below, we tried vainly to avoid them. There were no dry places in the boat, and at last we simply covered our heads with our Burberrys and endured the all-pervading water. The baling was work for the watch. Real rest we had none. The perpetual motion of the boat made repose impossible; we were cold, sore, and anxious. We moved on hands and knees in the semi-darkness of the day under the decking. The darkness was complete by 6 P.M., and not until 7 A.M. of the following day could we see one another under the thwarts. We had a few scraps of candle, and they were preserved carefully in order that we might have light at mealtimes. There was one fairly dry spot in the boat, under the solid original decking at the bows, and we managed to protect some of our biscuit from the salt water; but I do not think any of us got the taste of salt out of our mouths during the voyage.

The difficulty of movement in the boat would have had its humorous side if it had not involved us in so many aches and pains. We had to crawl under the thwarts in order to move along the boat, and our knees suffered considerably. When a watch turned out it was necessary for me to direct each man by name when and where to move, since if all hands had crawled about at the same time the result would have been dire confusion and many bruises. Then there was the trim of the boat to be considered. The order of the watch was four hours on and four hours off, three men to the watch. One man had the tiller ropes, the second man attended to the sail, and the third baled for all he was worth. Sometimes when the water in the boat had been reduced to reasonable proportions, our pump could be used. This pump, which Hurley had made from the Flinders bar case of our ship's standard compass, was quite effective, though its capacity was not large. The man who was attending the sail could pump into the big outer cooker, which was lifted and emptied overboard when filled. We had a device by which the water could go direct from the pump into the sea through a hole in the gunwale, but this hole had to be blocked at an early stage of the voyage, since we found that it admitted water when the boat rolled.

While a new watch was shivering in the wind and spray, the men who had been relieved groped hurriedly among the soaked sleeping bags and tried to steal a little of the warmth created by the last occupants; but it was not always possible for us to find even this comfort when we went off watch. The boulders that we had taken aboard for ballast had to be shifted continually in order to trim the boat and give access of the pump, which became choked with hairs from the moulting sleeping bags and finneskoe. The four reindeer-skin sleeping bags shed their hair freely owing to the continuous wetting, and soon became quite bald in appearance. The moving of the boulders was weary and painful work. We came to know every one of the stones by sight and touch, and I have vivid memories of their angular peculiarities even today. They might have been of considerable interest as geological specimens to a scientific man under happier conditions. As ballast they were useful. As weights to be moved about in cramped quarters they were simply appalling. They spared no portion of our poor bodies. Another of our troubles, worth mention here, was the chafing of our legs by our wet clothes, which had not been changed now for seven months. The insides of our thighs were rubbed raw, and the one tube of Hazeline cream in our medicine chest did not go far in alleviating our pain, which was increased by the bite of the salt water. We thought at the time that we never slept. The fact was that we would doze off uncomfortably, to be aroused quickly by some new ache or another call to effort. My own share of the general unpleasantness was accentuated by a finely developed bout of sciatica. I had become possessor of this originally on the floe several months earlier.

Our meals were regular in spite of the gales. Attention to this point was essential, since the conditions of the voyage made increasing calls upon our vitality. Breakfast, at 8 A.M., consisted of a pannikin of hot hoosh made from Bovril sledging ration, two biscuits, and some lumps of sugar. Lunch came at 1 P.M., and comprised Bovril sledging ration, eaten raw, and a pannikin of hot milk for each man. Tea, at 5 P.M., had the same menu. Then during the night we had a hot drink, generally of milk. The meals were the bright beacons in those cold and stormy days. The glow of warmth and comfort produced by the food and drink made optimists of us all. We had two tins of Virol, which we were keeping for an emergency; but, finding ourselves in need of an oil lamp to eke out our supply of candles, we emptied one of the tins in the manner that most appealed to us, and fitted it with a wick made by shredding a bit of canvas. When this lamp was filled with oil it gave a certain amount of light, though it was easily blown out, and was of great assistance to us at night. We were fairly well off as regarded fuel, since we had 6½ gallons of petroleum.

A severe southwesterly gale on the fourth day out forced us to heave to. I would have liked to have run before the wind, but the sea was very high and the *James Caird* was in danger of broaching to and swamping. The delay was vexatious, since up to that time we had been making sixty or seventy miles a day; good going with our limited sail area. We hove to under double-reefed mainsail and our little jigger, and waited for the gale to blow itself out. During that afternoon we saw bits of wreckage, the remains probably of some unfortunate vessel that had failed to weather the strong gales south of Cape Horn. The weather conditions did not improve, and on the fifth day out the gale was so fierce that we were compelled to take in the double-reefed mainsail and hoist our small jib instead. We put out a sea anchor to keep the *James Caird*'s head up to the sea. This anchor consisted of a triangular canvas bag fastened to the end of the painter and allowed to stream out from the bows. The boat was high enough to catch the wind, and, as she drifted to leeward, the drag of the anchor kept her head to windward. Thus our boat took most of the seas more or less end on. Even then the crests of the waves often would curl right over us and we shipped a great deal of water, which necessitated unceasing baling and pumping. Looking out abeam, we would see a hollow like a tunnel formed as the crest of a big wave toppled over on to the swelling body of water. A thousand times it appeared as though the *James Caird* must be engulfed; but the boat lived. The southwesterly gale had its birthplace above the Antarctic Continent, and its freezing breath lowered the temperature far toward zero. The sprays froze upon the boat and gave bows, sides, and decking a heavy coat of mail. This accumulation of ice reduced the buoyancy of the boat, and to that extent was an added peril; but it possessed a notable advantage from one point of view. The water ceased to drop and trickle from the canvas, and the spray came in solely at the well in the after part of the boat. We could not allow the load of ice to grow beyond a certain point, and in turns we crawled about the decking forward, chipping and picking at it with the available tools.

When daylight came on the morning of the sixth day out we saw and felt that the *James Caird* had lost her resiliency. She was not rising to the oncoming seas. The weight of the ice that had formed in her and upon her during the night was having its effect, and she was becoming more like a log than a boat. The situation called for immediate action. We first broke away the spare oars, which were encased in ice and frozen to the sides of the boat, and threw them overboard. We retained two oars for use when we got inshore. Two of the fur sleeping bags went over the side; they were thoroughly wet, weighing probably 40 lb. each, and they had frozen stiff during the night. Three men constituted the watch below, and when a man went down it was better to turn into the wet bag just vacated by another man than to thaw out a frozen bag with the heat of his unfortunate body. We now had four bags, three in use and one for emergency use in case a member of the party should break down permanently. The reduction of weight relieved the boat to some extent, and vigorous chipping and scraping did more. We had to be very careful not to put axe or knife through the

frozen canvas of the decking as we crawled over it, but gradually we got rid of a lot of ice. The *James Caird* lifted to the
endless waves as though she lived again.

About 11 A.M. the boat suddenly fell off into the trough of
the sea. The painter had parted and the sea anchor had gone.
This was serious. The *James Caird* went away to leeward, and
we had no chance at all of recovering the anchor and our
valuable rope, which had been our only means of keeping
the boat's head up to the seas without the risk of hoisting sail
in a gale. Now we had to set the sail and trust to its holding.
While the *James Caird* rolled heavily in the trough, we beat
the frozen canvas until the bulk of the ice had cracked off it
and then hoisted it. The frozen gear worked protestingly, but
after a struggle our little craft came up to the wind again, and
we breathed more freely. Skin frostbites were troubling us,
and we had developed large blisters on our fingers and
hands. I shall always carry the scar of one of these frostbites
on my left hand, which became badly inflamed after the skin
had burst and the cold had bitten deeply.

We held the boat up to the gale during that day, enduring
as best we could discomforts that amounted to pain. The boat
tossed interminably on the big waves under gray, threatening skies. Our thoughts did not embrace much more than the
necessities of the hour. Every surge of the sea was an enemy
to be watched and circumvented. We ate our scanty meals,
treated our frostbites, and hoped for the improved conditions that the morrow might bring. Night fell early, and in
the lagging hours of darkness we were cheered by a change
for the better in the weather. The wind dropped, the snow
squalls became less frequent, and the sea moderated. When
the morning of the seventh day dawned there was not much
wind. We shook the reef out of the sail and laid our course
once more for South Georgia. The sun came out bright and
clear, and presently Worsley got a snap for longitude. We
hoped that the sky would remain clear until noon, so that we
could get the latitude. We had been six days out without an
observation, and our dead reckoning naturally was uncer-

tain. The boat must have presented a strange appearance
that morning. All hands basked in the sun. We hung our
sleeping bags to the mast and spread our socks and other gear
all over the deck. Some of the ice had melted off the *James
Caird* in the early morning after the gale began to slacken,
and dry patches were appearing in the decking. Porpoises
came blowing round the boat, and Cape pigeons wheeled
and swooped within a few feet of us. These little black-and-
white birds have an air of friendliness that is not possessed by
the great circling albatross. They had looked gray against the
swaying sea during the storm as they darted about over our
heads and uttered their plaintive cries. The albatrosses, of
the black or sooty variety, had watched with hard, bright
eyes, and seemed to have a quite impersonal interest in our
struggle to keep afloat amid the battering seas. In addition to
the Cape pigeons an occasional stormy petrel flashed overhead. Then there was a small bird, unknown to me, that
appeared always to be in a fussy, bustling state, quite out of
keeping with the surroundings. It irritated me. It had practically no tail, and it flitted about vaguely as though in search
of the lost member. I used to find myself wishing it would find
its tail and have done with the silly fluttering.

We reveled in the warmth of the sun that day. Life was not
so bad, after all. We felt we were well on our way. Our gear
was drying, and we could have a hot meal in comparative
comfort. The swell was still heavy, but it was not breaking
and the boat rode easily. At noon Worsley balanced himself
on the gunwale and clung with one hand to the stay of the
mainmast while he got a snap of the sun. The result was more
than encouraging. We had done over 380 miles and were
getting on for halfway to South Georgia. It looked as though
we were going to get through.

The wind freshened to a good stiff breeze during the afternoon, and the *James Caird* made satisfactory progress. I had
not realized until the sunlight came how small our boat really
was. There was some influence in the light and warmth, some
hint of happier days, that made us revive memories of other

voyages, when we had stout decks beneath our feet, unlimited food at our command, and pleasant cabins for our ease. Now we clung to a battered little boat, "alone, alone, all, all alone, alone on a wide, wide sea." So low in the water were we that each succeeding swell cut off our view of the sky line. We were a tiny speck in the vast vista of the sea—the ocean that is open to all and merciful to none, that threatens even when it seems to yield, and that is pitiless always to weakness. For a moment the consciousness of the forces arrayed against us would be almost overwhelming. Then hope and confidence would rise again as our boat rose to a wave and tossed aside the crest in a sparkling shower like the play of prismatic colors at the foot of a waterfall. My double-barreled gun and some cartridges had been stowed aboard the boat as an emergency precaution against a shortage of food, but we were not disposed to destroy our little neighbors, the Cape pigeons, even for the sake of fresh meat. We might have shot an albatross, but the wandering king of the ocean aroused in us something of the feeling that inspired, too late, the Ancient Mariner. So the gun remained among the stores and sleeping-bags in the narrow quarters beneath our leaking deck, and the birds followed us unmolested.

The eighth, ninth, and tenth days of the voyage had few features worthy of special note. The wind blew hard during those days, and the strain of navigating the boat was unceasing, but always we made some advance toward our goal. No bergs showed on our horizon, and we knew that we were clear of the ice fields. Each day brought its little round of troubles, but also compensation in the form of food and growing hope. We felt that we were going to succeed. The odds against us had been great, but we were winning through. We still suffered severely from the cold, for, though the temperature was rising, our vitality was declining owing to shortage of food, exposure, and the necessity of maintaining our cramped positions day and night. I found that it was now absolutely necessary to prepare hot milk for all hands during the night, in order to sustain life till dawn. This meant lighting the Primus lamp in the darkness and involved an increased drain on our small store of matches. It was the rule that one match must serve when the Primus was being lit. We had no lamp for the compass and during the early days of the voyage we would strike a match when the steersman wanted to see the course at night; but later the necessity for strict economy impressed itself upon us, and the practice of striking matches at night was stopped. We had one watertight tin of matches. I had stowed away in a pocket, in readiness for a sunny day, a lens from one of the telescopes, but this was of no use during the voyage. The sun seldom shone upon us. The glass of the compass got broken one night, and we contrived to mend it with adhesive tape from the medicine chest. One of the memories that comes to me from those days is of Crean singing at the tiller. He always sang while he was steering, and nobody ever discovered what the song was. It was devoid of tune and as monotonous as the chanting of a Buddhist monk at his prayers; yet somehow it was cheerful. In moments of inspiration Crean would attempt "The Wearing of the Green."

On the tenth night Worsley could not straighten his body after his spell at the tiller. He was thoroughly cramped, and we had to drag him beneath the decking and massage him before he could unbend himself and get into a sleeping bag. A hard northwesterly gale came up on the eleventh day (May 5) and shifted to the southwest in the late afternoon. The sky was overcast and occasional snow squalls added to the discomfort produced by a tremendous cross sea—the worst, I thought, that we had experienced. At midnight I was at the tiller and suddenly noticed a line of clear sky between the south and southwest. I called to the other men that the sky was clearing, and then a moment later I realized that what I had seen was not a rift in the clouds but the white crest of an enormous wave. During twenty-six years' experience of the ocean in all its moods I had not encountered a wave so gigantic. It was a mighty upheaval of the ocean, a thing quite apart from the big white-capped seas that had been our tireless enemies for many days. I shouted, "For God's sake, hold on! It's got us!" Then came a moment of suspense that seemed drawn out into hours. White surged the foam of the breaking sea around us. We felt our boat lifted and flung forward like a cork in breaking surf. We were in a seething chaos of tortured water; but somehow the boat lived through it, half full of water, sagging to the dead weight and shuddering under the blow. We baled with the energy of men fighting for life, flinging the water over the sides with every receptacle that came to our hands, and after ten minutes of uncertainty we felt the boat renew her life beneath us. She floated again and ceased to lurch drunkenly as though dazed by the attack of the sea. Earnestly we hoped that never again would we encounter such a wave.

The conditions in the boat, uncomfortable before, had been made worse by the deluge of water. All our gear was thoroughly wet again. Our cooking stove had been floating about in the bottom of the boat, and portions of our last hoosh seemed to have permeated everything. Not until 3 A.M., when we were all chilled almost to the limit of endurance, did we manage to get the stove alight and make ourselves hot drinks. The carpenter was suffering particularly, but he showed grit and spirit. Vincent had for the past week ceased to be an active member of the crew, and I could not easily account for his collapse. Physically he was one of the strongest men in the boat. He was a young man, he had served on North Sea trawlers, and he should have been able to bear hardships better than McCarthy, who, not so strong, was always happy.

The weather was better on the following day (May 6), and we got a glimpse of the sun. Worsley's observation showed that we were not more than a hundred miles from the northwest corner of South Georgia. Two more days with a favorable wind and we would sight the promised land. I hoped that there would be no delay, for our supply of water was running very low. The hot drink at night was essential, but I decided that the daily allowance of water must be cut down to half a pint per man. The lumps of ice we had taken aboard had gone long ago. We were dependent upon the water we had brought from Elephant Island, and our thirst was increased by the fact that we were now using the brackish water in the breaker that had been slightly stove in in the surf when the boat was being loaded. Some sea water had entered at that time.

Thirst took possession of us. I dared not permit the allowance of water to be increased since an unfavorable wind might drive us away from the island and lengthen our voyage by many days. Lack of water is always the most severe privation that men can be condemned to endure, and we found, as during our earlier boat voyage, that the salt water in our clothing and the salt spray that lashed our faces made our thirst grow quickly to a burning pain. I had to be very firm in refusing to allow anyone to anticipate the morrow's allowance, which I was sometimes begged to do. We did the necessary work dully and hoped for the land. I had altered the course to the east so as to make sure of our striking the island, which would have been impossible to regain if we had run past the northern end. The course was laid on our scrap of chart for a point some thirty miles down the coast. That day and the following day passed for us in a sort of nightmare. Our mouths were dry and our tongues were swollen. The wind was still strong and the heavy sea forced us to navigate carefully, but any thought of our peril from the waves was buried beneath the consciousness of our raging thirst. The bright moments were those when we each received our one mug of hot milk during the long, bitter watches of the night. Things were bad for us in those days, but the end was coming. The morning of May 8 broke thick and stormy, with squalls from the northwest. We searched the waters ahead for a sign of land, and though we could see nothing more than had met our eyes for many days, we were cheered by a sense that the goal was near at hand. About ten o'clock that morning we passed a little bit of kelp, a glad signal of the proximity of land. An hour later we saw two shags sitting on a big mass of kelp, and knew then that we must be within ten or fifteen miles of the shore. These birds are as sure an indication of the proximity of land as a lighthouse is, for they never venture far to sea. We gazed ahead with increasing eagerness, and at 12:30 P.M., through a rift in the clouds, McCarthy caught a glimpse of the black cliffs of South Georgia, just fourteen days after our departure from Elephant Island. It was a glad moment. Thirst-ridden, chilled, and weak as we were, happiness irradiated us. The job was nearly done.

We stood in toward the shore to look for a landing place, and presently we could see the green tussock grass on the ledges above the surf-beaten rocks. Ahead of us and to the south, blind rollers showed the presence of uncharted reefs along the coast. Here and there the hungry rocks were close to the surface, and over them the great waves broke, swirling viciously and spouting thirty and forty feet into the air. The rocky coast appeared to descend sheer to the sea. Our need of water and rest was well-nigh desperate, but to have attempted a landing at that time would have been suicidal. Night was drawing near, and the weather indications were not favorable. There was nothing for it but to haul off till the following morning, so we stood away on the starboard tack until we had made what appeared to be a safe offing. Then we hove to in the high westerly swell. The hours passed slowly as we awaited the dawn, which would herald, we fondly hoped, the last stage of our journey. Our thirst was a torment and we could scarcely touch our food; the cold seemed to strike right through our weakened bodies. At 5 A.M. the wind shifted to the northwest and quickly increased to one of the worst hurricanes any of us had ever experienced. A great cross sea was running, and the wind simply shrieked as it tore the tops off the waves and converted the whole seascape into a haze of driving spray. Down into valleys, up to tossing heights, straining until her seams opened, swung our little boat, brave still but laboring heavily. We knew that the wind and set of the sea was driving us ashore, but we could do nothing. The dawn showed us a storm-torn ocean, and the morning passed without bringing us a sight of the land; but at 1 P.M., through a rift in the flying mists, we got a glimpse of the huge crags of the island and realized that our position had become desperate. We were on a dead lee shore, and we could gauge our approach to the unseen cliffs by the roar of the breakers against the sheer walls of rock. I ordered the double-reefed mainsail to be set in the hope that we might claw off, and this attempt increased the strain upon the boat. The *James Caird* was bumping heavily, and the water was pouring in everywhere. Our thirst was forgotten in the realization of our imminent danger, as we baled unceasingly, and adjusted our weights from time to time; occasional glimpses showed that the shore was nearer. I knew that Annewkow Island lay to the south of us, but our small and badly marked chart showed uncertain reefs in the passage between the island and the mainland, and I dared not trust it, though as a last resort we could try to lie under the lee of the island. The afternoon wore away as we edged down the coast, with the thunder of the breakers in our ears. The approach of evening found us still some distance from Annewkow Island, and, dimly in the twilight, we could see a snow-capped mountain looming above us. The chance of surviving the night, with the driving gale and the implacable sea forcing us on to the lee shore, seemed small. I think most of us had a feeling that the end was very near. Just after 6 P.M., in the dark, as the boat was in the yeasty backwash from the seas flung from this iron-bound coast, then, just when things looked their worst, they changed for the best. I have marveled often at the thin line that divides success from failure and the sudden turn that leads from apparently certain disaster to comparative safety. The wind suddenly shifted, and we were free once more to make an offing. Almost as soon as the gale eased, the pin that locked the mast to the thwart fell out. It must have been on the point of doing this throughout the hurricane, and if it had gone nothing could have saved us; the mast would have snapped like a carrot. Our backstays had carried away once

before when iced up and were not too strongly fastened now.
We were thankful indeed for the mercy that had held that
pin in its place throughout the hurricane.

We stood off shore again, tired almost to the point of apa-
thy. Our water had long been finished. The last was about a
pint of hairy liquid, which we strained through a bit of gauze
from the medicine chest. The pangs of thirst attacked us with
redoubled intensity, and I felt that we must make a landing
on the following day at almost any hazard. The night wore
on. We were very tired. We longed for day. When at last the
dawn came on the morning of May 10 there was practically
no wind, but a high cross sea was running. We made slow
progress toward the shore. About 8 A.M. the wind backed to
the northwest and threatened another blow. We had sighted
in the meantime a big indentation which I thought must be
King Haakon Bay, and I decided that we must land there. We
set the bows of the boat toward the bay and ran before the
freshening gale. Soon we had angry reefs on either side.
Great glaciers came down to the sea and offered no landing
place. The sea spouted on the reefs and thundered against
the shore. About noon we sighted a line of jagged reef, like
blackened teeth, that seemed to bar the entrance to the bay.
Inside, comparatively smooth water stretched eight or nine
miles to the head of the bay. A gap in the reef appeared, and
we made for it. But the fates had another rebuff for us. The
wind shifted and blew from the east right out of the bay. We
could see the way through the reef, but we could not approach it directly. That afternoon we bore up, tacking five
times in the strong wind. The last tack enabled us to get
through, and at last we were in the wide mouth of the bay.
Dusk was approaching. A small cove, with a boulder-strewn
beach guarded by a reef, made a break in the cliffs on the
south side of the bay, and we ran through the kelp and made
the passage of the reef. The entrance was so narrow that we
had to take in the oars, and the swell was piling itself right
over the reef into the cove; but in a minute or two we were
inside, and in the gathering darkness the *James Caird* ran in

on a swell and touched the beach. I sprang ashore with the short painter and held on when the boat went out with the backward surge. When the *James Caird* came in again three of the men got ashore, and they held the painter while I climbed some rocks with another line. A slip on the wet rocks twenty feet up nearly closed my part of the story just at the moment when we were achieving safety. A jagged piece of rock held me and at the same time bruised me sorely. However, I made fast the line, and in a few minutes we were all safe on the beach, with the boat floating in the surging water just off the shore. We heard a gurgling sound that was sweet music in our ears, and, peering around, found a stream of fresh water almost at our feet. A moment later we were down on our knees drinking the pure, ice-cold water in long draughts that put new life into us. It was a splendid moment.

HERBERT G. PONTING

(*1870–1935*)

DURING HERBERT PONTING'S LIFE he was widely known in England as a world traveler, master photographer, travel writer and lecturer. Now he is mostly remembered by the handful of admirers of his illustrations of *Scott's Last Expedition*. He met Scott in the autumn of 1909, at the height of his fame.

In his time he was by far the most gifted photographer of the Antarctic. Even from today's perspective he seems to be possibly the finest photographer so far to have worked in Antarctica, despite the limitations of his early equipment. He worked arduously, extensively, intensively and, above all, with great artistic effect. He made an invaluable record of the expedition. We are indebted to him for many famous photographs—for example those showing Scott in the hut on Cape Evans. He was equally good at dealing with landscapes and with men and animals. Scott prized not only his camera work but his lantern-slide lectures about exotic places given to members of the expedition. Ponting had a willingness, almost an eagerness, to teach others the art of photography. In his book about his experiences with the expedition Ponting reveals himself to be a sensitive and articulate writer.

Great White South

Having decided to establish winter-quarters at Cape Evans, Captain Scott, quick to recognise that fine weather meant everything to the success of my work, informed me that it would be as well to take all possible advantage of the exceptionally favourable weather conditions whilst the ice held, as, once it broke up, subjects now easily accessible would then become impossible of approach. I was to consider myself free to devote myself exclusively to my photographic work, and should not be expected to take any part in unloading the ship. Being thus freed from regulations drawn up for the observance of others, I worked almost ceaselessly, for there was no lack of subjects for my cameras.

I had noted some fine icebergs frozen into the sea ice about a mile distant. The morning after our arrival, I was just about to start across the ice to visit these bergs, with a sledge well loaded with photographic apparatus, when eight Killer whales appeared, heading towards the ice, blowing loudly. Since first seeing some of these wolves of the sea off Cape Crozier I had been anxious to secure photographs of them. Captain Scott, who also saw the approaching school, called out to me to try and obtain a picture of them, just as I was snatching up my reflex camera for that purpose. The whales dived under the ice, so, hastily estimating where they would be likely to rise again, I ran to the spot—adjusting the camera as I did so. I had got to within six feet of the edge of the ice —which was about a yard thick—when to my consternation it suddenly heaved up under my feet and split into fragments around me; whilst the eight whales, lined up side by side and almost touching each other, burst up from under the ice and blew off steam.

The head of one was within two yards of me. I saw its nostrils open, and at such close quarters the release of its pent-up breath was like a blast from an air-compressor. The noise of the eight simultaneous blows sounded terrific, and I was enveloped in the warm vapour of the nearest 'spout,' which had a strong fishy smell. Fortunately the shock sent me backwards, instead of precipitating me into the sea, or my Antarctic experiences would have ended somewhat prematurely.

As the whales rose from under the ice, there was a loud 'booming sound'—to use the expression of Captain Scott, who was a witness of the incident—as they struck the ice with their backs. Immediately they had cleared it, with a rapid movement of their flukes (huge tail fins) they made a tremendous commotion, setting the floe on which I was now isolated rocking so furiously that it was all I could do to keep from falling into the water. Then they turned about with the deliberate intention of attacking me. The ship was within sixty yards, and I heard wild shouts of 'Look out!' 'Run!' 'Jump, man, jump!' 'Run, quick!' But I could not run; it was all I could do to keep my feet as I leapt from piece to piece of the rocking ice, with the whales a few yards behind me, snorting and blowing among the ice-blocks. I wondered whether I should be able to reach safety before the whales reached me; and I recollect distinctly thinking, if they did get me, how very unpleasant the first bite would feel, but that it would not matter much about the second.

The broken floes had already started to drift away with the current, and as I reached the last fragment I saw that I could not jump to the firm ice, for the lead was too wide. The whales behind me were making a horrible noise amongst the broken ice, and I stood for a moment hesitating what to do. More frantic shouts of 'Jump, man, jump!' reached me from my friends. Just then, by great good luck, the floe on which I stood turned slightly in the current and lessened the distance. I was able to leap across, not, however, a moment too soon. As I reached security and looked back, a huge black and tawny head was pushed out of the water at the spot, and rested on the ice, looking round with its little pig-like eyes to see what had become of me. The brute opened his jaws wide, and I saw the terrible teeth which I had so narrowly escaped.

I wasted no time in sprinting the sixty or seventy yards to my sledge, by which Captain Scott was standing. I shall never forget his expression as I reached it in safety. During the next year I saw that same look on his face several times, when someone was in danger. It showed how deeply he felt the responsibility for life, which he thought rested so largely on himself. He was deathly pale as he said to me: 'My God! that was about the nearest squeak I ever saw!'

There were two dogs tethered out on the ice near the scene of this incident, and we came to the conclusion that it was an organized attempt by the whales to get the dogs— which they had doubtless taken for seals—into the water. I had happened on the scene at an inopportune moment, and I have no doubt they looked upon me as fair game as well.

Captain Scott, at the end of his description of this incident in his Journal, stated:

'One after the other their huge hideous heads shot vertically into the air through the cracks that they had made. As they reared them to a height of 6 or 8 feet it was possible to see their tawny head markings, their small glistening eyes and their terrible array of teeth—by far the largest and most terrifying in the world. There cannot be a doubt that they looked up to see what had happened to Ponting and the dogs.

The latter were horribly frightened, and strained at their chains, whining; the head of one Killer must certainly have been within five feet of one of the dogs. After this, whether they thought the game insignificant, or whether they missed Ponting is uncertain; but the terrifying creatures passed on to other hunting grounds and we were able to rescue the dogs.

'Of course we have known well that Killer whales continually skirt the edge of the floes, and that they would undoubtedly snap up anyone who was unfortunate enough to fall into the water; but the fact that they could display such deliberate cunning, that they were able to break ice of such thickness (at least 2½ feet), and that they could act in unison, was a revelation to us. It is clear that they are endowed with singular intelligence, and in future we shall treat that intelligence with every respect.'

This incident certainly inspired *me* with a wholesome respect for these devils of the sea, and I never took any chances with them afterwards.

The next day just as I was about to leave the ship to visit the bergs, a school of *Orcas* again appeared, heading for the ship in close formation. I leant over the poop rail, with my eyes deep in the hood of my large reflex camera, waiting for the whales to draw nearer, when, as I was about to release the shutter, the view disappeared from the finder, and light flooded the camera; at the same moment I heard something splash in the water. On examining the camera, what was my consternation to find that the lens-board had dropped into the sea, carrying with it the finest lens of my collection—a nine-inch Zeiss double protar, worth about £25, which had been presented to me some years ago by the Bausch and Lomb Optical Company of Rochester, U.S.A. This was a serious loss, as the lens was not only my favourite on account of its superb qualities, but I had used it in many foreign lands, and therefore regarded it with affection. I had none other capable of completely taking its place, and all my subsequent scenic work was done with other and less suitable objectives.

I retailed the story of the loss of the lens—which now lies in a watery grave, 200 fathoms deep, at the bottom of McMurdo Sound—in a letter to the makers, which was duly posted on the return of the ship to New Zealand. When the *Terra Nova* came to relieve us next year, there was a parcel for me containing a replica of the instrument, and a letter from this courteous firm, requesting that I would accept the new lens as a substitute.

The continued glorious fine weather which at this time we experienced, though a godsend to us all, had on me rather an exhausting effect, for as long as it lasted I was loath to take rest. I knew that at any hour it might end, a storm arise, and the sea-ice break up; then there would be an end to my chances of getting any pictures of the stranded icebergs, and other features of our surroundings.

The sun at this season is nearly as high in these regions at midnight as at midday, so if the light was not right on a subject at noon, the chances were that it would be twelve hours later. For the first four nights I scarcely slept at all, as this continuous daylight was too novel and too wonderful to permit of sleep; it seemed waste of precious time to lose one single hour. I determined that lost opportunities should be as few as human endurance would permit. Afterwards I had cause for congratulation that neither time nor chances had been wasted, for the ice was rapidly decaying, and five days later it was so rotten round the stranded bergs that I was no longer able to approach them.

In one of these bergs there was a grotto. This, I decided, should be the object of my first excursion. It was about a mile from the ship, and though a lot of rough and broken ice surrounded it, I was able to get right up to it. A fringe of long icicles hung at the entrance of the grotto, and passing under these I was in the most wonderful place imaginable. From outside, the interior appeared quite white and colourless, but, once inside, it was a lovely symphony of blue and green. I made many photographs in this remarkable place—than which I secured none more beautiful the entire time I was in the South. By almost incredible good luck the entrance to the cavern framed a fine view of the *Terra Nova* lying at the ice-foot, a mile away.

During this first and subsequent visits, I found that the colouring of the grotto changed with the position of the sun; thus, sometimes green would predominate, then blue, and then again it was a delicate lilac. When the sun passed round to the west—opposite the entrance to the cavern—the beams that streamed in were reflected by myriads of crystals, which decomposed the rays into lovely prismatic hues, so that the walls appeared to be studded with gems. Curiously enough, this wonderful effect was only to be obtained when wearing nonactinic goggles. The place then became a veritable Aladdin's Cave of beauty. I was loath to leave it all; but after having made sure of my pictures, I hurried back to persuade Captain Scott to come and see the sight, which he did, and was as delighted as I was with its wonders. Uncle Bill[1] came too, and made some sketches.

The cavern was about forty yards in length, and it had been formed by the berg turning partially over and carrying an ice-floe upwards, about eight feet thick, which had frozen into its present position. The difference of structure of the floe-ice on one side of the cavern, and the berg-ice on the other was very marked. It was great good fortune that I had been able to get the picture showing the ship framed by the grotto's entrance; a few hours later the berg had swung round many degrees in the current, and the ship was no longer to be seen from within.

Taylor and Wright came out to investigate the phenomenon in the afternoon, and with ice-axes cut steps up the floe that formed the outer part of the tunnel, whilst I kinematographed the Alpine feat. It made an excellent film. Then we all explored the cave, which closed up rapidly towards the further end. After squeezing through a passage with a 'fat man's misery' in it, and climbing through a narrow sloping

1 Edward Wilson.—C.N.

tunnel, we found ourselves high in the open air, near the summit of the berg. As we emerged, Wright had a slip and narrowly escaped falling into the water, fifty feet below. Fortunately he managed to regain his footing—thereby depriving a Killer whale, which immediately afterwards spouted in the pool, of a change of diet for lunch.

This pool was a most alluring feature of the vicinity, and its beauties were perpetuated in many pictures. When unruffled by the breeze, it was a faithful mirror of the sky, and penguins were continually leaping out of it, to rest awhile or roost on the ice. They took little or no notice of me as I made my photographs. Whilst I was engaged on one of them, I heard a sound behind me, and on looking round I saw a Killer whale—with open jaws, and eight feet of its length out of water—leaning on the ice, surveying me with interest. I didn't wait to pack my things. I almost threw them on to the sledge, and pulled off to a safer distance from the water—half expecting, as I did so, to feel the brute burst the ice under me, as I knew it was not very thick hereabouts.

When the temperature was comparatively high, the currents rapidly eroded the ice away underneath, whilst the appearance of the surface changed little. One might be walking along on sound ice; then suddenly tread on a place where it was not an inch thick. One had to feel one's way carefully along, when in doubt, by testing it with a ski-stick. In places the current ran swiftly below, and it was not a pleasant feeling when my legs went through; it made me think how hopeless would be my plight if I went through to the shoulders, and help were not at hand; but such incidents as a leg going through soon became so frequent that they ceased to have the thrill of novelty. I always threw myself flat when I felt the ice giving way underfoot, and I think it saved me a wetting, at least, more than once. Now, I shudder at the risks I took so recklessly in those first days, not realising the imminence of the dangers which, a week later, experience had taught me to hold in greater respect.

During those midnight days, when others slept and only

the night watch and I were awake, some of the most memorable of my Antarctic experiences befell me. It was in those 'night' hours, too, as the sun paraded round the southern heavens, that I secured some of the best of my Polar studies. One of these was 'The Death of an Iceberg'—which represents a berg in the last stage of decay, from the action of the sun and currents. This picture always recalls to me one of the most dismaying episodes of my life. The adventure with the Killer whales had been exciting enough; I had relished the thrill of it. But there was nothing either pleasurable or thrilling about the incident which occurred previous to the taking of this photograph.

There was not so much as a zephyr astir, and the mercury stood only a few degrees below the freezing point, as I started off once more to the bergs that were such a paradise for my work. No sound broke the stillness of the nightless night, save the occasional squawk of a penguin, or the blowing of a whale, perhaps half-a-dozen miles away.

As I neared the bergs, I was perspiring freely from the effort of dragging my sledge; and the yellow goggles, which I wore as protection against snow blindness, became clouded over, so that I could not see. I was just about to stop to wipe them, when I felt the ice sinking under me. I could not see a yard ahead because of my clouded goggles, but I felt the water wet my feet, and I heard a soft hissing sound as the ice gave way around me. I realised instantly that if the heavy sledge, to which I was harnessed, broke through, it would sink like a stone, dragging me down with it. For a moment the impulse was to save myself, by slipping out of the harness, at the expense of all my apparatus. But I went to the Great White South to illustrate its wonders, and without my cameras I was helpless. I therefore instantly resolved that I would save my precious kit, or go down with it. We would survive or sink together.

A flood of thought rushed through my brain in those fateful moments. I seemed to visualise the two hundred fathoms of water below me, infested with those devils, and wondered how long it would take the sledge to drag me to the bottom. Would I drown, or would an *Orca* snap me up before I got there?

Though the ice sank under my feet, it did not break; but each step I expected to be my last. The sledge, dragging through the slush, became like lead; and as the water rose above my boots, I was unable to pull it further. Just then, with perspiration dripping from every pore, I felt my feet touch firm ice. With one supreme, final effort, which sapped the last ounce of strength that was left, I got on to it, and managed to drag the sledge on to it too; then I collapsed. I was so completely exhausted that it was quite a long time before my trembling muscles ceased to quake. When finally my knees would hold me up, I took the photograph.

In adventure one never takes anything too seriously. Incidents of peril are quickly relegated to the limbo of the past. The moment such episodes are over—no matter how imminently life itself may have been at stake—they become mere reminiscences, to be cast aside, and perhaps seldom or never referred to again, until the pen searches them out from the treasure-house of memory.

Having taken the desired photograph, and recorded a very beautiful Polar scene, I lay down on the ice—at the edge of the pool where the reflections appear in the picture—to peer into the profundity that I had so nearly become more intimately acquainted with. A great shaft of sunlight pierced the depths like a searchlight, and, by shading my eyes, with my head close to the water, I could see a hundred feet down into the sea, which was all alive with minute creatures. As I watched, a slim silvery fish darted by, and then a seal rushed into the field of view, from the surrounding blackness—not in pursuit of the fish, but flying in evident terror. The cause of its terror immediately appeared. The horror hove into view without apparent effort, looking like some grim leviathan of war—a submarine; and a thing of war it really was for the seal. It was the dreaded Killer again, in close pursuit of its prey. It came so close to me that I could distinctly see the evil gleam in its eye, and the whole outline of its sleek and sinister shape. For a single second I lay, transfixed with interest at the sight. Then I remembered, and fled to a safer place.

WE SAW COMPARATIVELY LITTLE of Polar bird life at Cape Evans. There were only the amphibious penguins and skua-gulls. McCormick's Antarctic skua-gull—which was named after Mr. McCormick, the naturalist of Sir James Ross's 1840 Expedition—was, so far as one could discover, the only flying-bird that breeds on Ross Island; it was certainly the only bird that bred at Cape Evans whilst we were there. A few Giant petrels visited our promontory occasionally, but though several were shot, nothing was learned of their nesting habits, for they breed many hundreds of miles further north. When in the air they were an imposing sight, for they have a spread of wing some six feet or more from tip to tip; but aground they were ugly, ungainly, disgusting creatures—with big beaks—that would gorge to repletion on the refuse of a fresh-ly-killed seal, and then squat on the floes and doze for hours. They were very timid, and on the approach of anyone, first they vomited the contents of their stomachs to relieve them-selves of the weight, and then ran with outstretched wings for twenty or thirty yards ere they could gather sufficient way to enable them to leave the ice—similarly as an aero-plane 'taxies' over the ground before developing sufficient speed to rise into the air.

But the skua-gulls were with us for six months of the year, and nested within a hundred hards of our Hut. We did not find them altogether pleasant neighbours, for they were ex-tremely noisy and of a most quarrelsome disposition; throughout the summer their raucous screaming never ceased, day or night, around us. They are great scavengers, and the spilling of blood always attracted them in numbers. We first became intimately acquainted with them when the ship moored alongside the icefoot at Cape Evans, to dis-

charge her cargo. Immediately they evinced a lively interest
in the scraps thrown overboard from the galley, and soon
exhibited their carnivorous propensities. No sooner had the
first penguin been killed by the dogs than skuas flocked to the
scene of the tragedy, and were quickly picking at the victim's
remains.

These birds are greedy and selfish to the point of folly.
After the cook had taken the titbits from a slaughtered seal,
a dozen or so skuas would instantly gather about the carcase,
and quarrel so furiously over the remains that sometimes the
flesh froze as they fought, and finally they would have to
abandon what, but for their avidity, would have been sufficient to provide a feast for a hundred—as even their sharp
beaks could no longer make any impression on the meat. We
found that a good deal of work could be saved in the flensing
of seal-skins by simply laying the pelts on the ice, hair-side
downwards; the skuas rapidly cleaned them of every particle
of blubber.

Though numbers of these rapacious birds frequented our
vicinity, we soon found that they had no kindred feeling
whatever for each other. Each individual regarded its neighbours as its mortal enemies, as indeed they were, for skuas—
whose normal food consists of offal, small fish, crustacea and
anything else they can find in the sea—prey also on the eggs
and chicks of penguins, and on each other's eggs and young.
But, curiously enough, though a skua will at once pounce
down upon, carry off, and devour a neighbour's eggs or
chicks, if left unguarded, yet I have never seen one touch a
dead adult of its own species. Many gulls were shot around
our Hut; but their bodies lay unmolested by their kind—this
respect for the dead being one of the few pleasant characteristics of a fowl which I describe for lack of more agreeable
creatures to write about.

The skua-gull's only other virtues are its personal appearance and its love of cleanliness. It has a passion for fresh
water, and whilst the snow lakes were open on our cape,
scores would congregate in the largest of these to gambol and

cleanse themselves in the waters for hours on end, squawking their harsh cries, meanwhile, in delight. I never saw them venture under the cascade during the few days that it rippled down the rocks; but there were always many in the pond above. Standing in the shallows, they would stretch and flap their wings, and scream at the heavens; then, ruffling their feathers, they would settle down, and, with much splashing, send the cold refreshing water all over their bodies, working it well into the skin with evident pleasure—judging by the chorus of shrill cries that accompanied the process. When this diversion was no longer possible, on account of the frost, occasionally they would cleanse themselves in the sea; but only on the sunniest of days, and in a desultory manner, as though it were a duty, and never with any of the visible signs of enjoyment that characterised their frolics in the lake.

Estimated by outward and visible signs, the skua-gull is a gentleman, and his mate a dainty, well-dressed lady—appearances being thus deceptive, for, except for their looks and cleanliness, there is nothing refined about either male or female; both are scamps and malefactors. Full-grown skuas are about four feet from tip to tip, and there is little apparent difference between the cock and hen. Their plumage is a symphony in browns, varying from a soft fawn-coloured breast, to rich, dark-brown wing and tail feathers, which are well graduated, with lighter edges; and often there is a golden tinge about the neck of the male. On the pinions there is a broad streak of white, which gives the birds a remarkably handsome appearance when on the wing; this white band is less marked on the upper side of the feathers.

Unlike the penguins—who greeted us as friends—the skuas regarded us as enemies, and became exceedingly fierce if we approached their nests. They were nesting when we landed, and I spent much time endeavouring to illustrate their habits—a none-too-easy task, which was rendered more difficult by the fact that some of our party failed to comprehend that the gulls were but exhibiting a natural instinct in objecting to our presence near their nests, and in endeavouring to frighten us away by threatening manoeuvres and harsh cries. Finding themselves attacked by several of our number, the gulls quickly regarded us all as enemies, whereas some of us were friends, and anxious only to study their habits. I endeavoured to gain their confidence, and found that they would not molest me as long as they felt I had no evil intentions.

The skuas began to manifest the desire to nest in December, and many sites were submitted to trial before the location where the eggs were destined to be laid was finally decided upon. The nest was merely a slight hollow scooped out in the kenyte-covered ground, where there was fine gravel. The hen birds would try out one place after another, so that the cape was pitted with such 'scoops' that were never used. These unused nests puzzled me greatly, until I discovered the reason for their numbers. About the end of the year two eggs were laid, three inches long, of a greenish-brown colour with dark brown splotches. The eggs were incubated for three weeks.

During this period, if anyone appeared near the nest the hen bird would utter piercing screams and squawks of fear, and, leaving the eggs, would follow the invader with bitter cries, whereupon she was quickly joined by her mate. The pair would then swoop down upon the interloper, as though with intent to attack; but courage usually failed at the last moment, just as the blow seemed imminent, and they would rise again without striking. The menace, however, was sufficient to make one careful, and when one day I did get a blow on the head—and a good hard one too—I deemed it wise to hold a ski-stick above me for protection in future. This was a certain safeguard, as the birds then went for the stick, and not for me. One could not always be on the watch, however, and as time went on I received several sounding whacks. The skuas never struck with their beaks or claws, but always with the joint of the wing, and the blow was usually delivered from behind.

At Cape Royds the gulls were even more savage than in our own vicinity, and the above expedient availed us nothing against the disgusting practice they there had of vomiting on interlopers. They would fly towards us from the rear, and, carefully making allowance for speed and distance, discharge a nauseating shower of filth. Photography had to be done despite such discomforts, and though I protected myself with canvas and constant watchfulness, I was more than once the victim of this revolting habit—whilst the air was rent by what sounded to me very much like screams of sardonic laughter. The skuas at Cape Evans, though exceedingly truculent, were altogether better-mannered, and never exhibited this unpleasant trait. We accounted for this by reasoning that probably the same birds return yearly to the same locality, and that those at Cape Royds had learnt to adopt such defensive measures during the sojourn there of the Shackleton Expedition.

Once, at Cape Royds, when the skua chicks were hatching, I decided to kinematograph the process. Having selected a nest where the chicks were about due to appear, I set up the camera, focussed it on the eggs, and then went away—so that the mother might return and become accustomed to the machine. Later, I went to the nest again, and, finding that one of the chicks had now pipped the shell, I exposed a few feet of film. The mother was then permitted to return for half an hour, when more film was used—and so on for several hours. More than one nest was used to complete the film of the hatching of the eggs, as had I interrupted the process too frequently with the same clutch of eggs, they would have been chilled and the chicks killed.

When I was recording the final phase of one of the chick's kicking off the last bits of shell, the parents were swooping wildly around me, screaming with rage and fear as they heard the 'peeping' of the struggling little one. Just as I had finished the work and rose from my kneeling position, I received two blows in rapid succession, one on the back of the head and the other in the right eye. As I held both my arms close to my face for protection, two more blows were delivered, one just at the back of the ear, which almost bowled me over. Suffering acutely, I lay on the ground for an hour or more, my eye streaming with water, and I could see nothing with it. I really thought the eye was done for—as it probably would have been, had I not been wearing a heavy tweed hat with a wide brim. The joint of the gull's wing struck the brim of the hat, and beat it down against the eye; but for that wide brim I should certainly have received the blow full in the eye, and probably have lost it.

The infuriated birds made no further attempt to molest me as I lay on the ground, nor did they attack the camera either —seemingly comprehending that it was an inanimate thing that could do them no injury. Had they not attacked me, no harm would have resulted to the chick, for I had just finished the picture; but by the time I had recovered sufficiently to take the camera away, the chick was frozen stiff, the parents had forsaken it and were nowhere to be seen. My eye was weak for many days afterwards; but fortunately it had suffered no permanent damage, and it ultimately got all right again.

Once, when I was photographing a clutch of eggs in the nest, and the owners were circling around, screaming loudly, another skua swooped down, and, snatching up one of the unprotected eggs in its beak, made off with it—the lawful owners following in hot and clamorous pursuit. Before they had gone far, the robber dropped the egg, which broke on the rocks; but the owners continued the chase, bent, I assume, on administering summary justice; though I did not see the end of the incident. Later, I learned by witnessing repetitions of such offences, that any egg left unprotected for a moment was certain to be thus stolen.

Having discovered this thieving propensity of the skuas, it was easy to understand why each nesting pair of the miscreants regarded their neighbours with apprehension and hatred.

Though two eggs were laid, and sometimes both were

hatched, I noticed no instance where the mother had more than one chick after the first week. I do not know what became of the other: whether some cannibal neighbour made off with it, or whether the pangs of hunger had made the dainty morsel too tempting to one or other of the responsible pair, for—yes, I will state it, though it seems too horrible —I even suspect these unprincipled birds of the crime of eating their own young. Whether my suspicions be well-founded or not, I must in common fairness state that the surviving youngster was always watched, protected and provided for with irreproachable care.

One day I came upon what I regarded as a real 'find.' Approaching a sitting mother, who flew away to give sufficient height and distance to swoop at me, I discovered that there were two eggs and a chick in the nest. Delighted with what I supposed was an unprecedented case, I photographed the happy family. On reporting my find at the Hut, I found that I'd been 'had.' Taylor, having been attacked by a gull, had killed it with a stick, and then had placed the orphan chick in a neighbouring nest. Extraordinary to relate, the returning gull had mothered the little stranger, instead of eating it—a departure from custom which could only be accounted for by the fact that the gull, being in a state of repletion, was hoarding the chick for the next meal. That any skua would voluntarily foster a strange chick with good intentions, I could not believe. The next day the chick was not there! Further comment would be superfluous!

The chicks are beautiful little creatures. Their down is a lovely pearl-grey, and they have blue-tinted beaks and legs. They can walk almost as soon as hatched, and seem to inherit, from the egg, the hatred of their kind which is so characteristic of the adult. When but a day old, any movement on the part of one of a pair would cause them to look daggers at each other; and less than a week after they were hatched they would sometimes fight furiously without any provocation whatever, whilst the parent bird looked on approvingly. Several times I tried to kinematograph one of these 'scraps,' without success. Whenever I appeared on the scene, the combatants forgot, for the time being, their dislike for each other, in their apprehension of what they regarded as a common foe. They glared fiercely at me, instead of at one another.

During the incubation of the eggs the cock relieved the hen periodically, whilst she went off to feed; and, later, when the chicks were hatched, he guarded them when she took a spell off for the same purpose. Returning to feed the little ones—or, perhaps I should say, little one; for, as I have already stated, there was never more than one after the first week—she would retch a few times, and then vomit forth a mass of half digested food on to the ground, which the chick would go for greedily. I spent many hours in trying to kinematograph this habit, but in vain. On each occasion when—after standing still and silent as a statue for long periods—I began to turn the handle, as the mother was about to regurgitate, the moment I stirred she was frightened and stopped at once. Though I tried every manner of ruse— including keeping my hand moving as though working the camera, until I was compelled to stop from fatigue—I never succeeded in recording this interesting trait by moving-pictures. It was the clicking of the camera that defeated me. I think, however, the coveted record would have been secured, but for an unfortunate incident. By dint of stalking one mother and her chick for nearly twenty consecutive hours, I had got them thoroughly accustomed to my presence and the camera; but whilst I went to take a few hours' sleep, someone killed the mother. When I returned to continue my vigil, she was lying dead on the ground, not twenty yards away; and another gull had doubtless carried off the unprotected chick, for it was no longer to be seen. Fortunately, however, I had already made a 'still' photograph of the mother disgorging for the chick; it was the only study of the kind I ever succeeded in getting. I vowed inwardly that when I returned home I would endeavour to have a noiseless kinematograph made, before I tried to secure moving-pictures of animals or birds at close quarters again.

One day I was watching a group of a dozen Giant petrels that were sitting on an ice-floe—gorged to lethargy on the offal of a dead seal—when the big ungainly creatures were suddenly harried by several skua-gulls. I thought at first this was merely fun, or mischief, on the part of the gulls, and was not a little surprised—never having credited them with a sense of humour. I was soon undeceived, however, for it proved to be merely a cunning manoeuvre on the part of these crafty birds to get a meal on the cheap. Before the heavy petrels could rise on the wing and free themselves of their aggressors by flight, they had to disgorge the contents of their stomachs, and as soon as they did so the skuas fell upon the feast. Really, each fresh insight that I gained into the habits of these unlovable birds increased my antipathy to them; but I think the limit of repulsion was reached when I saw a couple of skuas having a tug-of-war with a yard of a seal's intestines, which parted in the middle and sent the two ghouls sprawling—reminding me of a similar incident that I had seen several years before, on the banks of the Ganges near Benares, when a pair of vultures were all tangled with and tugging at the entrails of a corpse.

The one great redeeming feature of this Antarctic pariah is the excellence of its eggs. A polar appetite is calculated to relieve one of any little prejudices in the matter of food, and once one's antipathy to the bird is overcome sufficiently to try its eggs, one finds they are fit for an epicure. After all, barnyard fowls are not over squeamish about their diet, and I doubt if anything that a skua feeds on would be refused by them. Skuas' eggs, when boiled, are semi-transparent and jelly-like, and taste like the eggs of plovers—the only drawback in our case being that we could not get enough of them. The breast flesh of the skua-gull is quite good eating too.

As the chicks grew older, they quickly lost the pretty appearance they exhibited when in the down. They became ugly, leggy creatures, bristling with stubbs, that ran away as fast as they could go—with backward, furtive looks—on the approach of man. As winter drew near; as the daylight waned away; as the weather became frigid, and the sea froze over again, the gulls gradually diminished in numbers on our cape, until only those were left that watched their unprepossessing fledglings until they were able to take care of themselves. As soon as these ill-favoured youngsters were full-grown and independent, they and the last of the adult stragglers departed too, and there was a peace around the Hut such as we had not known since our arrival in the South.

And, let me confess it, I missed them. When they had gone, I wished them back again, I even *longed* to have them back; for they had provided me with many interesting days of study when there was little else to investigate. And their savage and revolting ways were, after all, but instincts well in keeping with the pitiless conditions under which Nature has decreed that these buccaneers of the South shall struggle for existence.

APSLEY CHERRY-GARRARD

(*1886-1959*)

THE PHOTOGRAPHS which Herbert Ponting took of Cherry-Garrard during Scott's second expedition seem to be of a frail and sensitive young man. Cherry-Garrard's activities in Antarctica, however, dramatically belie the impression of frailty.

Cherry-Garrard was twenty-four when he joined the expedition. Together with Wilson and Bowers, he took part in what is possibly the most extraordinary traverse in Antarctic history: the round-trip mid-winter trek from Cape Evans down around Hut Point to Cape Crozier, Ross Island. The goal was three Emperor penguin eggs, to be garnered from the Crozier rookery for scientific study. (The Crozier rookery is the southernmost rookery of the Emperor penguin, which lays and hatches its single annual egg on the ice in the austral winter under unbelievably inauspicious circumstances.) The trek was successful, although on more than one occasion the men came very close to dying. Wilson and Bowers perished with Scott on the polar journey.

Scott, on seeing the startlingly haggard condition of the three men as they returned to Cape Evans after an absence of some five weeks (during which they had manhauled their sledges in the austral night and had shivered more than slept in their tent), gave Cherry-Garrard's narrative its title by remarking that in his opinion it was the worst journey in the world. Cherry-Garrard's complete narrative describes much more than the mid-winter journey. In many ways it is a graphic report on Scott's second expedition. It is one of the finest tales ever told of man's behavior while pitted against nature. Cherry-Garrard was also a member of the party that went searching in November 1912 on the Ross Ice Shelf for the doomed Scott and his companions.

The Worst Journey in the World

Five days later and three men, one of whom at any rate is feeling a little frightened, stand panting and sweating out in McMurdo Sound. They have two sledges, one tied behind the other, and these sledges are piled high with sleeping-bags and camping equipment, six weeks' provisions, and a venesta case full of scientific gear for pickling and preserving. In addition there is a pickaxe, iceaxes, an Alpine rope, a large piece of green Willesden canvas and a bit of board. Scott's amazed remark when he saw our sledges two hours ago, "Bill, why are you taking all this oil?" pointing to the six cans lashed to the tray on the second sledge, had a bite in it. Our

weights for such travelling are enormous—253 lbs. a man.
It is mid-day but it is pitchy dark, and it is not warm.

As we rested my mind went back to a dusty, dingy office
in Victoria Street some fifteen months ago. "I want you to
come," said Wilson to me, and then, "I want to go to Cape
Crozier in the winter and work out the embryology of the
Emperor penguins, but I'm not saying much about it—it
might never come off." Well! this was better than Victoria
Street, where the doctors had nearly refused to let me go
because I could only see the people across the road as vague
blobs walking. Then Bill went and had a talk with Scott about
it, and they said I might come if I was prepared to take the
additional risk. At that time I would have taken anything.

After the Depôt Journey, at Hut Point, walking over that
beastly, slippery, sloping ice-foot which I always imagined
would leave me some day in the sea, Bill asked me whether
I would go with him—and who else for a third? There can
have been little doubt whom we both wanted, and that evening Bowers had been asked. Of course he was mad to come.
And here we were. "This winter travel is a new and bold
venture," wrote Scott in the hut that night, "but the right
men have gone to attempt it."

I don't know. There never could have been any doubt
about Bill and Birdie. Probably Lashly would have made the
best third, but Bill had a prejudice against seamen for a
journey like this—"They don't take enough care of themselves, and they *will* not look after their clothes." But Lashly
was wonderful—if Scott had only taken a four-man party and
Lashly to the Pole!

What is this venture? Why is the embryo of the Emperor
penguin so important to Science? And why should three sane
and common-sense explorers be sledging away on a winter's
night to a Cape which has only been visited before in daylight, and then with very great difficulty?

I have explained more fully in the Introduction to this book
the knowledge the world possessed at this time of the Emperor penguin, mainly due to Wilson. But it is because the

Emperor is probably the most primitive bird in existence that the working out of his embryology is so important. The embryo shows remains of the development of an animal in former ages and former states; it recapitulates its former lives. The embryo of an Emperor may prove the missing link between birds and the reptiles from which birds have sprung.

Only one rookery of Emperor penguins had been found at this date, and this was on the sea-ice inside a little bay of the Barrier edge at Cape Crozier, which was guarded by miles of some of the biggest pressure in the Antarctic. Chicks had been found in September, and Wilson reckoned that the eggs must be laid in the beginning of July. And so we started just after midwinter on the weirdest bird's-nesting expedition that has ever been or ever will be.

But the sweat was freezing in our clothing and we moved on. All we could see was a black patch away to our left which was Turk's Head: when this disappeared we knew that we had passed Glacier Tongue, which, unseen by us, eclipsed the rocks behind. And then we camped for lunch.

That first camp only lives in my memory because it began our education of camp work in the dark. Had we now struck the blighting temperature which we were to meet. . . .

There was just enough wind to make us want to hurry: down harness, each man to a strap on the sledge—quick with the floor-cloth—the bags to hold it down—now a good spread with the bamboos and the tent inner lining—hold them, Cherry, and over with the outer covering—snow on to the skirting and inside with the cook with his candle and a box of matches. . . .

That is how we tied it: that is the way we were accustomed to do it, day after day and night after night when the sun was still high or at any rate only setting, sledging on the Barrier in spring and summer and autumn; pulling our hands from our mitts when necessary—plenty of time to warm up afterwards; in the days when we took pride in getting our tea boiling within twenty minutes of throwing off our harness: when the man who wanted to work in his fur mitts was thought a bit too slow.

But now it *didn't* work. "We shall have to go a bit slower," said Bill, and "we shall get more used to working in the dark." At this time, I remember, I was still trying to wear spectacles.

We spent that night on the sea-ice, finding that we were too far in towards Castle Rock; and it was not until the following afternoon that we reached and lunched at Hut Point. I speak of day and night, though they were much the same, and later on when we found that we could not get the work into a twenty-four-hour day, we decided to carry on as though such a convention did not exist; as in actual fact it did not. We had already realized that cooking under these conditions would be a bad job, and that the usual arrangement by which one man was cook for the week would be intolerable. We settled to be cook alternately day by day. For food we brought only pemmican and biscuit and butter; for drink we had tea, and we drank hot water to turn in on.

Pulling out from Hut Point that evening we brought along our heavy loads on the two nine-foot sledges with comparative ease; it was the first, and though we did not know it then, the only bit of good pulling we were to have. Good pulling to the sledge traveller means easy pulling. Away we went round Cape Armitage and eastwards. We knew that the Barrier edge was in front of us and also that the break-up of the sea-ice had left the face of it as a low perpendicular cliff. We had therefore to find a place where the snow had formed a drift. This we came right up against and met quite suddenly a very keen wind flowing, as it always does, from the cold Barrier down to the comparatively warm sea-ice. The temperature was −47° F., and I was a fool to take my hands out of my mitts to haul on the ropes to bring the sledges up. I started away from the Barrier edge with all ten fingers frostbitten. They did not really come back until we were in the tent for our night meal, and within a few hours there were two or three large blisters, up to an inch long, on all of them. For many days those blisters hurt frightfully.

We were camped that night about half a mile in from the Barrier edge. The temperature was −56°. We had a baddish time, being very glad to get out of our shivering bags next morning (June 29). We began to suspect, as we knew only too well later, that the only good time of the twenty-four hours was breakfast, for then with reasonable luck we need not get into our sleeping-bags again for another seventeen hours.

The horror of the nineteen days it took us to travel from Cape Evans to Cape Crozier would have to be reexperienced to be appreciated; and any one would be a fool who went again: it is not possible to describe it. The weeks which followed them were comparative bliss, not because later our conditions were better—they were far worse—but because we were callous. I for one had come to that point of suffering at which I did not really care if only I could die without much pain. They talk of the heroism of the dying—they little know —it would be so easy to die, a dose of morphia, a friendly crevasse, and blissful sleep. The trouble is to go on. . . .

It was the darkness that did it. I don't believe minus seventy temperatures would be bad in daylight, not comparatively bad, when you could see where you were going, where you were stepping, where the sledge straps were, the cooker, the primus, the food; could see your footsteps lately trodden deep into the soft snow that you might find your way back to the rest of your load; could see the lashings of the food bags; could read a compass without striking three or four different boxes to find one dry match; could read your watch to see if the blissful moment of getting out of your bag was come without groping in the snow all about; when it would not take you five minutes to lash up the door of the tent, and five hours to get started in the morning. . . .

But in these days we were never less than four hours from the moment when Bill cried "Time to get up" to the time when we got into our harness. It took two men to get one man into his harness, and was all they could do, for the canvas was frozen and our clothes were frozen until sometimes not even two men could bend them into the required shape.

The trouble is sweat and breath. I never knew before how much of the body's waste comes out through the pores of the skin. On the most bitter days, when we had to camp before we had done a four-hour march in order to nurse back our frozen feet, it seemed that we must be sweating. And all this sweat, instead of passing away through the porous wool of our clothing and gradually drying off us, froze and accumulated. It passed just away from our flesh and then became ice: we shook plenty of snow and ice down from inside our trousers every time we changed our foot-gear, and we could have shaken it from our vests and from between our vests and shirts, but of course we could not strip to this extent. But when we got into our sleeping-bags, if we were fortunate, we became warm enough during the night to thaw this ice: part remained in our clothes, part passed into the skins of our sleeping-bags, and soon both were sheets of armourplate.

As for our breath—in the daytime it did nothing worse than cover the lower parts of our faces with ice and solder our balaclavas tightly to our heads. It was no good trying to get your balaclava off until you had had the primus going quite a long time, and then you could throw your breath about if you wished. The trouble really began in your sleeping-bag, for it was far too cold to keep a hole open through which to breathe. So all night long our breath froze into the skins, and our respiration became quicker and quicker as the air in our bags got fouler and fouler: it was never possible to make a match strike or burn inside our bags!

Of course we were not iced up all at once: it took several days of this kind of thing before we really got into big difficulties on this score. It was not until I got out of the tent one morning fully ready to pack the sledge that I realized the possibilities ahead. We had had our breakfast, struggled into our foot-gear, and squared up inside the tent, which was comparatively warm. Once outside, I raised my head to look round and found I could not move it back. My clothing had frozen hard as I stood—perhaps fifteen seconds. For four hours I had to pull with my head stuck up, and from that time we all took care to bend down into a pulling position before being frozen in.

By now we had realized that we must reverse the usual sledging routine and do everything slowly, wearing when possible the fur mitts which fitted over our woollen mitts, and always stopping whatever we were doing, directly we felt that any part of us was getting frozen, until the circulation was restored. Henceforward it was common for one or other of us to leave the other two to continue the camp work while he stamped about in the snow, beat his arms, or nursed some exposed part. But we could not restore the circulation of our feet like this—the only way then was to camp and get some hot water into ourselves before we took our foot-gear off. The difficulty was to know whether our feet were frozen or not, for the only thing we knew for certain was that we had lost all feeling in them. Wilson's knowledge as a doctor came in here: many a time he had to decide from our descriptions of our feet whether to camp or to go on for another hour. A wrong decision meant disaster, for if one of us had been crippled the whole party would have been placed in great difficulties. Probably we should all have died.

On June 29 the temperature was $-50°$ all day and there was sometimes a light breeze which was inclined to frostbite our faces and hands. Owing to the weight of our two sledges and the bad surface our pace was not more than a slow and very heavy plod: at our lunch camp Wilson had the heel and sole of one foot frost-bitten, and I had two big toes. Bowers was never worried by frost-bitten feet.

That night was very cold, the temperature falling to $-66°$, and it was $-55°$ at breakfast on June 30. We had not shipped the eider-down linings to our sleeping-bags, in order to keep them dry as long as possible. My own fur bag was too big for me, and throughout this journey was more difficult to thaw out than the other two: on the other hand, it never split, as did Bill's.

We were now getting into that cold bay which lies between the Hut Point Peninsula and Terror Point. It was known from old Discovery days that the Barrier winds are deflected from this area, pouring out into McMurdo Sound behind us, and into the Ross Sea at Cape Crozier in front. In consequence of the lack of high winds the surface of the snow is never swept and hardened and polished as elsewhere: it was now a mass of the hardest and smallest snow crystals, to pull through which in cold temperatures was just like pulling through sand. I have spoken elsewhere of Barrier surfaces, and how, when the cold is very great, sledge runners cannot melt the crystal points but only advance by rolling them over and over upon one another. That was the surface we met on this journey, and in soft snow the effect is accentuated. Our feet were sinking deep at every step.

And so when we tried to start on June 30 we found we could not move both sledges together. There was nothing for it but to take one on at a time and come back for the other. This has often been done in daylight when the only risks run are those of blizzards which may spring up suddenly and obliterate tracks. Now in darkness it was more complicated. From 11 A.M. to 3 P.M. there was enough light to see the big holes made by our feet, and we took on one sledge, trudged back in our tracks, and brought on the second. Bowers used to toggle and untoggle our harnesses when we changed sledges. Of course in this relay work we covered three miles in distance for every one mile forward, and even the single sledges were very hard pulling. When we lunched the temperature was −61°. After lunch the little light had gone, and we carried a naked lighted candle back with us when we went to find our second sledge. It was the weirdest kind of procession, three frozen men and a little pool of light. Generally we steered by Jupiter, and I never see him now without recalling his friendship in those days.

We were very silent, it was not very easy to talk: but sledging is always a silent business. I remember a long discussion which began just now about cold snaps—was this the normal condition of the Barrier, or was it a cold snap?—what constituted a cold snap? The discussion lasted about a week. Do things slowly, always slowly, that was the burden of Wilson's leadership: and every now and then the question, Shall we go on? and the answer Yes. "I think we are all right as long as our appetites are good," said Bill. Always patient, self-possessed, unruffled, he was the only man on earth, as I believe, who could have led this journey.

That day we made 3¼ miles, and travelled 10 miles to do it. The temperature was −66° when we camped, and we were already pretty badly iced up. That was the last night I lay (I had written slept) in my big reindeer bag without the lining of eider-down which we each carried. For me it was a very bad night: a succession of shivering fits which I was quite unable to stop, and which took possession of my body for many minutes at a time until I thought my back would break, such was the strain placed upon it. They talk of chattering teeth: but when your body chatters you may call yourself cold. I can only compare the strain to that which I have been unfortunate enough to see in a case of lock-jaw. One of my big toes was frost-bitten, but I do not know for how long. Wilson was fairly comfortable in his smaller bag, and Bowers was snoring loudly. The minimum temperature that night as taken under the sledge was −69°; and as taken on the sledge was −75°. That is a hundred and seven degrees of frost.

We did the same relay work on July 1, but found the pulling still harder; and it was all that we could do to move the one sledge forward. From now onwards Wilson and I, but not to the same extent Bowers, experienced a curious optical delusion when returning in our tracks for the second sledge. I have said that we found our way back by the light of a candle, and we found it necessary to go back in our same footprints. These holes became to our tired brains not depressions but elevations: hummocks over which we stepped, raising our feet painfully and draggingly. And then we remembered, and said what fools we were, and for a while we compelled ourselves to walk through these phantom hills. But it was no lasting good, and as the days passed we realized that we must suffer this absurdity, for we could not do anything else. But of course it took it out of us.

During these days the blisters on my fingers were very painful. Long before my hands were frost-bitten, or indeed anything but cold, which was of course a normal thing, the matter inside these big blisters, which rose all down my fingers with only a skin between them, was frozen into ice. To handle the cooking gear or the food bags was agony; to start the primus was worse; and when, one day, I was able to prick six or seven of the blisters after supper and let the liquid matter out, the relief was very great. Every night after that I treated such others as were ready in the same way until they gradually disappeared. Sometimes it was difficult not to howl.

I *did* want to howl many times every hour of these days and nights, but I invented a formula instead, which I repeated to myself continually. Especially, I remember, it came in useful when at the end of the march with my feet frost-bitten, my heart beating slowly, my vitality at its lowest ebb, my body solid with cold, I used to seize the shovel and go on digging snow on to the tent skirting while the cook inside was trying to light the primus. "You've got it in the neck—stick it—stick it—you've got it in the neck," was the refrain, and I wanted every little bit of encouragement it would give me: then I would find myself repeating "Stick it —stick it—stick it—stick it," and then "You've got it in the neck." One of the joys of summer sledging is that you can let your mind wander thousands of miles away for weeks and weeks. Oates used to provision his little yacht (there was a pickled herring he was going to have): I invented the compactest little revolving bookcase which was going to hold not books, but pemmican and chocolate and biscuit and cocoa and sugar, and have a cooker on the top, and was going to stand always ready to quench my hunger when I got home: and we visited restaurants and theatres and grouse moors, and we thought of a pretty girl, or girls, and . . . But now that was all impossible. Our conditions forced themselves upon us without pause: it was not possible to think of anything else. We got no respite. I found it best to refuse to let myself think of the past or the future—to live only for the job of the moment, and to compel myself to think only how to do it most efficiently. Once you let yourself imagine . . .

This day also (July 1) we were harassed by a nasty little wind which blew in our faces. The temperature was −66°, and in such temperatures the effect of even the lightest airs is blighting, and immediately freezes any exposed part. But we all fitted the bits of wind-proof lined with fur, which we had made in the hut, across our balaclavas in front of our noses, and these were of the greatest comfort. They formed other places upon which our breath could freeze, and the lower parts of our faces were soon covered with solid sheets of ice, which was in itself an additional protection. This was a normal and not uncomfortable condition during the journey: the hair on our faces kept the ice away from the skin, and for myself I would rather have the ice than be without it, until I want to get my balaclava off to drink my hoosh. We only made 2 ¼ miles, and it took 8 hours.

It blew force 3 that night with a temperature of −65.2°, and there was some drift. This was pretty bad, but luckily the wind dropped to a light breeze by the time we were ready to start the next morning (July 2). The temperature was then −60°, and continued so all day, falling lower in the evening. At 4 P.M. we watched a bank of fog form over the peninsula to our left and noticed at the same time that our frozen mitts thawed out on our hands, and the outlines of the land as shown by the stars became obscured. We made 2½ miles with the usual relaying, and camped at 8 P.M. with the temperature −65°. It really was a terrible march, and parts of both my feet were frozen at lunch. After supper I pricked six or seven of the worst blisters, and the relief was considerable.

I have met with amusement people who say, "Oh, we had minus fifty temperatures in Canada; they didn't worry *me,*" or "I've been down to minus sixty something in Siberia." And then you find that they had nice dry clothing, a nice night's sleep in a nice aired bed, and had just walked out after lunch for a few minutes from a nice warm hut or an overheated train. And they look back upon it as an experience to be remembered. Well! of course as an experience of cold this can only be compared to eating a vanilla ice with hot chocolate cream after an excellent dinner at Claridge's. But in our present state we began to look upon minus fifties as a luxury which we did not often get.

That evening, for the first time we discarded our naked candle in favour of the rising moon. We had started before the moon on purpose, but as we shall see she gave us little light. However, we owed our escape from a very sticky death to her on one occasion.

It was a little later on when we were among crevasses, with Terror above us, but invisible, somewhere on our left, and the Barrier pressure on our right. We were quite lost in the darkness, and only knew that we were running downhill, the sledge almost catching our heels. There had been no light all day, clouds obscured the moon, we had not seen her since yesterday. And quite suddenly a little patch of clear sky drifted, as it were, over her face, and she showed us three paces ahead a great crevasse with just a shining icy lid not much thicker than glass. We should all have walked into it, and the sledge would certainly have followed us down. After that I felt we had a chance of pulling through: God could not be so cruel as to have saved us just to prolong our agony.

But at present we need not worry about crevasses; for we had not reached the long stretch where the moving Barrier, with the weight of many hundred miles of ice behind it, comes butting up against the slopes of Mount Terror, itself some eleven thousand feet high. Now we were still plunging ankle-deep in the mass of soft sandy snow which lies in the windless area. It seemed to have no bottom at all, and since the snow was much the same temperature as the air, our feet, as well as our bodies, got colder and colder the longer we marched: in ordinary sledging you begin to warm up after a quarter of an hour's pulling, here it was just the reverse. Even now I find myself unconsciously kicking the toes of my right foot against the heel of my left: a habit I picked up on this journey by doing it every time we halted. Well no. Not always. For there was one halt when we just lay on our backs and gazed up into the sky, where, so the others said, there was blazing the most wonderful aurora they had ever seen. I did not see it, being so near-sighted and unable to wear spectacles owing to the cold. The aurora was always before us as we travelled east, more beautiful than any seen by previous expeditions wintering in McMurdo Sound, where Erebus must have hidden the most brilliant displays. Now most of the sky was covered with swinging, swaying curtains which met in a great whirl overhead: lemon yellow, green and orange.

The minimum this night was −65°, and during July 3 it ranged between −52° and −58°. We got forward only 2½ miles, and by this time I had silently made up my mind that we had not the ghost of a chance of reaching the penguins. I am sure that Bill was having a very bad time these nights, though it was an impression rather than anything else, for he never said so. We knew we did sleep, for we heard one another snore, and also we used to have dreams and nightmares; but we had little consciousness of it, and we were now beginning to drop off when we halted on the march.

Our sleeping-bags were getting really bad by now, and already it took a long time to thaw a way down into them at night. Bill spread his in the middle, Bowers was on his right, and I was on his left. Always he insisted that I should start getting my legs into mine before *he* started: we were rapidly cooling down after our hot supper, and this was very unselfish of him. Then came seven shivering hours and first thing on getting out of our sleeping-bags in the morning we stuffed our personal gear into the mouth of the bag before it could freeze: this made a plug which when removed formed a frozen hole for us to push into as a start in the evening.

We got into some strange knots when trying to persuade

our limbs into our bags, and suffered terribly from cramp in consequence. We would wait and rub, but directly we tried to move again down it would come and grip our legs in a vice. We also, especially Bowers, suffered agony from cramp in the stomach. We let the primus burn on after supper now for a time—it was the only thing which kept us going—and when one who was holding the primus was seized with cramp we hastily took the lamp from him until the spasm was over. It was horrible to see Birdie's stomach cramp sometimes: he certainly got it much worse than Bill or I. I suffered a lot from heartburn, especially in my bag at nights: we were eating a great proportion of fat and this was probably the cause. Stupidly I said nothing about it for a long time. Later when Bill found out, he soon made it better with the medical case.

Birdie always lit the candle in the morning—so called, and this was an heroic business. Moisture collected on our matches if you looked at them. Partly I suppose it was bringing them from outside into a comparatively warm tent; partly from putting boxes into pockets in our clothing. Sometimes it was necessary to try four or five boxes before a match struck. The temperature of the boxes and matches was about a hundred degrees of frost, and the smallest touch of the metal on naked flesh caused a frost-bite. If you wore mitts you could scarcely feel anything—especially since the tips of our fingers were already very callous. To get the first light going in the morning was a beastly cold business, made worse by having to make sure that it was at last time to get up. Bill insisted that we must lie in our bags seven hours every night.

In civilization men are taken at their own valuation because there are so many ways of concealment, and there is so little time, perhaps even so little understanding. Not so down South. These two men went through the Winter Journey and lived: later they went through the Polar Journey and died. They were gold, pure, shining, unalloyed. Words cannot express how good their companionship was.

Through all these days, and those which were to follow, the worst I suppose in their dark severity that men have ever come through alive, no single hasty or angry word passed their lips. When, later, we were sure, so far as we can be sure of anything, that we must die, they were cheerful, and so far as I can judge their songs and cheery words were quite unforced. Nor were they ever flurried, though always as quick as the conditions would allow in moments of emergency. It is hard that often such men must go first when others far less worthy remain.

There are those who write of Polar Expeditions as though the whole thing was as easy as possible. They are trusting, I suspect, in a public who will say, "What a fine fellow this is! we know what horrors he has endured, yet see, how little he makes of all his difficulties and hardships." Others have gone to the opposite extreme. I do not know that there is any use in trying to make a −18° temperature appear formidable to an uninitiated reader by calling it fifty degrees of frost. I want to do neither of these things. I am not going to pretend that this was anything but a ghastly journey, made bearable and even pleasant to look back upon by the qualities of my two companions who have gone. At the same time I have no wish to make it appear more horrible than it actually was: the reader need not fear that I am trying to exaggerate.

During the night of July 3 the temperature dropped to −65°, but in the morning we wakened (we really did wake that morning) to great relief. The temperature was only −27° with the wind blowing some 15 miles an hour with steadily falling snow. It only lasted a few hours, and we knew it must be blowing a howling blizzard outside the windless area in which we lay, but it gave us time to sleep and rest, and get thoroughly thawed, and wet, and warm, inside our sleeping-bags. To me at any rate this modified blizzard was a great relief, though we all knew that our gear would be worse than ever when the cold came back. It was quite impossible to march. During the course of the day the temperature dropped to −44°: during the following night to −54°.

The soft new snow which had fallen made the surface the next day (July 5) almost impossible. We relayed as usual, and

managed to do eight hours' pulling, but we got forward only
1½ miles. The temperature ranged between −55° and
−61°, and there was at one time a considerable breeze, the
effect of which was paralysing. There was the great circle of
a halo round the moon with a vertical shaft, and mock moons.
We hoped that we were rising on to the long snow cape
which marks the beginning of Mount Terror. That night the
temperature was −75°; at breakfast −70°; at noon nearly
−77°. The day lives in my memory as that on which I found
out that records are not worth making. The thermometer as
swung by Bowers after lunch at 5.51 P.M. registered
−77.5°, which is 109½ degrees of frost, and is I suppose as
cold as any one will want to endure in darkness and iced-up
gear and clothes. The lowest temperature recorded by a
Discovery Spring Journey party was −67.7°,[1] and in those
days fourteen days was a long time for a Spring Party to be
away sledging, and they were in daylight. This was our tenth
day out and we hoped to be away for six weeks.

Luckily we were spared wind. Our naked candle burnt
steadily as we trudged back in our tracks to fetch our other
sledge, but if we touched metal for a fraction of a second with
naked fingers we were frost-bitten. To fasten the strap buckles over the loaded sledge was difficult: to handle the cooker,
or mugs, or spoons, the primus or oil can was worse. How
Bowers managed with the meteorological instruments I do
not know, but the meteorological log is perfectly kept. Yet as
soon as you breathed near the paper it was covered with a
film of ice through which the pencil would not bite. To handle rope was always cold and in these very low temperatures
dreadfully cold work. The toggling up of our harnesses to the
sledge we were about to pull, the untoggling at the end of the
stage, the lashing up of our sleeping-bags in the morning, the
fastening of the cooker to the top of the instrument box, were
bad, but not nearly so bad as the smaller lashings which were

---

1 A thermometer which registered −77° at the Winter Quarters of
H.M.S. *Alert* on March 4, 1876, is preserved by the Royal Geographical
Society. I do not know whether it was screened.

now strings of ice. One of the worst was round the weekly food bag, and those round the pemmican, tea and butter bags inside were thinner still. But the real devil was the lashing of the tent door: it was like wire, and yet had to be tied tight. If you had to get out of the tent during the seven hours spent in our sleeping-bags you must tie a string as stiff as a poker, and re-thaw your way into a bag already as hard as a board. Our paraffin was supplied at a flash point suitable to low temperatures and was only a little milky: it was very difficult to splinter bits off the butter.

The temperature that night was −75.8°, and I will not pretend that it did not convince me that Dante was right when he placed the circles of ice below the circles of fire. Still we slept sometimes, and always we lay for seven hours. Again and again Bill asked us how about going back, and always we said no. Yet there was nothing I should have liked better: I was quite sure that to dream of Cape Crozier was the wildest lunacy. That day we had advanced 1½ miles by the utmost labour, and the usual relay work. This was quite a good march —and Cape Crozier is 67 miles from Cape Evans!

More than once in my short life I have been struck by the value of the man who is blind to what appears to be a common-sense certainty: he achieves the impossible. We never spoke our thoughts: we discussed the Age of Stone which was to come, when we built our cosy warm rock hut on the slopes of Mount Terror, and ran our stove with penguin blubber, and pickled little Emperors in warmth and dryness. We were quite intelligent people, and we must all have known that we were not going to see the penguins and that it was folly to go forward. And yet with quiet perseverance, in perfect friendship, almost with gentleness those two men led on. I just did what I was told.

It is desirable that the body should work, feed and sleep at regular hours, and this is too often forgotten when sledging. But just now we found we were unable to fit 8 hours marching and 7 hours in our sleeping-bags into a 24-hour day: the routine camp work took more than 9 hours, such were the conditions. We therefore ceased to observe the quite imaginary difference between night and day, and it was noon on Friday (July 7) before we got away. The temperature was −68° and there was a thick white fog: generally we had but the vaguest idea where we were, and we camped at 10 P.M. after managing 1 3/4 miles for the day. But what a relief. Instead of labouring away, our hearts were beating more naturally: it was easier to camp, we had some feeling in our hands, and our feet had not gone to sleep. Birdie swung the thermometer and found it only −55°. "Now if we tell people that to get only 87 degrees of frost can be an enormous relief they simply won't believe us," I remember saying. Perhaps you won't, but it was, all the same: and I wrote that night: "There is something after all rather good in doing something never done before." Things were looking up, you see.

Our hearts were doing very gallant work. Towards the end of the march they were getting beaten and were finding it difficult to pump the blood out to our extremities. There were few days that Wilson and I did not get some part of our feet frost-bitten. As we camped, I suspect our hearts were beating comparatively slowly and weakly. Nothing could be done until a hot drink was ready—tea for lunch, hot water for supper. Directly we started to drink then the effect was wonderful: it was, said Wilson, like putting a hot-water bottle against your heart. The beats became very rapid and strong and you felt the warmth travelling outwards and downwards. Then you got your foot-gear off—puttees (cut in half and wound round the bottom of the trousers), finnesko, saenne-grass, hair socks, and two pairs of woollen socks. Then you nursed back your feet and tried to believe you were glad—a frost-bite does not hurt until it begins to thaw. Later came the blisters, and then the chunks of dead skin.

Bill was anxious. It seems that Scott had twice gone for a walk with him during the Winter, and tried to persuade him not to go, and only finally consented on condition that Bill brought us all back unharmed: we were Southern Journey men. Bill had a tremendous respect for Scott, and later when we were about to make an effort to get back home over the Barrier, and our case was very desperate, he was most anxious to leave no gear behind at Cape Crozier, even the scientific gear which could be of no use to us and of which we had plenty more at the hut. "Scott will never forgive me if I leave gear behind," he said. It is a good sledging principle, and the party which does not follow it, or which leaves some of its load to be fetched in later is seldom a good one: but it is a principle which can be carried to excess.

And now Bill was feeling terribly responsible for both of us. He kept on saying that he was sorry, but he had never dreamed it was going to be as bad as this. He felt that having asked us to come he was in some way chargeable with our troubles. When leaders have this kind of feeling about their men they get much better results, if the men are good: if men are bad or even moderate they will try and take advantage of what they consider to be softness.

The temperature on the night of July 7 was $-59°$.

On July 8 we found the first sign that we might be coming to an end of this soft, powdered, arrowrooty snow. It was frightfully hard pulling; but every now and then our finnesko pierced a thin crust before they sank right in. This meant a little wind, and every now and then our feet came down on a hard slippery patch under the soft snow. We were surrounded by fog which walked along with us, and far above us the moon was shining on its roof. Steering was as difficult as the pulling, and four hours of the hardest work only produced 1¼ miles in the morning, and three more hours 1 mile in the afternoon—and the temperature was $-57°$ with a breeze—horrible!

In the early morning of the next day snow began to fall and the fog was dense: when we got up we could see nothing at all anywhere. After the usual four hours to get going in the morning we settled that it was impossible to relay, for we should never be able to track ourselves back to the second sledge. It was with very great relief that we found we could move both sledges together, and I think this was mainly due to the temperature which had risen to −36°.

This was our fourth day of fog in addition to the normal darkness, and we knew we must be approaching the land. It would be Terror Point, and the fog is probably caused by the moist warm air coming up from the sea through the pressure cracks and crevasses; for it is supposed that the Barrier here is afloat.

I wish I could take you on to the great Ice Barrier some calm evening when the sun is just dipping in the middle of the night and show you the autumn tints on Ross Island. A last look round before turning in, a good day's march behind, enough fine fat pemmican inside you to make you happy, the homely smell of tobacco from the tent, a pleasant sense of soft fur and the deep sleep to come. And all the softest colours God has made are in the snow; on Erebus to the west, where the wind can scarcely move his cloud of smoke; and on Terror to the east, not so high, and more regular in form. How peaceful and dignified it all is.

That was what you might have seen four months ago had you been out on the Barrier plain. Low down on the extreme right or east of the land there was a black smudge of rock peeping out from great snow-drifts: that was the Knoll, and close under it were the cliffs of Cape Crozier, the Knoll looking quite low and the cliffs invisible, although they are eight hundred feet high, a sheer precipice falling to the sea.

It is at Cape Crozier that the Barrier edge, which runs for four hundred miles as an ice-cliff up to 200 feet high, meets the land. The Barrier is moving against this land at a rate which is sometimes not much less than a mile in a year. Perhaps you can imagine the chaos which it piles up: there are pressure ridges compared to which the waves of the sea are like a ploughed field. These are worst at Cape Crozier itself, but they extend all along the southern slopes of Mount Terror, running parallel with the land, and the disturbance which Cape Crozier makes is apparent at Corner Camp some forty miles back on the Barrier in the crevasses we used to find and the occasional ridges we had to cross.

In the *Discovery* days[1] the pressure just where it hit Cape Crozier formed a small bay, and on the sea-ice frozen in this bay the men of the *Discovery* found the only Emperor penguin rookery which had ever been seen. The ice here was not blown out by the blizzards which cleared the Ross Sea, and open water or open leads were never far away. This gave the Emperors a place to lay their eggs and an opportunity to find their food. We had therefore to find our way along the pressure to the Knoll, and thence penetrate *through* the pressure to the Emperors' Bay. And we had to do it in the dark.

Terror Point, which we were approaching in the fog, is a short twenty miles from the Knoll, and ends in a long snow-tongue running out into the Barrier. The way had been travelled a good many times in *Discovery* days and in daylight, and Wilson knew there was a narrow path, free from crevasses, which skirted along between the mountain and the pressure ridges running parallel to it. But it is one thing to walk along a corridor by day, and quite another to try to do so at night, especially when there are no walls by which you can correct your course—only crevasses. Anyway, Terror Point must be somewhere close to us now, and vaguely in front of us was that strip of snow, neither Barrier nor mountain, which was our only way forward.

We began to realize, now that our eyes were more or less out of action, how much we could do with our feet and ears. The effect of walking in finnesko is much the same as walking in gloves, and you get a sense of touch which nothing else except bare feet could give you. Thus we could feel every small variation in surface, every crust through which our feet broke, every hardened patch below the soft snow. And soon we began to rely more and more upon the sound of our footsteps to tell us whether we were on crevasses or solid ground. From now onwards we were working among cre-

1 That is, during Scott's first expedition.—C.N.

vasses fairly constantly. I loathe them in full daylight when much can be done to avoid them, and when if you fall into them you can at any rate see where the sides are, which way they run and how best to scramble out; when your companions can see how to stop the sledge to which you are all attached by your harness; how most safely to hold the sledge when stopped; how, if you are dangling fifteen feet down in a chasm, to work above you to get you up to the surface again. And then our clothes were generally something like clothes. Even under the ideal conditions of good light, warmth and no wind, crevasses are beastly, whether you are pulling over a level and uniform snow surface, never knowing what moment will find you dropping into some bottomless pit, or whether you are rushing for the Alpine rope and the sledge, to help some companion who has disappeared. I dream sometimes now of bad days we had on the Beardmore and elsewhere, when men were dropping through to be caught up and hang at the full length of the harnesses and toggles many times in an hour. On the same sledge as myself on the Beardmore one man went down once head first, and another eight times to the length of his harness in 25 minutes. And always you wondered whether your harness was going to hold when the jerk came. But those days were a Sunday School treat compared to our days of blind-man's buff with the Emperor penguins among the crevasses of Cape Crozier.

Our troubles were greatly increased by the state of our clothes. If we had been dressed in lead we should have been able to move our arms and necks and heads more easily than we could now. If the same amount of icing had extended to our legs I believe we should still be there, standing unable to move: but happily the forks of our trousers still remained movable. To get into our canvas harnesses was the most absurd business. Quite in the early days of our journey we met with this difficulty, and somewhat foolishly decided not to take off our harness for lunch. The harnesses thawed in the tent, and froze back as hard as boards. Likewise our clothing was hard as boards and stuck out from our bodies in every imaginable fold and angle. To fit one board over the other required the united efforts of the would-be wearer and his two companions, and the process had to be repeated for each one of us twice a day. Goodness knows how long it took; but it cannot have been less than five minutes' thumping at each man.

As we approached Terror Point in the fog we sensed that we had risen and fallen over several rises. Every now and then we felt hard slippery snow under our feet. Every now and then our feet went through crusts in the surface. And then quite suddenly, vague, indefinable, monstrous, there loomed a something ahead. I remember having a feeling as of ghosts about as we untoggled our harnesses from the sledge, tied them together, and thus roped walked upwards on that ice. The moon was showing a ghastly ragged mountainous edge above us in the fog, and as we rose we found that we were on a pressure ridge. We stopped, looked at one another, and then *bang*—right under our feet. More bangs, and creaks and groans; for that ice was moving and splitting like glass. The cracks went off all round us, and some of them ran along for hundreds of yards. Afterwards we got used to it, but at first the effect was very jumpy. From first to last during this journey we had plenty of variety and none of that monotony which is inevitable in sledging over long distances of Barrier in summer. Only the long shivering fits following close one after the other all the time we lay in our dreadful sleeping-bags, hour after hour and night after night in those temperatures—they were as monotonous as could be. Later we got frost-bitten even as we lay in our sleeping-bags. Things are getting pretty bad when you get frost-bitten in your bag.

There was only a glow where the moon was; we stood in a moonlit fog, and this was sufficient to show the edge of another ridge ahead, and yet another on our left. We were utterly bewildered. The deep booming of the ice continued, and it may be that the tide has something to do with this, though we were many miles from the ordinary coastal ice.

We went back, toggled up to our sledges again and pulled in what we thought was the right direction, always with that feeling that the earth may open underneath your feet which you have in crevassed areas. But all we found were more mounds and banks of snow and ice, into which we almost ran before we saw them. We were clearly lost. It was near midnight, and I wrote, "It may be the pressure ridges or it may be Terror, it is impossible to say,—and I should think it is impossible to move till it clears. We were steering N.E. when we got here and returned S.W. till we seemed to be in a hollow and camped."

The temperature had been rising from −36° at 11 A.M. and it was now −27°; snow was falling and nothing whatever could be seen. From under the tent came noises as though some giant was banging a big empty tank. All the signs were for a blizzard, and indeed we had not long finished our supper and were thawing our way little by little into our bags when the wind came away from the south. Before it started we got a glimpse of black rock, and knew we must be in the pressure ridges where they nearly join Mount Terror.

It is with great surprise that in looking up the records I find that blizzard lasted three days, the temperature and wind both rising till it was + 9° and blowing force 9 on the morning of the second day (July 11). On the morning of the third day (July 12) it was blowing storm force (10). The temperature had thus risen over eighty degrees.

It was not an uncomfortable time. Wet and warm, the risen temperature allowed all our ice to turn to water, and we lay steaming and beautifully liquid, and wondered sometimes what we should be like when our gear froze up once more. But we did not do much wondering, I suspect: we slept. From that point of view these blizzards were a perfect Godsend.

We also revised our food rations. From the moment we started to prepare for this journey we were asked by Scott to try certain experiments in view of the Plateau stage of the Polar Journey the following summer. It was supposed that the Plateau stage would be the really tough part of the Polar Journey, and no one then dreamed that harder conditions could be found in the middle of the Barrier in March than on the Plateau, ten thousand feet higher, in February. In view of the extreme conditions we knew we must meet on this winter journey, far harder of course in point of weather than anything experienced on the Polar Journey, we had determined to simplify our food to the last degree. We only brought pemmican, biscuit, butter and tea: and tea is not a food, only a pleasant stimulant, and hot: the pemmican was excellent and came from Beauvais, Copenhagen.

The immediate advantage of this was that we had few food bags to handle for each meal. If the air temperature is 100 degrees of frost, then everything in the air is about 100 degrees of frost too. You have only to untie the lashings of one bag in a −70° temperature, with your feet frozen and your fingers just nursed back after getting a match to strike for the candle (you will have tried several boxes—metal), to realize this as an advantage.

The immediate and increasingly pressing disadvantage is that you have no sugar. Have you ever had a craving for sugar which never leaves you, even when asleep? It is unpleasant. As a matter of fact the craving for sweet things never seriously worried us on this journey, and there must have been some sugar in our biscuits which gave a pleasant sweetness to our mid-day tea or nightly hot water when broken up and soaked in it. These biscuits were specially made for us by Huntley and Palmer: their composition was worked out by Wilson and that firm's chemist, and is a secret. But they are probably the most satisfying biscuit ever made, and I doubt whether they can be improved upon. There were two kinds, called Emergency and Antarctic, but there was I think little difference between them except in the baking. A well-baked biscuit was good to eat when sledging if your supply of food was good: but if you were very hungry an underbaked one was much preferred.

By taking individually different quantities of biscuit, pemmican and butter we were able roughly to test the proportions of proteids, fats and carbo-hydrates wanted by the human body under such extreme circumstances. Bill was all for fat, starting with 8 oz. butter, 12 oz. pemmican and only 12 oz. biscuit a day. Bowers told me he was going for proteids, 16 oz. pemmican and 16 oz. biscuit, and suggested I should go the whole hog on carbohydrates. I did not like this, since I knew I should want more fat, but the rations were to be altered as necessary during the journey, so there was no harm in trying. So I started with 20 oz. of biscuit and 12 oz. of pemmican a day.

Bowers was all right (this was usual with him), but he did not eat all his extra pemmican. Bill could not eat all his extra butter, but was satisfied. I got hungry, certainly got more frost-bitten than the others, and wanted more fat. I also got heartburn. However, before taking more fat I increased my biscuits to 24 oz., but this did not satisfy me; I wanted fat. Bill and I now took the same diet, he giving me 4 oz. of butter which he could not eat, and I giving him 4 oz. of biscuit which did not satisfy my wants. We both therefore had 12 oz. pemmican, 16 oz. biscuit and 4 oz. butter a day, but we did not always finish our butter. This is an extremely good ration, and we had enough to eat during most of this journey. We certainly could not have faced the conditions without.

I will not say that I was entirely easy in my mind as we lay out that blizzard somewhere off Terror Point; I don't know how the others were feeling. The unearthly banging going on underneath us may have had something to do with it. But we were quite lost in the pressure and it might be the deuce and all to get out in the dark. The wind eddied and swirled quite out of its usual straightforward way, and the tent got badly snowed up: our sledge had disappeared long ago. The position was not altogether a comfortable one.

Tuesday night and Wednesday it blew up to force 10, temperature from −7° to + 2°. And then it began to modify and get squally. By 3 A.M. on Thursday (July 13) the wind had nearly ceased, the temperature was falling and the stars were shining through detached clouds. We were soon getting our breakfast, which always consisted of tea, followed by pemmican. We soaked our biscuits in both. Then we set to work to dig out the sledges and tent, a big job taking several hours. At last we got started. In that jerky way in which I was still managing to jot a few sentences down each night as a record, I wrote:

"Did 7½ miles during day—seems a marvellous run—rose and fell over several ridges of Terror—in afternoon suddenly came on huge crevasse on one of these—we were quite high on Terror—moon saved us walking in—it might have taken sledge and all."

To do seven miles in a day, a distance which had taken us nearly a week in the past, was very heartening. The temperature was between −20° and −30° all day, and that was good too. When crossing the undulations which ran down out of the mountain into the true pressure ridges on our right we found that the wind which came down off the mountain struck along the top of the undulation, and flowing each way, caused a N.E. breeze on one side and a N.W. breeze on the other. There seemed to be wind in the sky, and the blizzard had not cleared as far away as we should have wished.

During the time through which we had come it was by burning more oil than is usually allowed for cooking that we kept going at all. After each meal was cooked we allowed the primus to burn on for a while and thus warmed up the tent. Then we could nurse back our frozen feet and do any necessary little odd jobs. More often we just sat and nodded for a few minutes, keeping one another from going too deeply to sleep. But it was running away with the oil. We started with 6 one-gallon tins (those tins Scott had criticized), and we had now used four of them. At first we said we must have at least two one-gallon tins with which to go back; but by now our estimate had come down to one full gallon tin, and two full primus lamps. Our sleeping-bags were awful. It took me, even as early in the journey as this, an hour of pushing and thumping and cramp every night to thaw out enough of mine to get into it at all. Even that was not so bad as lying in them when we got there.

Only −35° but "a very bad night" according to my diary. We got away in good time, but it was a ghastly day and my nerves were quivering at the end, for we could not find that straight and narrow way which led between the crevasses on either hand. Time after time we found we were out of our course by the sudden fall of the ground beneath our feet— in we went and then—"are we too far right?"—nobody knows—"well let's try nearer in to the mountain," and so forth! "By hard slogging 2 3/4 miles this morning—then on in thick gloom which suddenly lifted and we found ourselves under a huge great mountain of pressure ridge looking black in shadow. We went on, bending to the left, when Bill fell and put his arm into a crevasse. We went over this and another, and some time after got somewhere up to the left, and both Bill and I put a foot into a crevasse. We sounded all about and everywhere was hollow, and so we ran the sledge down over it and all was well."[1] Once we got right into the pressure and took a longish time to get out again. Bill lengthened his trace out with the Alpine rope now and often afterwards, so he found the crevasses well ahead of us and the sledge: nice for us but not so nice for Bill. Crevasses in the dark *do* put your nerves on edge.

When we started next morning (July 15) we could see on our left front and more or less on top of us the Knoll, which is a big hill whose precipitous cliffs to seaward form Cape Crozier. The sides of it sloped down towards us, and pressing against its ice-cliffs on ahead were miles and miles of great pressure ridges, along which we had travelled, and which hemmed us in. Mount Terror rose ten thousand feet high on our left, and was connected with the Knoll by a great cup-like drift of wind-polished snow. The slope of this in one place runs gently out on to the corridor along which we had sledged, and here we turned and started to pull our sledges

1 My own diary.

up. There were no crevasses, only the great drift of snow, so hard that we used our crampons just as though we had been on ice, and as polished as the china sides of a giant cup which it resembled. For three miles we slogged up, until we were only 150 yards from the moraine shelf where we were going to build our hut of rocks and snow. This moraine was above us on our left, the twin peaks of the Knoll were across the cup on our right; and here, 800 feet up the mountain side, we pitched our last camp.

We had arrived.

What should we call our hut? How soon could we get our clothes and bags dry? How would the blubber stove work? Would the penguins be there? "It seems too good to be true, 19 days out. Surely seldom has any one been so wet; our bags hardly possible to get into, our wind-clothes just frozen boxes. Birdie's patent balaclava is like iron—it is wonderful how our cares have vanished."[1]

It was evening, but we were so keen to begin that we went straight up to the ridge above our camp, where the rock cropped out from the snow. We found that most of it was *in situ* but that there were plenty of boulders, some gravel, and of course any amount of the icy snow which fell away below us down to our tent, and the great pressure about a mile beyond. Between us and that pressure, as we were to find out afterwards, was a great ice-cliff. The pressure ridges, and the Great Ice Barrier beyond, were at our feet; the Ross Sea edge but some four miles away. The Emperors must be some-where round that shoulder of the Knoll which hides Cape Crozier itself from our view.

Our scheme was to build an igloo with rock walls, banked up with snow, using a nine-foot sledge as a ridge beam, and a large sheet of green Willesden canvas as a roof. We had also brought a board to form a lintel over the door. Here with the stove, which was to be fed with blubber from the penguins, we were to have a comfortable warm home whence we

1 My own diary.

would make excursions to the rookery perhaps four miles away. Perhaps we would manage to get our tent down to the rookery itself and do our scientific work there on the spot, leaving our nice hut for a night or more. That is how we planned it.

That same night "we started to dig in under a great boulder on the top of the hill, hoping to make this a large part of one of the walls of the hut, but the rock came close underneath and stopped us. We then chose a moderately level piece of moraine about twelve feet away, and just under the level of the top of the hill, hoping that here in the lee of the ridge we might escape a good deal of the tremendous winds which we knew were common. Birdie gathered rocks from over the hill, nothing was too big for him; Bill did the banking up outside while I built the wall with the boulders. The rocks were good, the snow, however, was blown so hard as to be practically ice; a pick made little impression upon it, and the only way was to chip out big blocks gradually with the small shovel. The gravel was scanty, but good when there was any. Altogether things looked very hopeful when we turned in to the tent some 150 yards down the slope, having done about half one of the long walls."[1]

The view from eight hundred feet up the mountain was magnificent and I got my spectacles out and cleared the ice away time after time to look. To the east a great field of pressure ridges below, looking in the moonlight as if giants had been ploughing with ploughs which made furrows fifty or sixty feet deep: these ran right up to the Barrier edge, and beyond was the frozen Ross Sea, lying flat, white and peaceful as though such things as blizzards were unknown. To the north and north-east the Knoll. Behind us Mount Terror on which we stood, and over all the grey limitless Barrier seemed to cast a spell of cold immensity, vague, ponderous, a breeding-place of wind and drift and darkness. God! What a place!

[1] My own diary.

"There was now little moonlight or daylight, but for the next forty-eight hours we used both to their utmost, being up at all times by day and night, and often working on when there was great difficulty in seeing anything; digging by the light of the hurricane lamp. By the end of two days we had the walls built, and banked up to one or two feet from the top; we were to fit the roof cloth close before banking up the rest. The great difficulty in banking was the hardness of the snow, it being impossible to fill in the cracks between the blocks which were more like paving-stones than anything else. The door was in, being a triangular tent doorway, with flaps which we built close in to the walls, cementing it with snow and rocks. The top folded over a plank and the bottom was dug into the ground."[1]

Birdie was very disappointed that we could not finish the whole thing that day: he was nearly angry about it, but there was a lot to do yet and we were tired out. We turned out early the next morning (Tuesday 18th) to try and finish the igloo, but it was blowing too hard. When we got to the top we did some digging but it was quite impossible to get the roof on, and we had to leave it. We realized that day that it blew much harder at the top of the slope than where our tent was. It was bitterly cold up there that morning with a wind force 4–5 and a minus thirty temperature.

The oil question was worrying us quite a lot. We were now well in to the fifth of our six tins, and economizing as much as possible, often having only two hot meals a day. We had to get down to the Emperor penguins somehow and get some blubber to run the stove which had been made for us in the hut. The 19th being a calm fine day we started at 9.30, with an empty sledge, two ice-axes, Alpine rope, harnesses and skinning tools.

Wilson had made this journey through the Cape Crozier pressure ridges several times in the *Discovery* days. But then they had daylight, and they had found a practicable way

1 *Ibid.*

close under the cliffs which at the present moment were between us and the ridges.

As we neared the bottom of the mountain slope, farther to the north than we had previously gone, we had to be careful about crevasses, but we soon hit off the edge of the cliff and skirted along it until it petered out on the same level as the Barrier. Turning left handed we headed towards the sea-ice, knowing that there were some two miles of pressure between us and Cape Crozier itself. For about half a mile it was fair going, rounding big knobs of pressure but always managing to keep more or less on the flat and near the ice-cliff which soon rose to a very great height on our left. Bill's idea was to try and keep close under this cliff, along that same *Discovery* way which I have mentioned above. They never arrived there early enough for the eggs in those days: the chicks were hatched. Whether we should now find any Emperors, and if so whether they would have any eggs, was by no means certain.

However, we soon began to get into trouble, meeting several crevasses every few yards, and I have no doubt crossing scores of others of which we had no knowledge. Though we hugged the cliffs as close as possible we found ourselves on the top of the first pressure ridge, separated by a deep gulf from the ice-slope which we wished to reach. Then we were in a great valley between the first and second ridges: we got into huge heaps of ice pressed up in every shape on every side, crevassed in every direction: we slithered over snow-slopes and crawled along drift ridges, trying to get in towards the cliffs. And always we came up against impossible places and had to crawl back. Bill led on a length of Alpine rope fastened to the toggle of the sledge; Birdie was in his harness also fastened to the toggle, and I was in my harness fastened to the rear of the sledge, which was of great use to us both as a bridge and a ladder.

Two or three times we tried to get down the ice-slopes to the comparatively level road under the cliff, but it was always too great a drop. In that dim light every proportion was distorted; some of the places we actually did manage to negotiate with ice-axes and Alpine rope looked absolute precipices, and there were always crevasses at the bottom if you slipped. On the way back I did slip into one of these and was hauled out by the other two standing on the wall above me.

We then worked our way down into the hollow between the first and second large pressure ridges, and I believe on to the top of the second. The crests here rose fifty or sixty feet. After this I don't know where we went. Our best landmarks were patches of crevasses, sometimes three or four in a few footsteps. The temperatures were lowish ($-37°$), it was impossible for me to wear spectacles, and this was a tremendous difficulty to me and handicap to the party: Bill would find a crevasse and point it out; Birdie would cross; and then time after time, in trying to step over or climb over on the sledge, I put my feet right into the middle of the cracks. This day I went well in at least six times; once, when we were close to the sea, rolling into and out of one and then down a steep slope until brought up by Birdie and Bill on the rope.

We blundered along until we got into a great cul-de-sac which probably formed the end of the two ridges, where they butted on to the sea-ice. On all sides rose great walls of battered ice with steep snow-slopes in the middle, where we slithered about and blundered into crevasses. To the left rose the huge cliff of Cape Crozier, but we could not tell whether there were not two or three pressure ridges between us and it, and though we tried at least four ways, there was no possibility of getting forward.

And then we heard the Emperors calling.

Their cries came to us from the sea-ice we could not see, but which must have been a chaotic quarter of a mile away. They came echoing back from the cliffs, as we stood helpless and tantalized. We listened and realized that there was nothing for it but to return, for the little light which now came in the middle of the day was going fast, and to be caught in absolute darkness there was a horrible idea. We started back on our tracks and almost immediately I lost my footing and rolled down a slope into a crevasse. Birdie and Bill kept their balance and I clambered back to them. The tracks were very faint and we soon began to lose them. Birdie was the best man at following tracks that I have ever known, and he found them time after time. But at last even he lost them altogether and we settled we must just got ahead. As a matter of fact, we picked them up again, and by then were out of the worst: but we were glad to see the tent.

The next morning (Thursday, June 20) we started work on the igloo at 3 A.M. and managed to get the canvas roof on in spite of a wind which harried us all that day. Little did we think what that roof had in store for us as we packed it in with snow blocks, stretching it over our second sledge, which we put athwartships across the middle of the longer walls. The windward (south) end came right down to the ground and we tied it securely to rocks before packing it in. On the other three sides we had a good two feet or more of slack all round, and in every case we tied it to rocks by lanyards at intervals of two feet. The door was the difficulty, and for the present we left the cloth arching over the stones, forming a kind of portico. The whole was well packed in and over with slabs of hard snow, but there was no soft snow with which to fill up the gaps between the blocks. However, we felt already that nothing could drag that roof out of its packing, and subsequent events proved that we were right.

It was a bleak job for three o'clock in the morning before breakfast, and we were glad to get back to the tent and a meal, for we meant to have another go at the Emperors that day. With the first glimpse of light we were off for the rookery again.

But we now knew one or two things about that pressure which we had not known twenty-four hours ago; for instance, that there was a lot of alteration since the *Discovery* days and that probably the pressure was bigger. As a matter of fact it has been since proved by photographs that the ridges now ran out three-quarters of a mile farther into the sea than they did ten years before. We knew also that if we entered the pressure at the only place where the ice-cliffs came down to the level of the Barrier, as we did yesterday, we could neither penetrate to the rookery nor get in under the cliffs where formerly a possible way had been found. There was only one other thing to do—to go over the cliff. And this was what we proposed to try and do.

Now these ice-cliffs are some two hundred feet high, and I felt uncomfortable, especially in the dark. But as we came back the day before we had noticed at one place a break in the cliffs from which there hung a snow-drift. It *might* be possible to get down that drift.

And so, all harnessed to the sledge, with Bill on a long lead out in front and Birdie and myself checking the sledge behind, we started down the slope which ended in the cliff, which of course we could not see. We crossed a number of small crevasses, and soon we knew we must be nearly there. Twice we crept up to the edge of the cliff with no success, and then we found the slope: more, we got down it without great difficulty and it brought us out just where we wanted to be, between the land cliffs and the pressure.

Then began the most exciting climb among the pressure that you can imagine. At first very much as it was the day before—pulling ourselves and one another up ridges, slithering down slopes, tumbling into and out of crevasses and holes of all sorts, we made our way along under the cliffs which rose higher and higher above us as we neared the black lava precipices which form Cape Crozier itself. We straddled along the top of a snow ridge with a razor-backed edge, balancing the sledge between us as we wriggled: on our right was a drop of great depth with crevasses at the bottom, on our left was a smaller drop also crevassed. We crawled along, and I can tell you it was exciting work in the more than half darkness. At the end was a series of slopes full of crevasses, and finally we got right in under the rock on to moraine, and here we had to leave the sledge.

We roped up, and started to worry along under the cliffs,

which had now changed from ice to rock, and rose 800 feet above us. The tumult of pressure which climbed against them showed no order here. Four hundred miles of moving ice behind it had just tossed and twisted those giant ridges until Job himself would have lacked words to reproach their Maker. We scrambled over and under, hanging on with our axes, and cutting steps where we could not find a foothold with our crampons. And always we got towards the Emperor penguins, and it really began to look as if we were going to do it this time, when we came up against a wall of ice which a single glance told us we could never cross. One of the largest pressure ridges had been thrown, end on, against the cliff. We seemed to be stopped, when Bill found a black hole, something like a fox's earth, disappearing into the bowels of the ice. We looked at it: "Well, here goes!" he said, and put his head in, and disappeared. Bowers likewise. It was a long-ish way, but quite possible to wriggle along, and presently I found myself looking out of the other side with a deep gully below me, the rock face on one hand and the ice on the other. "Put your back against the ice and your feet against the rock and lever yourself along," said Bill, who was already standing on firm ice at the far end in a snow pit. We cut some fifteen steps to get out of that hole. Excited by now, and thoroughly enjoying ourselves, we found the way ahead easier, until the penguins' call reached us again and we stood, three crystallized ragamuffins, above the Emperors' home. They were there all right, and we were going to reach them, but where were all the thousands of which we had heard?

We stood on an ice-foot which was really a dwarf cliff some twelve feet high, and the sea-ice, with a good many ice-blocks strewn upon it, lay below. The cliff dropped straight, with a bit of an overhang and no snow-drift. This may have been because the sea had only frozen recently; whatever the reason may have been it meant that we should have a lot of difficulty in getting up again without help. It was decided that some one must stop on the top with the Alpine rope, and clearly that one should be I, for with short sight and fogged spectacles which I could not wear I was much the least useful of the party for the job immediately ahead. Had we had the sledge we could have used it as a ladder, but of course we had left this at the beginning of the moraine miles back.

We saw the Emperors standing all together huddled under the Barrier cliff some hundreds of yards away. The little light was going fast: we were much more excited about the approach of complete darkness and the look of wind in the south than we were about our triumph. After indescribable effort and hardship we were witnessing a marvel of the natural world, and we were the first and only men who had ever done so; we had within our grasp material which might prove of the utmost importance to science; we were turning theories into facts with every observation we made,—and we had but a moment to give.

The disturbed Emperors made a tremendous row, trumpeting with their curious metallic voices. There was no doubt they had eggs, for they tried to shuffle along the ground without losing them off their feet. But when they were hustled a good many eggs were dropped and left lying on the ice, and some of these were quickly picked up by eggless Emperors who had probably been waiting a long time for the opportunity. In these poor birds the maternal side seems to have necessarily swamped the other functions of life. Such is the struggle for existence that they can only live by a glut of maternity, and it would be interesting to know whether such a life leads to happiness or satisfaction.

I have told how the men of the *Discovery* found this rookery where we now stood. How they made journeys in the early spring but never arrived early enough to get eggs and only found parents and chicks. They concluded that the Emperor was an impossible kind of bird who, for some reason or other, nests in the middle of the Antarctic winter with the temperature anywhere below seventy degrees of frost, and the blizzards blowing, always blowing, against his devoted back. And they found him holding his precious chick balanced upon his big feet, and pressing it maternally, or paternally (for both sexes squabble for the privilege) against a bald patch in his breast. And when at last he simply must go and eat something in the open leads near by, he just puts the child down on the ice, and twenty chickless Emperors rush to pick it up. And they fight over it, and so tear it that sometimes it will die. And, if it can, it will crawl into any ice-crack to escape from so much kindness, and there it will freeze. Likewise many broken and addled eggs were found, and it is clear that the mortality is very great. But some survive, and summer comes; and when a big blizzard is going to blow (they know all about the weather), the parents take the children out for miles across the sea-ice, until they reach the threshold of the open sea. And there they sit until the wind comes, and the swell rises, and breaks that ice-floe off; and away they go in the blinding drift to join the main pack-ice, with a private yacht all to themselves.

You must agree that a bird like this is an interesting beast, and when, seven months ago, we rowed a boat under those great black cliffs, and found a disconsolate Emperor chick still in the down, we knew definitely why the Emperor has to nest in mid-winter. For if a June egg was still without feathers in the beginning of January, the same egg laid in the summer would leave its produce without practical covering for the following winter. Thus the Emperor penguin is compelled to undertake all kinds of hardships because his children insist on developing so slowly, very much as we are tied in our human relationships for the same reason. It is of interest that such a primitive bird should have so long a childhood.

But interesting as the life history of these birds must be, we had not travelled for three weeks to see them sitting on their eggs. We wanted the embryos, and we wanted them as young as possible, and fresh and unfrozen, that specialists at home might cut them into microscopic sections and learn from them the previous history of birds through the evolutionary ages. And so Bill and Birdie rapidly collected five eggs, which we hoped to carry safely in our fur mitts to our igloo upon Mount Terror, where we could pickle them in the alcohol we had brought for the purpose. We also wanted oil for our blubber stove, and they killed and skinned three birds —an Emperor weighs up to 6½ stones.

The Ross Sea was frozen over, and there were no seals in sight. There were only 100 Emperors as compared with 2000 in 1902 and 1903. Bill reckoned that every fourth or fifth bird had an egg, but this was only a rough estimate, for we did not want to disturb them unnecessarily. It is a mystery why there should have been so few birds, but it certainly looked as though the ice had not formed very long. Were these the first arrivals? Had a previous rookery been blown out to sea and was this the beginning of a second attempt? Is this bay of sea-ice becoming unsafe?

Those who previously discovered the Emperors with their chicks saw the penguins nursing dead and frozen chicks if they were unable to obtain a live one. They also found decomposed eggs which they must have incubated after they had been frozen. Now we found that these birds were so anxious to sit on something that some of those which had no eggs were sitting on ice! Several times Bill and Birdie picked up eggs to find them lumps of ice, rounded and about the right size, dirty and hard. Once a bird dropped an ice nest egg as they watched, and again a bird returned and tucked another into itself, immediately forsaking it for a real one, however, when one was offered.

Meanwhile a whole procession of Emperors came round under the cliff on which I stood. The light was already very bad and it was well that my companions were quick in returning: we had to do everything in a great hurry. I hauled up the eggs in their mitts (which we fastened together round our necks with lampwick lanyards) and then the skins, but failed to help Bill at all. "Pull," he cried, from the bottom: "I am pulling," I said, "But the line's quite slack down here," he shouted. And when he had reached the top by climbing up on Bowers' shoulders, and we were both pulling all we knew Birdie's end of the rope was still slack in his hands. Directly we put on a strain the rope cut into the ice edge and jammed

—a very common difficulty when working among crevasses. We tried to run the rope over an ice-axe without success, and things began to look serious when Birdie, who had been running about prospecting and had meanwhile put one leg through a crack into the sea, found a place where the cliff did not overhang. He cut steps for himself, we hauled, and at last we were all together on the top—his foot being by now surrounded by a solid mass of ice.

We legged it back as hard as we could go: five eggs in our fur mitts, Birdie with two skins tied to him and trailing behind, and myself with one. We were roped up, and climbing the ridges and getting through the holes was very difficult. In one place where there was a steep rubble and snow slope down I left the ice-axe half way up; in another it was too dark to see our former ice-axe footsteps, and I could see nothing, and so just let myself go and trusted to luck. With infinite patience Bill said: "Cherry, you *must* learn how to use an ice-axe." For the rest of the trip my wind-clothes were in rags.

We found the sledge, and none too soon, and now had three eggs left, more or less whole. Both mine had burst in my mitts: the first I emptied out, the second I left in my mitt to put into the cooker; it never got there, but on the return journey I had my mitts far more easily thawed out than Birdie's (Bill had none) and I believe the grease in the egg did them good. When we got into the hollows under the ridge where we had to cross, it was too dark to do anything but feel our way. We did so over many crevasses, found the ridge and crept over it. Higher up we could see more, but to follow our tracks soon became impossible, and we plugged straight ahead and luckily found the slope down which we had come. All day it had been blowing a nasty cold wind with a temperature between −20° and 30°, which we felt a good deal. Now it began to get worse. The weather was getting thick and things did not look very nice when we started up to find our tent. Soon it was blowing force 4, and soon we missed our way entirely. We got right up above the patch of rocks which marked our igloo and only found it after a good deal of search.

I have heard tell of an English officer at the Dardanelles who was left, blinded, in No Man's Land between the English and Turkish trenches. Moving only at night, and having no sense to tell him which were his own trenches, he was fired at by Turk and English alike as he groped his ghastly way to and from them. Thus he spent days and nights until, one night, he crawled towards the English trenches, to be fired at as usual. "Oh God! what can I do!" some one heard him say, and he was brought in.

Such extremity of suffering cannot be measured: madness or death may give relief. But this I know: we on this journey were already beginning to think of death as a friend. As we groped our way back that night, sleepless, icy, and dog-tired in the dark and the wind and the drift, a crevasse seemed almost a friendly gift.

"Things must improve," said Bill next day, "I think we reached bed-rock last night." We hadn't, by a long way.

It was like this.

We moved into the igloo for the first time, for we had to save oil by using our blubber stove if we were to have any left to travel home with, and we did not wish to cover our tent with the oily black filth which the use of blubber necessitates. The blizzard blew all night, and we were covered with drift which came in through hundreds of leaks: in this wind-swept place we had found no soft snow with which we could pack our hard snow blocks. As we flensed some blubber from one of our penguin skins the powdery drift covered everything we had.

Though uncomfortable this was nothing to worry about overmuch. Some of the drift which the blizzard was bringing would collect to leeward of our hut and the rocks below which it was built, and they could be used to make our hut more weather-proof. Then with great difficulty we got the blubber stove to start, and it spouted a blob of boiling oil into Bill's eye. For the rest of the night he lay, quite unable to stifle his groans, obviously in very great pain: he told us afterwards that he thought his eye was gone. We managed to cook a meal somehow, and Birdie got the stove going afterwards, but it was quite useless to try and warm the place. I got out and cut the green canvas outside the door, so as to get the roof cloth in under the stones, and then packed it down as well as I could with snow, and so blocked most of the drift coming in.

It is extraordinary how often angels and fools do the same thing in this life, and I have never been able to settle which we were on this journey. I never heard an angry word: once only (when this same day I could not pull Bill up the cliff out of the penguin rookery) I heard an impatient one: and these groans were the nearest approach to complaint. Most men would have howled. "I think we reached bed-rock last night," was strong language for Bill. "I was incapacitated for a short time," he says in his report to Scott.[1] Endurance was tested on this journey under unique circumstances, and always these two men with all the burden of responsibility which did not fall upon myself, displayed that quality which is perhaps the only one which may be said with certainty to make for success, self-control.

We spent the next day—it was July 21—in collecting every scrap of soft snow we could find and packing it into the crevasses between our hard snow blocks. It was a pitifully small amount but we could see no cracks when we had finished. To counteract the lifting tendency the wind had on our roof we cut some great flat hard snow blocks and laid them on the canvas top to steady it against the sledge which formed the ridge support. We also pitched our tent outside the igloo door. Both tent and igloo were therefore eight or nine hundred feet up Terror: both were below an outcrop of rocks from which the mountain fell steeply to the Barrier behind us, and from this direction came the blizzards. In front of us the slope fell for a mile or more down to the

[1] *Scott's Last Expedition*, vol. ii, p. 42.

ice-cliffs, so wind-swept that we had to wear crampons to walk upon it. Most of the tent was in the lee of the igloo, but the cap of it came over the igloo roof, while a segment of the tent itself jutted out beyond the igloo wall.

That night we took much of our gear into the tent and lighted the blubber stove. I always mistrusted that stove, and every moment I expected it to flare up and burn the tent. But the heat it gave, as it burned furiously, with the double lining of the tent to contain it, was considerable.

It did not matter, except for a routine which we never managed to keep, whether we started to thaw our way into our frozen sleeping-bags at 4 in the morning or 4 in the afternoon. I think we must have turned in during the afternoon of that Friday, leaving the cooker, our finnesko, a deal of our foot-gear, Bowers' bag of personal gear, and many other things in the tent. I expect we left the blubber stove there too, for it was quite useless at present to try and warm the igloo. The tent floor-cloth was under our sleeping-bags in the igloo.

"Things must improve," said Bill. After all there was much for which to be thankful. I don't think anybody could have made a better igloo with the hard snow blocks and rocks which were all we had: we would get it air-tight by degrees. The blubber stove was working, and we had fuel for it: we had also found a way down to the penguins and had three complete, though frozen eggs: the two which had been in my mitts smashed when I fell about because I could not wear spectacles. Also the twilight given by the sun below the horizon at noon was getting longer.

But already we had been out twice as long in winter as the longest previous journeys in spring. The men who made those journeys had daylight where we had darkness, they had never had such low temperatures, generally nothing approaching them, and they had seldom worked in such difficult country. The nearest approach to healthy sleep we had had for nearly a month was when during blizzards the temperature allowed the warmth of our bodies to thaw some of the ice in our clothing and sleeping-bags into water. The wear and tear on our minds was very great. We were certainly weaker. We had a little more than a tin of oil to get back on, and we knew the conditions we had to face on that journey across the Barrier: even with fresh men and fresh gear it had been almost unendurable.

And so we spent half an hour or more getting into our bags. Cirrus cloud was moving across the face of the stars from the north, it looked rather hazy and thick to the south, but it is always difficult to judge weather in the dark. There was little wind and the temperature was in the minus twenties. We felt no particular uneasiness. Our tent was well dug in, and was also held down by rocks and the heavy tank off the sledge which were placed on the skirting as additional security. We felt that no power on earth could move the thick walls of our igloo, nor drag the canvas roof from the middle of the embankment into which it was packed and lashed.

"Things must improve," said Bill.

I do not know what time it was when I woke up. It was calm, with that absolute silence which can be so soothing or so terrible as circumstances dictate. Then there came a sob of wind, and all was still again. Ten minutes and it was blowing as though the world was having a fit of hysterics. The earth was torn in pieces: the indescribable fury and roar of it all cannot be imagined.

"Bill, Bill, the tent has gone," was the next I remember—from Bowers shouting at us again and again through the door. It is always these early morning shocks which hit one hardest: our slow minds suggested that this might mean a peculiarly lingering form of death. Journey after journey Birdie and I fought our way across the few yards which had separated the tent from the igloo door. I have never understood why so much of our gear which was in the tent remained, even in the lee of the igloo. The place where the tent had been was littered with gear, and when we came to reckon up afterwards we had everything except the bottom piece of the cooker, and the top of the outer cooker. We never saw these again. The most wonderful thing of all was that our finnesko were lying where they were left, which happened to be on the ground in the part of the tent which was under the lee of the igloo. Also Birdie's bag of personal gear was there, and a tin of sweets.

Birdie brought two tins of sweets away with him. One we had to celebrate our arrival at the Knoll: this was the second, of which we knew nothing, and which was for Bill's birthday, the next day. We started eating them on Saturday, however, and the tin came in useful to Bill afterwards.

To get that gear in we fought against solid walls of black snow which flowed past us and tried to hurl us down the slope. Once started nothing could have stopped us. I saw Birdie knocked over once, but he clawed his way back just in time. Having passed everything we could find in to Bill, we got back into the igloo, and started to collect things together, including our very dishevelled minds.

There was no doubt that we were in the devil of a mess, and it was not altogether our fault. We had had to put our igloo more or less where we could get rocks with which to build it. Very naturally we had given both our tent and igloo all the shelter we could from the full force of the wind, and now it seemed we were in danger not because they were in the wind, but because they were not sufficiently in it. The main force of the hurricane, deflected by the ridge behind, fled over our heads and appeared to form by suction a vacuum below. Our tent had either been sucked upwards into this, or had been blown away because some of it was in the wind while some of it was not. The roof of our igloo was being wrenched upwards and then dropped back with great crashes: the drift was spouting in, not it seemed because it was blown in from outside, but because it was sucked in from within: the lee, not the weather, wall was the worst. Already everything was six or eight inches under snow.

Very soon we began to be alarmed about the igloo. For some time the heavy snow blocks we had heaved up on to the canvas roof kept it weighted down. But it seemed that they were being gradually moved off by the hurricane. The tension became well-nigh unendurable: the waiting in all that welter of noise was maddening. Minute after minute, hour after hour—those snow blocks were off now anyway, and the roof was smashed up and down—no canvas ever made could stand it indefinitely.

We got a meal that Saturday morning, our last for a very long time as it happened. Oil being of such importance to us we tried to use the blubber stove, but after several preliminary spasms it came to pieces in our hands, some solder having melted; and a very good thing too, I thought, for it was more dangerous than useful. We finished cooking our meal on the primus. Two bits of the cooker having been blown away we had to balance it on the primus as best we could. We then settled that in view of the shortage of oil we would not have another meal for as long as possible. As a matter of fact God settled that for us.

We did all we could to stop up the places where the drift was coming in, plugging the holes with our socks, mitts and other clothing. But it was no real good. Our igloo was a vacuum which was filling itself up as soon as possible: and when snow was not coming in a fine black moraine dust took its place, covering us and everything. For twenty-four hours we waited for the roof to go: things were so bad now that we dare not unlash the door.

Many hours ago Bill had told us that if the roof went he considered that our best chance would be to roll over in our sleeping-bags until we were lying on the openings, and get frozen and drifted in.

Gradually the situation got more desperate. The distance between the taut-sucked canvas and the sledge on which it should have been resting became greater, and this must have been due to the stretching of the canvas itself and the loss of the snow blocks on the top: it was not drawing out of the walls. The crashes as it dropped and banged out again were louder. There was more snow coming through the walls, though all our loose mitts, socks and smaller clothing were stuffed into the worst places: our pyjama jackets were stuffed between the roof and the rocks over the door. The rocks were lifting and shaking here till we thought they would fall.

We talked by shouting, and long before this one of us proposed to try and get the Alpine rope lashed down over the roof from outside. But Bowers said it was an absolute impossibility in that wind. "You could never ask men at sea to try such a thing," he said. He was up and out of his bag continually, stopping up holes, pressing against bits of roof to try and prevent the flapping and so forth. He was magnificent.

And then it went.

Birdie was over by the door, where the canvas which was bent over the lintel board was working worse than anywhere else. Bill was practically out of his bag pressing against some part of a long stick of some kind. I don't know what I was doing but I was half out of and half in my bag.

The top of the door opened in little slits and that green Willesden canvas flapped into hundreds of little fragments in fewer seconds than it takes to read this. The uproar of it all was indescribable. Even above the savage thunder of that great wind on the mountain came the lash of the canvas as it was whipped to little tiny strips. The highest rocks which we had built into our walls fell upon us, and a sheet of drift came in.

Birdie dived for his sleeping-bag and eventually got in, together with a terrible lot of drift. Bill also—but he was better off: I was already half into mine and all right, so I turned to help Bill. "Get into your own," he shouted, and when I continued to try and help him, he leaned over until his mouth was against my ear, "*Please*, Cherry," he said, and his voice was terribly anxious. I know he felt responsible: feared it was he who had brought us to this ghastly end.

The next I knew was Bowers' head across Bill's body. "We're all right," he yelled, and we answered in the affirmative. Despite the fact that we knew we only said so because we knew we were all wrong, this statement was helpful.

Then we turned our bags over as far as possible, so that the bottom of the bag was uppermost and the flaps were more or less beneath us. And we lay and thought, and sometimes we sang.

I suppose, wrote Wilson, we were all revolving plans to get back without a tent: and the one thing we had left was the floor-cloth upon which we were actually lying. Of course we could not speak at present, but later after the blizzard had stopped we discussed the possibility of digging a hole in the snow each night and covering it over with the floor-cloth. I do not think we had any idea that we could really get back in those temperatures in our present state of ice by such means, but no one ever hinted at such a thing. Birdie and Bill sang quite a lot of songs and hymns, snatches of which reached me every now and then, and I chimed in, somewhat feebly I suspect. Of course we were getting pretty badly drifted up. "I was resolved to keep warm," wrote Bowers, "and beneath my debris covering I paddled my feet and sang all the songs and hymns I knew to pass the time. I could occasionally thump Bill, and as he still moved I knew he was alive all right—what a birthday for him!" Birdie was more drifted up than we, but at times we all had to hummock ourselves up to heave the snow off our bags. By opening the flaps of our bags we could get small pinches of soft drift which we pressed together and put into our mouths to melt. When our hands warmed up again we got some more; so we did not get very thirsty. A few ribbons of canvas still remained in the wall over our heads, and these produced volley of cracks like pistol shots hour after hour. The canvas never drew out from the walls, not an inch. The wind made just the same noise as an express train running fast through a tunnel if you have both the windows down.

I can well believe that neither of my companions gave up hope for an instant. They must have been frightened, but they were never disturbed. As for me I never had any hope at all; and when the roof went I felt that this was the end. What else could I think? We had spent days in reaching this place through the darkness in cold such as had never been experienced by human beings. We had been out for four weeks under conditions in which no man had existed previously for more than a few days, if that. During this time we had seldom slept except from sheer physical exhaustion, as men sleep on the rack; and every minute of it we had been fighting for the bed-rock necessaries of bare existence, and always in the dark. We had kept ourselves going by enormous care of our feet and hands and bodies, by burning oil, and by having plenty of hot fatty food. Now we had no tent, one tin of oil left out of six, and only part of our cooker. When we were lucky and not too cold we could almost wring water from our clothes, and directly we got out of our sleeping-bags we were frozen into solid sheets of armoured ice. In cold temperatures with all the advantages of a tent over our heads we were already taking more than an hour of fierce struggling and cramp to get into our sleeping-bags—so frozen were they and so long did it take us to thaw our way in. No! Without the tent we were dead men.

And there seemed not one chance in a million that we should ever see our tent again. We were 900 feet up on the mountain side, and the wind blew about as hard as a wind can blow straight out to sea. First there was a steep slope, so hard that a pick made little impression upon it, so slippery that if you started down in finnesko you never could stop: this ended in a great ice-cliff some hundreds of feet high, and then came miles of pressure ridges, crevassed and tumbled, in which you might as well look for a daisy as a tent: and after that the open sea. The chances, however, were that the tent had just been taken up into the air and dropped somewhere in this sea well on the way to New Zealand. Obviously the tent was gone.

Face to face with real death one does not think of the things that torment the bad people in the tracts, and fill the good people with bliss. I might have speculated on my chances of going to Heaven; but candidly I did not care. I could not have wept if I had tried. I had no wish to review the evils of my past. But the past did seem to have been a bit wasted. The road to Hell may be paved with good intentions: the road to Heaven is paved with lost opportunities.

I wanted those years over again. What fun I would have with them: what glorious fun! It was a pity. Well has the Persian said that when we come to die we, remembering that God is merciful, will gnaw our elbows with remorse for thinking of the things we have not done for fear of the Day of Judgment.

And I wanted peaches and syrup—badly. We had them at the hut, sweeter and more luscious than you can imagine. And we had been without sugar for a month. Yes—especially the syrup.

Thus impiously I set out to die, making up my mind that I was not going to try and keep warm, that it might not take too long, and thinking I would try and get some morphia from the medical case if it got very bad. Not a bit heroic, and entirely true! Yes! comfortable, warm reader. Men do not fear death, they fear the pain of dying.

And then quite naturally and no doubt disappointingly to those who would like to read of my last agonies (for who would not give pleasure by his death?) I fell asleep. I expect the temperature was pretty high during this great blizzard, and anything near zero was very high to us. That and the snow which drifted over us made a pleasant wet kind of snipe marsh inside our sleeping-bags, and I am sure we all dozed a good bit. There was so much to worry about that there was not the least use in worrying: and we were so *very* tired. We were hungry, for the last meal we had had was in the morning of the day before, but hunger was not very pressing.

And so we lay, wet and quite fairly warm, hour after hour while the wind roared round us, blowing storm force continually and rising in the gusts to something indescribable. Storm force is force 11, and force 12 is the biggest wind which can be logged: Bowers logged it force 11, but he was always so afraid of overestimating that he was inclined to underrate. I think it was blowing a full hurricane. Sometimes awake, sometimes dozing, we had not a very uncomfortable time so far as I can remember. I knew that parties which had come to Cape Crozier in the spring had experienced blizzards which lasted eight or ten days. But this did not worry us as much as I think it did Bill: I was numb. I vaguely called to mind that Peary had survived a blizzard in the open: but wasn't that in the summer?

It was in the early morning of Saturday (July 22) that we discovered the loss of the tent. Some time during that morning we had had our last meal. The roof went about noon on Sunday and we had had no meal in the interval because our supply of oil was so low: nor could we move out of our bags except as a last necessity. By Sunday night we had been without a meal for some thirty-six hours.

The rocks which fell upon us when the roof went did no damage, and though we could not get out of our bags to move them, we could fit ourselves into them without difficulty. More serious was the drift which began to pile up all round and over us. It helped to keep us warm of course, but at the same time in these comparatively high temperatures it saturated our bags even worse than they were before. If we did not find the tent (and its recovery would be a miracle) these bags and the floor-cloth of the tent on which we were lying were all we had in that fight back across the Barrier which could, I suppose, have only had one end.

Meanwhile we had to wait. It was nearly 70 miles home and it had taken us the best part of three weeks to come. In our less miserable moments we tried to think out ways of getting back, but I do not remember very much about that time. Sunday morning faded into Sunday afternoon,—into Sunday night,—into Monday morning. Till then the blizzard had raged with monstrous fury; the winds of the world were there, and they had all gone mad. We had bad winds at Cape Evans this year, and we had far worse the next winter when the open water was at our doors. But I have never heard or felt or seen a wind like this. I wondered why it did not carry away the earth.

In the early hours of Monday there was an occasional hint of a lull. Ordinarily in a big winter blizzard, when you have lived for several days and nights with that turmoil in your ears, the lulls are more trying than the noise: "the feel of not to feel it."[1] I do not remember noticing that now. Seven or eight more hours passed, and though it was still blowing we could make ourselves heard to one another without great difficulty. It was two days and two nights since we had had a meal.

We decided to get out of our bags and make a search for the tent. We did so, bitterly cold and utterly miserable, though I do not think any of us showed it. In the darkness we could see very little, and no trace whatever of the tent. We returned against wind, nursing our faces and hands, and settled that we must try and cook a meal somehow. We managed about the weirdest meal eaten north or south. We got the floor-cloth wedged under our bags, then got into our bags and drew the floor-cloth over our heads. Between us we got the primus alight somehow, and by hand we balanced the cooker on top of it, minus the two members which had been blown away. The flame flickered in the draughts. Very slowly the snow in the cooker melted, we threw in a plentiful supply of pemmican, and the smell of it was better than anything on earth. In time we got both tea and pemmican, which was full of hairs from our bags, penguin feathers, dirt and debris, but delicious. The blubber left in the cooker got burnt and gave the tea a burnt taste. None of us ever forgot that meal: I enjoyed it as much as such a meal could be enjoyed, and that burnt taste will always bring back the memory.

It was still dark and we lay down in our bags again, but soon a little glow of light began to come up, and we turned out to have a further search for the tent. Birdie went off before Bill and me. Clumsily I dragged my eider-down out of my bag on my feet, all sopping wet: it was impossible to get it back and I let it freeze: it was soon just like a rock. The sky to the south

1 Keats.

was as black and sinister as it could possibly be. It looked as though the blizzard would be on us again at any moment.

I followed Bill down the slope. We could find nothing. But, as we searched, we heard a shout somewhere below and to the right. We got on a slope, slipped, and went sliding down quite unable to stop ourselves, and came upon Birdie with the tent, the outer lining still on the bamboos. Our lives had been taken away and given back to us.

We were so thankful we said nothing.

The tent must have been gripped up into the air, shutting as it rose. The bamboos, with the inner lining lashed to them, had entangled the outer cover, and the whole went up together like a shut umbrella. This was our salvation. If it had opened in the air nothing could have prevented its destruction. As it was, with all the accumulated ice upon it, it must have weighed the best part of 100 lbs. It had been dropped about half a mile away, at the bottom of a steep slope: and it fell in a hollow, still shut up. The main force of the wind had passed over it, and there it was, with the bamboos and fastenings wrenched and strained, and the ends of two of the poles broken, but the silk untorn.

If that tent went again we were going with it. We made our way back up the slope with it, carrying it solemnly and reverently, precious as though it were something not quite of the earth. And we dug it in as tent was never dug in before; not by the igloo, but in the old place farther down where we had first arrived. And while Bill was doing this Birdie and I went back to the igloo and dug and scratched and shook away the drift inside until we had found nearly all our gear. It is wonderful how little we lost when the roof went. Most of our gear was hung on the sledge, which was part of the roof, or was packed into the holes of the hut to try and make it drift-proof, and the things must have been blown inwards into the bottom of the hut by the wind from the south and the back draught from the north. Then they were all drifted up. Of course a certain number of mitts and socks were blown away and lost, but the only important things were Bill's fur mitts, which were stuffed into a hole in the rocks of the hut. We loaded up the sledge and pushed it down the slope. I don't know how Birdie was feeling, but I felt so weak that it was the greatest labour. The blizzard looked right on top of us.

We had another meal, and we wanted it: and as the good hoosh ran down into our feet and hands, and up into our cheeks and ears and brains, we discussed what we would do next. Birdie was all for another go at the Emperor penguins. Dear Birdie, he never would admit that he was beaten—I don't know that he ever really was! "I think he (Wilson) thought he had landed us in a bad corner and was determined to go straight home, though I was for one other tap at the Rookery. However, I had placed myself under his orders for this trip voluntarily, and so we started the next day for home."[1] There could really be no common-sense doubt: we had to go back, and we were already very doubtful whether we should ever manage to get into our sleeping-bags in very low temperature, so ghastly had they become.

I don't know when it was, but I remember walking down that slope—I don't know why, perhaps to try and find the bottom of the cooker—and thinking that there was nothing on earth that a man under such circumstances would not give for a good warm sleep. He would give everything he possessed: he would give—how many —years of his life. One or two at any rate—perhaps five? Yes—I would give five. I remember the sastrugi, the view of the Knoll, the dim hazy black smudge of the sea far away below: the tiny bits of green canvas that twittered in the wind on the surface of the snow: the cold misery of it all, and the weakness which was biting into my heart.

For days Birdie had been urging me to use his eider-down lining—his beautiful dry bag of the finest down—which he had never slipped into his own fur bag. I had refused: I felt that I should be a beast to take it.

We packed the tank ready for a start back in the morning

[1] Bowers.

and turned in, utterly worn out. It was only −12° that night, but my left big toe was frost-bitten in my bag which I was trying to use without an eider-down lining, and my bag was always too big for me. It must have taken several hours to get it back, by beating one foot against the other. When we got up, as soon as we could, as we did every night, for our bags were nearly impossible, it was blowing fairly hard and looked like blizzing. We had a lot to do, two or three hours' work, packing sledges and making a depôt of what we did not want, in a corner of the igloo. We left the second sledge, and a note tied to the handle of the pickaxe.

"We started down the slope in a wind which was rising all the time and −15°. My job was to balance the sledge behind: I was so utterly done I don't believe I could have pulled effectively. Birdie was much the strongest of us. The strain and want of sleep was getting me in the neck, and Bill looked very bad. At the bottom we turned our faces to the Barrier, our backs to the penguins, but after doing about a mile it looked so threatening in the south that we camped in a big wind, our hands going one after the other. We had nothing but the hardest wind-swept sastrugi, and it was a long business: there was only the smallest amount of drift, and we were afraid the icy snow blocks would chafe the tent. Birdie lashed the full biscuit tin to the door to prevent its flapping, and also got what he called the tent downhaul round the cap and then tied it about himself outside his bag: if the tent went he was going too.

"I was feeling as if I should crack, and accepted Birdie's eider-down. It was wonderfully self-sacrificing of him: more than I can write. I felt a brute to take it, but I was getting useless unless I got some sleep which my big bag would not allow. Bill and Birdie kept on telling me to do less: that I was doing more than my share of the work: but I think that I was getting more and more weak. Birdie kept wonderfully strong: he slept most of the night: the difficulty for him was to get into his bag without going to sleep. He kept the meteorological log untiringly, but some of these nights he had to give it up for the time because he could not keep awake. He used to fall asleep with his pannikin in his hand and let it fall: and sometimes he had the primus.

"Bill's bag was getting hopeless: it was really too small for an eider-down and was splitting all over the place: great long holes. He never consciously slept for nights: he did sleep a bit, for we heard him. Except for this night, and the next when Birdie's eider-down was still fairly dry, I never consciously slept; except that I used to wake for five or six nights running with the same nightmare—that we were drifted up, and that Bill and Birdie were passing the gear into my bag, cutting it open to do so, or some other variation,—I did not know that I had been asleep at all."[1]

"We had hardly reached the pit," wrote Bowers, "when a furious wind came on again and we had to camp. All that night the tent flapped like the noise of musketry, owing to two poles having been broken at the ends and the fit spoilt. I thought it would end matters by going altogether and lashed it down as much as I could, attaching the apex to a line round my own bag. The wind abated after 1½ days and we set out, doing five or six miles before we found ourselves among crevasses."[2]

We had plugged ahead all that day (July 26) in a terrible light, blundering in among pressure and up on to the slopes of Terror. The temperature dropped from −21° to −45°. "Several times [we] stepped into rotten-lidded crevasses in smooth wind-swept ice. We continued, however, feeling our way along by keeping always off hard ice-slopes and on the crustier deeper snow which characterizes the hollows of the pressure ridges, which I believed we had once more fouled in the dark. We had no light, and no landmarks to guide us, except vague and indistinct silhouetted slopes ahead, which were always altering and whose distance and character it was impossible to judge. We never knew whether we were approaching a steep slope at close quarters or a long slope of

1 My own diary.
2 Bowers.

Terror, miles away, and eventually we travelled on by the ear, and by the feel of the snow under our feet, for both the sound and the touch told one much of the chances of crevasses or of safe going. We continued thus in the dark in the hope that we were at any rate in the right direction."[1] And then we camped after getting into a bunch of crevasses, completely lost. Bill said, "At any rate I think we are well clear of the pressure." But there were pressure pops all night, as though some one was whacking an empty tub.

It was Birdie's picture hat which made the trouble next day. "What do you think of *that* for a hat, sir?" I heard him say to Scott a few days before we started, holding it out much as Lucille displays her latest Paris model. Scott looked at it quietly for a time: "I'll tell you when you come back, Birdie," he said. It was a complicated affair with all kinds of nose-guards and buttons and lanyards: he thought he was going to set it to suit the wind much as he would set the sails of a ship. We spent a long time with our housewifes before this and other trips, for everybody has their own ideas as to how to alter their clothing for the best. When finished some looked neat, like Bill: others baggy, like Scott or Seaman Evans: others rough and ready, like Oates and Bowers: a few perhaps more rough than ready, and I will not mention names. Anyway Birdie's hat became improper immediately it was well iced up.

"When we got a little light in the morning we found we were a little north of the two patches of moraine on Terror. Though we did not know it, we were on the point where the pressure runs up against Terror, and we could dimly see that we were right up against something. We started to try and clear it, but soon had an enormous ridge, blotting out the moraine and half Terror, rising like a great hill on our right. Bill said the only thing was to go right on and hope it would lower; all the time, however, there was a bad feeling that we might be putting any number of ridges between us and the mountain. After a while we tried to cross this one, but had

---

1 Wilson in *Scott's Last Expedition*, vol. ii, p. 58.

to turn back for crevasses, both Bill and I putting a leg down. We went on for about twenty minutes and found a lower place, and turned to rise up it diagonally, and reached the top. Just over the top Birdie went right down a crevasse, which was about wide enough to take him. He was out of sight and out of reach from the surface, hanging in his harness. Bill went for his harness, I went for the bow of the sledge: Bill told me to get the Alpine rope and Birdie directed from below what we could do. We could not possibly haul him up as he was, for the sides of the crevasse were soft and he could not help himself."[1]

"My helmet was so frozen up," wrote Bowers, "that my head was encased in a solid block of ice, and I could not look down without inclining my whole body. As a result Bill stumbled one foot into a crevasse and I landed in it with both mine [even as I shouted a warning[2]], the bridge gave way and down I went. Fortunately our sledge harness is made with a view to resisting this sort of thing, and there I hung with the bottomless pit below and the ice-crusted sides alongside, so narrow that to step over it would have been quite easy had I been able to see it. Bill said, 'What do you want?' I asked for an Alpine rope with a bowline for my foot: and taking up first the bowline and then my harness they got me out."[3] Meanwhile on the surface I lay over the crevasse and gave Birdie the bowline: he put it on his foot: then he raised his foot, giving me some slack: I held the rope while he raised himself on his foot, thus giving Bill some slack on the harness: Bill then held the harness, allowing Birdie to raise his foot and give me some slack again. We got him up inch by inch, our fingers getting bitten, for the temperature was $-46°$. Afterwards we often used this way of getting people out of crevasses, and it was a wonderful piece of presence of mind that it was invented, so far as I know, on the spur of the moment by a frozen man hanging in one himself.

"In front of us we could see another ridge, and we did not

1 My own diary.
2 Wilson.
3 Bowers.

know how many lay beyond that. Things looked pretty bad. Bill took a long lead on the Alpine rope and we got down our present difficulty all right. This method of the leader being on a long trace in front we all agreed to be very useful. From this moment our luck changed and everything went for us to the end. When we went out on the sea-ice the whole experience was over in a few days, Hut Point was always in sight, and there was daylight. I always had the feeling that the whole series of events had been brought about by an extraordinary run of accidents, and that after a certain stage it was quite beyond our power to guide the course of them. When on the way to Cape Crozier the moon suddenly came out of the cloud to show us a great crevasse which would have taken us all with our sledge without any difficulty, I felt that we were not to go under this trip after such a deliverance. When we had lost our tent, and there was a very great balance of probability that we should never find it again, and we were lying out the blizzard in our bags, I saw that we were face to face with a long fight against cold which we could not have survived. I cannot write how helpless I believed we were to help ourselves, and how we were brought out of a very terrible series of experiences. When we started back I had a feeling that things were going to change for the better, and this day I had a distinct idea that we were to have one more bad experience and that after that we could hope for better things.

"By running along the hollow we cleared the pressure ridges, and continued all day up and down, but met no crevasses. Indeed, we met no more crevasses and no more pressure. I think it was upon this day that a wonderful glow stretched over the Barrier edge from Cape Crozier: at the base it was the most vivid crimson it is possible to imagine, shading upwards through every shade of red to light green, and so into a deep blue sky. It is the most vivid red I have ever seen in the sky."[1]

1 My own diary.

It was −49° in the night and we were away early in −47°. By mid-day we were rising Terror Point, opening Erebus rapidly, and got the first really light day, though the sun would not appear over the horizon for another month. I cannot describe what a relief the light was to us. We crossed the point outside our former track, and saw inside us the ridges where we had been blizzed for three days on our outward journey.

The minimum was −66° the next night and we were now back in the windless bight of Barrier with its soft snow, low temperatures, fogs and mists, and lingering settlements of the inside crusts. Saturday and Sunday, the 29th and 30th, we plugged on across this waste, iced up as usual but always with Castle Rock getting bigger. Sometimes it looked like fog or wind, but it always cleared away. We were getting weak, how weak we can only realize now, but we got in good marches, though slow—days when we did 4½, 7¼, 6¾, 6½, 7½ miles. On our outward journey we had been relaying and getting forward about 1½ miles a day at this point. The surface which we had dreaded so much was not so sandy or soft as when we had come out, and the settlements were more marked. These are caused by a crust falling under your feet. Generally the area involved is some twenty yards or so round you, and the surface falls through an air space for two or three inches with a soft 'crush' which may at first make you think there are crevasses about. In the region where we now travelled they were much more pronounced than elsewhere, and one day, when Bill was inside the tent lighting the primus, I put my foot into a hole that I had dug. This started a big settlement: sledge, tent and all of us dropped about a foot, and the noise of it ran away for miles and miles: we listened to it until we began to get too cold. It must have lasted a full three minutes.

In the pauses of our marching we halted in our harnesses the ropes of which lay slack in the powdery snow. We stood panting with our backs against the mountainous mass of frozen gear which was our load. There was no wind, at any rate no more than light airs: our breath crackled as it froze. There was no unnecessary conversation: I don't know why our tongues never got frozen, but all my teeth, the nerves of which had been killed, split to pieces. We had been going perhaps three hours since lunch.

"How are your feet, Cherry?" from Bill.

"Very cold."

"That's all right; so are mine." We didn't worry to ask Birdie: he never had a frost-bitten foot from start to finish.

Half an hour later, as we marched, Bill would ask the same question. I tell him that all feeling has gone: Bill still has some feeling in one of his but the other is lost. He settled we had better camp: another ghastly night ahead.

We started to get out of our harnesses, while Bill, before doing anything else, would take the fur mitts from his hands, carefully shape any soft parts as they froze (generally, however, our mitts did not thaw on our hands), and lay them on the snow in front of him—two dark dots. His proper fur mitts were lost when the igloo roof went: these were the delicate dog-skin linings we had in addition, beautiful things to look at and to feel when new, excellent when dry to turn the screws of a theodolite, but too dainty for straps and lanyards. Just now I don't know what he could have done without them.

Working with our woollen half-mitts and mitts on our hands all the time, and our fur mitts over them when possible, we gradually got the buckles undone, and spread the green canvas floor-cloth on the snow. This was also fitted to be used as a sail, but we never could have rigged a sail on this journey. The shovel and the bamboos, with a lining, itself lined with ice, lashed to them, were packed on the top of the load and were now put on the snow until wanted. Our next job was to lift our three sleeping-bags one by one on to the floor-cloth: they covered it, bulging over the sides—those obstinate coffins which were all our life to us. . . . One of us is off by now to nurse his fingers back. The cooker was unlashed from the top of the instrument box; some parts of it were put on the bags with the primus, methylated spirit can, matches and so forth; others left to be filled with snow later. Taking a pole in each hand we three spread the bamboos over the whole. "All right? Down!" from Bill; and we lowered them gently on to the soft snow, that they might not sink too far. The ice on the inner lining of the tent was formed mostly from the steam of the cooker. This we had been unable to beat or chip off in the past, and we were now, truth to tell, past worrying about it. The little ventilator in the top, made to let out this steam, had been tied up in order to keep in all possible heat. Then over with the outer cover, and for one of us the third worst job of the day was to begin. The worst job was to get into our bags: the second or equal worst was to lie in them for six hours (we had brought it down to six): this third worst was to get the primus lighted and a meal on the way.

As cook of the day you took the broken metal framework, all that remained of our candlestick, and got yourself with difficulty into the funnel which formed the door. The enclosed space of the tent seemed much colder than the outside air: you tried three or four match-boxes and no match would strike: almost desperate, you asked for a new box to be given you from the sledge and got a light from this because it had not yet been in the warmth, so called, of the tent. The candle hung by a wire from the cap of the tent. It would be tedious to tell of the times we had getting the primus alight, and the lanyards of the weekly food bag unlashed. Probably by now the other two men have dug in the tent; squared up outside; filled and passed in the cooker; set the thermometer under the sledge and so forth. There were always one or two odd jobs which wanted doing as well: but you may be sure they came in as soon as possible when they heard the primus hissing, and saw the glow of light inside. Birdie made a bottom for the cooker out of an empty biscuit tin to take the place of the part which was blown away. On the whole this was a success, but we had to hold it steady—on Bill's sleeping-bag, for the flat frozen bags spread all over the floor space.

Cooking was a longer business now. Some one whacked out the biscuit, and the cook put the ration of pemmican into the inner cooker which was by now half full of water. As opportunity offered we got out of our day, and into our night foot-gear—fleecy camel-hair stockings and fur boots. In the dim light we examined our feet for frostbite.

I do not think it took us less than an hour to get a hot meal to our lips: pemmican followed by hot water in which we soaked our biscuits. For lunch we had tea and biscuits: for breakfast, pemmican, biscuits and tea. We could not have managed more food bags—three were bad enough, and the lashings of everything were like wire. The lashing of the tent door, however, was the worst, and it *had* to be tied tightly, especially if it was blowing. In the early days we took great pains to brush rime from the tent before packing it up, but we were long past that now.

The hoosh got down into our feet: we nursed back frostbites: and we were all the warmer for having got our dry foot-gear on before supper. Then we started to get into our bags.

Birdie's bag fitted him beautifully, though perhaps it would have been a little small with an eider-down inside. He must have had a greater heat supply than other men; for he never had serious trouble with his feet, while ours were constantly frost-bitten: he slept, I should be afraid to say how much, longer than we did, even in these last days: it was a pleasure, lying awake practically all night, to hear his snores. He turned his bag inside out from fur to skin, and skin to fur, many times during the journey, and thus got rid of a lot of moisture which came out as snow or actual knobs of ice. When we did turn our bags the only way was to do so directly we turned out, and even then you had to be quick before the bag froze. Getting out of the tent at night it was quite a race to get back to your bag before it hardened. Of course this was in the lowest temperatures.

We could not burn our bags and we tried putting the lighted primus into them to thaw them out, but this was not very successful. Before this time, when it was very cold, we lighted the primus in the morning while we were still in our bags: and in the evening we kept it going until we were just getting or had got the mouths of our bags levered open. But returning we had no oil for such luxuries, until the last day or two.

I do not believe that any man, however sick he is, has a much worse time than we had in those bags, shaking with cold until our backs would almost break. One of the added troubles which came to us on our return was the sodden condition of our hands in our bags at night. We had to wear our mitts and half-mitts, and they were as wet as they could be: when we got up in the morning we had washer-women's hands—white, crinkled, sodden. That was an unhealthy way to start the day's work. We really wanted some bags of saennegrass for hands as well as feet; one of the blessings of that kind of bag being that you can shake the moisture from it: but we only had enough for our wretched feet.

The horrors of that return journey are blurred to my memory and I know they were blurred to my body at the time. I think this applies to all of us, for we were much weakened and callous. The day we got down to the penguins I had not cared whether I fell into a crevasse or not. We had been through a great deal since then. I know that we slept on the march; for I woke up when I bumped against Birdie, and Birdie woke when he bumped against me. I think Bill steering out in front managed to keep awake. I know we fell asleep if we waited in the comparatively warm tent when the primus was alight—with our pannikins or the primus in our hands. I know that our sleeping-bags were so full of ice that we did not worry if we spilt water or hoosh over them as they lay on the floor-cloth, when we cooked on them with our maimed cooker. They were so bad that we never rolled them up in the usual way when we got out of them in the morning: we opened their mouths as much as possible before they froze, and hoisted them more or less flat on to the sledge. All three of us helped to raise each bag, which looked rather like a squashed coffin and was probably a good deal harder. I know that if it was only − 40° when we camped for the night we considered quite seriously that we were going to have a warm one, and that when we got up in the morning if the temperature was in the minus sixties we did not enquire what it was. The day's march was bliss compared to the night's rest, and both were awful. We were about as bad as men can be and do good travelling: but I never heard a word of complaint, nor, I believe, an oath, and I saw self-sacrifice standing every test.

Always we were getting nearer home: and we were doing good marches. We were going to pull through; it was only a matter of sticking this for a few more days; six, five, four . . . three perhaps now, if we were not blizzed. Our main hut was behind that ridge where the mist was always forming and blowing away, and there was Castle Rock: we might even see Observation Hill tomorrow, and the Discovery Hut furnished and trim was behind it, and they would have sent some dry sleeping-bags from Cape Evans to greet us there. We reckoned our troubles over at the Barrier edge, and assuredly it was not far away. "You've got it in the neck, stick it, you've got it in the neck"—it was always running in my head.

And we *did* stick it. How good the memories of those days are. With jokes about Birdie's picture hat: with songs we remembered off the gramophone: with ready words of sympathy for frost-bitten feet: with generous smiles for poor jests: with suggestions of happy beds to come. We did not forget the Please and Thank you, which mean much in such circumstances, and all the little links with decent civilization which we could still keep going. I'll swear there was still a grace about us when we staggered in. And we kept our tempers—even with God.

We *might* reach Hut Point to-night: we were burning more oil now, that one-gallon tin had lasted us well: and burning more candle too; at one time we feared they would give out. A hell of a morning we had: − 57° in our present state. But it was calm, and the Barrier edge could not be much farther now. The surface was getting harder: there were a few wind-blown furrows, the crust was coming up to us. The sledge was dragging easier: we always suspected the Barrier sloped downwards hereabouts. Now the hard snow was on the surface, peeping out like great inverted basins on which we slipped, and our feet became warmer for not sinking into soft snow. Suddenly we saw a gleam of light in a line of darkness running across our course. It was the Barrier edge: we were all right now.

We ran the sledge off a snow-drift on to the sea-ice, with the same cold stream of air flowing down it which wrecked my hands five weeks ago: pushed out of this, camped and had a meal: the temperature had already risen to $-43°$. We could almost feel it getting warmer as we went round Cape Armitage on the last three miles. We managed to haul our sledge up the ice foot, and dug the drift away from the door. The old hut struck us as fairly warm.

Bill was convinced that we ought not to go into the warm hut at Cape Evans when we arrived there—tomorrow night! We ought to get back to warmth gradually, live in a tent outside, or in the annexe for a day or two. But I'm sure we never meant to do it. Just now Hut Point did not prejudice us in favour of such abstinence. It was just as we had left it: there was nothing sent down for us there—no sleeping-bags, nor sugar: but there was plenty of oil. Inside the hut we pitched a dry tent left there since Depôt Journey days, set two primuses going in it; sat dozing on our bags; and drank cocoa without sugar so thick that next morning we were gorged with it. We were very happy, falling asleep between each mouthful, and after several hours discussed schemes of not getting into our bags at all. But some one would have to keep the primus going to prevent frost-bite, and we could not trust ourselves to keep awake. Bill and I tried to sing a part-song. Finally we sopped our way into our bags. We only stuck *them* three hours, and thankfully turned out at 3 A.M., and were ready to pack up when we heard the wind come away. It was no good, so we sat in our tent and dozed again. The wind dropped at 9.30: we were off at 11. We walked out into what seemed to us a blaze of light. It was not until the following year that I understood that a great part of such twilight as there is in the latter part of the winter was cut off from us by the mountains under which we travelled. Now, with nothing between us and the northern horizon below which lay the sun, we saw as we had not seen for months, and the iridescent clouds that day were beautiful.

We just pulled for all we were worth and did nearly two miles an hour: for two miles a baddish salt surface, then big undulating hard sastrugi and good going. We slept as we walked. We had done eight miles by 4 P.M. and were past Glacier Tongue. We lunched there.

As we began to gather our gear together to pack up for the last time, Bill said quietly, "I want to thank you two for what you have done. I couldn't have found two better companions —and what is more I never shall."

I am proud of that.

Antarctic exploration is seldom as bad as you imagine, seldom as bad as it sounds. But this journey had beggared our language: no words could express its horror.

We trudged on for several more hours and it grew very dark. There was a discussion as to where Cape Evans lay. We rounded it at last: it must have been ten or eleven o'clock, and it was possible that some one might see us as we pulled towards the hut. "Spread out well," said Bill, "and they will be able to see that there are three men." But we pulled along the cape, over the tide-crack, up the bank to the very door of the hut without a sound. No noise from the stable, nor the bark of a dog from the snowdrifts above us. We halted and stood there trying to get ourselves and one another out of our frozen harnesses—the usual long job. The door opened— "Good God! here is the Crozier Party," said a voice, and disappeared.

Thus ended the worst journey in the world.

RICHARD E. BYRD

(*1888–1957*)

THE AMERICAN EXPLORER and navigator Richard E. Byrd was the first man to fly over both geographic poles. More than any other person, he was responsible for the introduction and wide use of aircraft in Antarctic exploration. He led five successive Antarctic expeditions. During the first of these (1928–30), he constructed the station Little America on the Ross Ice Shelf near the site of Amundsen's base off the Bay of Whales, and made numerous geographical discoveries, including the Rockefeller Mountains, Marie Byrd Land (named in honor of his wife) and the Edsel Ford Mountains. It was on November 29, 1929 that he first flew over the South Pole.

Returning to Antarctica in 1934, he continued to make significant geographical discoveries. During this second expedition he wintered over alone at Bolling Advanced Weather Station, located on the ice shelf some 125 miles south of Little America. It appears from his narrative that although he went ostensibly to take weather readings of the continent's interior he also wanted to experience the extreme solitude of a solitary austral winter. His interest in testing man's ability to endure great stress recalls Scott's efforts to push man to his physical limits during manhauled sledging traverses.

Byrd came close to dying from carbon monoxide poisoning at Bolling Station. Realizing that he was mentally and physically losing control, he tried to keep his condition a secret from Little America because he feared that a perilous midwinter attempt to rescue him would be undertaken. His increasingly erratic and irrational radio messages during the scheduled radio contacts, however, gave him away and a successful rescue was made.

An aloof, reserved member of an old Virginia family, Byrd was reluctant to publish the personal details of the near-tragedy that occurred at Bolling Station but was persuaded by friends and colleagues to do so. He belongs to that select group of well-educated, intelligent, gifted and imaginative naval officers (beginning with Cook and including Scott and Shackleton) who produced remarkably fine narratives from their Antarctic experiences.

Alone

May was a round boulder sinking before a tide. Time sloughed off the last implication or urgency, and the days moved imperceptibly one into the other. The few world

news items which Dyer read to me from time to time[1]
seemed almost as meaningless and blurred as they might to
a Martian. My world was insulated against the shocks running
through distant economies. Advance Base was geared to different laws. On getting up in the morning, it was enough for
me to say to myself: Today is the day to change the barograph
sheet, or, Today is the day to fill the stove tank. The night was
settling down in earnest. By May 17th, one month after the
sun had sunk below the horizon, the noon twilight was dwin-
dling to a mere chink in the darkness, lit by a cold reddish
glow. Days when the wind brooded in the north or east, the
Barrier became a vast stagnant shadow surmounted by swollen masses of clouds, one layer of darkness piled on top of the
other. This was the polar night, the morbid countenance of
the Ice Age. Nothing moved; nothing was visible. This was
the soul of inertness. One could almost hear a distant creak-
ing as if a great weight were settling.

Out of the deepening darkness came the cold. On May
19th, when I took the usual walk, the temperature was 65°
below zero. For the first time the canvas boots failed to protect my feet. One heel was nipped, and I was forced to return
to the hut and change to reindeer mukluks. That day I felt
miserable; my body was racked by shooting pains—exactly as
if I had been gassed. Very likely I was; in inspecting the
ventilator pipes next morning I discovered that the intake
pipe was completely clogged with rime and that the outlet
pipe was two-thirds full. Next day—Sunday the 20th—was
the coldest yet. The minimum thermometer dropped to
72° below zero; the inside thermograph, which always read
a bit lower than the instruments in the shelter, stood at
−74°; and the thermograph in the shelter was stopped dead
—the ink, though well laced with glycerine, and the lubri-
cant were both frozen. So violently did the air in the fuel tank
expand after the stove was lit that oil went shooting all over
the place; to insulate the tank against similar temperature

1 That is, over the radio.

spreads I wrapped around it the rubber air cushion which by some lucky error had been included among my gear. In the glow of a flashlight the vapor rising from the stovepipe and the outlet ventilator looked like the discharge from two steam engines. My fingers agonized over the thermograph, and I was hours putting it to rights. The fuel wouldn't flow from the drums; I had to take one inside and heat it near the stove. All day long I kept two primus stoves burning in the tunnel.

Sunday the 20th also brought a radio schedule; I had the devil's own time trying to meet it. The engine balked for an hour; my fingers were so brittle and frostbitten from tinkering with the carburetor that, when I actually made contact with Little America, I could scarcely work the key. "Ask Haines come on," was my first request. While Hutcheson searched the tunnels of Little America for the Senior Meteorologist, I chatted briefly with Charlie Murphy. Little America claimed only −60°. "But we're moving the brass monkeys below," Charlie advised. "Seventy-one below here now," I said. "You can have it," was the closing comment from the north.

Then Bill Haines's merry voice sounded in the earphones. I explained the difficulty with the thermograph. "Same trouble we've had," Bill said. "It's probably due to frozen oil. I'd suggest you bring the instrument inside, and try soaking it in gasoline, to cut whatever oil traces remain. Then rinse it in ether. As for the ink's freezing, you might try adding more glycerine." Bill was in a jovial mood. "Look at me, Admiral," he boomed. "I never have any trouble with the instruments. The trick is in having an ambitious and docile assistant." I really chuckled over that because I knew, from the first expedition, what Grimminger, the Junior Meteorologist, was going through: Bill, with his back to the fire and blandishment on his tongue, persuading the recruit that duty and the opportunity for self-improvement required him to go up into the blizzard to fix a balky trace; Bill humming to himself in

the warmth of a shack while the assistant in an open pit kept
a theodolite trained on the sounding balloon soaring into the
night, and stuttered into a telephone the different vernier
readings from which Bill was calculating the velocities and
directions of the upper air currents. That day I rather wished
that I, too, had an assistant. He would have taken his turn on
the anemometer pole, no mistake. The frost in the iron cleats
went through the fur soles of the mukluks, and froze the balls
of my feet. My breath made little explosive sounds on the
wind; my lungs, already sore, seemed to shrivel when I
breathed.

Seldom had the aurora flamed more brilliantly. For hours
the night danced to its frenetic excitement. And at times the
sound of Barrier quakes was like that of heavy guns. My
tongue was swollen and sore from drinking scalding hot tea,
and the tip of my nose ached from frostbite. A big wind, I
guessed, would come out of this still cold; it behooved me to
look to my roof. I carried gallons of water topside, and poured
it around the edges of the shack. It froze almost as soon as it
hit. The ice was an armor plating over the packed drift.

At midnight, when I clambered topside for an auroral
"ob," a wild sense of suffocation came over me the instant I
pushed my shoulders through the trapdoor. My lungs gasped,
but no air reached them. Bewildered and perhaps a little
frightened, I slid down the ladder and lunged into the shack.
In the warm air the feeling passed as quickly as it had come.
Curious but cautious, I again made my way up the ladder.
And again the same thing happened; I lost my breath, but I
perceived why. A light air was moving down from eastward;
and its bitter touch, when I faced into it, was constricting the
breathing passages. So I turned my face away from it, breathing into my glove; and in that attitude finished the "ob."
Before going below, I made an interesting experiment. I put
a thermometer on the snow, let it lie there awhile, and discovered that the temperature at the surface was actually
5° colder than at the level of the instrument shelter, four feet

higher. Reading in the sleeping bag afterwards, I froze one finger, although I shifted the book steadily from one hand to the other, slipping the unoccupied hand into the warmth of the bag.

OUT OF THE COLD and out of the east came the wind. It came on gradually, as if the sheer weight of the cold were almost too much to be moved. On the night of the 21st the barometer started down. The night was black as a thunderhead when I made my first trip topside; and a tension in the wind, a bulking of shadows in the night indicated that a new storm center was forming. Next morning, glad of an excuse to stay underground, I worked a long time on the Escape Tunnel by the light of a red candle standing in a snow recess. That day I pushed the emergency exit to a distance of twenty-two feet, the farthest it was ever to go. My stint done, I sat down on a box, thinking how beautiful was the red of the candle, how white the rough-hewn snow. Soon I became aware of an increasing clatter of the anemometer cups. Realizing that the wind was picking up, I went topside to make sure that everything was secured. It is a queer experience to watch a blizzard rise. First there is the wind, rising out of nowhere. Then the Barrier unwrenches itself from quietude; and the surface, which just before had seemed as hard and polished as metal, begins to run like a making sea. Sometimes, if the wind strikes hard, the drift comes across the Barrier like a hurrying white cloud, tossed hundreds of feet in the air. Other times the growth is gradual. You become conscious of a general slithering movement on all sides. The air fills with tiny scraping and sliding and rustling sounds as the first loose crystals stir. In a little while they are moving as solidly as an incoming tide, which creams over the ankles, then surges to the waist, and finally is at the throat. I have walked in drift so thick as not to be able to see a foot ahead of me; yet, when I glanced up, I could see the stars shining through the thin layer just overhead.

Smoking tendrils were creeping up the anemometer pole when I finished my inspection. I hurriedly made the trapdoor fast, as a sailor might batten down a hatch; and knowing that my ship was well secured, I retired to the cabin to ride out the storm. It could not reach me, hidden deep in the Barrier crust; nevertheless the sounds came down. The gale sobbed in the ventilators, shook the stovepipe until I thought it would be jerked out by the roots, pounded the roof with sledge-hammer blows. I could actually feel the suction effect through the pervious snow. A breeze flickered in the room and the tunnels. The candles wavered and went out. My only light was the feeble storm lantern.

Even so, I didn't have any idea how really bad it was until I went aloft for an observation. As I pushed back the trap-door, the drift met me like a moving wall. It was only a few steps from the ladder to the instrument shelter, but it seemed more like a mile. The air came at me in snowy rushes; I breasted it as I might a heavy surf. No night had ever seemed so dark. The beam from the flashlight was choked in its throat; I could not see my hand before my face.

My windproofs were caked with drift by the time I got below. I had a vague feeling that something had changed while I was gone, but what, I couldn't tell. Presently I noticed that the shack was appreciably colder. Raising the stove lid, I was surprised to find that the fire was out, though the tank was half full. I decided that I must have turned off the valve unconsciously before going aloft; but, when I put a match to the burner, the draught down the pipe blew out the flame. The wind, then, must have killed the fire. I got it going again, and watched it carefully.

The blizzard vaulted to gale force. Above the roar the deep, taut thrumming note of the radio antenna and the anemometer guy wires reminded me of wind in a ship's rigging. The wind direction trace turned scratchy on the sheet; no doubt drift had short-circuited the electric contacts, I decided. Realizing that it was hopeless to attempt to try to keep them clear, I let the instrument be. There were other ways of getting the wind direction. I tied a handkerchief to a bamboo pole and ran it through the outlet ventilator; with a flashlight I could tell which way the cloth was whipped. I did this at hourly intervals, noting any change of direction on the sheet. But by 2 o'clock in the morning I had had enough of this periscope sighting. If I expected to sleep and at the same time maintain the continuity of the records, I had no choice but to clean the contact points.

The wind was blowing hard then. The Barrier shook from the concussions overhead; and the noise was as if the entire physical world were tearing itself to pieces. I could scarcely heave the trapdoor open. The instant it came clear I was plunged into a blinding smother. I came out crawling, clinging to the handle of the door until I made sure of my bearings. Then I let the door fall shut, not wanting the tunnel filled with drift. To see was impossible. Millions of tiny pellets exploded in my eyes, stinging like BB shot. It was even hard to breathe, because snow instantly clogged the mouth and nostrils. I made my way toward the anemometer pole on hands and knees, scared that I might be bowled off my feet if I stood erect; one false step and I should be lost forever.

I found the pole all right; but not until my head collided with a cleat. I managed to climb it, too, though ten million ghosts were tearing at me, ramming their thumbs into my eyes. But the errand was useless. Drift as thick as this would mess up the contact points as quickly as they were cleared; besides, the wind cups were spinning so fast that I stood a good chance of losing a couple of fingers in the process. Coming down the pole, I had a sense of being whirled violently through the air, with no control over my movements. The trapdoor was completely buried when I found it again, after scraping around for some time with my mittens. I pulled at the handle, first with one hand, then with both. It did not give. It's a tight fit, anyway, I mumbled to myself. The drift has probably wedged the corners. Standing astride the hatch, I braced myself and heaved with all my strength. I might just as well have tried hoisting the Barrier.

Panic took me then, I must confess. Reason fled. I clawed at the three-foot square of timber like a madman. I beat on it with my fists, trying to shake the snow loose; and, when that did no good, I lay flat on my belly and pulled until my hands went weak from cold and weariness. Then I crooked my elbow, put my face down, and said over and over again, You damn fool, you damn fool. Here for weeks I had been defending myself against the danger of being penned inside the shack; instead, I was now locked out; and nothing could be worse, especially since I had only a wool parka and pants under my windproofs. Just two feet below was sanctuary— warmth, food, tools, all the means of survival. All these things were an arm's length away, but I was powerless to reach them.

There is something extravagantly insensate about an Antarctic blizzard at night. Its vindictiveness cannot be measured on an anemometer sheet. It is more than just wind: it is a solid wall of snow moving at gale force, pounding like surf.[1] The whole malevolent rush is concentrated upon you as upon a personal enemy. In the senseless explosion of sound you are reduced to a crawling thing on the margin of a disintegrating world; you can't see, you can't hear, you can hardly move. The lungs gasp after the air sucked out of them, and the brain is shaken. Nothing in the world will so quickly isolate a man.

Half-frozen, I stabbed toward one of the ventilators, a few feet away. My mittens touched something round and cold. Cupping it in my hands, I pulled myself up. This was the outlet ventilator. Just why, I don't know—but instinct made me kneel and press my face against the opening. Nothing in the room was visible, but a dim patch of light illuminated the floor, and warmth rose up to my face. That steadied me.

Still kneeling, I turned my back to the blizzard and considered what might be done. I thought of breaking in the win-

1 Because of this blinding, suffocating drift, in the Antarctic winds of only moderate velocity have the punishing force of full-fledged hurricanes elsewhere.–R.E.B.

dows in the roof, but they lay two feet down in hard crust, and were reinforced with wire besides. If I only had something to dig with, I could break the crust and stamp the windows in with my feet. The pipe cupped between my hands supplied the first inspiration; maybe I could use that to dig with. It, too, was wedged tight; I pulled until my arms ached, without budging it; I had lost all track of time, and the despairing thought came to me that I was lost in a task without an end. Then I remembered the shovel. A week before, after leveling drift from the last light blow, I had stabbed a shovel handle up in the crust somewhere to leeward. That shovel would save me. But how to find it in the avalanche of the blizzard?

I lay down and stretched out full length. Still holding the pipe, I thrashed around with my feet, but pummeled only empty air. Then I worked back to the hatch. The hard edges at the opening provided another grip, and again I stretched out and kicked. Again no luck. I dared not let go until I had something else familiar to cling to. My foot came up against the other ventilator pipe. I edged back to that, and from the new anchorage repeated the maneuver. This time my ankle struck something hard. When I felt it and recognized the handle, I wanted to caress it.

Embracing this thrice-blessed tool, I inched back to the trapdoor. The handle of the shovel was just small enough to pass under the little wooden bridge which served as a grip. I got both hands on the shovel and tried to wrench the door up; my strength was not enough, however. So I lay down flat on my belly and worked my shoulders under the shovel. Then I heaved, the door sprang open, and I rolled down the shaft. When I tumbled into the light and warmth of the room, I kept thinking, How wonderful, how perfectly wonderful.

MY WRIST WATCH had stopped; the chronometers showed that I had been gone just under an hour. The stove had blown out again, but I did not bother to light it. Enough warmth remained for me to undress. I was exhausted; it was all I could do to hoist myself into the bunk. But I did not sleep at first. The blizzard scuffled and pounded gigantically overhead; and my mind refused to drop the thought of what I might still be doing if the shovel hadn't been there. Still struggling, probably. Or maybe not. There are harder ways to die than freezing to death. The lush numbness and the peace that lulls the mind when the ears cease listening to the blizzard's ridiculous noise, could make death seem easy.

The wind was still blowing, but not so violently, when I awakened at 7 o'clock the next morning. Dressing in the yellow light of the storm lantern, I shivered in every bone. My clothes, rigid with frost, lay in a grotesque heap on the floor, exactly as they had fallen a few hours before; they crackled like paper when I put them on. Starting up the ladder, I thought glumly, It will be stuck again for sure. Therefore, I had no misgivings at finding the door jammed. Armed with a saw, a shovel, alpine rope, and a lantern, I walked to the far end of the Escape Tunnel. It didn't take long to breach a hole in the roof, which was less than two feet thick at this point.

Before leaving the tunnel, I drove a stout stick into the roof, to which I made fast one end of the line. With the other end secured to my belt, I clambered to the surface over a ladder made of boxes. The drift was still heavy, but with a flashlight it was possible to see a yard or two. After a couple of false stabs I finally fetched the anemometer pole. The drift packed in the cups was almost as compact as cement; I cleaned them out and scraped the contact points. It was an abominable task; but it had to be done, because the fouling slowed down the cups and hence the wind-speed reading. Yet, after what I had been through the night before, there was little reason to complain.

For once "daily promenade" was missed. Every moment that could be spared from the instruments and my own personal needs was devoted to leveling drift around the shack. Luckily the new snow wasn't packed hard. I just shoveled it into the air and let the wind dissipate it to leeward. That done, I sealed off the breach in the Escape Tunnel with the sides of a couple of food boxes and reopened the hatch. The faint lightening in the gloom that came with midday was draining away; heavy shadows were pressing down through the ghostly billowing of drift. But the wind was spent; and so was the cold, temporarily. The temperature kited to 10° below. Safe in the bunk, I slept the sleep of a man who had been working a hundred years.

Thursday the 24th was unbelievably warm. At the 8 A.M. "ob" the maximum thermometer read 2° above zero. The wind still haunted the east; and puffs of drift came erratically from that quarter, thickening the steady fall of snow from the sky. I was nearly an hour late meeting the radio schedule, because the antenna had been blown down and I didn't find out until after I had checked the transmitter and receiver. I made a hurried splice at a break and re-rigged the antenna temporarily on two poles. Dyer was still calling patiently when I made contact. My signals, he said, were weak but intelligible. Beyond discussing arrangements for me to participate in a special broadcast, we had little to talk about. At Little America the temperature was 25° above zero, and Bill Haines officially announced a "heat wave."

I was informed that on Saturday Little America was broadcasting a special program to the Chicago World Fair; would I mind adding my greetings? Certainly not. It was agreed that I should spell out in code, "Greetings from the bottom of the world," which message was to be picked up and relayed by Little America's more powerful transmitter. I reduced the message to dots and dashes and practiced religiously. When Saturday came, Charlie Murphy broke the news, just before the broadcast, that New York now wanted me to spell, "Antarctic greetings," instead. "I'm given to understand," he said sententiously, "they intend to translate the damn thing into fireworks."

"Let it be on their own heads, then," I said.

Charlie chuckled. "If the fireworks are supposed to spell out what you send, then Chicago is in for the wildest display since the Fire."

As excited as an actor making his debut, I sat at Advance Base listening to the broadcast from Little America; and, when somebody said, "We shall now attempt to make contact with Admiral Byrd," I reached for the key and worked it furiously. But it went for naught. Dyer reported a few minutes after that he had heard it clearly, but Chicago hadn't heard anything. "No doubt the fireworks went off anyway," he observed dryly.

Bill Haines's forecast of a "heat wave" was no jest. That afternoon the thermometer rose to 18° above zero—the second highest point it ever reached. The wind, dallying in the east, flooded the Barrier with warm air from the distant ocean. From then until the end of the month the coldest temperature recorded was 23° below zero; and most of the time it was above zero or close to it.[1] Snow fell in a relentless flutter; the Barrier became a concentrated gloom, except when the moon, fetched back on its fortnightly errand, was able to break through the cloud rack and bathe it briefly in an astringent light.

May 25

This is my sixty-fourth day at Advance Base, and it just so happened that I had some leisure time. I have been taking advantage of this to think back over my stay here and take stock of my situation.

There are three things for which I am particularly thankful. The first is that my records so far are complete (though blotted and splotched a bit). The second is that my defenses are perfected, and the third is that I have become well adjusted to conditions—especially psycho-

---

1 Studied as a whole, the records show that May was not exactly a hot month. The cold passed 40° below zero 20 days out of the 31, crossed 50° below, 12 days; crossed 60° below, 3 days; and 70° below, 2 days.–R.E.B.

logically. I feel able now to withstand any assaults the beleaguering night may launch. Indeed, I look forward to the rest of my sojourn with pleasure.

Though I am not quite as heavy as when I came out here, I feel all right. I was probably a bit overweight, anyway. Perhaps the fumes have had something to do with the lost pounds, though because of my precautions I think I am getting less fumes than at first.

I am finding that life here has become largely a life of the mind. Unhurried reflection is a sort of companion. Yes, solitude is greater than I anticipated. My sense of values is changing, and many things which before were in solution in my mind now seem to be crystallizing. I am better able to tell what in the world is wheat for me and what is chaff. In fact, my definition of success itself is changing. Just lately my views about man and his place in the cosmic scheme have begun to run something like this:

If I had never seen a watch and should see one for the first time, I should be sure its hands were moving according to some plan and not at random. Nor does it seem any more reasonable for me to conceive that the precision and order of the universe is the product of blind chance. This whole concept is summed up in the word harmony. For those who seek it, there is inexhaustible evidence of an all-pervading intelligence.

The human race, my intuition tells me, is not outside the cosmic process and is not an accident. It is as much a part of the universe as the trees, the mountains, the aurora, and the stars. My reason approves this; and the findings of science, as I see them, point in the same direction. And, since man is a part of the cosmos and subject to its laws, I see no reason to doubt that these same natural laws operate in the psychological as well as in the physical sphere and that their operation is manifest in the workings of the consciousness.

Therefore, it seems to me that convictions of right and

wrong, being, as they are, products of the consciousness, must also be formed in accordance with these laws. I look upon the conscience as the mechanism which makes us directly aware of them and their significance and serves as a link with the universal intelligence which gives them form and harmoniousness.

I believe further that the age-tested convictions of right and wrong, in which individual aberrations must have been largely canceled out, are as much a manifestation of cosmic law and intelligence as are all other phenomena.

Therefore, the things that mankind has tested and found right make for harmony and progress—or peace; and the things it has found wrong hinder progress and make for discord. The right things lead to rational behavior—such as the substitution of reason for force—and so to freedom. The wrong things lead to brute force and slavery.

But the peace I describe is not passive. It must be won. Real peace comes from struggle that involves such things as effort, discipline, enthusiasm. This is also the way to strength. An inactive peace may lead to sensuality and flabbiness, which are discordant. It is often necessary to fight to lessen discord. This is the paradox.

When a man achieves a fair measure of harmony within himself and his family circle, he achieves peace; and a nation made up of such individuals and groups is a happy nation. As the harmony of a star in its course is expressed by rhythm and grace, so the harmony of a man's life-course is expressed by happiness; this, I believe, is the prime desire of mankind.

"The universe is an almost untouched reservoir of significance and value," and man need not be discouraged because he cannot fathom it. His view of life is no more than a flash in time. The details and distractions are infinite. It is only natural, therefore, that we should never see the picture whole. But the universal goal—the attainment of harmony—is apparent. The very act of perceiving this goal and striving constantly toward it does much in itself to bring us closer and, therefore, becomes an end in itself.

SNOW WAS STILL FALLING on Thursday the 31st. The morning was dreary and stagnant; the temperature about 5° above. The calendar warned: "Radio schedule." I went about the preparations methodically. Before me now are the messages which I dispatched to Little America that day. One was to Chief Pilot June and Navigator Rawson, reminding them to swing the planes for compass deviations. Another was to my wife, suggesting that she take up with my secretary, Miss McKercher, and my representatives in the United States ways and means of reducing the expedition's expenses.

Dyer took these messages down, then read them back. Poulter, he said, had already arrived in the radio shack in response to my summons. I had a long talk with him and Charlie Murphy over the proposed operations, and was particularly emphatic about the dangers from crevasses confronting the tractors. Poulter finished his business with me; and Charlie Murphy stayed to finish a few matters, one having to do with the engagement of an ice pilot for the *Jacob Ruppert* on her return voyage to Little America in December. We talked back and forth nearly an hour and a half. From my desk in the shack I could hear the engine in the tunnel; for some reason it started skipping. "Wait," I spelled out to Dyer. Unhooking the lantern, I went into the tunnel. The air was thick with exhaust gases. Thinking the mixture was at fault, I bent over the carburetor and tinkered with the needle valve. This had little effect. I remember straightening up. And that was the last conscious act of mine that I do remember. The next thing I recall, I was down on my hands and knees; and through the drowsiness, like an echo from far away, came an insistent notion that something terribly important ought to be done. What it was exactly my mind couldn't tell; and I felt helpless to do anything about it. I don't know how long I remained in that position. It may be that the cold aroused me. Anyhow, after a little while I crawled into the shack. The radio desk emerged from the blur, and then I remembered what I was supposed to do. I fumbled for the key and signed off, thinking how hard it was to spell out what I had to say. If any acknowledgment came, I did not hear it; for I couldn't get the earphones on.[1]

My actions thereafter are uncertain; I don't really know which were nightmare and which were fact. I remember lying on the bunk, fully dressed, and hearing as if with surprise, the irregular beat of the engine in the tunnel and realizing that I must shut it off to escape asphyxiation. I rolled off the bunk and staggered to the door. Dizziness seized me, and my heart turned fantastic somersaults; but, as from a great distance, I could see the gray fumes of the exhaust smoke curling under the top sill; and the upper half of the tunnel, when I entered, was so foggy that I could not see as far as the alcove where the engine lay.

Very probably I dropped to my hands and knees, as I must have appreciated the necessity for keeping my head under the fumes and in the uncontaminated air near the floor. Anyhow, I was on my knees when I reached into the recess and threw the ignition switch. When I turned around, the light was gone in the doorway; this was puzzling until I recalled that the only light in the shack was the electric bulb over the radio desk, which burned only while the engine supplied current. Luckily the lantern was still burning on a box, where I had set it down before adjusting the engine. Pushing the lantern ahead of me, I crawled back to the shack and to the bunk.

Whatever did, in fact, occur during the rest of this last day in May, this I do know: that much of it was probably fantasy —a slow and wearying fantasy. Perhaps I did in truth roll off

1 The radio log at Little America shows that twenty minutes or so elapsed between the time I said, "Wait" and the time I signed off, saying, "See you Sunday." This fixes approximately the interval I was in the tunnel.–R.E.B.

the bunk and try to replace the sheets on the register drum; else how to account for the vague recollection of seeing the glass frame on the floor some time in the afternoon. But the rest of it—the skyrocketing pain in my forehead and eyes, the nausea, the violent beating of my heart, the illusion of being a thin flame drawn between two voids—they could not have been real. Only the cold was real: the numbness in the hands and feet, creeping like a slow paralysis through my body. At least, I could cope with cold. I grasped for the throat of the sleeping bag, and eased in.

Once the ticking of the clocks roused me out of the stupor. I have no sure memory of winding them; but, so strong was the compulsion of habit, I do remember thinking bitterly that they ought to be wound and that the register and ther-mograph sheets ought to be changed. Evidently I performed these tasks; for the instruments were still going next day; and the records, now in the possession of the U. S. Weather Bureau, show that the sheets were shifted at 2 P.M., two hours late. My only distinct memory from that period was arousing and thinking that I was blind. My eyes were open, but I could see nothing. Then I realized that I must be facing the wall. The lantern was out (from lack of fuel, I learned presently), but a dim glow showed in the side of the stove.

There is nothing more panicky than the loss of sight. I shall never forget the agony in Floyd Bennett's voice when we pulled him, terribly smashed up, from the debris of our crash landing. "I'm done for," he whispered; "I can't see any-thing." His face was a smear of oil; when I wiped it away and he could see again, the expression that transfigured his face was beautiful.

IT IS PAINFUL for me to dwell on the details of my collapse, particularly as the affairs of Advance Base are now receding into the gentling haze of the past. The subject is one that does not easily bear discussion, if only because a man's hurt, like his love, is most seemly when concealed. From my youth I have believed that sickness was somehow humiliating, something to be kept hidden. But the consequences of this collapse were never to depart during the rest of my stay at Advance Base; and my struggle against the one universal certainty played too large a part in my experience there to be omitted from this account.

I have a pretty clear idea concerning much that happened, almost too clear, in fact. I shall not, however, depend upon memory alone. During the days that followed, I set forth in the diary—as far as I was able—what I knew and remembered. How natural is the instinct which drives a man alone to pencil and paper, as if his destiny required the right last word and period.

The afternoon ran out its time; though my eyes would not stop aching and the pain would not quit my temples, just lying in the sleeping bag quieted the hammering of my heart. Gradually my mind cleared, and I tried to reconstruct the events preceding the episode in the tunnel. The exhaust vent over the engine, I decided, must have filled with rime, causing the poisonous gases to back into the tunnel. I was pretty sure that it was carbon monoxide. The instantaneous way I was struck down, the absence of any consciousness of suffocation bespoke these things, plus the symptoms—the splitting headaches, the nausea, the stabbing pains in my body and eyes, the hot and cold rushes of dizziness. What had saved me in the tunnel was the fact of my being dropped as though poleaxed. Since monoxide rises, the air at the bottom of the tunnel must have been all right; and the oxygen entering my blood brought me around.

All this represented a mind groping for bearings. To know I had escaped disaster in one form was only a preliminary step in the process of preparing to avert it in another. The fact was manifest that I was helpless, at least for the time being. I barely had strength to light the candle standing on the tin ledge directly over my head. If so simple a movement could empty me of the little strength that had returned, what chance did I have of bringing in food and fuel from the tunnels, let alone attending to the instruments? I could live many days without food. I could suck snow to quench thirst.

But, ill and weak as I was, I could not live long without heat; and the fuel tank had to be filled every three days. Pondering such difficult matters was too much for me; my mind went blank again. When I awakened and looked at my wrist watch, the time was 7 o'clock. I wasn't quite so weak, and my body craved water.

So I drew the flashlight from the sleeping bag and propped it on the edge of the bunk in order to direct the beam toward the stove. With this to guide me, I slipped from the bunk, clinging to the side for support. Waves of dizziness swept from head to foot, but after a little while I was able to reach the chair and push it toward the stove. A little water remained in the bucket on the stove; I dipped it out with a can. The first few swallows my stomach threw up; nevertheless, I persevered until I had at least a cupful down. Wondering why my teeth chattered so, I put my hand against the stove. It was out—no longer than a few minutes, evidently, else the water would have frozen. *Thursday . . . Thursday . . . the day to fill the tank.* So the tank was dry, as was the lantern; and if I wanted to have light and warmth, both must be filled at once.

The notes which I jotted down a few days afterwards insist this stranger reeling in the dark acted with the utmost deliberation. Perhaps so. Between the pain and the weakness it was hard for more than one thought to find a lodgment. I managed to pull on my parka and mittens. Then I lifted the empty tank from the stand. Holding it by the handle with one hand and the flashlight with the other, I started into the tunnel. The nearest fuel drum—by the grace of God equipped with a spigot—was only fourteen feet from the door; but to make the distance I had to stop and put around my neck the loop attached to the flashlight so as to free one hand with which to steady myself. I walked slowly and uncertainly; as, years ago, I had walked for the first time after being desperately ill of typhoid fever while on a midshipman cruise to England.

The funnel lay on top of a barrel. I fitted it into the tank;

and, while the tank was filling, I rested on a box. But, though I had the strength to lift the tank (it weighed about twenty-one pounds filled to the brim), I could not carry it far. After a few steps my heart was pounding, and the dizziness returned. I let go and slumped on the tool box, near the head of the tunnel. For how long? I really don't know. Long enough, anyhow, to be shaken by the cold. If I couldn't carry the tank, perhaps I could pull it, which was what I did—a few feet at a time. At least, I remember doing that.

Inside the shack, I poured half a gallon or so of the precious stuff into a pitcher; this would do for the lantern. A lot spilled on the floor. Presently I succeeded in lifting the tank itself to the stand behind the stove. With that a feeling of relief possessed me for a moment. I could now hold off the cold for at least two days, and maybe three if I economized. Nevertheless, I didn't attempt to light the stove, dreading the effort and knowing that I ought to be in the bunk; but, craving light after the long darkness, I did light the lantern. The light was so cheery that I was encouraged to attempt an observation at 10 P.M. (Actually 8 P.M. my old time; for, a day or two previously, I had advanced my clock two hours, as an experiment in moonlight saving, so to speak.)

That was a mistake. I was able to climb the ladder all right, resting at every rung; I pushed the door back with my head, waited a moment, and then hobbled to the instrument shelter, feeling dizzy and utterly forlorn. I guessed the wind's velocity as being seventeen miles per hour (the register trace shows an actual wind speed of only seven miles), and noted the absence of aurora. But I was unspeakably weak and sick again when I reached the bottom of the ladder. I must sleep. I must sleep, something was saying inside me. In the Escape Tunnel I groped around until I found the box of phenobarbital pills. With the box in my hand I stumbled to the hut. I got my parka, pants, and shoes off; but the shirt was beyond me. Using the chair as a step, I hung the lantern from its peg above the bunk, then climbed in, weighed down by a sense of complete futility.

The instant the candle died, the darkness dropped like a blow. Sleep was the great hunger; but it would not come, so cruel was the pain in my head and back and legs. As I lay there, the intimation came that I would not recover. Carbon monoxide poisoning is an insidious thing. Once the haemoglobin in the blood stream and the lungs is broken down, it takes the liver and spleen a long time to restore the oxygen-carrying material. Even with the best of hospital care this is a matter of weeks and sometimes months. For me the worst of the cold and the darkest part of the night were yet to come. The sun was nearly three months away. I could not persuade myself that I had the strength to meet it. To some men sickness brings a desire to be left alone; animal-like, their one instinct is to crawl into a hole and lick the hurt. It used to be so with me. But that night, as never before, I discovered how alone I was; and the realization evoked an indescribable desire to have about me those who knew me best. Remembering the meticulous preparations, the safeguards which I had thrown about myself, my soul was bitter with reproaches. My fort had become an ambush. Nothing within the power of the night or cold had made it so. My stupidity was to blame, and this I should have feared before the others.

Even in my stupor I seem to have recognized that the gasoline engine was not solely responsible. The engine dealt the blow which knocked me down, but long before then I had partially perceived a developing weakness. I remembered the notches I had taken up in my belt; the headaches and hurt in my eyes earlier in the month. Maybe the frost in my lungs was at fault. Maybe something was organically wrong with me. But I doubted that these by themselves could have depleted me so much. What reason I could muster indicted the stinking stove as the principal villain. Monoxide poisoning is not necessarily an instantaneous matter. It may be a gradual and cumulative process, brought about by intermittent exposure to the chemistry of the fumes. And the more I thought about the leaky joints in the stove, the more I blamed it.

But all this was shadowy in my mind that last night in May. I wavered between self-recrimination and hopefulness, between pain and an emptiness devoid of feeling. I knew that I was in a frightful mess, one that would involve my family, the expedition, and God only knew whom else. But it was hard to see what could be done about that. I lighted the candle, intending to write certain messages; but no paper was within reach. After a little while I blew out the candle. In my hand was the box of sleeping pills. I was reluctant to take one, not from squeamishness but from the fear that the drug would weaken me further. So, telling myself I would wait until 4 o'clock before resorting to the sedative, I put the box down. Sometime after 3 o'clock I drifted off into a dream of horrors.

JUNE 1ST WAS A FRIDAY. A black Friday for me. The nightmare left me, and about 9 o'clock in the morning I awakened with a violent start, as if I had been thrown down a well in my sleep. I found myself staring wildly into the darkness of the shack, not knowing where I was. The weakness that filled my body when I turned in the sleeping bag and tried to throw the flashlight on my wrist watch was an eloquent reminder. I was Richard E. Byrd, United States Navy (Ret.), temporarily sojourning at Latitude 80° 08' South, and not worth a damn to myself or anybody else. My mouth was dry and tasted foul. God, I was thirsty. But I had hardly strength to move. I clung to the sleeping bag, which was the only source of comfort and warmth left to me, and mournfully debated the little that might be done.

Two facts stood clear. One was that my chances of recovering were slim. The other was that in my weakness I was incapable of taking care of myself. These were desperate conclusions, but my mood allowed no others. All that I could reasonably hope for was to prolong my existence for a few days by hoarding my remaining resources; by doing the necessary things *very slowly* and with *great deliberation.* So long as he did that and maintained the right frame of mind, even a very ill man should be able to last a time. So I reasoned, anyway. There was no alternative. My hopes of survival had to be staked on the theory.

But you must have *faith*—you must have faith in the outcome, I whispered to myself. It is like a flight, a flight into another unknown. You start and you cannot turn back. You must go on and on and on, trusting your instruments, the course you have plotted on the charts, and the reasonableness of events. Whatever goes wrong will be mostly of your own making; if it is to be tragedy, then it will be the commonplace tragedy of human vulnerability.

My first need was warmth and food. The fire had been out about twelve hours; I had not eaten in nearly thirty-six. Toward providing those necessities I began to mobilize my slender resources. If there had been a movie camera to record my movements, the resulting picture could have been passed off as slow motion. Every act was performed with the utmost patience. I lifted the lantern—and waited. I edged out of the sleeping bag—and rested on the chair beside the stove. I pulled on my pants, hiking them up a little bit at a time. Then the shirt. Then the socks. And shoes. And finally the parka. All this took a long time. I was shaking so from the cold that, when my elbow struck the wall, the sound was like a peremptory knock at the door. Too miserable to stick it out, I retreated to the sleeping bag; half an hour later the chill in my body drove me into a fresh attempt to reach the stove.

Faintness seized me as I touched foot to the floor. I barely made the chair. There I sat for some minutes, not moving, just staring at the candle. Then I turned the valve, and with the stove lids off waited for the wick to become saturated with the cold, sluggish oil. Thirst continued to plague me. Several inches of ice were in the water bucket. I dropped it on the floor, bottom up. A sliver of ice fell out, which I sucked until my teeth rattled from the cold. A box of matches was on the table. I touched one to the burner. A red flame licked over the metal ring; it was a beautiful thing to see. I sat there ten or fifteen minutes at least, absorbing the column of warmth. The flame burned red and smoky, when it should have been blue and clear; and, studying it, I knew that this was from faulty combustion and was one source of my misfortunes. This fire was my enemy, but I could not live without it.

Thus this never-ending day began. To describe it all would be tedious. Nothing really happened; and yet, no day in my life was more momentous. I lived a thousand years, and all of them were agonizing. I won a little and lost a lot. At the day's end—if it can be said to have had an end—all that I could say was that I was still alive. Granting the conditions, I had no right to expect more. Life seldom ends gracefully or sensibly. The protesting body succumbs like a sinking ship going down with the certificate of seaworthiness nailed fast to the wheelhouse bulkhead; but the mind, like the man on the bridge, realizes at last the weakness of the hull and ponders the irony. If the business drags out long enough, as mine did, the essence of things in time becomes pitifully clear; except that by then it is wadded into a tight little scrap ready to be thrown away, as the knowledge is of no earthly use.

My thirst was the tallest tree in a forest of pain. The Escape Tunnel was a hundred miles away, but I started out, carrying the bucket and lantern. Somewhere along the way I slipped and fell. I licked the snow until my tongue burned. The Escape Tunnel was too far. But in the food tunnel my boots had worn a rut eighteen inches wide and six inches deep, which was full of loose snow. The snow was dirty, but I scraped the bucket along until it was nearly full, then pulled it into the shack, a foot or so at a time.

Snow took a long time to melt in the bucket, and I could not wait. I poured a little into a pan and heated it with alcohol tablets. It was still a soggy mass of snow when I raised it to my lips. My hands were shaking, and the water spilled down the front of my parka; then I vomited, and all that I had drunk came up. In a little while I tried again, taking sips too small to be thrown up. Then I crawled on top of the sleeping bag, drawing a heavy blanket over my shoulders, hoping I should somehow regain strength.

Nevertheless, I was able to do a number of small things, in a series of stealthy, deliberate sorties from the bunk. I attended to the inside thermograph and register, changing the sheets, winding the clocks, and inking the pens. The outlet ventilator was two-thirds filled with ice; I could just reach it from the bunk with a stick which had a big nail in the end. After every exertion I rested; the pain in my arms and back and head was almost crucifying. I filled a thermos jug with warm water, added powdered milk and sugar, and carried the jug into the sleeping bag. My stomach crawled with nauseous sensations; but, by taking a teaspoonful at a time, I finally managed to get a cupful down. After a while the weakness left me, and I felt strong enough to start for the instrument shelter. I reached the hatch and pushed it open, but could go no farther. The night was a gray fog, full of shadows, like my mood. In the shack I lost the milk I had drunk. On the verge of fainting, I made for the bunk.

I WON'T EVEN ATTEMPT to recall all the melancholy thoughts that drifted through my mind that long afternoon. But I can say truthfully that at no time did I have any feeling of resignation. My whole being rebelled against my low estate. As the afternoon wore on, I felt myself sinking. Now I became alarmed. This was not the first time I had ever faced death. It had confronted me many times in the air. But then it had seemed altogether different. In flying things happen fast: you make a decision; the verdict crowds you instantly; and, when the invisible and neglected passenger comes lunging into the cockpit, he is but one of countless distractions. But now death was a stranger sitting in a darkened room, secure in the knowledge that he would be there when I was gone.

Great waves of fear, a fear I had never known before, swept through me and settled deep within. But it wasn't the fear of suffering or even of death itself. It was a terrible anxiety over the consequences to those at home if I failed to return. I had done a damnable thing in going to Advance Base, I told myself. Also, during those hours of bitterness, I saw my whole life pass in review. I realized how wrong my sense of values had been and how I had failed to see that the simple, homely, unpretentious things of life are the most important.

Much as I should have liked to, I couldn't consider myself a martyr to science; nor could I blame the circumstances that had prevented staffing the base with three men, according to the original plan. I had gone there looking for peace and enlightenment, thinking that they might in some way enrich my life and make me a more useful man. I had also gone armed with the justification of a scientific mission. Now I saw both for what they really were: the first as a delusion, the second as a dead-end street. My thoughts turned to gall and wormwood. I was bitter toward the whole world except my family and friends. The clocks ticked on in the gloom, and a subdued whir came from the register at my feet. The confidence implicit in these unhurried sounds emphasized my own debasement. What right had they to be confident and unhurried? Without me they could not last a day.

The one aspiration I still had was to be vindicated by the tiny heap of data collected on the shelf in the Escape Tunnel. But, even as I seized upon this, I recognized its flimsiness; a romanticized rationalization, as are most of the things which men are anxious to be judged by. We men of action who serve science serve only a reflection in a mirror. The tasks are difficult, the objectives remote; but scholars sitting in bookish surroundings tell us where to go, what to look for, and even what we are apt to find. Likewise, they pass dispassionate judgment on whatever we bring back. We are nothing more than glamorous middlemen between theory and fact, materialists jobbing in the substance of universal truths.

Beyond the fact that I had suffered to secure them, what did I know about the theoretical significance of the records in the Escape Tunnel, of the implications which might differentiate them from a similar heap of records gathered at Keokuk? I really didn't know. I was a fool, lost on a fool's errand, and that was how I should be judged.

At the end only two things really matter to a man, regardless of who he is; and they are the affection and understanding of his family. Anything and everything else he creates are insubstantial; they are ships given over to the mercy of the winds and tides of prejudice. But the family is an everlasting anchorage, a quiet harbor where a man's ships can be left to swing to the moorings of pride and loyalty.

THE CHILL went out of the shack; and the heat from the stove, accumulating in a layer under the ceiling, wrapped the bunk as in a blanket. A little after 6 o'clock, as nearly as I could remember afterwards, I sipped the last of the milk in the thermos jug. My body needed stronger nourishment, but I possessed nothing like the strength to cook a meal. I nibbled an Eskimo biscuit and a piece of chocolate, but my stomach was turning somersaults. So I got up and refilled the thermos jug with hot water and powdered milk, a really desperate task, as I had to cling to the table to keep from falling. The next several hours are a blank. Later, when I was able to make notes of what had happened to me, I could not remember anything at all. Perhaps I slept. When I looked at my watch again the time was about 9:30. I was dazed and exhausted. The idea came to me that I ought to put out the stove to give myself a needed rest from the fumes; besides, there was no telling when I should have strength to fill the tank again. As I twisted the valve, the room went black. The next thing I knew I was on the floor. I pulled myself up by the stove. It was still warm; so I could not have been out very long.

I dropped into the chair, convinced that the end was near.

Up till now I had been sustained by a conviction that the only way I could nullify my mistake and make reparation to my family was by transcending myself and surviving. But I had lost. I flung my arms across the table, and put my head down, spilling a cup of water I had in my hand. My bitterness evaporated, and the only resentment I felt was concentrated on myself. I lay there a long time, sobbing, "What a pity, what an infinite pity!" So my pride was gone as well. A Virginian, I was brought up to believe that a gentleman never gives way to his feelings. I felt no shame then, although I do now. Fear was gone, also. When hope goes, uncertainty goes, too; and men don't fear certainties.

The only conscious resolve left was to write a message to my wife—a last groping touch of the hand. Beyond the very personal things, I wanted her to understand why I had not tried to inform Little America of my plight (forgetting that it needed no explanation) and my reasons for going to Advance Base. There had to be that. Pencil and paper were on a shelf nearby. When I went to reach out, my arm would not come free; my sleeve had frozen in the spilled water. I wrenched it loose. The frenzy to write supplied its own strength. After the first few paragraphs my mind calmed. But I was too weak to write sitting up. My head kept jerking forward; and, now that the fire was out, the shack was unbearably cold.

The bunk was a continent's breadth away, and I had to cross an interminable plateau to reach it. Safe at last in the sleeping bag, I lay still many minutes, shivering and gasping for breath. Then I finished the letter; and, as I did so, I thought of the last entry in Scott's diary: "For God's sake, look after our people." I had often pondered that simple phrase, but only intellectually. That night I understood what Scott meant. It seemed a pity that men must undergo a cataclysmic experience to perceive this simplest of truths.

The lantern flicked and grew dim. I managed to light two candles which stood on a ledge over the bunk. Just as the second one flamed, the lantern went out. Then, after a while,

I wrote a letter to my mother, and another to my children, a few messages, very brief, of instruction to Dr. Poulter and Charlie Murphy concerning the welfare of the expedition, and a final letter to the men at Little America. On the shelf was the green metal box which held my personal papers. I have had it for years. In this I stowed the letters to my family. The ensuing periods are not very clear. I may have lapsed into a coma. A sensation of freezing came; my next recollection is of hoisting myself into a sitting position and composing a message to Murphy regarding the disposal of my papers. This, with the other messages, I secured with a string to the nail from which the lantern usually hung.

Something approaching gratitude flowed into me. Over my head the two candles still burned. Both were red. one stood in a cracked china holder. The other was planted in its own tallow. I looked up at them, thinking vaguely that, when they went out, I should never again see anything so friendly. After a little while I doused the wicks against the wall. Presently another reaction set in. My mind wandered off into a vision of the past, in which I seemed to be wrestling again for the welterweight championship of the Naval Academy. An agonizing pain was in my body; I had given up all hope of winning; there remained only an insane determination not to bring shame to my mother in the gallery. It was vivid, and the reason it was vivid was that I was again in almost the same situation, except that the stakes were infinitely greater and the chances of winning even less. Then the same determination that had kept me fighting on to the finish that day again came surging back. I saw that, although I seemed absolutely washed up, there was a chance I was mistaken. Anyway, I would have another try.

PAUL SIPLE

(*1908-1968*)

IN 1928 A NATION-WIDE SEARCH was conducted to select a Boy Scout to accompany Richard E. Byrd on the latter's first Antarctic expedition. Paul Siple was chosen. This event was to be the turning point of Siple's life. Not only did he prove his value to the expedition; after serving in several subsequent expeditions he became recognized as an Antarctic expert. He was chief biologist of Byrd's 1933–35 expedition. During the International Geophysical Year (1957–58), when the United States boldly and for the first time in history set up a permanent station at the Pole, Siple was named as the station's scientific leader. He was among the small group of men who first wintered over at the Pole. During his active years he made important contributions to the body of knowledge of the continent. In the following pages he vividly and sensitively describes what it was like to live at the Pole during that first experimental year.

Living at the Pole

"Will it be pitch dark?" one of Tuck's Navy men had asked me when he first arrived at the Pole.

"Not very often," I had assured him, though he was far from convinced.

All my previous experience in Antarctica's winter night had been centered at Little America off the Bay of Whales on the Ross Ice Shelf. What would happen at the geographic South Pole some 800 miles inland was something we would experience for the first time in man's long history on earth.

Three times I had spent winter nights at Little America. There the sun disappeared for four months beginning in late April, and during the first and last months of the winter night there was enough light to permit work outdoors several hours a day. During May, even though the sun dropped deeper below the horizon each day, we had a twilight around noon. And even during the two real months of total darkness at Little America there was a flush of pale reddish light to the north over the Ross Sea, for at most the noon sun lay only about 12° below the horizon.

The dark we faced at the South Pole, however, would be deeper and would last far longer. For our night would last six months instead of the four at Little America, and the sun at its farthest point from us on June 22 would lie a full 23½° below our horizon instead of 12°.

Our neighboring Antarctic IGY[1] stations would fare better

1 International Geophysical Year.

than we with respect to the amount of light they would have.
The British, Argentine and Chilean stations on the Graham-
Palmer Peninsula[1] north of the Antarctic Circle would, of
course, have sunrises and sunsets every day in the year. The
sun would not rise very high nor would their day be very long
on midwinter day (June 22), but nevertheless they would
have several hours of light each day. The U.S. Wilkes Station,
France's D'Urville Station, Russia's Mirny and Oasis stations,
Australia's Mawson and Davis stations, Japan's Showa Station,
Belgium's Baudoin Station and Norway's Maudheim Station
were all so close to the Antarctic Circle that they would
celebrate midwinter season with gaudy brilliant sunsets with
the sun barely, if at all, below the horizon at noon.

Other stations, like Little America, McMurdo, Ellsworth,
Byrd, Hallett, New Zealand's Scott Station,[2] Argentina's Bel-
grano Station, and British Halley Bay, Shackleton and South
Ice would have respectable polar nights but they would be
nowhere near as long or dark as ours would be at the Pole
Station.

Inside the polar areas the four seasons of the year take on
a meaning of their own. Summer and winter are of course the
periods of 24-hour sun and sunlessness respectively. Fall and
spring apply to the periods when there are true sunrises and
sunsets. How long these periods last depends on one's latitude. At Little America halfway between the Antarctic Circle and the Pole fall and spring last for two months each. The
length of the sunup and sundown periods during these
two months ranges from one minute to 23 hours and 59 minutes.

The twilight season at the South Pole lingers from sunset
on March 22 until May 4 when the sun's angle, from its
position below our horizon, was 18°. This latter date represented the real beginning of the dark period. Just how dark
it is when the sun is 18° below the horizon can be garnered
from the fact that a smaller 6° to 8° angle represents twilight

1 Now known as the Antarctic Peninsula.
2 Now known as Scott Base.

back in civilization, or the time for turning on streetlights. Twilight lasts much longer in the polar regions than anywhere else because of the relatively flat trajectory of the sun's rays. It is longest at the Poles themselves, where twilight lasts for a whole month.

During this prolonged twilight from March 22 until May 4, when we walked outdoors we could distinguish an ominous and ever-increasing gray arc rising farther from the horizon opposite the sun each day. It was the earth shadow, a phenomenon rarely noticed in temperate latitudes where the sun sets in a matter of minutes rather than weeks as at the Pole. This earth shadow is actually the portion of the atmosphere completely shaded from the setting sun by the earth, and here at the Pole was separated from the sunlit portion of the atmosphere by a distinct gray line which rose higher in the sky each day. As it advanced across the sky, the oranges, yellows and pinks of the sunset seemed actually to increase in brilliance and intensity. It was my observation on such days that the beauty of the sunset at the Pole surpassed that at any other point on the globe. For with the occasional red of the sky and the white surface, we were living in a pink world. And then before my eyes, our pink world would turn green or purple or a host of other pastel shades.

The ending of the astronomical twilight was another matter, however. Now not even the faintest glimmer of twilight loomed over our horizon. Yet oddly, only 300 miles above our cone of darkness the sun shone brightly into space all the while. But this offered little compensation to us on the ground, for there is no side emanation from a beam of light, and there were not enough atmospheric particles of moisture or dust that high up to reflect back any light to us. The sun's rays went by us invisibly, as they do in the sky until the moon or a planet reflects them to let us know they are there. Sunlight, or even the indirect light the sun sheds, is one of the accepted blessings of life. Without it, apprehension crept into the hearts of the uninitiated.

This was so even though the South Pole winter night frequently has periods of light from other sources. For two winter weeks each month, the black sky would be punctured by the light of the moon as it swung around the sky from right to left. During the first week the moon would spiral its way upward and ride higher in the sky each day. The second week it would creep down toward the horizon and then disappear. In addition the Pole sky, except on cloudy days, would be dotted with starlight and occasional auroral light. It would only be on these cloudy days that the blackness would be all-encompassing.

The men's reaction to the winter night varied from individual to individual. A few of the men expressed their apprehension about the unknown perils ahead in blustering aggressiveness or in elaborate practical jokes as some men do when depressed. Others turned to the hamset for reassurance that there still was an outside world. Oz, our builder, sawed wood and pounded nails as nonchalantly as if he were back home in Pennsylvania. Some of the other men grew quieter while others grew noisier.

I realized what was running through most minds. We were like men who had been fired off in rockets to take up life on another planet. We were in a lifeless, and almost featureless, world. However snug and comfortable we might make ourselves, we could not escape from our isolation. We were now face to face with raw nature so grim and stark that our lives could be snuffed out in a matter of minutes. Every day would bring us new problems to solve and our ingenuity would be taxed over and over again. And all this to carry out a somewhat difficult fragment of the world-wide scientific program of the International Geophysical Year.

An occasional overheard conversation gave me good evidence of the concern the men felt at living in a dark, womanless wasteland. The blink of an eye revealed the wonder that crossed a mind. There was no escape now from the truly lethal wall that separated us from the rest of mankind.

The perils of polar life were many. A fire could toss us to the bitter mercies of a savage, unknown land. If a man were lost outdoors he could not hope to survive more than a few hours. After that he would run out of energy and his body would cool down to the danger point. There was danger also from the restricted vision possible in the darkness, cold and wind-drifting snow. A man wandering only a hundred yards from camp under such conditions might lose his way and never be found. Vapor from a man's breath could freeze his eyelashes shut in an instant and make him believe he had gone blind. His breath would come in gasps and his joints would ache. The intense pain of the cold on fingers and toes could easily distract him, and even destroy his ability to reason clearly.

The dark presented its own danger, for there were no landmarks to help a man find his way. It was like walking out on the ocean where every wave was like every other. If the stars were out, it was possible to fathom your direction—if you knew your stars. But even then it was possible to walk right past the station. Jack and I found this out one time when we walked out 200 yards to collect snow samples. We thought we were walking parallel to the thousand-foot seismic tunnel when suddenly we crossed it and almost fell in. Had this fortuitous accident not occurred and given us our bearings, we might have gotten well lost.

The wind also presented a danger. If it was strong (and it often blew in excess of 30 miles an hour), it was natural to turn your face away when traveling downwind. But returning to camp a man would also tend to avert his face and might easily wander off course. With the surface rough, walking was often a matter of stumbling along and this, too, would tend to turn a man off his path. Then again, the winds blew up snow and drift and made the horizon indistinct. Herb Hansen, one of our Met men, got religion polarwise as the result of a wind on one occasion. Out to check meteorological observations, he became befuddled due to the wind and drifts. For safety we had placed flags along the route to the meteorological station, but Herb could not find them. He changed his direction several times when he saw he was lost, though he managed to keep himself from growing panicky. Then by sheer accident he found himself at camp. "Guess where I've been?" he whispered when he got indoors.

There was danger also in the very temperature outdoors. My early observations led me to believe that the winter night temperature might easily reach a low of −120° F. If such cold was combined with even a modest wind, a man had little chance for lengthy survival, for almost any wind would triple the body's rate of cooling. I had spent years developing tables to show the effect of wind chill on humans, and the prospects of outdoor movement at this temperature were nil. . . .

STILL ANOTHER DANGER to be faced was the possibility that an ice fog would roll over you outdoors. An ice fog is a mass of crystals of ice that float and form a fog. An ice fog could render the camp invisible from a very short way off. Our camp formed its own ice fogs as a result of the clouds of steam which poured from exhaust pipes and condensed on contact with the frigid air, erasing most outside markers from sight.

So in a physical sense we at the Pole were 18 men in a box. Only with the aid of our "box" could we survive, yet it bound us in. There was no way we could make our way to the outside world. Nor was there any possibility that we could be rescued should tragedy strike. We would have to remain put until the next summer—in October or November—come what might.

There was also the very large problem of how the men would stand each other's company in the daily rub and grind that would be their steady routine for months without respite. Friction was bound to arise from a variety of a minor details, from the way a man chewed to how he closed a door or talked. There would be the monotony of constantly seeing the same faces when one rose, ate, worked and relaxed. Whatever a man was inherently would be intensified during the close-quarters winter night. A mean man would grow meaner; a kind man would grow kinder.

Men in a box; that was what we were.

"THIS IS A POORLY DEVISED arrangement for running a small isolated camp," I had said to Jack Tuck[1] even before the winter night set in. "A split command for eighteen men can lead to all sorts of troubles unless we can consciously work together as a team. It's the kind of thing that always happens when men plan an expedition they know they won't be on themselves. They always let their theories run rampant at the expense of what they know is practical."

Fortunately Jack readily agreed to eliminate any local distinction between the scientific staff and the naval support group. To have the camp divided nine and nine into "sheep and goats" was asking for serious trouble.

I told our eighteen men frankly that though they were strangers to each other when they came to the Pole, by the time they left they would know each other better than they knew their own families. For there would be no real escape from one another, no possibility of getting away, and no other men to see and listen to for almost a year. "We are all in the same dark pickle barrel," I told them.

Leadership in a small and isolated community has to be planned and carried out with precision, yet it must also appear matter-of-fact or it will be offensive. One of Admiral Byrd's chief tenets regarding leadership in the Antarctic was that a leader had to remain aloof to keep group morale high. This, he felt, gave a sense of security to the men by causing them to believe their leader was different from and somehow

1 The station's Navy leader.—C.N.

superior to them, whether he really was or not. In addition, where a leader had to make arbitrary decisions it was important that he not get too close to the men under his command. At the same time, therapeutic leadership was also essential, so that a man would be willing first of all to come to you with personal problems, and second, that he would feel you were interested in his welfare.

There are other important ingredients in successful Antarctic leadership. One is to avoid a caste system. All men must be put on an equal basis and no favoritism must be shown any individual. Each troublesome person has to be treated on the basis of his own character. For instance, some individuals must be handled with sympathy; others with a firm hand. Another, and perhaps the key, factor in maintaining group discipline is to place great reliance on the "group-pressure system." Because there can be no strong-arm leadership in isolated living, the wise leader lets the group "ride" a man who is shirking his duty or becoming obnoxious. But the leader's sense of timing must be right. When the riding is overdone or when it is unfair, he must step in to get things back on an even keel. At the same time, when he does step in he must handle the problem in such a manner as to make clear that no one can get away with shirking or obnoxious behavior.

Sometimes men would come to me and complain that certain individuals were egging them on to an eventual fight. Others complained that they were irritated by persons they disliked. "So you don't like him," I would say. "Then live *around* him. And remember that you don't have to live with him after you leave here."

On minor infractions, a man will not be offended by group discipline. On one occasion, for instance, Junior Waldron and Mel Havener played a tape recorder until 2:30 A.M. and kept most of the barracks building awake. Early the next morning while Junior was still asleep, the men entered his room, turned on his lights, beat on the walls and clanged pot covers together. Junior got the point and later went around and apologized for his thoughtlessness.

Our men at the South Pole Station had undergone extensive psychological testing before being finally selected. This was important in weeding out men who suffered from claustrophobia or mental disorders. The men were also tested for manly interests and qualities.

As a matter of fact, one striking characteristic of the men on all six of the Antarctic expeditions I have gone on is that almost all were of the type popularly known as "he-men." Expeditions may have brought men together in a womanless world, yet paradoxically the men who went on such adventures had a great regard for women. They might get along without them during a stay in the Antarctic but they did not like it one bit.

Only a single instance stands out in my mind where this was apparently not so. We had the misfortune on an earlier expedition to have a man who had hidden his tendency toward homosexuality. But the strain of keeping his feelings pent up within him proved too great a burden during the winter night and he attempted suicide rather than reveal them. Later when we returned to civilization he succeeded in doing away with himself.

The true penalties then for living in the isolation of the Antarctic were the absence of women and families, exotic foods, knowledge of what was going on in the outside world and a general lack of privacy. Away from the influence of women, men have a tendency to become unkempt and sometimes surly as they suppress their heartfelt emotions behind a hardened exterior of sham gruffness. Even though Chet's food was excellent, men drooled over the thought of a special meal they had enjoyed back in civilization. As for news of the outside world, I knew from previous experiences that it would be years after I returned before I would catch up with news events and deaths that had occurred during my absence. I often missed the entire birth, life and burial of a popular piece of music without ever having heard of it.

Privacy was not possible in a camp the size of the South Pole Station. Yet even in a crowded base such as ours, men somehow found opportunity for solitude. At the Pole, for instance, when I went to bed I could almost draw a blind on my life at the Pole and enter into another world mentally in which I would read and think about matters away from the Pole. In fact, I resented it a bit when someone invaded the privacy of my secret life and thoughts, so that in a true sense this forced solitude was isolation within isolation.

Whenever Admiral Byrd was asked what men missed most on Antarctic expeditions, he would reply with the single word "temptation." This was a splendid summation. Whatever a man cannot have, he wants. Things taken for granted become priceless in their absence. Perhaps one of our Pole men (just which one I do not recall) put it well when I asked him what he missed most. "Tomatoes," he blurted. "Both kinds."

This year, only the Russians brought women along to the Antarctic: women scientists and stewardesses served aboard Soviet IGY ships. From all reports they were capable and were no problem. The only American women to get to the Antarctic in 1957 were two Pan-American stewardesses who stayed at McMurdo for just a few hours.

Another thing the men missed at the Pole were pets. I had suggested bringing in birds and fish, but this suggestion had been rejected. On earlier expeditions we had had many dogs and the men had lavished attention on them. Jack Tuck's Bravo was the only pet at the South Pole, but he was by and large a one-man dog. When Jack was ill on one occasion, Bravo lay at the foot of his bunk and would not take his eyes off Jack. And when Jack went off to the snow mine for his hours of exhausting digging, Bravo fretted continuously, looking all about the camp for Jack until he returned. (A Bravo fence kept him out of the snow mine.) I wrestled occasionally with Bravo, and Doc Taylor let him tug ferociously on his sweater sleeve in a make-believe tug of war, but no man cared to expose a hand when he dropped left-overs into Bravo's dish in the mess hall.

The pressures of close-quarters living were numerous but never serious at the Pole Station. Nevertheless, in the course of our year there, every man had at least a minor personality problem involving someone else. Doc Taylor made his own investigation of daily attitudes with a unique chart that he devised.

He distributed a clip board, paper and pencil to each man. They were to record their state of mind for the entire day and whether they had had a good night's sleep. Doc Taylor devised a scale from a low of 1 to a high of 5, and instructed the men to insert the proper number in the DAY and NIGHT columns. When a man was a bit sad and his self-determined rating was low, others would nod and say, "Gee, let's get him a radio contact with his family." Generally this worked won-ders and produced a 5 for that day.

The men all recognized that a bad night was invariably followed by a bad day. But a bad day was not always followed by a bad night. Once during the winter night, I had worked late for several consecutive days and felt myself keyed up. Two nights in a row I gave myself a 2. Then I had a hamgram from Ruth, and the poor pattern changed abruptly.

When Doc Taylor summarized his 1–5 Day and Night Study, he said to me, "Paul, you are going to be surprised at my astounding discovery that the average is 3, or normal."

At one time Doc considered moving from our Jamesway to the barracks building where ratings were lower and some of the men were having petty arguments with one another. But Jack and I dissuaded him and it was for the best.

Well-meaning psychologists back in the States hoped to make use of our experience living in isolation during the six-month winter night by using us as guinea pigs to supply them with data. Of course there was nothing wrong with this proposal, for we were a unique breed on the face of the earth and the scientific value of a study of our small isolated group could have borne fruitful results. However, some of the tests they sent us to take from their far-off position proved injurious to Station morale.

Each man was to take one of these tests at the outset of the winter night and again at its middle and end. Each test consisted of true-and-false questions, paragraphs to be completed, pictures to explain, and questions regarding opinions of others in camp. This last test was dangerous because it forced each man to examine himself and the camp clinically and to take apart his buddies. Other tests seemed condescending in attitude to our hard-working crew.

Certainly there was nothing wrong in asking a man several times in the course of a period of months to complete a paragraph beginning: "A woman is a . . ." Where a man might initially write a dull paragraph, by the time winter ended he would often reach new heights of lyrical description. But the pictures he was asked to explain and the Buddy Test were another matter.

The first time the men took the picture-explanation test they explained the scenes as they saw them. However, when the same five pictures came up again in the second testing, most of the men were smart enough to realize that their interpretation of the pictures was intended to reveal any deterioration they had suffered in the interim. As a result, none explained them seriously. Some deliberately wrote lewd explanations that would have singed the eyes of most readers. Others made up the most preposterous tales their minds could devise.

For instance, one of the pictures depicted a man standing on a piece of floe ice with one arm raised, the shore in the background and a ship to one side. It obviously was intended to raise a melodramatic concept of a man adrift on an ice floe. "If those psychologists are looking for something screwy," one of the men said with a laugh, "then I'll give them something."

His explanation ran as follows:

A bunch of guys on the ship got tight. Looking over
the rail, they saw that the bay ice had broken up. "What
do you say we fit it all back together again like a jigsaw
puzzle?" one of them shouted.

They managed to fit all the pieces together again with
the exception of one piece that they could not find. One
man had continued the search, and just before he was
ready to give up he found the piece of ice. So here he
stood standing on that last piece and yelling back to the
boat, "Guys, I found it!"

The Buddy Test, however, was the test that almost caused
serious trouble. It revealed poor psychological thinking on
the part of the psychologists, for the questions asked were of
a nature disruptive to our continued peace in camp. The
Buddy Test required each man to list his best friends among
the Pole personnel, as well as those he disliked most. Then
he had to explain why he liked and disliked the persons in
question.

The men, who had never given consideration to such matters, now found themselves forced to choose sides. "Those
psychologists are trying to split us up," one man charged.
"I'm not going to do it."

The entire Station was soon up in arms at the Buddy Test.
Wisely, Doc Taylor destroyed the papers. Then he got in
touch with the psychologists by radio and persuaded them to
call off further Buddy Tests at the Pole or other such isolated
small communities.

In general, the men were too busy to get into serious trouble. The IGY men especially had to run from morning to
night to complete their observations, and in between times
often had to straighten out serious problems involving maintenance of their instruments. The cold slowed down cameras, made emulsions alter chemical composition, cracked
vital parts of instruments—and sapped human energy. Then

there were the community tasks that always seemed to pop up just as they felt like relaxing. Jack's crew, too, had their work problems. The question of maintaining radio contact with the outside world plagued us continually; new electrical and heating difficulties cropped up unexpectedly; tractor and Weasel repairs for the coming summer were hampered by the absence of spare parts and the necessity to devise adequate substitutes.

The threat of fire was always on our minds. Once Mel Havener and Floyd Johnson were working on a gasoline-powered Herman-Nelson heater in the warming room of the inflation shelter when the stove caught fire. Luckily their fire extinguisher was next to them and they managed to extinguish the blaze before the gasoline fire spread. Another time one of our jet heaters backfired and started a fire in the science building. But here again it was quickly put out, though the stove was ruined by the powdered extinguishing matter.

Boredom and too much leisure time had caused trouble on some of the earlier expeditions I went on. But these were not our problem at the Pole. Nevertheless, we did have some. For instance, at the outset there was some resentment on the part of various individuals in Jack's Navy support crew against the IGY men. These tensions were based primarily on the fact that the scientists were better paid and were doing professional work. Some of the Navy men groused and referred to the IGY personnel as "sand crabs." However, this early ceased to be a problem when the IGY men took on some of the heaviest manual labor connected with buttoning up the camp for winter and carried the load in supplying the camp with fresh snow for the melter, as well as sharing housemouse and mess duties. In addition, five of the IGY men lived in the barracks building and were not standoffish in any respect.

There were special built-in tensions, however, involving the entire IGY group. Contributing chiefly to these was the men's feeling that they were being forgotten by the IGY national group back in Washington. Added to this was a concern that the ground rules laid down for their scientific observations were at times needlessly bureaucratic and tended to impede the men's efforts. Actually, they were right on both counts, though it was my business to persuade them to ignore these irksome matters. As a new organization, the IGY had quickly become even more bureaucratic than the government at times and far too impersonal. Of course, they had a multitude of problems and insufficient time or help. Seldom however did the national staff take time to get in touch with our Station by radio, and when they did, all too often it was to register some petty complaint. Also, our science staff was being made to understand that they were simply employees who could be ordered to carry out certain tasks while conclusions would be drawn by the desk sitters in Washington.

There were also minor arbitrary rulings that momentarily took the heart out of our hard-working and capable men. One of these was a shortsighted regulation that they were not to discuss their work on the ham radio set with other IGY scientists at other Antarctic stations. The men were shocked by this order and morale suffered until we were able to get this dictum removed. Another odd display occurred on the winter night "Midnight," June 22, when we were ordered not to reply to congratulatory messages from foreign IGY stations in the Antarctic, since this would tend to tie up the radio sets. However, we boldly ignored this, for not to have exchanged messages would have been taken as a show of rudeness by the leaders of other stations in the Antarctic, some of whom I knew well.

I was not greatly upset by these frictions, however, for I had often observed on earlier expeditions, as well as during the war, that field groups and headquarters often tend to feel the other is performing below par, particularly when communications are poor. Perhaps the old saying that distance makes the heart grow fonder is not all that correct.

It was not enough for Jack and me to sit and wait until problems arose. Nor was it wise to make decisions without consulting some of the other men: especially when we knew a decision would be unpopular.

The result was that we set up a council of five which met infrequently but at critical times. Besides Jack and I, other members of the council were Doc Taylor, Ed Flowers and Willi Hough. From time to time this council recommended men for outstanding work not in their field. It was of interest to me how proud the recipients were to receive our type-written notations: ON BEHALF OF ALL MEMBERS OF THE STA-TION WE WISH TO EXPRESS OUR APPRECIATION FOR THE EXCELLENT JOB YOU HAVE VOLUNTARILY DONE FOR THE BENEFIT OF ALL HANDS.

In addition to this camp council there was another council, a streamlined affair consisting of Jack, Doc and myself which met informally almost daily to take up immediate problems. A young man of humor, kindness and the highest integrity and ability, Doc Taylor's basic thought on the subject of morale maintenance was a call for strict discipline. But in a camp such as ours, this would only have caused morale to deteriorate. In the first place, strict discipline cannot be maintained without the threat of punishment and there were no facilities for a court-martial at the Pole Station. And secondly, we were a mixed group of military and civilians, and it is not easy to order civilians around under the best of circumstances. Therefore, Jack and I saw to it that disciplin-ing was done indirectly, slowly and without any onus of pun-ishment.

Morale is a word of many meanings, as I so well learned on other expeditions. Admiral Byrd, on his first expedition, brought along a morale officer whose job it was to keep our spirits high. This man was remarkable in a sense because he equated good morale with an ability to play the ukulele. He had brought along boxes of ukuleles and was prepared to teach us how to strum the strings to keep us from growing morose or homesick. Unfortunately, the men considered it a morale booster not to have him or his ukuleles around.

One of the surprising things about any major expedition is

the way in which leadership qualities will arise from unsuspected quarters. On one expedition I appointed a man as my executive officer who had had excellent leadership training. He had been an officer in the armed forces and was obviously accustomed to exercising authority. Or so I thought. For I found he was unable to handle men. He lacked the ability to give simple instructions with the necessary finesse.

Fortunately I had a noncommissioned officer who rose to the occasion and I let him take over. He had the knack of jollying men into distasteful tasks and using enough force when necessary to show them he meant business. He instinctively said the right thing at the right time, and spoke in a voice that commanded respectful co-operation.

Cliff Dickey, who was Jack Tuck's electronics specialist, was one who showed such latent leadership qualities. Almost from the outset he proved to be a strong and stabilizing influence among Jack's enlisted men. The men recognized that he was always cheerful, reliable and sympathetic. If Chet Segers was being snowed under with galley work, Dickey was always the first to offer to help out as well as to talk other men into lending Chet a hand.

Jack often came to rely on Cliff to straighten out many matters affecting morale. For instance, one of our radio operators let personal messages go untyped and frequently failed to meet schedules when there were messages or patches. The result was that a crisis brewed. Quickly Jack turned over basic responsibility to Dickey and soon everyone was pleased with the ham service and the personal attention Cliff gave them.

I knew from previous expeditions how important word from home was to morale. On the negative side, I was concerned about the effects of illness and poor health on camp morale. One thing I worried about repeatedly was what would happen to our teeth at the South Pole. Doc Taylor had taken a short course in dentistry before coming to the Pole, for we considered it essential on the basis of previous expeditions to have a man with dental training available.

My previous sojourns at Little America had found our camps repeatedly weakened by recurring attacks of mouth trouble. Hardly a man got by without losing fillings or even a tooth and sometimes spending long nights of misery nursing aching molars. For reasons never properly determined, the Third Expedition of 1939–41 had had tooth trouble of almost epidemic proportions. Dr. Russell Frazier, physician on that expedition, discovered something strange when he tried to treat teeth. The smallest injection of adrenalin with novocaine resulted in sending a man into adrenalin shock. Frazier reported that an abnormal amount of adrenalin was secreted in glands during the long, dark winter night. This he suggested was the reason for much of the cabin fever that overtakes explorers and prospectors.

Doc Taylor had an almost completely opposite experience with teeth at the South Pole. Only John Guerrero needed a filling. Why we were so free of mouth trouble is still a happy mystery. Was it our high elevation? Our better mouth hygiene and care? I suspected that even though the air we breathed was colder than at McMurdo, for instance, it had less thermal capacity than the somewhat warmer sea-level air because of our altitude. This could mean there was less differential expansion between the fillings and the teeth. There may be something to my theory, for McMurdo kept a dentist busy almost full-time.

An important factor in maintaining morale in the Antarctic was to make certain that the routine did not become onerous. If a man could not be assured of a change from time to time, both his work and attitude suffered. But how was this possible when a tight schedule must be maintained?

The answer lay in declaring holidays and holding celebrations that were somehow sandwiched into the routine. For instance, we declared a holiday with the appearance of the full moon each month. This meant a special meal and a special effort at camaraderie. Chet never let us down on such occasions. In addition, those with no urgent morning duties could rise late, and at the end of the day we enjoyed a movie.

Holidays were also declared when the sun went down, at the mid-winter point, at eclipses of the moon, on birthdays —even Bravo's—and at such times as Jack and I thought the men deserved a holiday even without a special occasion. My idea was to hold them frequently and at irregular intervals. Bravo's first birthday came in August and we all celebrated it. Chet baked a special cake for Bravo with one lonely candle on top. Jack lighted the candle and Bravo wandered over to the cake as if he knew something was expected of him. With one loud sniff he blew out the candle, to the surprise of all except Jack.

These special occasions gave the men a chance to "let their hair down." This was especially true when the meal was unusual. There was one occasion when Doc Taylor and I spent almost an entire day preparing a unique *smörgåsbord* dinner of twenty-five separate dishes, including one of vitamin pills.

Ours was not a singing crowd, though a few were proud of "talents" who were woefully lacking in talent. One small group, labeling itself the "Three Lonesome Polecats," actually went so far as to make a tape recording of several songs. Someone suggested that when the sun returned and the planes landed, the recording should be sent to some individual deserving major punishment. On earlier expeditions when movie shows were few, the men had put on local talent shows that were always amusing and well done, though of a sort for a stag audience only. At the South Pole, a show such as this would not have been possible. There, talents were of a different sort, with Doc Taylor devoting a well-attended lecture to future fathers on "How to Deliver a Baby," and Bob Benson putting the group into hysterics with a seemingly serious talk on "How to Locate an Earthquake."

Another chance for a change of pace was offered by the physical phenomena surrounding us. Whenever one appeared, the men reacted excitedly and afterwards exhibited renewed enthusiasm for their regular activities.

Actually, when the men first came to the Pole what most

impressed each in turn was the "nothingness" of this south-ernmost spot. There was no other place in the world where there was less to look at. The eye could not feast on a distant mountain, the ocean, birds, foliage—or even a crevasse. The nearest mountain peak lay 300 miles away and the ocean was 800 miles off. But as they began looking closer, they saw new things each time. There was beauty in the snow surface that was not apparent at the outset. The snow had different shapes and forms, from massive drifts to sastrugi-carved fields and on down to exquisite tiny crystals. Optical phenomena were all about us and some of them were awe-some. We may have been people in solitary confinement, but the beauty of what lay about us was awe-inspiring.

Certain types of men have a hard time in the Antarctic. Those who come without good motivation are generally un-happy. And those who come because of romanticism are quickly disillusioned. For the cold and the dark and the hard work necessary to stay alive hit them like a tidal wave. On one expedition one of our men had come simply to take pictures with the hope of returning to the United States and making his fortune on the lecture platform. The unexpected work demanded of him brought on a sullenness that led to group razzing and he was happy only when he embarked for home. Even his picture collection was a sad one!

It is easy for a man to lose face in the Antarctic and when he does it is difficult to regain it. The code of the Antarctic is cruel in many ways. A man who walks away from a task, no matter how justified he is, soon finds himself without friends. For the code is that when a man shows a weakness, he is letting the group down.

On one expedition when I was off on a trail trip, one of the dog drivers twisted his knee. He had the opportunity of suf-fering his way along and perhaps injuring his knee further or returning to camp in a tractor. The decision was left to him and he chose to come back by the tractor. To the other men his action implied a quitting attitude and he was all but ostracized when his trail companions returned. The next spring when Admiral Byrd asked me to lead a trail party, I, like the other party leaders, took untried men with me and ignored the man with the "trick knee." I was fearful that he might let the others down on the trail. And yet, there was no logic to what I did. Robert Scott had taken the same attitude toward Shackleton when he fell ill on the trail early in the century. But Shackleton had gone on to become a great explorer in his own right. And the man I helped ostracize later became a leader on other expeditions to the Antarctic.

Perhaps the reason for such unusual group behavior stems from the belief that only "he-men" are worthy companions on an expedition. Thus those whose physical abilities fall off through illness or state of mind are for the moment no longer "he-men." Oddly, on one expedition a man who was physically weak used counterpsychology to win group acceptance. He made sport of his own inabilities and the other men accepted him wholeheartedly, perhaps because they could look at him and feel more like "he-men" themselves.

This code of the Antarctic was employed at our South Pole Station, though I worked strenuously to see that it did not get out of hand. Earl Johnson and Junior Waldron had been among our hardest workers during the frightful interim when the McMurdo runways gave out. At that time there were only twelve of us at the Pole, and Junior and Earl worked almost around the clock at necessary tasks. For this they both paid heavily: Earl developed high-altitude nosebleeds as well as a hernia; Junior's leg went bad and sent him to bed for days at a time. Doc Taylor put both men on light duty and the others in our small group accepted his decision.

However, when the rest of our crew arrived and settled down to life at the Pole, trouble broke out. Two of the enlisted men who had not been present to witness the period when Earl and Junior worked so hard took to riding them as slackers, a charge that had no basis whatsoever. One of the men, who had a latent mean streak, took to writing nasty notes in the maintenance logbook that Earl kept. One of them read: *Why don't you cut snow, slob?*

This same individual also challenged Earl and Junior to fight him. "Don't rise to the bait," I cautioned them. "Jack and I have our eyes on him and if the time comes, Jack will handle the situation."

They followed my advice and in time the riding stopped, though the complications that ensued were many. For example, Moose Remington, our glaciologist, lived in the barracks building, along with the Navy men and our Met crew. Moose, who was an outgoing and friendly sort, became the champion of anyone being ridden by others. As a result, he soon found himself being ridden along with Earl, Junior and John Guerrero.

Moose was another who became ill at the Pole. A flyer in the South Pacific during World War II, he had contracted malaria there and at the Pole he came down with the tropical disease known as amebiasis. In his usual generous enthusiasm, Moose had offered to cut all the snow for the camp in the snow mine when that operation began. He had even erected a sign: REMINGTON MINES, INC. *Visitors Welcome, Hours* 0001.5–2400, 7 *Days a Week*. However, when he became ill he could not work in the snow mine for a while, and the code of the Antarctic was applied to him by some of the men.

Living at close quarters, the men often found some things in the manners of others to be highly irritating. Sometimes they allowed their imaginations to run away with them in a search for reasons why a man who had been friendly yesterday was standoffish today. On one occasion Doc Taylor was baffled by one of the men who was down in the dumps. Doc sent him to me, expressing concern that he could do nothing for him. After a talk with this man, he left me smiling and happy, and his face had resumed its normal color.

"What happened?" Doc asked me. "What was your cure?"

"Nothing much," I told him. "He had an idea I was down on him and had stopped considering him as a friend."

In calling attention to shortcomings, it was necessary to consider the personality of the individual involved. In the case of a man who was the ringleader of a small group riding one of the men, I called him in one day and brought up the problem. But I didn't challenge him directly. Instead I said, "Some of the men have been picking on—— ——. Would you see what you can do to get them to stop this nonsense?" The riding toned down considerably after that.

When Willi Hough fell behind in the required hours of digging in the snow mine, I knew he was exceedingly busy in his ionosphere work. Yet camp morale demanded that each man somehow find time to do his digging stint. Willi had a sense of humor and I relied on it to straighten out the problem. One night, when all the men were together, I said to the wall, "I wonder if there's any truth to that rumor that Willi Hough has been released from his responsibilities in the snow mine." The men roared and Willi's mouth fell open. Then he smiled. And the next day I found him in the snow mine working hard.

Occasionally one of the men did things unwittingly that hurt the feelings of the others. Arlo Landolt was a delight to have at the Pole. Hard-working and brilliant, he had to spend a great deal of time developing film in the science darkroom. He and Willi were fearful someone might mess up the chemicals or dirty up film and thus possibly destroy valuable scientific records. They put a padlock on the door. I was besieged almost immediately by irate Station members who considered a locked door in such a small closed community to be a personal insult. A feud was in the making and I had to call Arlo and Willi in. "Hang a key on the hook beside the door," I told them, "and issue an invitation for visitors to come by appointment. But don't make it appear as if you have staked out the darkroom as your private kingdom." They were both quick to get the point.

It is difficult to judge a person on short acquaintance. Bob Benson was a case in point. When Bob first got to the Pole, some of the men resented his immaturity. He talked about his home state of Minnesota as if he were a paid employee of the Minnesota Chamber of Commerce, and also spoke of his most excellent professors at the University of Minnesota as if they were superhuman. In addition, he was an overzealous camera bug. In the midst of the early work jobs he would rush away to get his camera, and return to announce, "I'm going to take a picture of the moon!" Some of the others kidded him a great deal about his moon pictures. "That's the same moon that's over Minnesota," they would tell him. But Bob stuck to his moon shots and eventually got pictures that could not be duplicated away from the Pole.

Every expedition I have gone on has included the same general types of men. Each had one man who was the strongest and most dependable man in camp. In ours it was Ed Flowers. There also was always the heaviest eater and camp wit. Bob Benson was both at the Pole. And then there was the camp practical joker. Ours was Moose Remington.

I recall that on my first expedition, when I was "Byrd's Boy Scout," we had a man who pulled the most outlandish of stunts. Once in the dead of night he got the night watchman to come running into the barracks screaming, "The Barrier's broken!" The men hurriedly gathered their gear in an effort to save what they could before Little America was swept out to sea. Of course, it was a false alarm, and the men were ready to commit mayhem when they found out.

On another occasion, he put flash powder in the toilet and triggered it to go off with a roar when the seat was lowered. One of the men, who was not aware of the surprise awaiting him, went to the head while the men gathered outside in suspense. A moment later they were rewarded by an explosion that shook the building. They waited for the victim to come running out, but he did not appear. The men who had laughed until they almost cried now grew worried. They banged on the door and called out his name. Finally they broke the door loose. The man inside stared at them blank-faced and said, "What's the matter, gentlemen?"

Some of Moose Remington's jokes backfired too. One World Day especially, Arlo could not physically keep up with the demand that he take observations every fifteen minutes around the clock in his Aurora Tower. As a consequence he made them for eighteen hours and Moose and Bob Benson spelled him for the remaining six. To get to the Tower from his office in the science building, Arlo had to go through two trap doors while climbing a ladder. The men had asked Arlo to put a rope on the trap doors so they could open them easily, but Arlo had procrastinated. He was smaller than they and could manage more easily to maneuver the doors in the narrow shaft.

Moose decided to teach Arlo a lesson. When Arlo woke up from a short sleep and came to resume his observations, Moose told him that Bob had fallen down the hatch and broken a leg. Arlo suffered immediate remorse, but when his eye caught the open record book and saw that Bob had initialed observations several hours after the alleged hour of the accident, he suspected a trick and refused to act alarmed. Moose responded by accusing him of being calloused and unconcerned about his friend.

All this happened at six A.M. and Arlo cornered me shortly after that to ask if Bob was really hurt. Nothing about this so-called joke was funny to me. Even worse, Arlo and Moose were peeved at each other, and I had to spend the better part of a day straightening out both their perspectives so they would resume their friendship.

Sometimes in the Antarctic a man will get in wrong with his companions and only by an unusual exploit on his part can he alter his reputation. We had one such man who underwent considerable riding from some of the men because he did not work as hard as they, nor was his approach as serious. Although he exhibited as much enthusiasm as the other men, it was mostly vocal. Some of the men complained that he would show up exceedingly late for assigned tasks and then find some reason to quit early.

Gradually the group brought pressure to bear on him. Several men began to comment openly about his bragging, poor work habits and general lack of co-operation. I watched this situation develop, but without too much concern since the man in question obviously possessed a thick skin and was accustomed to being the butt of jokes. However, the group-pressure system in time made inroads on his morale, though it did not cause him to step-up his work. At a crucial point I spoke to a few of the men who were riding him the hardest. But even this did not alter the group's harsh opinion.

And then came a disaster which proved to be a fortuitous event. The ham radio set, one of our leading morale boosters, went out of order. The original set had had a weak power-amplifier "final" and the power had gradually dwindled with use. Cliff Dickey, our electronics man, had worked frantically to keep the set in operation, though he had no repair parts. But gradually, continued operation of the hamset caused it to deteriorate beyond Cliff's ability to repair it, and finally the set gave out.

"What are we going to do now?" Jack Tuck asked me.

There was nothing I could suggest. We both recognized that the hamset was actually our mail system. It was simple to predict a quick drop in the men's spirits with the loss of opportunity to remain in touch with loved ones back in civilization.

It was at this point that the man toward whom the group had shown little kindliness or good will asked for permission to work on the hamset. There were the usual silent sneers because of his previous performance on other tasks.

Several weeks had already passed by now, however, and there was nothing to lose by granting him permission. "How can you do anything?" I asked. "We don't have any repair parts."

"I can make them from bits and pieces of other unserviceable equipment," he said.

With a perseverance he had never before revealed, he set to work. Wires and tubes gradually fell into place and then one day we were on the air again! His achievement had a profound effect on the way men regarded him. Instead of a person who had been reviled, he now emerged a hero. The men recognized that he was far smarter than most of them had realized. As for the man himself, after his electronics achievement he began straightening out. He took his work more seriously, came up with several excellent ideas and became in every way a worthy member of our camp.

On one of our holidays, while we were lingering at the mess table after a meal, one of the men asked, "Tell us, Doc, now that we're well past the middle of the winter night, how are we doing in comparison to other men you've wintered over with?"

I told them I thought they were doing well. "Better in fact than any of the other camps."

Each group I had lived with had gotten along well together, but here at the Pole we had been even more like a big family, with far less bickering and squabbling than one would find in most families. The men were pleased and asked for more evidence of their success as compared to other expeditions.

"Well, maybe I can actually let you judge for yourselves."

I brought in my tape recorder and a small tape some of the construction crew Seabees had made for one of our wintering-over men. Admittedly the tape had been recorded on our less than sober Christmas Eve, but still in my judgment it illustrated the uninhibited degeneration which language could undergo. I explained as I put on the tape that this recording showed how we might all be acting and talking if we devoted no attention to our manner of speech.

It was a short tape and lasted no more than five or ten minutes. The man to whom it was addressed, who was able on occasion to give vent to colorful language himself, blushed. No one wanted to hear the second side of the tape.

Intentionally I have told here the actual nature of the minor frictions that arose among the men. Actually our small isolated station was blessed with a minimum of personality problems. Yet certainly they were real when they occurred and could have been serious had the men not exercised their own self-control. Each man in our group had his virtues and his weaknesses. We were an average cross section of Americans descended from a wide variety of European stock.

Close *esprit de corps* prevents many writers from presenting a full account of their difficulties. I have dared to, for any less frankness might hold us suspect. Humans just don't live without impinging on one another, even in civilization.

All things considered, our group-pressure control system worked well. Other stations which tried to rely on court-martial or arbitration of disputes by long-distance appeal to higher authority outside their Station found that they were stymied. Neither the Navy or IGY wanted the disgrace of a public hearing.

We had to solve our own problems. No one else could help.

EDMUND HILLARY

(*1919–*)

EDMUND HILLARY is well known as one of the two men (the other was Tenzing Norgay) to make the first ascent of Mount Everest (May 1953). He was knighted for this feat. Less known about him are his Antarctic contributions.

Born in Auckland, New Zealand, and an apiarist by profession, he chose the site for Scott Base, the New Zealand station on Ross Island, and helped to erect the station. He was a member of the station's first wintering-over team. In 1956 the British Commonwealth Transantarctic Expedition was begun, its goal being to traverse the continent: from the Weddell Sea to the Ross Sea via the Pole. (In 1914–16 Ernest Shackleton had attempted unsuccessfully to make this traverse.) Hillary led his nation's section of the expedition. His

main task was to set up depots from Ross Island to the Pole
to support Vivian Fuchs's party, which would make the full
traverse. Hillary reached the Pole in a tractor January 4,
1958, becoming, after Scott, the first man to reach the Pole
overland. The following brief account describes crevasses
that he and his depot-laying party encountered.

Crevasses

We started up again at 11 P.M. and experienced no difficulty
in crossing the bridges we had marked over the crevasses. At
each satisfactory bridge we built a high snow cairn as a
marker to the crossing party. I walked on ahead for half an
hour or so, prodding at anything that looked suspicious but
finally decided that there were no more breaks.

Derek was now taking a turn in the lead tractor. I set up
the sun compass for him and then assured him that the way
ahead was clear. He didn't look very convinced but started
up his tractor and gave the wave for the vehicles to move off.
Somewhat fatigued after my tramping around I jumped
aboard the caboose as it came past and relaxed for a few
moments on the bunk. But not for long! We couldn't have
covered more than half a mile when suddenly everything
stopped once more. I scrambled outside to see three drivers
clustered around something behind the lead tractor—it was
a large hole in the snow—another crevasse. I walked carefully up to join them and was suitably impressed by the dimensions of the crevasse. "Some day," I thought, "the tractor
just won't scramble out, it will go straight down. If you ask
me we're being jolly lucky." Derek looked at me in an accusing manner. "I thought you said there were no more cre-

vasses?" I acknowledged my fallibility but expressed my surprise, for according to my experience in the matter there just shouldn't have been one. It looked as though there was still plenty to learn about crevasses.

After a lot of probing I found a safe bridge a hundred yards to the left and we brought the rest of the tractor train across. Then I walked on ahead for another mile or so, examining every inch of the way, but didn't find anything else and before long we were rolling steadily southwards.

Once we were fully clear of these crevasses we made quite good time over improving country and covered twenty miles in under five hours. Then the surface changed considerably and became very hard with unusual knobs of ice all over the place. The sky was thinly overcast and grey and the landscape had an eerie air about it. It seemed a fruitful ground for crevasses, so our nerves and muscles tensed up and our concentration increased. We clanked on over this hard surface while the ice hummocks became more pronounced and the slopes ahead grew a good deal steeper. The icy knobs were now lined across our path in a more regular fashion, and we came to a halt in front of some suspicious looking ground. We had covered twenty-eight point three miles in two-thirds of a day's run and as we were now in no particular hurry while we awaited a reply from Fuchs I decided we'd camp here and do a thorough reconnaissance. The slope in front of us looked as if it would give us a rather trying day and I knew we'd attack it with more determination if we were fresh.

According to the sledge wheel we were now fifty-six miles from D700 and I was delighted to find that we had averaged nearly two miles per gallon. If we kept this up for a while we would build up a small reserve to counteract any difficult surfaces we might strike later. My altimeter didn't seem very reliable, but it now showed a reading of 8,700 feet which bore out our impression that we had been gaining height over the last two days. I wanted to turn on to a due south heading at the sixty mile mark so I needed an accurate fix of our position. Before going to bed I shot the sun's altitude and plotted a position line. After a few hours sleep the raucous clang of the alarm brought me out of bed again at 2.30 P.M. for a noon sight.

I pulled on my boots, threw on a down jacket, and then scrambled out of the caboose. I walked into a scene of complete desolation. The hard glazed surface swept away to the horizon in every direction, peppered with twisted knobs of ice five or six feet high and all looking somehow barren and ominous. The sun was visible through a thin layer of cloud, but the subdued lighting cast an air of gloom over the landscape. A bitter wind moaned quietly around our sleeping camp, but this was the only sound apart from the harsh rasp of my own breathing in the frigid air. "Crickey," I thought, "we seem a heck of a long way from anywhere at the moment. I suppose it's something like this on the moon!" I turned my thoughts to more tangible matters and completed my sun observations, and then, with a last glance at this mournful scene, I scrambled back into the caboose with frozen hands and a slight chill around my heart.

I always found it difficult to go off to sleep again after getting up for the noon sight so tossed and turned until the alarm went off for the 5.30 P.M. radio schedule. This time, to my relief, there were only routine messages to pass, and I had a useful exchange of information and general organisation with Scott Base. This was Sunday night so we all listened to the radio session "Calling Antarctic" from Radio New Zealand. For half an hour we were transported back to the familiar scene in New Zealand and enjoyed the items of local interest and bits of gossip . . . five scraggy specimens in a cramped wooden box in the middle of Antarctica . . . and it took quite a mental effort to stir ourselves out into the cold again and get back to the familiar routine of starting up frozen tractors.

Conditions weren't particularly pleasant. There was a strong wind and a low ground drift, even though the temperature was a very modest $-4°$ F. I walked ahead of the tractor train to examine the route and soon realised that we were right on the edge of the crevasses. There were hundreds of them and some of them were monsters, fifty or sixty feet wide. Fortunately they were all plugged with snow, and a lot of careful prodding showed that these bridges seemed to be fairly solid. Only at their edges where they abutted on to the walls of the crevasses were the bridges somewhat shaky, and here it was usually possible to jab an ice-axe through the crust and open up a deep hole underneath. But even these holes were rarely more than two feet wide. The most unpleasant feature about the bridges was that they appeared to have shrunk a little and slipped down into the crevasses, with the result that the tractors would have to thump down a foot or two on to the bridge and then climb steeply out the far side.

I gave the signal to start and we drove our vehicles carefully over the first few crevasses, dropping down on to the bridges with bated breath and then heaving a sigh of relief when we clawed our way up on to the solid ground beyond. Hours passed as we probed our way forward, surrounded now by a vast sea of crevasses and never coming to the end of them. The bridges were holding well and it was only the last tractor that was really getting into any trouble. By the time the first two vehicles had crossed there was usually a respectable hole in the crevasse, and the third tractor would drop suddenly into this only to be wrenched out again as the rope came tight under the relentless forward surge of the two front vehicles. After three hours of this exacting work we stopped for a breather and a cup of tea.

I didn't like the way the crevasses were changing. Instead of being easily identified and well plugged with snow, we were now finding a lot which were enormous voids bridged over with a thin layer of snow and with only a hairline crack on the surface to denote their presence. A mistake with one of these could be fatal. I decided to go ahead for quite a distance and carefully examine every inch of the way and flag or cairn the safe bridges. Three of us roped up together, and we probed our way ahead investigating every suspicious crack. Whenever I broke through into a large hole I lay down on my stomach and put my head well down into the crevasse to judge its direction and try and pick a solid bridge. In this fashion we worked our way up to the crest of the slope and came to a complicated area of crevasses. No longer did they sweep across the slope in regular lines, but here they seemed to be coming from every direction. Despite constant probing it was hard to find a satisfactory way through them, and our final route proved to be a sinuous one which would throw a severe strain on the steering abilities of our tractors. We marked the route through this portion with particular care and then continued on for another half-mile, when we were delighted to find that the crevasses were reducing in size and frequency, and the terrain was flattening out into what looked like safer ground. Feeling rather heartened we trudged back to the tractors, rechecking the route as we went.

We started the vehicles and moved off once more. All went well. We wound our way past ice hummocks, dropped down on to sunken lids of crevasses, dodged thinly covered holes, and made excellent progress. Only the third tractor was caused any discomfort as it jarred into the holes gouged out in the lips of the crevasses by the first two vehicles. Murray Ellis was in the lead tractor and was doing a magnificent job charging over the bridges with great aplomb. We approached the crest of the slope and its complicated crevasse area. I quickly rechecked our route and then waved to Murray to come on. With engines revving furiously the vehicles headed towards me, raced over the bridges, whipped between the flags, around the snow cairns and wended their sinuous way across the dangerous area. They were two-thirds through and still going well when Murray failed to keep the lead tractor close in to one of the flags and swung about ten feet wide on a corner. Before I could utter a shout he was safely across and so was the next tractor. But suddenly the whole train came to an abrupt halt with the Terylene rope twanging under the strain. I rushed back to the third vehicle, to see Derek Wright standing beside it, white and shaken, and looking at the caboose behind.

What an unpleasant sight it was! Underneath the caboose the bridge of an enormous crevasse had sunk away leaving it suspended over a vast gaping hole. The skis of the caboose had jammed into the forward wall of the crevasse and this had brought the train to a halt. The caboose was precariously perched, supported on one side by its drawbar and on the other by the steel wire rope which connected it to the two heavy sledges behind. I leaned carefully over and gave the caboose a light push and it rocked rather alarmingly and then settled back into the same position. Lying on my stomach I looked down into the crevasse. It disappeared away into the darkness in both directions, and I could see it was enormous in extent, even underneath our poled route. But at least the bridge over it there was thick and substantial. It seemed a miracle that all three tractors had successfully crossed where the much lighter caboose had broken through, and the consequences of a tractor tumbling into that hole didn't bear thinking about.

There was a funny side to the incident. At D700 we had been discussing the question of photography on our tractor trip and had been bemoaning the fact that generally when we were in any sort of spectacular trouble that might photograph rather well, we were all far too busy to bother about it. We had resolved that if we struck bad crevasse trouble again we would make the effort to photograph it. Well, here we were in somewhat spectacular trouble, but there was only one snag. All of our cameras, both movie and still, were inside the caboose and nobody was at all anxious to get them out as a slight change in balance might tip the caboose over on its side with disastrous consequences.

We attacked the caboose problem with determination. First of all we dug sloping ramps down through the front lip of the crevasse, deep enough until the tips of the runners rested in them. Then we unhitched the sledges from the caboose, and although it settled a little into the crevasse it still remained delicately poised. A good hearty tug should do the rest. We started the tractors, I gave the signal, and the three vehicles moved together as one. The caboose jerked suddenly forward and its back came free and dropped into the crevasse. But the runners had entered the steep ramps we had dug for them, and the whole structure was dragged irresistibly to the surface and thumped down on to an even keel again. I clambered inside and was relieved to find that although gear was loose all over the place no irreparable damage had been done.

That was the first stage completed. Getting the two sledges from the other side of the crevasse was going to be harder. These sledges contained all our supplies of fuel and food, and our camping gear, and they were close up to the far side of the big hole. The marked route was ten or fifteen feet to the left and we'd have to try and get them over this. In order to drag them sideways on to this route I'd have to get a tractor well out to the right on rather shaky ground. With considerable care I prodded around over a wide area and identified the crevasses. It was all horribly unstable but I soon located the best of it. Feeling not a little like a parachutist making a jump, I unhitched the lead tractor, clambered aboard and then drove cautiously over my proved route out to the right of the tractor train. Somewhat to my surprise I came to no grief, so backed with extreme care up to the edge of a large bridged crevasse in order to get as near a right angle as possible to the two sledges. We connected the tractor and the sledges with a long rope over the intervening crevasses and I began to plunge forward with the vehicle, jerking the sledges around sideways off their dead end route, and trying to get them into line to cross safely over the original marked route. The scheme worked. Slowly the sledges came around into position and were ready to be dragged across the bridge. I drove back to the other vehicles again and hitched on to the sledges in a direct line across the bridge. Then, using every bit of power in the motor I drove forward as hard as I could go, and like a bullet out of a gun each sledge shot across the bridge to safety.

Shuffling around on our crevasse free spot we connected up our sledges and vehicles once more into the full tractor train. Then we started off over the flagged route, taking particular care now to stick very closely indeed to the flags and cairns. It was an enormous relief to us when the crevasses started becoming less frequent and smaller in size and when we finally emerged on open going. It was 3.30 A.M. The band of crevasses had been three and a half miles wide and it had taken us six and a half hours to get through them. We stopped for another cup of tea and built a huge cairn to indicate where we had come out of the area.

This had proved to be a particularly large area of crevasses and stretched away for many miles in either direction. It was such an extensive formation, in fact, that it gave the impression of being the edge of the icecap where the vast sheet of polar ice started to flow down on its slow but relentless progress towards the sea. If this were true it would mean a considerable reduction in our crevasse troubles as we would be entering the comparatively undisturbed expanses of the high plateau.

CHRONOLOGY

*Some Important Dates
in the Exploration of Antarctica*

1739   J. B. C. Bouvet de Lozier, a Frenchman, reaches 55° S. He also discovers Bouvet Island.

1772   Marion Dufresne, a Frenchman, discovers the Crozet and Prince Edward Islands.

1772   Y. J. de Kerguelen-Trémarec, a Frenchman, discovers the Kerguelen Islands.

1774   James Cook, an Englishman, is the first to cross the Antarctic Circle. He reaches a farthest south of 71° 10′ at 106° 54′ W.

1790–1822   The sealing era in Antarctica.

1790–92   Daniel F. Greene of Connecticut visits South Georgia. He heads the first American expedition to approach the continent.

1810   Frederick Hasselborough, an Australian, discovers Macquarie Island.

1819   William Smith, an Englishman, sights land in 62° 42′ S.

1820   Nathaniel B. Palmer of Connecticut discovers an archipelago, for a time called Palmer Peninsula and now known as the Antarctic Peninsula.

1821   John Davis of Connecticut makes what is apparently the first landing on the mainland.

1821   Thaddeus Bellingshausen, a Russian, makes the first sighting of land within the Antarctic Circle.

1823   James Weddell, an Englishman, discovers the Weddell Sea and reaches a farthest south of 74° 15′.

1832   John Biscoe, an Englishman, discovers the Biscoe Islands and the Graham Coast.

1839–40   Charles Wilkes, an American, makes a series of land sightings which lead him to conclude, correctly, that he has discovered a land mass of continental proportions.

1840   J. S. C. Dumont d'Urville, a Frenchman, discovers the Adélie Coast.

1841   James Clark Ross, an Englishman, discovers the Ross Sea, Victoria Land, Ross Island and the Ross Ice Shelf and makes a farthest southing of 78° 10′ at 161° 27′ W.

1874   George S. Nares, an Englishman, makes the first crossing of the Antarctic Circle by steamer.

1897–98   Adrien de Gerlache, a Belgian, leads a Belgian expedition in the *Belgica*. Because the ship is trapped in the pack ice, the crew is the first to winter over in the Antarctic.

1898–99   Part of a British expedition under C. E. Borchgrevink is the first to winter over ashore.

1901–04   Robert Falcon Scott's first Antarctic expedition, based on Ross Island, makes the first extensive land exploration of the continent. In 1902 Scott, Ernest Shackleton and Edward Wilson, using sledges, achieve a new southing of 82° 17'.

1907–09   Ernest Shackleton's first Antarctic expedition, based on Ross Island, makes the first ascent of Mount Erebus, reaches the magnetic pole and pioneers the Beardmore Glacier route to the polar plateau. Shackleton and three companions reach a farthest south of 88° 23'.

1910–12   Robert Falcon Scott commands his second and last Antarctic expedition.

1911   Roald Amundsen, a Norwegian, and four companions are the first to reach the South Pole.

1912   Scott and four companions reach the Pole and die on their way back toward Ross Island.

1914–16   Ernest Shackleton commands his second and ill-fated Antarctic expedition. His ship *Endurance* is crushed by the pack ice.

1928   Hubert Wilkins, an Australian, makes the first airplane flight over the continent.

1928–30   Richard E. Byrd leads his first Antarctic expedition, based on the Ross Ice Shelf.

Byrd makes the first flight over the Pole.

1933–35   Byrd leads his second expedition and winters over alone at an advance base south of Little America II.

1935   Mrs. Klarius Mikkelsen, a whaling captain's wife, is the first woman to set foot on the continent.

1935   Lincoln Ellsworth, an American, makes the first trans-Antarctic flight.

1939–41   Byrd commands the United States Antarctic Service Expedition.

1946–47   Byrd heads Operation Highjump, the largest Antarctic expedition in history.

1946–48   The Ronne Antarctic Research Expedition includes the first two women to winter over on the continent.

1955   Four United States Navy planes are the first to fly to the continent from another land mass, New Zealand.

1956   The first plane lands at the Pole.

1957–58   The International Geophysical Year is accompanied by extensive scientific activity on the continent.

1958   A tractor group headed by Vivian E. Fuchs, an Englishman, and supported by Edmund Hillary, a New Zealander, makes the first overland crossing of Antarctica.

1959   The Antarctic Treaty is signed.

1961   A United States plane makes the first winter flight to Antarctica.

1962   The United States activates the continent's first nuclear reactor, located at McMurdo Station, Ross Island.

1964   The Antarctic Treaty signatories pronounce the region south of 60° S a special conservation area.

1966   A United States Air Force pure jet aircraft is the first of its kind to land on the continent.

1967   Scientists discover the jawbone of a freshwater vertebrate, evidence that Antarctica was probably once linked to neighboring continents.

1969   The first women visit the Pole.

SOURCES

JAMES COOK, A *Voyage Towards the South Pole, and Round the World*, two volumes, London, 1777, Vol. I, Book II, Chapter VI, pp. 251–76.

GEORGE FORSTER, A *Voyage Round the World in his Britannic Majesty's Sloop, Resolution, Commanded by Capt. James Cook, During the Years 1772, 3, 4 and 5*, two volumes, London, 1777, Vol. I, Book II, Chapter III, pp. 527–55.

THADDEUS BELLINGSHAUSEN, *The Voyage of Captain Bellingshausen to the Antarctic Seas 1819–1821*, two volumes, London, 1945, translated from the Russian by several hands and edited by Frank Debenham, Vol. I, pp. 104–21.

JAMES WEDDELL, *A Voyage Towards the South Pole*, London, 1825, pp. 8–43.

CHARLES WILKES, *Narrative of the United States Exploring Expedition*, five volumes, Philadelphia, 1845, Vol. II, pp. 281–306.

JAMES CLARK ROSS, *A Voyage of Discovery and Research in the Southern and Antarctic Regions, During the Years 1839–43*, London, 1847, pp. 209–46.

ROALD AMUNDSEN, *The South Pole*, two volumes, London and New York, 1913, translated from the Norwegian by A.G. Chater, Vol. II, pp. 96–134.

ROBERT FALCON SCOTT, *Scott's Last Expedition*, arranged by Leonard Huxley, two volumes, London, 1913, Vol. I, pp. 543–95.

ERNEST SHACKLETON, *South*, New York, 1920, pp. 158–83.

HERBERT G. PONTING, *The Great White South*, London, 1921, pp. 63–71, 217–26.

APSLEY CHERRY-GARRARD, *The Worst Journey in the World*, two volumes, London, 1922, Vol. I, pp. 233–99.

RICHARD E. BYRD, *Alone*, New York, 1938, pp. 146–83.

PAUL SIPLE, *90° South*, New York, 1959, pp. 241–48, 306–23.

EDMUND HILLARY, *No Latitude for Error*, New York, 1961, pp. 195–201.

ABOUT THE AUTHOR

*CHARLES NEIDER, a lover of Antarctica, has made
two trips to the white continent. The first was sponsored by the United States Navy in 1969. The second,
sponsored by the National Science Foundation and
the Chapelbrook Foundation, was made in December 1970 and January 1971 in order to research his
forthcoming book,* Ross Island, Antarctica. *At the request of the National Science Foundation he has prepared the only historical guide to Ross Island, the
site of McMurdo Station, the U. S. outpost for scientific research in Antarctica.*

*During his second trip he camped on Cape Royds,
Ross Island, where he slept in Ernest Shackleton's
hut, and on Cape Evans, Ross Island, where he slept
in Robert Falcon Scott's last hut. Also, while being
transported from McMurdo Station to Cape Bird,
where he was due to camp, he was involved in a
near-fatal helicopter accident. The helicopter
crashed close to the summit of Mount Erebus, the
continent's largest and most active volcano, at an
altitude of over twelve thousand feet and a temperature of* −30°F. *He and three companions were rescued twelve hours after the crash. During this second*

trip he took 2,600 color photographs of Antarctica. Neider, born in 1915, is one of the very few literary men to work in the Antarctic. He is a novelist, critic, editor, and Mark Twain scholar. One of his novels, The Authentic Death of Hendry Jones, *was made into the movie,* One-Eyed Jacks. *He lives in Princeton, New Jersey, with his wife and daughter.*

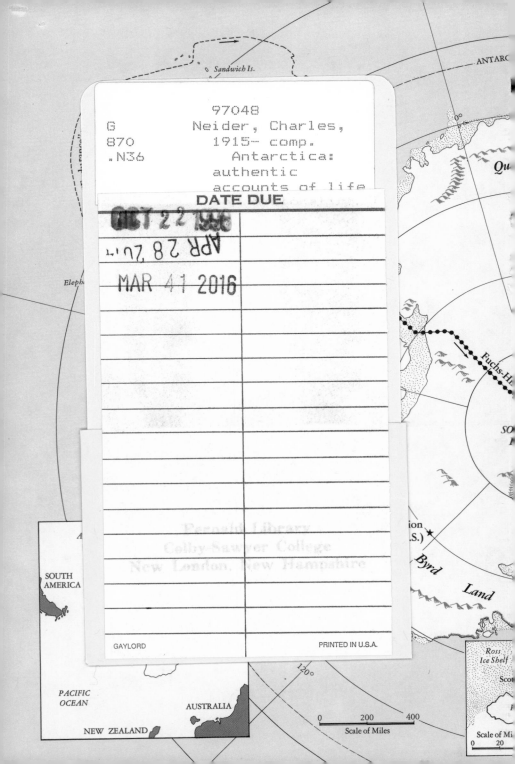